THE CAGE

Gordon Weiss was the United Nations Spokesman in Sri Lanka for two years during the recent civil war. For two decades, he worked as a journalist and for international organisations in numerous conflict and natural disaster zones. He is currently a Visiting Scholar at the University of Sydney, Australia.

GORDON WEISS

The Cage

The Fight for Sri Lanka and the Last Days of the Tamil Tigers

VINTAGE BOOKS
London

Published by Vintage 2012

2 4 6 8 10 9 7 5 3

First published in Great Britain in 2011 by
The Bodley Head

Vintage
Random House, 20 Vauxhall Bridge Road,
London SW1V 2SA

www.vintage-books.co.uk

Addresses for companies within The Random House Group Limited
can be found at: www.randomhouse.co.uk/offices.htm

The Random House Group Limited Reg. No. 954009

A CIP catalogue record for this book
is available from the British Library

ISBN 9780099548478

Penguin Random House is committed to a sustainable future for
our business, our readers and our planet. This book is made from
Forest Stewardship Council® certified paper.

Printed and bound in Great Britain by Clays Ltd, St Ives plc

This book was inspired by my grandmother Suzanne,
who urged me to risk and rove,

And is dedicated to my grandfather Karel 1902–1945,
who walked with me.

Contents

Acknowledgements

My special gratitude to Katey Grusovin, intrepid film-maker and roving intellect, who endured the most turgid phase of my manuscript, kept my spirits up through the long months of writing and surrendered her Seal Rocks house with its kangaroo-strewn lawn; to Owen Harries, Senior Fellow of the Lowy Institute, adviser to statespeople and leaders and editor emeritus of the *National Interest* in Washington, DC, who generously and repeatedly critiqued the most important elements of this book until I was satisfied; and to my resolute agent Jonah Straus, who from the distant shores of New York City cultivated this project with dedication and aplomb, and brought it to publication.

My particular thanks also to Louise Arbour, President of the International Crisis Group; Chandana Keerthi Bandara and the BBC's Sinhala and Tamil Service at Bush House; Alex Bellamy, Professor of International Security at the Griffith Asia Institute, for his always warm listening; Andy Brooks of UNICEF; Dr Samuel Doe, UN post-conflict specialist; the Hon. John Dowd AO, Chancellor of Southern Cross University and President of the Australian Section of the International Commission of Jurists; Chris du Toit, for his example; Eric Ellis, for his insights into Sri Lanka's political elites; David Feith of Monash University; Basil Fernando of the Asian Human Rights Commission; Yolanda Foster at Amnesty International, London, for help obtaining archives of the JVP insurrection; Tom Gilliatt of Pan Macmillan for his measured guidance; the unique Clare Goddard for her Norwich respite and access to her rich library, from which I extracted work on the theosophists; Erika Goldman of Bellevue Publishing in New York City, who always barracked for my voice of experience; Natalie Grove, for her interest and substantive contributions to this project; the BBC's Sri Lanka Bureau chief Charles

Havilland; Ron Haviv, photographer of VII Photo Agency, who generously contributed his photos from Sri Lanka; 'Mr Heidel', a Sinhalese intellectual and gentleman who provided me with the bulk of the most important and difficult-to-obtain texts on Sri Lanka's Buddhism, ethnography and history, and whose compassion gave me great hope; Dr Anthony Hippisley for his close attention to the text; Rajan Hoole of the University Teachers for Human Rights, whose courageous and exhaustive labours speak for themselves; Vincent Hubin, a devoted United Nations civil servant and racquets partner who provided so much of the data that tracked the fate of civilians caught in the siege; my great comrade Morten Hvaal, whose military expertise, journalistic sense, experience of the siege of Sarajevo and close observations of governments at war, quite apart from the sheer joy of his friendship, served as a vital point of reference in Sri Lanka; the courageous staff of the International Committee of the Red Cross who served in Sri Lanka, and bore witness; Alfred Ironside, Director of Communications at the Ford Foundation; Alan Keenan, the Sri Lanka expert at the International Crisis Group; Warren Jacobs, for his insights into fast attack craft and 'brown water' tactics; David Keen of the London School of Economics, for his fascinating chapters from *Endless War*; Damien Kingsbury of Deakin University's Faculty of International Relations; Ara Koopelien, for photo research; Ogi and Emily Krunic of USAID, for cartographic advice; Martin Krygier, Gordon Samuels Professor of Law and Social Theory at the University of New South Wales Centre for Interdisciplinary Studies of Law; Rich Lang of Rhode Island, intellectual, friend and doppelgänger, for his valuable critiques; John Lee, the China expert at the Centre for Independent Studies in Sydney (and new father); Iain Levine, Programme Director at Human Rights Watch, for his efforts on behalf of this book; Jake Lynch at the University of Sydney's Centre for Peace and Conflict Studies; Javier Marroquin, friend, author and aid worker, who shared his memorable experiences of Sri Lanka, as he has shared so much, and Judith, for the weeks of writing in Barcelona; Ravi Nessman, the South Asia Bureau Chief for the Associated Press, a humorous companion who kindly read through the manuscript and offered valuable advice; the staff of London's Overseas Development Institute; Ana Pararajasingham, for his generous outreach; Kay Peddle, my hard-working, attentive and elegant editor at Random House, who spotted the potential in this story; Jacobo Quintanilla, for his help and good friendship; David Rampton of the School of Oriental and African Studies, for his insights into the JVP; Philip Reeves of National Public Radio; Richard Rigby, former Australian ambassador to China, and now head of the China Institute at the Australian National University; Jim Ross, the Legal and Policy Director at Human Rights Watch, for his expert attention to aspects of international law addressed in the book, as well as for his generous, sharp, expeditious and warmly delivered Yuletide review of one of the final versions of the manuscript; Jane Selley, for her close attention to the text; Justice Carolyn Simpson of the NSW Supreme Court; Will Sulkin, my publisher at Random House, who had the courage and curiosity to first take this project on; Captain Timothy Visscher, who explained the intricacies and explored the implications of the Long Range Information Tracking system with me; Lal Wickrematunge, former police officer, now publisher of Colombo's doggedly courageous the *Sunday Leader* and brother of the murdered Lasantha; Professor Clive Williams, Visiting Fellow, Strategic & Defence Studies Centre, School of International, Political & Strategic Studies at the Australian National University, for his lucid and restrained analysis of the LTTE; Clara Womersley, Random House publicist, for her enthusiastic support; my colleagues and friends at the United Nations, whose valuable work goes often unsung; staff at the British Library for their help; contributing members of the Sinhalese communities of Australia, France and the UK, who did not wish to be named, yet reviewed the chapters on the JVP, the early history of Sri Lanka, as well as my conclusions; contributing members of Australia's Tamil community who did not wish to be named; and the many, many full-hearted and boisterous Sri Lankans of casual encounters and more profound friendships, who shed so much light on the complexity of the island.

My thanks, not least, to all my family – my father Zdenek and mother Angela for her vigilant reading of the text and proof suggestions, my stepfather Alwyn for the legal reading, my sister Rachael for her Sheffield cottage, sisters Suzanne and Alexandra, nieces and nephews – but above all others to my daughters Anna and Catalina, and to their mother Olga, who brought joy and warmth, insistently, even as they endured the months of writing.

List of Illustrations

Picture section

Maps

The author and publisher have made every effort to trace and contact the relevant primary copyright holders for each image. The publishers would be pleased to correct any omissions or errors in any future editions.

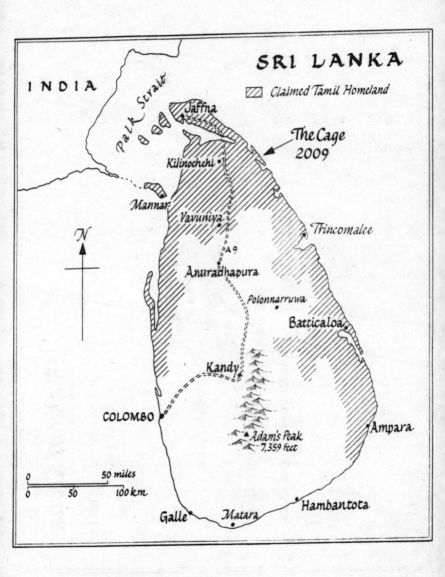

SRI LANKA

Claimed Tamil Homeland

INDIA

Palk Strait

Jaffna

The Cage
2009

Kilinochchi

Mannar

Vavuniya

Trincomalee

A 9

Anuradhapura

Polonnaruwa

Batticaloa

Kandy

COLOMBO

Adam's Peak
7,359 feet

Ampara

0   50 miles
0   50   100 km

Galle   Matara   Hambantota

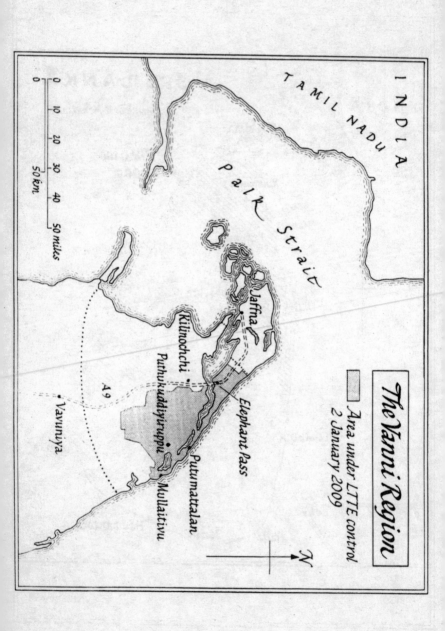

The Vanni Region

Area under LTTE control
2 January 2009

N

INDIA

TAMIL NADU

Palk Strait

Jaffna

Elephant Pass

Kilinochchi

Puthukuddiyiruppu

Putumattalan

Mullaitivu

Vavuniya

A9

0 10 20 30 40 50 km
0 50 miles

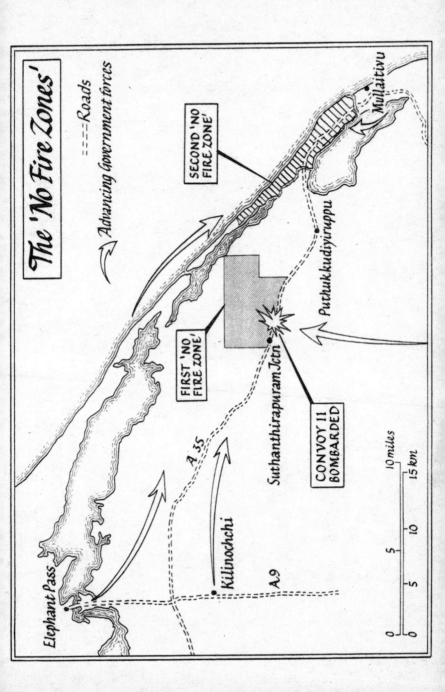

The 'No Fire Zones'

=== Roads

↗ Advancing Government forces

Elephant Pass

Kilinochchi

A 35

A 9

FIRST 'NO FIRE ZONE'

SECOND 'NO FIRE ZONE'

Mullaitivu

Puthukkudiyiruppu

Suthanthirapuram Jctn

CONVOY 11 BOMBARDED

0   5   10miles

0   5   10   15 km

Preface

In the first few months of 2009, thousands of children were killed and maimed as Sri Lanka's army initially besieged and then destroyed the notorious Tamil Tiger guerrillas whom it had battled for thirty years. Along with the Tigers, around 330,000 Tamil civilians had been snared in a siege of epic proportions as the insurgents fell back on a small pocket of land on the island's north-east coast to make a final stand. While government artillery hammered at the Tiger lines, and pitched battles were fought, children died along with their families at the ragged edges of the combat, felled by shellfire, gunshot wounds and diseases beneath the baking sun. Trapped and short of manpower, the Tigers pressed cohorts of untested boys and girls, some barely in their teens, into the lines of battle. Today, the lost lives of these innocents are just brief and inconsequential footnotes in the narrative of world events. This was the reality of the Cage.

At the same time, several hundred kilometres to the south, I was working with the United Nations in Colombo, and despite occasional bomb blasts and air raids, my young daughters were being comfortably schooled in the city. As most parents understand, it is a form of anguish to observe children suffering, even if they are not your own. Over the years, I had seen countless children endure a variety of torments in war and disaster zones around the world. In Sri Lanka, even though I could not bear witness, I was close enough to the levers of action to believe that they were being wounded and killed in large numbers each day. Meanwhile, the government of Sri Lanka insisted that its efforts to 'rescue' civilians were bloodless. It attributed any deaths to the Tamil Tigers, who had indeed induced or forced civilians to fall back with them into the narrowing siege pocket, and who also killed civilians

who tried to escape. After the final battle, the government rejected
international calls for an investigation into the conduct of the war, and
instead commissioned a domestic inquiry vaguely mandated to look at
the 'root causes' of the conflict over the previous seven years.

To avoid futility, however, or a convenient cover-up of the final
death toll, one must search much further back in time. To begin
with, many thousands of Tamils fled Sri Lanka after island-wide
riots in 1983 that killed between 1,000 and 3,000 people. Chilling
photographs show thin Tamil men, stripped of their clothes,
cowering before machete-wielding mobs of Sinhalese, or waiting
with tyres around their necks for the terrible moment when they
would be set alight by their tormentors. Black July, as it is known,
has become a sort of Kristallnacht in the collective memory of Sri
Lanka's Tamils, a government-orchestrated pogrom that burned families out of their homes and drove them from their country.
One direct consequence was a flood of thousands of Tamil recruits to
a ragtag guerrilla outfit of several dozen men who called themselves
the Tamil Tigers. Another was the multiplication of the global Sri
Lankan Tamil diaspora that went on to fund them.

Black July, however was not the first such bloodletting, and Tamils
were not the first large-scale victims. In 1971, and again in the late 1980s,
a generation of young Marxist Sinhalese revolted against the state and
its ruling elders. Tens of thousands of youths (as well as some Buddhist
monks) were killed in ensuing massacres by government forces.
Sinhalese soldiers and policemen dumped the bodies of these teenagers into rivers, or burned them on the white sands on which tourists
lounge today, or left their heads impaled on roadside stakes as warnings
to other rebel youths. The sheer scale of these earlier responses fore-
shadowed those that would follow against the Tamil, and predominantly
Hindu, separatist rebellion in this endemically violent country, and
reflect directly on the events of 2009. These Sinhalese revolts also reveal
something about the way in which those who govern Sri Lanka wield
power and repress memory, revelations that encourage a broader view
of the island's ailments beyond just the ethnic paradigm.

Nor did the problems of this troubled nation start with these revolts.
To begin to grapple with the tensions that in time would culminate in
fully fledged revolution, one must refer back to the emergence of nationalism in the nineteenth century and the evolution of independence from

Britain in the twentieth. The island has a well-deserved reputation for the striking beauty of its landscapes, its ancient 'lost' cities and its welcoming and intelligent people who so eloquently advertise their antique cultures. Upon independence in 1948, it was widely held that Sri Lanka (or Ceylon as it was then known), positioned astride the great sea trade routes of the Indian Ocean and benefiting from the railways, roads and administration of British colonialism, would become an economic powerhouse in Asia. It was predicted that the new nation would trump Singapore, South Korea and even Japan. But Sri Lanka's fault lines gave rise to surprising contradictions that foiled these glittering prospects.

One such contradiction, particularly to the Western mind, but also to many Sri Lankans, lies with the Buddhism practised by two thirds of the country's twenty million people. The year 2011 is held to mark the 2,600th anniversary of Buddha's enlightenment, and the birth of one of the world's great religions. Yet in marked contrast to this commemoration, Sri Lanka is home to a violently nationalist coterie of Buddhist monks, some of whom now sit in parliament.[1] Despite a famously peaceable philosophy, these clerics preach bloodshed and domination over the country's minorities. In the government of President Mahinda Rajapaksa, the man who led the country to victory over the Tigers, their ideology has been a fundamental political force. The relatively recent political gestation of ideas that have given these monks an influence beyond their numbers includes a toxic mixture of religion, nationalism and xenophobia, as well as a blood-and-soil claim to territory based on obscure two-thousand-year-old Buddhist texts. It jars Western preconceptions of Buddhism to see saffron-robed monks angrily speechifying in a house of parliament.[2]

Each contradiction unmasks others. Sri Lanka, which was born a liberal democratic state in 1948, has spawned governments that use the familiar language of liberal democrats while deploying death squads to kill journalists, students and political opponents. Since 1972, the independence of the country's police force and judicial institutions has been increasingly degraded to serve the predilections of its leaders. Its parliament today is little more than a small group of oppositionists overwhelmed by a gaggle of provincial potentates and party sycophants, who gather to rubber-stamp the wishes of the country's president and his family, in return for the spoils of government. Its once free press has been largely cowed into serving the dominant ideology of politicised Sinhalese Buddhism. In 2008, the island could fairly be called one of the most dangerous places in the world to be a journalist or humanitarian worker, and between 2006 and 2009, dozens died just doing their jobs. As Sri Lanka has developed into a middle-income country, with high rates of literacy and leading health indices, its authoritarianism has actually deepened, and ordinary citizens now have less say over their own lives than at independence.

In a similarly unexpected vein, this crowded nation, smaller than Scotland but with four times the population, bred a globalised national liberation group that became notorious for its depraved violence and the tenacity of its fight. In their struggle for a tiny sovereign state, the Tamil Tigers killed a head of state and systematised the use of suicide bombers, female shock troops and child soldiers. Their ingenuity became a pioneering model for other transnational terrorist organisations emerging in the twenty-first century. The Tigers established a vast network of finance and fund-raising in Tamil communities throughout the world, mustered a fleet of merchant ships and imported the arms, machinery and knowledge that it required to build an army, navy, special forces capability and even a meagre air force in Sri Lanka. At some critical junctures, it seemed possible that they might succeed in carving out their Tamil nation state in the north of the island. Most foreign observers believed that they were militarily unbeatable.

Beyond these paradoxes, the total victory of the Sri Lankan government over the Tamil Tigers reflects a number of global trends that ought to concern us. One is the renewed validation of terror when exercised by governments. The final episode of this war coincided with the last of the Bush years. Post-9/11, the Tamil Tigers had lost important international support, and their networks of finance and trafficking came under intense scrutiny. Western governments, who were getting better at understanding and fighting the nexus between terror and international crime, turned on the Tamil Tiger groups on their soil. The latitude bred by the US-invoked 'global war on terror' was not lost on the Sri Lankan government, which soon adopted the language and rationale of the West. Secretary of defence Gotabaya Rajapaksa, the president's brother and one of many Rajapaksas now participating in the machinery of the Sri Lankan state, gave an interview to Reuters in 2007 in which he asked rhetorically about the difference between US anti-terror measures and those of Sri Lanka: '[In the US] they say covert operations . . . in Sri Lanka they call it abductions. This is playing with words,' he explained.[3] As the International Red Cross, for a century and a half the guardian of international humanitarian law, has observed, the global reaction against terror has reinforced the right of governments to use it.[4]

Another trend, now well noted, is the geo-strategic 'Great Game' being played out between the US and China in the Indian Ocean, a region that over the next two decades is set to become the economic powerhouse of the world. The south-eastern tip of Sri Lanka lies six nautical miles off the world's busiest and most important sea route into the oil hub of the Middle East. China has long had a significant presence on the island (Sri Lanka was among the first to recognise the 1949 communist takeover of China), but the commissioning of a billion-dollar deep-sea port in the once impoverished home town of Sri Lanka's president Mahinda Rajapaksa has significantly boosted the permanent Chinese naval presence in the Indian Ocean. As a corollary of these interests, China effectively blocked international action that might have prevented or moderated the mass killing of civilians at the end of the war. The Sri Lanka story, therefore, is a modest but significant sign of the new balancing of power between the US and China, a contest that is arguably the single most important political story in the decades ahead. It is symptomatic of the new 'Beijing Consensus', the notion that countries such as Sri Lanka can achieve economic prosperity, underwritten by China, without the inconvenience of domestic political freedoms expected by bothersome Western allies who still insist on notions of a shared moral order amongst nations.

Further to this is Sri Lanka's participation in what has been called the 'democratic recession'.[5] Around the world, the countries that became democracies in the 1970s, and following the end of the Cold War, are in decline. This decay is well illustrated in Sri Lanka, where the pay-off for aspiring to membership of a club led by Western liberal democracies is no longer quite as alluring as it was. With China as backstop, the Rajapaksa regime felt no compunction about thumbing its nose at murmurs of concern from a number of countries, and playing the 'rogue regime' card. Sri Lankan government officials have made a number of deals with Iran, Libya, Myanmar and Venezuela since Mahinda Rajapaksa was elected to the presidency in 2005.

Quite apart from the nose-diving trajectory of political freedom on the island, Sri Lanka highlights the effects of this recession on the UN. For example, at a time when the UN Human Rights Council had issued a dozen resolutions condemning Israel's invasion of Gaza, it produced only one resolution on Sri Lanka, which ignored credible allegations of war crimes by government forces. The comforting notion of a progressive respect and shared regard between nations for democratic norms, based on key human rights agreements such as the Universal Declaration of Human Rights, can be assumed less now than at any time since the end of the Cold War. What the Sri Lankan government now touts as 'the Sri Lanka model' for solving civil conflict will lead to more 'wars between the people',[6] in which the international fraternity of nations will be increasingly unable to interfere, and about which fewer nations will be troubled to object. Liberal peace-building (or nation-making) has at the very least been knocked off balance atop its pedestal, and with it much of the power of the 'carrot' of conditional foreign aid, and the 'stick' of international intercession to dissuade large-scale abuses by governments against their own people.

One question that is very reasonably asked in relation to the war in Sri Lanka is what else was the government supposed to do? Should they have stood back while the Tamil Tigers ran riot over the corpse of Sri Lankan unity? With the Tigers, under their enigmatic 'Supreme Leader' Velupillai Prabakharan, having proved their record of appalling violence, was armed conflict not the only solution? Given the guerrillas' record of duplicity and intransigence in negotiations, how could the Sri Lankan state trust any of the ceasefires they asked for, and is the world not better off now without the arms-trafficking Tamil Tigers? When the Sri Lankan Army (SLA), which for thirty-seven months had worked its way meticulously across the territory controlled by the Tigers, at great cost to young Sinhalese soldiers, finally bottled up Prabakharan, his son and heir and his senior commanders in a bunker, shielded by tens of thousands of trapped civilians, was it not best that they took no risk that he might escape?

I went to Sri Lanka as a supporter of that state's essential right to protect its sovereign territory, and I left with much the same view. However, I believe that the tactical choices the SLA was directed to make, and which contributed to the deaths of so many civilians, warrant a credible judicial investigation of the kind that the Sri Lankan state, in its current guise, is no longer capable of mounting. The large-scale deaths of civilians had less to do with a necessary absolute victory over the Tamil Tigers, and more to do with the nature of government spawned by the island's history as a modern nation state. It would be a mistake for Sri Lankans to gloss over the fact of these deaths; those who hope for a genuine peace and for the preservation of their democracy must eventually look full in the face at a violent past that has killed so many from every ethnic group. Bearing in mind the decisive role of the Chinese diplomat and philosopher Chang Peng-chun in framing the Universal Declaration of Human Rights in 1948, I do not share the view of some Asian leaders that individual human rights are less important in Sri Lanka than they are in New York City or the *banlieues* of Paris.[7]

I met and often spoke in depth with hundreds of diplomats, journalists, statespeople, intelligence officers, artists, civic and business leaders, Buddhist, Catholic and Hindu priests, activists, politicians, students, old JVP (Janatha Vimukthi Peramuna, or People's Liberation Front) revolutionaries, writers, ordinary soldiers, Tamil Tiger cadres, government functionaries, defence attachés, analysts, academics and many ordinary folk. The vast majority of Sri Lankans I met came across as kind and curious, and demonstrated that kindness with consideration and generosity. Most of the island's Buddhist monks do not advocate the extreme views of a minority who have courted and won political power. A coterie of elderly, mostly Sinhalese people whom I befriended, and who recalled a very different Sri Lanka, were particularly crucial in the fashioning of my views, and have served as a constant reminder of the rich intellectual and cultural life of their extraordinary land. Most of these people will, however, not be mentioned, and where I have been specific, I have almost invariably masked the identity of my source. This is especially necessary with the numerous Sinhalese sources both abroad and within Sri Lanka whom I consulted during my research, because of the implicit dangers for those seen as traitors. Sri Lanka continues to be a dangerous and unpredictable place for dissenters, particularly given the passage in September 2010 of the 18th Constitutional Amendment, which gives virtually unfettered power to the Rajapaksa brothers.

I was introduced to Gotabaya Rajapaksa – brother of the president, secretary of defence and the most powerful man in Sri Lanka – by an explosion that rent the air and sounded across Colombo like the sunset cannon. He had just survived a suicide attack on his convoy by a bomb-laden autorickshaw. Hours later, having been protected from the blast by his armour-plated BMW, he was photographed embracing the president, their warm smiles broadcasting the good fortune of his escape. For me, on my second day on the island, it was the first of many bomb blasts. I went on to encounter Gotabaya and his brothers and sister at meetings, official events and private functions. I did not meet or come to know much about Velupillai Prabakharan aside from what I read, or from stories told to me by people who had met him, although I communicated directly with others of the Tiger leadership, such as Thamilshevan, Nadesan and Pulidevan, all of whom were eventually killed. In the writing of this book, it seemed to me that the two chief protagonists in the final confrontation, Prabakharan and Gotabaya, were two sides of the same coin. Both had fought with courage and conviction over decades of civil war, albeit on opposite sides. Both were stamped with a practised brutality, neither trusted negotiation and both prepared assiduously for what they believed would be their final confrontation – albeit that each predicted an opposing outcome – in what is now known as Eelam War IV.

I was warned before going to Sri Lanka that when I left, I would know the country less well than when I arrived, and in a sense this is true. One learns of Sri Lanka's ethnic, religious, political and social complexities with a degree of exasperation. Nobody knows Sri Lanka better than her citizens, and a brief survey of the academic works available on caste, on nationalism and identity and on Sri Lankan history that have been written by Sri Lankans, as well as by other experts in the field, will describe a large body of work examining the great questions facing modern Sri Lanka. If the academic world in general is fraught with tiny squabbles and great confrontations, then one can only imagine the depth and emotion of such discussions in the hothouse atmosphere of the island nation, where the expression of ideas contrary to powerful interests can be perilous. This book is not intended as a substitute for the refined and considerable studies available to the interested reader, but as an accessible and lively account of recent Sri Lankan history, as a brief exploration of the antecedents to that history, and as a discussion of how the struggle of the Tamil Tigers reflects on global current affairs. I am not an expert on Sri Lanka, and do not strive to be one. My observations were honed by the three years I lived there, and the two decades during which I have spent a great deal of time in other conflict-ridden countries. As such, they are best characterised as the reflections of an informed observer.

There are aspects with which I have dealt lightly. I have not dwelt on the initial phase of the end of the war, which was the recapture of the eastern side of Sri Lanka between 2006 and 2007. I witnessed a part of those events myself, but I did not deem them central to the story that I wanted to tell, despite the fact that they were a dress rehearsal for what was to follow. Nor have I addressed in any depth the so-called 'Plantation Tamils', a community that in many ways has endured more discrimination and hardship than any other in Sri Lanka, because once again it does not go to the heart of what I think is most central to this tale. The successful, and now largely expatriate, Burgher community (those of mixed European and Sri Lankan ancestry) is barely mentioned. And Muslim Sri Lankans might think that I have forgotten their important role in the island's history, because of the sparse mentions I make of this industrious and cautious community that itself was the victim of ethnic cleansing at the hands of the Tamil Tigers. For that matter, I have not dealt in close detail with the matter of figures of dead and wounded, how they are calculated and how reliable those sources might be. I make the point in the text that it is for others to get closer to that particular particle of truth. Readers will find that Chapter Two, my survey of Ceylon's ancient and modern history up to the Sinhala Only Act of 1956, is dense, but not, I hope, unnecessarily so.

Almost three quarters of a century ago, in the heart of civilised Europe, my own grandfather and dozens of other relatives were taken from their homes and killed because of their ethnicity. From the age of about four, looking at a name inscribed on a gold fob watch, I was conscious of the scar left by the vanishing of my father's father. It is a silence even when spoken, an absence filled with emotional upheaval, though it eludes any clumsy assembly of words. From my own life I know that very distant and indistinct memories have a habit of hanging heavily over our present. So it has always been a source of wonder to me that men will coolly kill with satisfaction those whose only wrong is that they are of a different stripe, or hold a linguistic or religious distinction. As I have travelled through and worked in dozens of landscapes ruined by conflict, the fate of my own family in Auschwitz has thus coloured my view of the world. One misleading tendency seen at the end of the Sri Lankan war was the ascription of the root causes of the conflict to the formation of the Tamil Tigers, as if their popular support had arisen from nowhere. Yet the depth of hatred engendered by conflicting identities is palpable in Sri Lanka, and one only has to read the bile spilled across the online comments boxes following any articles written on this subject to get a taste of this continuing resentment. Although this book takes a detailed look at Sri Lanka and her circumstances, I am more interested in the general lessons that might throw light on the innumerable conflicts around the world, and those that will follow in our new era of 'small wars' and evolving hegemons.

Many readers will think this is a book solely about Sri Lanka, but I do not intend it that way. The recent European experience shows us that the divide between orderly, law-abiding societies and those that descend into a collective madness governed by hatred is a thin one. Civilisation, with all its supreme accomplishments, is a fragile veneer that must be constantly repaired. Even though Sri Lanka is uniquely Sri Lankan, the island serves as a cipher for the human condition, and all our woes. We cannot discuss grand ideologies, the greed and brutality of politicians, murderous clerics, the culpability of leadership, ethnic cleansing, murder and love between neighbours or the experimentation with different political systems without looking within at our own examples, and to the resuscitation of our own societies. The lesson of Sri Lanka is that we must always be sentinel to the weaknesses in our human design.

Finally, the international community was closely entwined in Sri Lanka throughout these final months, with the UN in a pre-eminent role, and the UN Secretary General Ban Ki-moon personally engaged in attempts to dissuade the government from using excessive force. It is impossible to examine the alleged crimes that were committed without a look at the guardian organisation of post-World War Two ideals, which had its boots on the ground and its staff in the thick of the action as thousands of men, women and children perished. The UN has many faces and many purposes, but it is justly famous for its role in peacekeeping and humanitarian operations that are at the cutting edge of an evolving intimacy linking nations to each other's affairs. These operations are comprised of complex moral, political and physical choices made by international civil servants who are often deeply committed and hard-working people trying to do their duty in apparently impossible situations. While the fact remains that responsibility rests with those upon whom it falls, I largely avoid decisive judgements about the UN's role, but I do record the critical views of those who have accused the UN of failing in aspects of its fundamental duties or, in the words of a *Le Monde* correspondent regarding the UN's role in Sri Lanka, of building on successive failures through 'excessive diplomatic prudence'.[8]

As the spokesman and communications adviser attached to the UN team during the years that included the end of the war, my job was to advise on the best way to procure, shape and disseminate information to support the UN's actions on the ground. I must therefore say a word about the International Civil Service Oath I took when I joined the UN, in which I swore not to divulge information obtained as a result of the office I held, whether or not I continued to work with the organisation. I have tried to balance the requirements of that oath with the compulsion to tell the story of those unprotected civilians who died during this conflict, and Sri Lanka's own tragic tale. I have done my best to interpret and use publicly available information, and have not drawn on confidential correspondence or internal reports, discussions and confrontations over proposed courses of action that were available to me solely by virtue of the position that I held. I have also striven to avoid passing personal judgement on the actions, or lack thereof, of colleagues. Inevitably, the convictions that have guided my interpretations were formed by the fact that I was close to events, and occasionally a privileged participant. I have freely made use of the testimony of associates who wanted their own perceptions to be known, and who wished to attach their names to that testimony from the simple belief that the death of so many should not pass unmarked.

CHAPTER ONE

The Lion's Victory

As the mist lifted on the morning of 19 May 2009, a soldier leaned down to a body on the smouldering and largely silent marshland battlefield. He tugged the slack shoulder to free it from the muddy patch in which it lay, and turned the corpse to face the sun. Like the hundreds of other troops inspecting the bodies strewn among the marshy tufts and sandy stretches of this desolate edge of the island, this soldier knew precisely for whom he was searching. Nevertheless, he must have been startled by the fleshy, mustachioed face that instantly stood out from the hundreds of other dead scattered among the mangroves, a face that stared back at him through dull, half-closed eyes, lips barely apart as if to utter a final command.

A bullet had pierced the forehead and the cranial cap was blasted away, but the otherwise intact figure of the corpulent founder and leader of the Tamil Tigers lay where he had fallen some hours ago. His brown face had been drained of blood, leaving a pallid waxwork that seemed to illuminate the oddness of this iconic figure lying in a mud patch, as though it were a discarded picture torn from a page in *Life* magazine. Despite the dirt, his uniform was neat and undamaged, as if he had emerged from a hidden bunker at the last possible moment to meet his death headlong. A holstered pistol was clamped to a belt around his thick midriff, along with six unused pouches of ammunition, and clipped to his chest was an identity card with his name, picture and the serial number '001'. Among the few possessions found in his small kit bag was a bottle of grape-scented hand lotion purchased in Singapore – an incongruous detail that the newspapers in Colombo would later seize on to discredit the fallen leader's reputation for rigid asceticism.

The Sinhalese soldier who chanced upon the corpse of Velupillai Prabakharan at the edge of the Nandikadal lagoon on the north-east coast of Sri Lanka had not even been born when the dead man began his career of violent insurgency. In 1975, when just twenty-one years old, and already with a reputed taste for rebellion and guns, Prabakharan assassinated the Tamil mayor of Jaffna with a single shot to the head as he prepared for prayer at a Hindu temple. Although Sri Lanka's tourist brochures boast of the island's balmy beaches, its soaring white Buddhist shrines, the warmth of its people and its sweeping mountain tea estates, this brutal temple killing was in fact a more fitting symbol of the young state, marred by ethnic, religious, caste and class warfare.

All through this young soldier's boyhood, the name of Prabakharan loomed large in the speeches of politicians, and was decried in interviews with the policemen and generals who tried to hunt him and his Tamil Tiger guerrillas down. The few photos that existed of his square-jawed face, either scowling or bearing a shy smile that mocked the cut of his fatigues, had for thirty years featured almost daily in Sri Lankan newspapers and on television screens, above articles detailing the mounting atrocities committed by Tamil Tiger forces. The stocky figure personified the claim of Tamil nationalists to a third of Sri Lanka's territory and, for the Sinhalese community, a fear of 'the other' that lived among them.

Prabakharan's shy manner and soft voice belied the orders he regularly issued to his guerrilla cells: to bomb buses full of women and children, assassinate heads of state, sink or seize ships, murder child monks and kill prisoners.[1] The mantra of the global Tamil Tiger propaganda network was that the Liberation Tigers of Tamil Eelam (LTTE),* as they called themselves, represented the right to Sri Lankan Tamil self-determination based around an independent state that would be known as Tamil Eelam. The fanaticism and commitment of the Tiger fighters recalled to observers the struggles of other post-colonial liberation movements such as the Palestinian Liberation Organisation, whose repugnant acts in the name of freedom seemed nevertheless to embody an elemental human instinct for justice and identity. Tamil Tiger fighters strung vials of cyanide around their necks in case of capture, and as a symbol of their readiness to die for 'the Movement'.[2]

---

* This book uses the term 'Tamil Tigers' in preference to the LTTE.

On the sandy spit that morning, the soldier radioed his position to his unit commander. He in turn raised the officer commanding Sri Lanka's 58th battlefield division – the division that had fought the Tamil Tigers until their final destruction at the edge of the lagoon. The brigadier was driven in a jeep from his forward command headquarters through an abandoned tent city that sprawled across the narrow pock-marked spit, a wasteland of torn plastic sheeting, bodies and burned-out vehicles. Since February, the tents had sheltered around 330,000 men, women and children besieged by the SLA, which pounded the area with heavy weapons in an effort to crush the Tamil Tiger guerrillas operating within the siege zone.

Over many weeks, as the Tiger strength waned, army assaults pierced the guerrillas' defences, and tens of thousands of civilians escaped in small batches or great waves. They struggled across the shallow lagoon that divided the government and Tiger forces, carrying their weak, wounded, elderly and young. Some were too exhausted or frightened to tend to those who were struck by bullets as they escaped, and ignored those who sank below the surface of the lagoon. The tent city, and anyone injured or left huddling in the trenches, was consumed as government troops moved in for the final kill. It was a conflagration of grenades and gunfire. In their flight, the refugees had left thousands of their dead in unmarked graves or simply lying in the open, discarded in the frantic rush to escape.

The battlefield was now silent – the groans of the wounded and dying had ceased. The brigadier walked the final few hundred metres across waterlogged grasslands, surrounded by his bodyguards, who shielded him against any surviving Tiger still lurking amid the charred and battered terrain. The brigadier examined the plastic face and swollen carcass of his fallen adversary, the insignia and pistol and the contents of his kitbag. He plucked the identity card from the chest of the dead man, and turned to proclaim the death of Velupillai Prabakharan, the 'Supreme Leader' of the Tamil Tigers, to the troops mustered around him. Then he beckoned to a staff member, who handed him a field radiophone, and rang through to the SLA commander based at the Ministry of Defence Joint Operations Headquarters in Colombo. Major General Sarath Fonseka in turn telephoned the news through to the man who had appointed him to lead the army: his former comrade-in-arms and now the most powerful man in Sri Lanka, the defence secretary Gotabaya Rajapaksa.

If the Sinhalese possessed an equal to Prabakharan's ruthlessness, commitment and grit, it was the defence secretary, a yeoman from the island's Sinhalese south. Gotabaya was no politician or insipid bureau-crat. A tough fifty-nine-year-old former colonel in the SLA, he had fought in some of the hardest engagements against the Tamil Tigers in the 1980s, when he had very nearly been killed. In 2005, his brother Mahinda had enticed him back to Sri Lanka with a promise of full support for a war against the Tamil Tigers – should he win his own planned bid for the presidency. Gotabaya, then retired from the army and working as a computer systems administrator at Loyola Law School, Los Angeles, always believed the SLA had been consistently betrayed in the field by weak political leadership. Mahinda's prospec-tive presidency promised revenge, glory and the possibility of a new political dynasty built on a military victory that had eluded the Sri Lankan government for almost three decades.

Within months of the end of the war in 2009, General Sarath Fonseka and Gotabaya Rajapaksa fell out with each other, with Gota-baya accusing the general of treason, and Fonseka accusing the defence secretary of war crimes. In 2006, however, with victory over the Tamil Tigers still a dubious and distant prospect, the two men had begun planning the eradication of the Tamil Tiger menace once and for all. They persuaded China to provide them with the arms they so badly needed, and began training troops and refining deployment and oper-ational tactics in preparation for the bloody war that was to follow. For the duration of this final stage of the civil war, Fonseka and Gotabaya worked closely, buoyed by one military success after another, as the army slashed its way through Tiger defences to the north. That morning, after taking the news from Fonseka, Gotabaya informed his brother, the president, that Prabakharan was dead and Mahinda's place in history assured.

Back in the northern marshes, four soldiers carried the bier with Prabakharan's body through a crowd of hundreds of weary and excited soldiers, each of whom raised his weapon above his head, like Roman legionaries cheering the fall of a Teutonic chieftain. Bearing their load steadily, they marched along a rivulet while troops lined the banks and leaned forward to snap pictures of the scene on mobile phones – images that soon spread throughout Sri Lanka and around the world to the watching and waiting Tamil diaspora. An army photographer caught the triumphal procession in a photo that made its way to the front page of the *New York Times* the following day. The lifeless and dishevelled body, picked over by so many hands, traverses a sea of smiling green-clad soldiers, whose outstretched arms might have been raised in a salute had it not been for the mobile phones grasped in their hands.

As the sun rose higher, the soldiers slowly bore the bulky corpse through the muddy pools of the bog and lowered it on to a dry sandy bank for closer examination by an SLA forensic team. The experts studied the uniform and the great gaping wound in the skull. They compared the pudgy face with the few photographs that existed of the reclusive Prabakharan, including those from a family album that had been found in an abandoned bunker the month before. They also took a swab from his mouth for a DNA comparison with the body of his son, twenty-two-year-old Charles Anthony, anointed heir to the Tiger leadership, whose body had been recovered from the battlefield and positively identified just two days earlier.

The forensic teams had already identified the bodies of the other senior Tiger leaders as they were dredged from bogs or dragged from the dune faces where they had fallen. They laid the fighters in long, stinking ranks, their corpses engorged, burned and mutilated, their arms outstretched, their flesh marked by chemical burns or cyanide, their faces contorted. When their *noms de guerre* appeared in the television broadcasts that day – Nadesan, Puleedevan, Charles Anthony, Kittu, Manimekala, Kannadasan, Rangan, Arul Vendan, Anna Thurai, Soosei, Rangan, Thomas, Purani, Bhanu – they read like the rolling credits from an epic and familiar film, one that had been watched many times. It was a reminder of the peculiar intimacy of the savage conflict that had consumed this small island nation for thirty years. Each name had been a minor hero in the pantheon of Tamil fighters who stood up to the Sri Lankan security forces, men and women deified by the hopes of the Tamil people. Tamils in Sri Lanka and around the world mourned the deaths of their too mortal gods.

For the Sinhalese, who account for three quarters of Sri Lanka's twenty million people, the deaths of the guerrillas inspired a very different reaction. As each dead Tamil commander was identified, word spread rapidly throughout the country by news service text messages, and was passed from mobile phone to computer screen, to

Facebook page, and Twittered and Googled for every fine detail of their demise. In the street cafés of the capital, each television news flash brought volleys of firecrackers that echoed in the streets. Strangely, though, that last day there was little of the air of celebration one might have expected at the end of such an epoch. How should some mark the end of fear, and others the end of hope? The scattered crackle of fireworks seemed disjointed and half-hearted, an almost muted struggle to believe that this long civil war, which had killed well over 100,000 people during three decades, might have ended. Most Sri Lankans had only ever known the state to be at war. They had lived with the daily fear of Tamil Tiger attacks for so long that they felt numbed shock instead of joy. For well over half of the country's independence, road-blocks, mass searches, urban bomb blasts, arbitrary arrests, casual police brutality and lawlessness had been the norm.

Government death squads and 'disappearances' had become a feature of public life. Armed men hauled their victims from the streets and off to their deaths on isolated beaches or in paddy fields. Although the majority of the victims during the war had been young Tamil men, the government also targeted opposition leaders and lawyers, human rights activists and academics, humanitarian workers and journalists. In January 2009, in one of the most brazen assassinations in the country's history, Lasantha Wickrematunge, a national newspaper editor embroiled in a legal dispute with the government, was shot and killed by masked gunmen in a Colombo street. Wickrematunge had predicted his own death in an editorial, quoting the words of Martin Niemöller, the German theologian and resister to Nazi terror:

> They came first for the Communists,
> and I didn't speak up because I wasn't a Communist.
> Then they came for the trade unionists,
> and I didn't speak up because I wasn't a trade unionist.
> Then they came for the Jews,
> and I didn't speak up because I wasn't a Jew.
> Then they came for me,
> and by that time no one was left to speak up.[3]

Outside of Sri Lanka, the news of the deaths of Prabakharan and the senior leadership came as a shock to most informed observers, who knew the Tigers' reputation for tenacity. They had grown from a core band of around three dozen members in 1983 to a small army of some 5,000 battle-hardened fighters by 1987. Not only had they held back the numerically superior armed forces of the Sri Lankan state for three decades; they had once decimated an expeditionary force from the world's fourth largest army. The Indian intervention force sent to bring peace to the island battled the Tigers for three years in the streets and jungles of the north, until forced to withdraw in humiliation, leaving more than a thousand of their dead. In May 1991, the Tiger leadership sent an operative to India to kill the Indian political leader who had been responsible for the presence of the Indian army in Sri Lanka. Former Prime Minister Rajiv Gandhi died in a suicide bomb-blast of steel ball bearings and ceremonial marigold petals.

Now, in May 2009, those guerrilla leaders lay dead around the Nandikadal lagoon, and thousands of civilians had been killed or wounded over the final five months of fighting. Some still lay dying on the battlefield amidst the detritus, while Sri Lanka's government brazenly declared that no civilians had died at the hands of its forces. The US, Britain, France, Mexico and a number of other countries had tried to stop the bloodshed through the UN Security Council, reasoning with the government that with Prabakharan and the Tigers surrounded, they would gain more by preserving civilian lives. Newly elected US president Barack Obama had urged the regime to show restraint, and his Secretary of State Hillary Clinton had offered the services of the US navy to evacuate Tamil civilians, leaving the SLA free to deal with those who remained bearing arms. The Sri Lankan government, backed by Russia and China in the Security Council, refused all entreaties.

Until the very end, the Tigers had been no pushover. Throughout the 1980s and 1990s, steeled by the battles fought against the Sri Lankan and Indian armies, the Tiger forces had evolved from classic fleet-footed, Kalashnikov-armed guerrilla units into a conventional combat force capable of holding and defending territory. Their de facto state in northern Sri Lanka gradually expanded through battle, and their strength of arms, military capabilities and organisational might grew. They boasted a naval unit of small attack craft, known as the 'Sea Tigers', which sank Sri Lankan warships and pirated merchant ships on the high seas. They also ran a merchant fleet of more than a dozen cargo vessels, which engaged in legitimate trade and carriage of goods worldwide, as well as arms and people smuggling. Known as the 'Sea Pigeons' and crewed by Tamil seamen, these vessels frequented Japan, Indonesia, Singapore, Turkey, France, Italy and Ukraine, and served as warehouses to store and manufacture munitions. The Tigers slowly built the world's first – and to date only – insurgent air force, which launched night-time bombing raids on Colombo and military bases across the island, while small suicidal penetration teams mounted daring assaults on naval bases and public utilities deep inside government territory. In 2001, one such unit attacked Colombo's Bandaranaike airport, blowing up twenty-six military and civilian aircraft, including six Air Lanka jets, in full view of hundreds of startled European holidaymakers.

For a decade, the Tigers held almost a third of the territory of Sri Lanka, including a swathe of its richest agricultural land and one quarter of its coastline. In the areas they ruled, they had constructed an efficient administration that mimicked the workings of a fully fledged state, with perhaps a fifth of Sri Lanka's 2.5 million Tamils living under their writ. The Tigers built a parallel system of government that included courts of law, municipal administration, a police force, a customs service, a tax and legislative code, a banking system, and a television and radio network. They sought recognition for their homeland, and took heart from the internationally backed independence movements for Timor Leste and Kosovo. In what they called Eelam (a Tamil word implying separation), a small portion of the Tamil inhabitants of Sri Lanka began to enjoy the fruits of an independence long denied by the Sri Lankan state, including the right to use their own language.

The growth of the Tamil Tiger organisation mirrored the changes that took place in global trade, finance and communications following the end of the Cold War. The Tigers exploited the loosening governance of state borders and international financial transactions, and the flourishing trade in eastern European and Chinese weapons. Their transnational multifaceted corporate operation steadily accumulated global resources that were then used to fund their liberation struggle. European motorists refuelled their cars at petrol stations that served as legitimate fronts for Tiger earnings and money laundering. A dedicated finance department known as the 'KP Department' operated from offices abroad, and managed the growing web of complex income generation. An efficient propaganda and political operation took root in dozens of countries amongst the million-strong Tamil diaspora. International sympathy for the liberation struggle confounded successive Sinhalese governments, which wavered between a militant policy toward the Tigers and one of unsuccessful peacemaking. The growth of a de facto Tamil state and a network on foreign soil fuelled Sinhalese suspicions that the world beyond Sri Lanka cared little for the majority Buddhist population, and that India in particular, with a population of sixty million Tamils in its southern states, harboured territorial designs over northern Sri Lanka. After all, it was India that had connived to train Tamil guerrillas on Indian soil, and to export them back to Sri Lanka.

In 2006, the Sri Lankan army under Gotabaya's control began its push to reclaim the sovereign territory held by the Tigers. That push culminated three years later, when the remnants of the Tamil Tiger force was caged on a small sand spit the size of New York City's Central Park. The Tigers' refusal to surrender unconditionally, their forced retention and recruitment of civilians and the government's determination to destroy the leadership at all costs created the conditions for a bloodbath.[4] Contrary to denials by the government, UN international staff had witnessed the wholesale bombardment by government forces of unarmed civilians. The United Nations High Commissioner for Human Rights, among others, cautioned the regime that it might have committed war crimes.

Sri Lanka's government celebrated their victory in grand style with military parades, promotions for army commanders and medals for the troops. Town councils, businesses and schools erected posters and billboards of the president, lavishing him with praise. President Rajapaksa gave offerings in gratitude to the Buddha in the Temple of the Tooth in the highland town of Kandy, an honour not bestowed by the high priests on any person since the last independent Sri Lankan kingdom almost two centuries ago. He gave speeches pronouncing in an expansive manner that there would 'no longer be any minorities, just Sri Lankans'. Towering cutouts of the Rajapaksa brothers stood in the middle of internment camps where the hundreds of thousands of Tamils who had survived the siege now languished in captivity. As his motorcade swept past in the streets of the capital, people bowed and kissed the earth. Young professionals surveyed by a national newspaper opined that Rajapaksa ought to be appointed king, since he had in their view 'rescued Sri Lanka'.

History casts a harsh light on the work of kings, as the 'Sun King' Prabakharan had discovered. The defeat of the Tamil Tigers brought great relief for a majority of Sri Lanka's people, who had lived for a quarter of a century in fear of terrorism. But for millions of others, the Tigers were the one force standing between them and an oppressive state that had institutionalised discrimination and denied them their identity. The grievances that had given rise to the Tigers did not disappear with their destruction at the Nandikadal lagoon. Nor was their end a harbinger of the end of mass violence in Sri Lanka. On the contrary, all the signs indicate that the government of Sri Lanka will continue to distance itself from its secular, democratic and liberal foundation. There is no hint of a political offering that will remove the *casus belli* for which the Tamil Tigers fought, and thus perhaps no escape from the island's cycle of violence.

The Tamils and Sinhalese have shared Sri Lanka for thousands of years, in varying states of domination and cooperation. Around 18 per cent of the island's population are Tamils; roughly 12.5 per cent of those are held to be Sri Lankan Tamils, as opposed to Indian Tamils, a difference that is relatively meaningless to outsiders, but replete with fine distinctions for *all* Sri Lankans. The Tamils are a Dravidian people, virtually indistinguishable from the Tamils of southern India, while the largely Buddhist Sinhalese trace their lineage back to northern India, and make up a little under three quarters of the island's population. These two main ethnic groups use separate alphabets and each speaks a language that is unintelligible to the other. Ancient Sri Lanka had been ruled by rival Sinhalese and Tamil kingdoms whose origins remain the subject of competing historical accounts. As in similar 'ethnic' conflicts, Sri Lanka's political class has used selective interpretations of an indistinct past, based on narratives of 'them and us', to shape and pursue power. The story of that pursuit is what must be examined next.

CHAPTER TWO

Paradise Found

On 16 May 1880, a tall American soldier with a distinguished bearing disembarked from a merchant ship in the elegant, languid and over-heated port of Colombo to begin a new phase in his life. At forty-eight years of age, Colonel Henry Steel Olcott had already carved a remarkably diverse career across a range of professions and passions that today might earn him the sobriquet of 'unsettled'. Forced to leave university due to his father's bankruptcy, this restless and enquiring man had journeyed from farmer to journalist, soldier in the American Civil War to insurance lawyer and distinguished commissioner in the investigation of the assassination of Abraham Lincoln. He was involved in some of the great movements of his era, from the abolition of slavery to temperance and women's suffrage. To his admirers in Ceylon, he would become known as 'the Awakener'.

The first real steps in Olcott's journey to Ceylon* were taken in 1874, when he attended a series of seances in Vermont. This brush with the metaphysical fired a spiritual revelation in him, which inspired him to write a book called *People From the Other World*. Spiritualism has faded in the public imagination of the twenty-first century, but in the middle of the nineteenth, Europe and America were peppered with drawing-room seances. In darkened rooms professional spiritualists put the middle classes in contact with their dead children, remonstrative parents, disinheriting aunts and a full cast of historical luminaries who had passed to the other side but kept themselves available for consultations. Every small town in the US could expect a well-advertised visit from a medium versed in the art of hypnosis, levitation, mind-reading and hoodwinking.

---

* The terms 'Ceylon' and 'Sri Lanka' are used interchangeably throughout this chapter.

Its most serious adherents, however, regarded spiritualism as the emerging global religion that was bound to subvert Christianity – 'Dead, dead, stone dead! Your Christianism is dead!' as one spiritualist would have it.[1] This ambitious status allowed it to claim a great many belief systems by vague or total assimilation, from animism and Zoro-astrianism to philosophy and astrology. From the vague stirrings of spiritual possibilities beyond the dominant Christian churches emerged a sturdy residual interest in the great religions of the Orient. In 1875, Olcott had been one of the founders of the Theosophist Society, dedi-cated to the exploration of 'universal brotherhood; comparative religion, philosophy and science; and the unexplained laws of nature and the powers latent in man'.

The Sri Lankan civil servant and essayist Sam Wijesinha wrote of Olcott, 'It is a curious thing that Buddhism, which was introduced into Ceylon by one foreigner . . . should have been "rediscovered" in Ceylon, 2,000 years later, by another foreigner, an American.'[2] Some of Olcott's more fervent followers suggested that he was a reincarnation of that first foreigner, Mahinda, whose father, the great north Indian Mauryan emperor and Buddhist convert Ashoka, had sent his son to establish Buddhism on the island in 246 BC. By the time of Olcott's arrival in 1880, Buddhism had been all but extinguished in India for more than a millennium, so that Ceylon, at the tip of the subcontinent, was the last redoubt of Theravada Buddhism, and its Sinhalese practitioners the keepers of the flame.

Olcott had come to save Ceylon's Buddhism. His fellow theosophist, the German-Russian aristocrat Madame Helena Blavatsky, brimful with foggy Wagnerian fantasies of hierarchical racialism, accompanied him down the gangplank. After 500 years of European colonialism, Ceylon's temples had crumbled, and its *bhikkhu* orders declined. In Olcott's view, the aggressive incursions of Western missionaries on one hand, and osmosis with Hindu practices on the other, had usurped authentic Buddhist traditions. Nevertheless, he had detected the poten-tial for a popular backlash. In the mid 1860s, a series of public debates in Ceylon had pitted Christian theologians against *bhikkhus*, and the latter had proven more than capable of matching the churchmen. In 1873, the *bhikkhu* Migettuvatte Gunanada achieved a kind of immor-tality in the most famous debate before the arrival of Olcott. The thrill that this intellectual contest apparently generated amongst the island's

Buddhist adherents is testimony to the hold on the Buddhist masses of a well-argued point, and to the respect that the oratorical tradition arouses in general in Sri Lankans today.[3]

These debates sounded the first notes of the Buddhist awakening into which Olcott stepped, having read an account of the oratorical contest back home in America. Once in Ceylon, he saw that the *bhikkhus* were outcasts in their own land, and that Buddhism was encircled, if not actually in decline and decay. While the Buddhist temples were destitute and the *bhikkhus* beggarly, Christian priests were closely integrated with the British colonial establishment, the churches were well funded and their congregations booming. Christian practice was a pathway to social acceptance and worldly success, whereas Buddhism seemed mired in archaism and regression. The religion of the *bhikkhus*, their vows of poverty and their very simplicity worked against the grain of the times. The torpid lack of interest of peasants in their temples seemed to pale beside the evangelising energies of missionaries, with the *bhikkhus* more concerned with arcane doctrinal differences than with retaining their followers.

Olcott's arrival is also a convenient point of departure in this story because the most significant roots of the island's modern conflict are little more than a century old.[4] In this regard, Sri Lanka can usefully be compared with Israel, another modern nation state that embraces two major ethnic groups while rejecting the full occupancy rights of one. Both are littered with ancient ruins, and with recorded chronicles (the Old Testament in the case of Israel, and the Mahavamsa and other Buddhist chronicles in the case of Sri Lanka) that, having been selectively interpreted to give fervid meaning to the past, suggest a stillborn vision of the future. Both countries have used shreds of what is known of the ancient past to support inflexible claims to modern nation states which bear scant resemblance to the earlier forms of society that once stood in their place. Both have used these glorified 'compensatory fantasies'[5] to diminish, ignore or suppress the identity and place of other minority claimants whose history is rooted in the same soil.

Sri Lanka's position on the map, dangling at the tip of India like a pearl earring, provides the setting for her history. The stepping stones of small islands that trickle sixty kilometres across the Palk Straits between southern Tamil India and northern Tamil Sri Lanka, known as Adam's Bridge, were once a land bridge, and the country 'is in the cultural and historical sense part of the vast Indian composite as truly as if its northern straits were a peninsula'. A Stone Age aboriginal population of 2,000 Vedda people are all that remains today of the earliest human groups who are thought to have populated the island for more than 100,000 years. Around 1000 BC, a culture with black and red ceramics, iron, horses and irrigation intrudes into the archaeological narrative with evidence of a shared regional culture, spanning central and southern India and ancient Sri Lanka. Around 500 BC, in a turn of events that corresponds with passages of the story chronicled by the Mahavamsa, as well as parts of the Indian epic poem the Ramayana, fragmentary evidence emerges of the arrival of north Indian habitation on the island.[6]

The rest of the world has been writing about Sri Lanka for two millennia. On Ptolemy's second-century map the fulsomely drawn island of Taprobane, as the ancient Greeks knew Sri Lanka, represents in its exaggerated proportions the breathless tales of infinite riches and beauty carried home by Roman, Greek, Arab and Chinese traders.[7] These merchants told stories of a lush land with fruit trees growing wild, bejewelled and sensuously half-clothed women and gleaming white *dagabas* bulging like mushrooms from the dark soil to rise above the green jungle canopy. Marco Polo stopped in Ceylon in around 1293 on his way back from seventeen years at the court of the Chinese emperor Kublai Khan. He added to the manifold claims to Sri Lanka's beauty when he wrote: 'In the land of Seilan there is an exceeding high mountain . . . the Great Khan heard how on that mountain there was the sepulchre of our first father Adam.'

In 1347, about fifty years after Marco Polo's visit, the great Moorish traveller Ibn Batuta landed in Serendib (the Arabic name for the island, from which the word 'serendipity' originates) on a pilgrimage to visit the mountain of which Polo had written. Known today as Adam's Peak, the mountain in the rugged central highlands is claimed by Muslims to be a giant footprint left by Adam; the same feature is revered by Buddhists as the footprint of Buddha and by Hindus as that of Shiva. Batuta also visited the court of the island's most powerful king, the Tamil Pararasasekaram III, at his seat of Jaffna, as well as the cities of Galle, Kuranegala and Colombo, the last of which he noted was the largest and finest city in Ceylon. Like ancient Greece or Renaissance Italy, Ceylon was a land of disparate city-state kingdoms, with power radiating outwards, increasingly feeble and vague the further from the throne, occasionally overlapping or conflicting with the interests of other seats of power.

The occupants of the island begin to write about themselves around the fourth century AD with the Dipavamsa chronicle, the first in an almost unbroken line of *bhikkhu*-authored histories that have monopolised modern Sri Lankans' understanding of the past.[8] Written in Pali, an ancient literary Indo-Aryan language, the Dipavamsa was a tale woven from mnemonic verses, ancient Pali texts and Sinhala commentaries. The *bhikkhu* text most central to contemporary Sinhalese nationalist dogma, however, is the Mahavamsa, which was written in the sixth century by a *bhikkhu* called Mahanama, an uncle of the reigning king.

The Mahavamsa records the arrival of the first Sinhalese on the island, the tearaway Prince Vijaya – the Victorious One – exiled by his king from northern India with a retinue of 700 men in 483 BC (the year also said to be that of the death of Buddha). Vijaya was the product of a union between a lion (Sinha) and a fair-skinned north Indian princess, and soon after landing on the island he coupled with an unprepossessing *yaksha*, one of Ceylon's original inhabitants. The legend roughly accords with the archaeological evidence of a sudden north Indian influence. It describes three visits to the island by Buddha, and his supposed subsequent deathbed anointing of the island and its faithful people to a role as guardians of 'true' Buddhism. It lists the reigns of a variety of successive rulers in fairly short order, until it reaches a great culminating battle in the second century BC, in which the island's Sinhalese king Duttugemenu kills a neighbouring Tamil king called Elara.

The Buddhist author of the chronicle has much to say about this Manichean battle, which today is a story familiar to every schoolchild in the island. Most immediately, Sinhalese nationalists have promoted this fabled primordial triumph as a metaphor for the current struggle between competing Tamil and Sinhalese claims to their rightful roles in the modern state.[9] More fundamentally, the Mahavamsa is cited as literal evidence for the Sinhalese claim to the whole island as a matter of historical record and right. With the killing of Elara by Duttugemenu, the true faith of Buddhism is rescued from extinction, the menacing Tamil horde is drubbed and the Sinhalese nation and the island itself are saved – for the Sinhalese.[10] Just as the Old Testament is treated as the literal command of God and an immutable force of nature by Zionist nationalists to dislodge the claims of others, so the Mahavamsa is deemed to be the literal transmission of the Buddha's will. The undue emphasis on this simple tale masks a vastly more complex tableau.

If one begins by standing in the fragrant air of the ruined jungle city of Polonnaruwa, in the centre of the country, one of the great capitals of the Ceylonese kings, it is possible to grasp the far more uncertain, disordered yet undeniable strands of history of this tangled land. The city had been founded around the third century AD, and had fallen to south Indian Tamil invaders only a few decades before Marco Polo landed in 1293. Polonnaruwa is a mossy-stoned marvel of cultural syncretism that conflicts with the rudimentary version of history derived from the selective readings of the Mahavamsa preferred by Sri Lanka's Sinhalese nationalists. The site is littered with shrines dedicated to both Buddha and the Hindu god Shiva, and in its shapes and on its walls, in the Gandharian curve of a Buddha's gown or the soaring peak of a *dagaba* lifted straight from Angkor Wat in Cambodia, one sees the complex threads of received cultures woven over two millennia into the island's magnificent history. In its wonderful stone halls, pillared temples, lotus baths and statues, laid out next to a vast silver lake whose shores are encrusted with the muddy footprints of sunbathing elephants, the continual flows of cultural confluence between India and Sri Lanka, together with other momentous civilisations throughout Asia, are displayed like a huge archaeological and ethnological map.

These flows came to the island in many forms. Buddhism was the shared dominant religion in both India and Ceylon for more than a thousand years up to the early Middle Ages. There were dozens of waves of outright Tamil invasion over the millennia – 'a never-failing source of harassment' – as well as the custom of marriage between the ruling elites that saw the scions of Indian dynasties (as well as their considerable retinues) marrying into the island, and Ceylonese princes and princesses marrying into the mainland royal houses. But beyond these well-recorded exchanges, there was the constant traffic of trade, excursions, borrowed ideas, shared artisans and internal migration. The Sinhalese anthropologist Siran Deraniyagala wrote in 1996 that from the Palaeolithic period onwards, the 'unimpeded gene-flow between southernmost India and Sri Lanka (in both directions)' was what created the people one encounters today in the streets of Colombo or Jaffna.

Today many academics challenge the simplistic proto-nationalist interpretation of the Mahavamsa. In times that were constantly uncertain, and when power was both local and always under contest, the tale of Duttugemenu vanquishing Elara was as much an allegorical political tract as it was a stab at recording history that even then was a retelling of events more than five hundred years old. It reminded the king for whom it was written of the transient nature of personal power, and of the importance of the sangha – and by extension the central role of Buddhism – as a source of constancy and a pillar of his reign.

To many historians, the Mahavamsa also provides evidence that contradicts ideas central to the 'exclusive' version of history favoured by Sri Lanka's Sinhalese nationalists, versions of which can be read in the newspapers or seen on television daily on the island. For example, it indicates the equally ancient presence of Tamils in Sri Lanka, undermining claims that they have only been on the island in significant numbers for the past few hundred years. Far from a monolithic contest pitting one race against another, Duttugemenu's battle against Elara was in fact the epilogue of a series of some thirty-two battles, fought mostly against other Sinhalese kings and princes. From the Mahavamsa, it is evident that there were many Tamils in Duttugemenu's army, while many Sinhalese fought for Elara. The battle represents a small episode in an exceptionally long series of conflicts between squabbling chiefs, princes and kings who ranged across Ceylon's landscape for two thousand years prior to the arrival of European invaders. Each pretender to power left behind signs of his impact in the form of the kinds of edifices, statuary and stone inscriptions one encounters in the ruins of Polonnaruwa.

Polonnaruwa was, however, before its abandonment around the time of Polo's visit, certainly the centre of a resistance to aggressive Hindu expansionism. Since the fifth century AD, three great Tamil dynasties, the Chola, the Pandyas and the Pallavas, had competed for dominance in southern India, and their excursions frequently spilled over into Ceylon. In Polonnaruwa, the struggle against successive invading Tamil armies forced the distillation, for the first time, of a distinct Sinhalese identity derived from a mixture of language, people and Buddhist religious practices. By the thirteenth century, Buddhism in the outpost island off the Indian subcontinent was a lonely echo of a religion that had once dominated the entire Asian region. Abandoning their claim over the lands of central Ceylon in the face of these invasions, the Sinhalese kings retreated to the south-west quadrant of the island, while a Tamil kingdom solidified in Jaffna. From the thirteenth century through to the first quarter of the twentieth, 'a vast forest belt separated the Sinhalese from the Tamils of the north and east'.[11] From the early sixteenth century, a Ceylon exhausted by invasion fell under varying degrees of domination from the emerging eastward expansion of the seafaring mercantile empires of the Portuguese, followed by the Dutch and finally the British. Polonnaruwa, consumed by jungle, was forgotten until its rediscovery and unearthing by the British in the nineteenth century.

Like forgotten Polonnaruwa, the Mahavamsa was in effect lost to the world until 'found' and translated into English by amateur scholars in 1838. The British uncritically elevated the chronicle as proof of the ancient Sinhalese lineage on the island, to the exclusion of other potential claimants who could point to no such equivalent text.[12] In keeping with the romantic imaginings of the time, the Sinhalese were hailed as a kind of lost civilisation, an Aryan outpost dangling from the dark Dravidian underbelly of India. It is odd to contemplate today that it was not until the British governor commissioned a Sinhala translation in 1877 that a majority of Sinhalese became aware of the existence of the Mahavamsa.[13] That translation coincided with the first glimmers of Buddhism's reawakening, and with the adolescence of a precocious Sinhalese political mystic called Anagarika Dharmapala, who served as secretary and translator to Olcott when the American arrived in Ceylon in 1880.

When Olcott stepped ashore in Sri Lanka, the Singer sewing machine company's first Colombo shop had been open just a few years, a harbinger of a future garment industry central to the island's economy in the twenty-first century. That year, British advertisers were using images of the Buddha to market everything from towelling, sewing machines and crockery, to spoons and salt. Colombo was dotted with colonial buildings and brick bungalows, which characterised the broad and easy luxury of the colonial Briton's life. In between and all around were the mud, thatch and wooden post huts in which the vast majority of the Ceylonese lived. Asia's oldest grand hotel, the glittering white Galle Face Hotel, the future vacation abode of monarchs and film stars, had been open for a decade on the Colombo shorefront, next to the old Dutch fortress and its green parade ground where British troops mustered for weekly parades.

British engineers were building the basic network of road and rail links throughout the island that still stood the country in good stead well into independence, linking plantation with port. The British colony was thriving due to its plantation economy, as well as its central position on Asian and European sea routes. A new class of Sinhalese entrepreneurs, made rich by the concessions they held over tax collection, the brewing of alcohol and running gambling and cock-fights, invested their capital in land, plantations and graphite mining. Many of these *mudaliyars*, as they were known, had long records of loyal service to the Portuguese, Dutch and then English rulers.[14] They formed a self-styled feudal class that yielded families like the Senanayakes and the Bandaranaikes, the first prime ministers of independent Ceylon, as well as the large family conglomerates that still dominate Sri Lanka. Colonial 'wasteland' acts continued to benefit these enterprising families and created a class of landless peasants.[15]

A disastrous blight had wiped out the embryonic highland coffee industry, leaving planters no choice but to replace the sorry crop with tea trees imported from Assam in northern India. Within a decade, Thomas Lipton's clippers made Ceylon's tea world famous – the time-less image of a Tamil 'tea plucker' in bright headdress hoisting a basket on her back became iconic in Britain and around the world. Unable to find sufficient labour on the island for the gruelling task of harvesting coffee and tea on the steep mountain slopes, the British encouraged poor Tamils from southern India to make the short crossing over the Palk Straits and then to trek into the interior – a terrible march into bonded labour during which thousands died from disease and exhaustion. Between 1830 and 1900, hundreds of thousands of Indian Tamils arrived in Ceylon to work the vast tracts of land opened up by the British for the booming plantation economy. By the first decade of the twentieth century, the number of Indian Tamils equalled that of native Ceylonese Tamils.[16]

Kandy, an elegant city in the heart of the rugged hill country, lies just north-west of Adam's Peak. It is considered the cultural heartland of Sinhalese consciousness because of its bitterly fought resistance to European invaders for more than two centuries. Long after the lowland coastal regions had succumbed to European merchants and troops, the last king of Kandy surrendered to the British in 1815, helped along by his feudal chiefs, who had tired of his bloody reign. Kandy had been founded in the thirteenth century after the fall of Polonnaruwa, and had been one of the three kingdoms that dominated the island at the time of the Portuguese incursion in 1505. By 1880, however, the Kandyan royal palace and the great temple holding the Tooth Relic of the Buddha were appurtenances in a city of courthouses, tennis courts, churches, barracks, planters' clubs and Victorian houses. Nevertheless, it was said that whoever controlled the Tooth Relic of Kandy controlled the sovereignty of Ceylon, and even today, the senior clerics of the leading Buddhist orders seated in Kandy are the first to be visited for blessings by newly appointed army commanders, incumbent politicians and victorious presidents.[17]

When the British unseated the last king of Kandy in 1815, they united Ceylon for perhaps the first time in its history. The feudal chiefs who formed the king's court acceded to British rule under a treaty that in theory preserved Buddhism's special place in the affairs of state.* But the finely tuned nexus between politics and religion had been embodied in the person of the king, and in practice the intimate connection of Buddhism with governance ended with his abdication. His dynasty was Hindu and originally from southern India. The kings had preserved and protected Theravada Buddhism and the sangha even as they selected Hindu brides for their Buddhist princes. The rule of this last royal dynasty was yet another reflection of the coexistence of Tamils and Sinhalese communities that characterised the island, and of syncretic worship. Tamils and Sinhalese had lived for more than two thousand years as neighbours, and so too did they pray. Hundreds of temples across the island are constructed in a style that 'reflects the fusion of Buddhism and Hinduism'.[18]

In 1880, the vestiges of Portuguese encroachment on to the island littoral in the sixteenth century could be detected in some coastline

---

* A small but notable footnote to the treaty is the fact that only three of the signatory chiefs signed in Sinhala. The rest, including the Sinhalese ancestor of future prime minister Sirimavo Bandaranaike, wrote in Tamil.

communities where Portuguese was still spoken, despite the intervening two centuries of Dutch followed by British rule. One of the later Ceylonese chronicles, the Rajavaliya, reported the Portuguese landing in terms that presaged the violence of their impact: 'Information was brought to the King that there was in the harbour a race of very white and beautiful people who wear boots and hats of iron and never stop in one place. They eat a sort of white stone and drink blood . . .'[19] The landing of the Portuguese had been the beginning of another dark age of invasion. The colonisers destroyed vast numbers of Hindu and Buddhist temples with apparent relish, plundering their treasures and claiming their ravaged lands. As one Ceylonese wrote, the bigotry and cruelty of the Portuguese towards the Ceylonese 'would be incredible, if there was not the testimony of their own historians'.[20] Jesuit priests are recorded taking to grand and ancient shrines with iron bars. The Portuguese seized the Tooth Relic and took it to Goa, where it was reportedly pounded into dust and burned (although according to Buddhists it reconstituted itself, took wing and arrived safely back home). Despite their rapacious impact, they were able to convert to Christianity many of the coastal landowning communities, both Tamil and Sinhalese, who today hold names such as de Silva, Fonseka, Perera and Don Carolis. Within a century of the Portuguese landing, trade and tax privileges, as well as proximity, meant that half of the country's coastal dwellers professed to worship in Christian churches.

Even further north, on the Jaffna peninsula proper, the Tamil population was making the most of the opportunities offered by British colonial rule. The Jaffna kingdom had succumbed to the Portuguese in 1619, almost a century after the conquerors had smashed the temples of the southern Sinhalese kingdom of Kotte. Despite its famous vegetables and fruit, the hot and relatively arid peninsula held little of the industrial-scale plantation or mineral promise of the bulk of Sinhalese Ceylon. The Tamils fished, farmed and smuggled goods from India across the Palk Straits.

American missionaries, who had come to the peninsula to teach and proselytise, left the Tamils with one great benefit they would exercise under the British: the English language. The British, it is often said, favoured the Tamils; in fact the Tamils simply exploited one of the limited advantages they held. From the 1830s, the British had recruited from the native population the bedrock of a civil service. At the time, around three quarters of the student population were located in missionary schools in Tamil areas. Jaffna also boasted one of Asia's earliest medical schools, thanks to the foresight of its political leaders. Tamils travelled easily between British-ruled India and Jaffna. With their English and academic skills, the Tamils started as errand boys, clerics and managers, before they evolved to become doctors, lawyers, engineers and senior civil servants, who oversaw much of the administration of the country. [21]

This critical role was a cause for complaint in independent Sri Lanka and would become one of the subtexts for the culling of Tamils from the education system in 1972, in an act defended by the government as 'affirmative action'. But in 1880, and indeed for the following four decades, there was no sense of resentment by the Sinhalese at the success of Tamils in the civil service and the professions. In 1899, for example, the leading Buddhist journal had this to say about one of the great Tamil civil servants, Ponnambalam Ramanathan, also an early theosophist with a passionate interest in the Buddhist revival: 'The Buddhists owe Mr Ramanathan a deep debt of gratitude. His interest in the question of the *Vesak* holiday and the Buddhist Temporalities Bill . . . and a host of other services towards Buddhism have endeared him immensely to the Buddhists of Ceylon.' [22]

Around the same time, Ramanathan's brother Arunachalam wrote a short monograph, *Sketches of Ceylon History*, an untroubled and generous recounting of what was then known about Ceylonese history, in which he decried the sparse appreciation that most Ceylonese had for their own grand narrative. [23] In his book, Arunachalam, who was also one of the island's leading civil servants, celebrated its two majority communities, the Sinhalese and the Tamils, whom he evidently saw as the heirs to an ancient lineage of grand history, having shared the land for more than two thousand years. Tamil civil servants were considered politically mature and progressive, and represented the interests of all communities with an even-handedness and pedantic capability that irked a succession of British governors. The two brothers were famous for shaping the vision of an independent Ceylon, and Ramanathan in particular for championing Buddhist causes. In 1880, the communal divisions that mattered most were those of caste and religion, and it was this debate that Colonel Olcott joined.

*   *   *

Within two weeks of their arrival in Ceylon, Olcott and Blavatsky had taken Buddhist precepts at a Buddhist monastery in Galle, and thus became the first Westerners formally received into Theravada Buddhism. Olcott recognised the disadvantages Buddhism faced, and turned next to organise change with the practised hand of a campaigner. His determination ignited the Buddhist monastic orders, alarmed the British colonial authorities and churchmen and left a legacy so profound that it is easily visible in Sri Lanka today.

The first warning the complacent church received was the establishment in 1880 of a chapter of the Buddhist Theosophical Society in Colombo to serve as campaign headquarters. 'As the Christians have their Society for the diffusion of Christian knowledge,' said Olcott, 'so this should be a society for the diffusion of Buddhist knowledge.' Over the next three years, during his intermittent stays in Ceylon, he sold subscriptions, organised defence committees, wrote and distributed anti-Christian tracts, toured the provinces in a home-made bullock cart and conducted mass healings. He also wrote a simple catechism of basic Buddhist principles – 'an antidote to Christianity', as he described it – that was translated into twenty languages and is still widely used in Sri Lankan schools today.

In 1884, Olcott travelled to London to intercede with the British colonial authorities, who were investigating the cause of a riot in Colombo a year earlier between Buddhists and Christians that had killed two men. Ceylon's governor Sir James Longden had claimed that the unexpected revival of Buddhism in just a few short years was a cause of the riots, as well as the role of Olcott, who had, he said, 'brought the energy of Western propagandism to [the revival's] aid'. 'The outer evidence of it is to be seen in the rebuilding of old shrines . . . the larger offerings made to the Temples . . . a greater number of ordinations held with greater publicity . . . and the preparation of Buddhist Catechisms in the native and even in the English language.'[24] Olcott left London with agreements in hand that recognised the right of Buddhists to practise rituals hitherto forbidden, such as the beating of tom-toms in processions, and the celebration of their holidays. On 28 April 1885, the first Ceylonese Vesak* under the British was celebrated as a national holiday.

---

* An annual event that marks the birth and death of Buddha.

Over the following ten years, the society supported the building of three hundred Buddhist schools and funded the education of Buddhist teachers, effectively undermining what had been the unchallenged Christian control of Ceylonese youth through the education system. Significantly, Olcott inspired a generation of Buddhist intellectuals and *bhikkhus* who were impressed by the conviction and unflagging efforts of the American in his campaign to reverse the decline of Buddhism.

The most important of these disciples, and one who is central to the tale of troubled independent Sri Lanka, was the son of one of Colombo's richest merchants, who had amassed a fortune under colonial rule. Don David Hewavitarne was just sixteen years old when he met Olcott, a meeting that took him to the heart of Buddhist revivalism in both India and his own country. While still a teenager, he renounced the wealth of his family, took a vow of celibacy, donned the rough yellow cloth of a devotee of Buddha and, changing his name to Anagarika Dharmapala (meaning 'homeless one'), fashioned himself into a sackcloth religious activist, halfway between peasant revolutionary and touring celebrity orator.

Dharmapala remains revered in modern Sri Lanka, and almost every town in Sinhalese areas has a road named after him. In the south, families garland his image and venerate his statue. His Facebook page proudly celebrates the baton of Buddhist revivalism that he carried into the twentieth century. But Dharmapala, who became translator and assistant to Olcott when still a teenager, would in time transform his mentor's revival of universal Buddhism into an acutely politicised nationalist revival, notable for the xenophobia and exclusivity that lay at its heart. Seizing on the Mahavamsa chronicle that had so recently been translated from English into Sinhala, he identified the Sinhalese inextricably with their Buddhism, the soil of Ceylon as much a part of them as their blood and the Tamils as their eternal enemies.

Whereas Olcott saw Buddhism as a worldly and scientific philosophy for all people and all ages, Dharmapala, with his dreamy spiritualism and capacious intellect, came to regard Buddhist practice in Ceylon as a vehicle for Sinhalese hegemony – and an inheritance for the Sinhalese alone. He took the energy and organisational skills of his mentor and adapted them to serve the Sinhalese Buddhist national project he envisioned. He had the marketing sense of a modern celebrity, exemplified by the conceit with which he managed his photographed image. His extraordinary charisma was apparent when, in 1893, Olcott sponsored his protégé's trip to the World Parliament of Religion in Chicago, where the *St Louis Observer* wrote of him: 'With black curly locks thrown from his broad brow, his clean, clear eyes fixed upon the audience, his long, brown fingers emphasizing the utterances of his vibrant voice he looked the very image of a propagandist and one trembled to know that such a figure stood at the head of the movement to consolidate all the disciples of Buddha and to spread the light of Asia throughout the world.'

Dharmapala touted simplistic interpretations of the Mahavamsa and Duttugemenu's battle with Elara to support his notion of an ethnically pure Aryan Sinhalese people. He articulated a Sinhalese Utopia that seized the threads of a disordered and stirring Buddhist consciousness and wove them into a simple, bright, appealing and fabled tableau of the past 2,500 years. His sermons, harangues and boudoir political invocations meshed the identities and interests of an emergent Sinhalese ruling class with their mass power base: the millions of Sinhalese consumers who formed two thirds of Ceylon's population at the turn of the nineteenth century.

Dharmapala's criticism of the Sinhalese masses upon whom he practised his arousing rhetoric was scorching. He accused them of barbarism, drunkenness, poor hygiene and superstitious ignorance: 'If there is a semi-civilized utterly selfish race in Asia it is the Sinhalese.' His ideology fused his own internal contradictions – blatant misogyny and a rumoured proclivity for children – with the nationalist project. He imposed values on Sinhalese women that subdued a famous and distinctive island sensuality.[25] He commandeered the history and culture of the Sinhalese and ritualised numerous aspects of their ordinary life – food, clothing, worship and language – packaging these elements into digestible messages that could be carried through the country by pamphleteers, street actors, touring gramophones, newspapers, *bhikkhus*, union activists and the burgeoning mass temperance movement with which he was allied.

He took Olcott's vision of Buddhism as a philosophy for the modern world, and converted it instead into a reference point for anti-colonialism. He equated British rule in Ceylon with the throttling of Buddhism by Hinduism in India: 'What the Brahmans had been then the British are today.' Using his formidable instinct for propaganda, he campaigned for the restoration of important Buddhist pilgrimage sites in India, where he blamed the near extinction of Buddhism on its violent suppression at the hands of Hindu and Muslim conquerors a thousand years before.

Dharmapala's professed concern for humanity at large – 'the lion's roar', as he called it – carried with it a significant measure of dislike for other races that belied the global love for man that he touted. In the newspapers he founded, he exerted an overtly racist and exclusivist muscle that has become reflexive in much of the ordinary political and social discourse of Sri Lanka today.

> This bright, beautiful island was made into a Paradise by the Aryan Sinhalese before its destruction was brought about by the barbaric vandals. Christianity and polytheism are responsible for the vulgar practices of killing animals, stealing, prostitution, licentiousness, lying and drunkenness ... The ancient, historic, refined people, under the diabolism of vicious paganism, introduced by the British administrators, are now declining slowly away.[26]

Central to his thesis was the notion of a vulnerable and encircled pure Sinhalese race polluted by 'Semitic and savage ideas' and exploited by 'cunning foreign Semites' schooled in the arts of commerce. As a propagandist, he generated a rhetoric that licensed the increasingly extreme expressions of contempt for other nationalities that would follow in the twentieth century.

> The Muhammedans, an alien people ... by Shylockian methods became prosperous like the Jews. The Sinhalese, sons of the soil, whose ancestors for 2358 years had shed rivers of blood to keep the country free of alien invaders ... are in the eyes of the British only vagabonds. The Alien South Indian Muhammedan come to Ceylon, sees the neglected, illiterate villagers, without any experience in trade ... and the result is that the Muhammedan thrives and the sons of the soil go to the wall.[27]

By the early twentieth century, this highly politicised version of Buddhism had trumped the original apolitical ambitions of the Theosophical Society, and Dharmapala had successfully situated Buddhism in the vanguard of a Sinhalese national awakening. As is so often the case with great partnerships, the falling out between Olcott and Dharmapala, when it came, was bitter. By 1905, the protégé Dharmapala had renounced his earlier adulation and labeled Olcott 'a cheat, imposter . . . fraud . . . and timeserver', even as he anointed himself a bodhisattva devoted to working for 'Buddha and Humanity'.

By the time of his death in 1933, Dharmapala's narrow and inflexible self-portrait of the Sinhalese as a chosen people situated on their island paradise since time immemorial was fixed in the popular imagination. His intoxicating political Buddhism had been propagated among generations of Buddhists educated in schools originally founded by Olcott, and inflamed by popular Sinhalese newspapers that catered to the newly literate masses. The stage was set for a nation that in the achievement of its own identity and independence in 1948 saw denial of the identity of others in their midst – Tamils, Muslims, Christians – as their right. As the modern state took form, excessive Sinhalese Buddhist nationalism would dismiss the complementary claims of other of the island's communities to Ceylon's scroll chronicles, stone inscriptions, shattered pillars, soaring effigies, earthen burial mounds and sites of pilgrimage.

In 1915, Ceylon marked the centenary of the abdication of the last king of Kandy. Muslims complained that an activist at Adam's Peak had distributed offensive political leaflets printed by Dharmapala's press. Zealous intolerance spilled over as Sinhalese mobs attacked Muslim traders throughout south-west Ceylon. Thousands of houses were burned, mosques desecrated and pillaged and more than two dozen people murdered. The ostensible spark was a long-standing resentment at police ordinances preventing the beating of tom-toms outside mosques and churches by marchers during Buddhist processions (over which Olcott had won concessions in 1884).[28]

As the mobs attacked, they shouted slogans such as 'There is no English Government. This is the day of the Buddhists. This is our flag.'* The genuine grievances held by Buddhists over restrictions on their traditional practices were organised into an economic opportunity to trounce the tiny and successful Malabar Indian Moor community, who bore the brunt of the attacks. The reaction of the

---

* The Buddhist flag used throughout Sri Lanka was designed in 1885 by a committee that included the father of Anagarika Dharmapala. It was later modified by Colonel Olcott, who then introduced it to Japan and Burma.

colonial police force provides an early model for the kind of brutality that is institutional in Sri Lanka today. The police killed dozens of people, including Dharmapala's brother. Many were arrested for incitement, and military tribunals conducted the trials of the ring-leaders.

The result of the riots was that, while Dharmapala's style of chau-vinism continued to fester in the popular imagination, his influence on the engine of the Ceylonese independence movement sputtered. As the British colonial authorities stamped out the embers of the 1915 riots, an elite group of Sinhalese and Tamils grasped the potential of independence based on a gradual legal transfer of power from Britain to Ceylon. This elite was composed of men who had an interest – polit-ical, economic and cultural – in sustaining the paternalistic hand of the state, since many of them had long been the direct beneficiaries of colonial rule. An advisory body to the governor known as the legisla-tive council, made up of one representative drawn from each of the European, Sinhalese, Tamil and Burgher communities, had existed since 1833.[29] This early inclusive British political reform set the tone for what would be, a little over a century later, a seamless transition to independence, as well as for the cloying intimacy of Ceylonese political life.

Many of the same families who represented their communities on the council during the nineteenth century took up the reins of power when the British departed in the twentieth. The grandfather of the two Ponnambalam brothers – a friend to Disraeli and Gladstone – repre-sented the Tamils for much of the nineteenth century, while an ancestor of future prime minister S.W.R.D. Bandaranaike was the first Sinhalese representative to the legislative council. Thus the council had two effects critical to the exercise of power in future independent Ceylon. First, it established an oligarchy of families who retained political control right up until the twenty-first century, when the advent of the Rajapaksas decisively broke its hold. Second, and far more dangerous, it aligned communal identities into early blocs of power, which mattered little in 1833 when exercised by a few lofty men in the gover-nor's chamber, but was hugely significant when subject to the weight of an electorate a century later.

During the few years following the 1915 riots, and unlike in India, where the Indian National Congress policy of peaceful confrontation was met with violence and a stubborn colonial administration, the English-speaking elite steered the island comfortably towards self-rule. In 1917 a Tamil, Ponnambalam Arunachalam, was elected by the acclaim of the largely Sinhalese elite, in recognition of his stature as spokesman for both communities, to lead the first organised political body in negotiations for independence. Paradoxically, however, the Ceylon National Congress would expose the manifold schisms so fundamental in this island society. The legacy of stable governance that the British hoped to leave at independence would fall victim to complex allegiances of race, religion, caste, region and economics in an increasingly ugly bid for dominance.

The most obvious of the schisms that came to dominate Ceylon was that between Tamils and Sinhalese. But it might well have been another, as elite politicians defined their politics and reconfigured their cultural allegiances in the bid for popular support. The high-country Kandyans claimed a Sinhalese purity of culture that had been preserved through their stubborn military resistance to European invaders. They marked themselves as quite distinct from all other Sinhalese. The people of the littoral areas, particularly around Colombo, had fought, been defeated by, traded and intermarried with Asian and European invaders, taken foreign names and assumed the religion of the colonisers. Further south, in what is popularly known today as the island's deep south Sinhalese belt, this assimilative tendency waned, and a great majority of the Sinhalese retained their Buddhism. (It is no surprise that the anarchic and violent Sinhalese Marxist uprisings of the late twentieth century, which will be dealt with in the next chapter, should have emerged from this area of Sri Lanka.) The Kandyans were adamant that they should be recognised as a constituent minority in a future state, separate and distinct from all low-country people.

The Tamils, who comprised about a quarter of the population, were equally divided. While caste distinctions cut across both majority communities like a knife, they are on the whole more stubbornly fixed in Tamil social organisation than in that of the Sinhalese.[30] Regional differences were equally important. The Tamils of the northern Jaffna peninsula distinguished themselves from those of the eastern seaboard by virtue of caste and history (this distinction would later fatally weaken the Tamil Tiger insurgency, when a vital eastern commander betrayed them). The imported Plantation Tamils, situated in the centre

of the island, equal in number to the indigenous Tamils and by then
well established in Ceylon for generations, were considered so dispen-
sable that at independence in 1948, Tamil politicians colluded with the
Sinhalese-dominated government to deny almost a million of them
citizenship and equal rights in the budding state. Close to half a million
were deported 'home' to India.[31]

In addition to the schismatic majority groups, the island was sown
with a plethora of smaller communities, equally complex and riven.
The small but powerful Muslim population included a variety of
discrete groups, from the Borah to the much larger Malay and
Moors, the latter further divided into the Indian, Ceylon and coast.
To add to the general confusion, the Moors mostly spoke Tamil,
while asserting that their language was no indication of any relationship with those who spoke Tamil and worshipped as Hindus. The
Christian Burghers were coffee-skinned mixed-blood children of
Dutch and Portuguese extraction. There were Europeans, Jews,
Yemenis, Sindhis, Chinese, Eurasians and Zoroastrian Parsees, as
well as a variety of African groups who had arrived as slaves with the
Portuguese and who retained distinctively African customs. Finally
there was a tiny group of some two thousand Veddas, descendants
of the island's original inhabitants. Apart from race, religion,
language, region, class, caste and socio-economic group, there were
abiding distinctions between urban and rural, the educated and the
illiterate and, increasingly as the country moved towards independence, different political creeds.

In 1921, elections were held for the first legislative council to be
dominated by a majority of elected members. An expanded voter
population cast their slips along ethnic lines, and suddenly the position
that the Tamils had long held as one of the two main ethnic groups,
with equal representation as advisers to governors, dropped away to
reveal a stark reality. In a single blow, the customary equal balance
between Tamil and Sinhalese representatives was laid waste. Independence would mean that the fate of the minorities now rested permanently
with a Sinhalese majority. The Ceylon National Congress, which had
attempted to bring a steady and united hand to the impending challenge of self-rule, now appeared to be merely thin brushwork over the
serious cracks in communal harmony exposed by looming independence. A crestfallen Arunachalam, who reluctantly joined a political bloc

of aggrieved Tamils that sought power-sharing guarantees, personified the new Tamil insecurity.[32]

Despite this, the tiny, clubbish Ceylonese ruling elite that dominated the path to self-rule continued to sustain a tone of gentlemanly anti-communalism, as if by habit. During the 1920s, the mass forces generated by Dharmapala's proselytisation seethed and organised beneath the surface of public political life. The English newspapers of the capital (the only ones that mattered to the educated English-speaking privileged class, arriviste and aspiring) kept up a gentle discourse that lent confidence to the political process and reassured the British governor. References to race were considered poor taste. In contrast, the heaving Sinhalese press, geared to a booming population narrowly educated in the vernacular, was alive with 'a fine weave of myths, orientalist writings and popular perceptions . . . In this imagined past where the [Sinhalese] self was being shaped, the question of who was a migrant took a new turn.'[33]

These newspapers were owned by an emerging class of prosperous Sinhalese entrepreneurs for whom the issue of 'ownership' – political, economic and cultural – was of crucial importance during a period in which tropical Ceylon's economy had stagnated after decades of growth. These same men funded Dharmapala's presses, which were grooming the future electorate. Just as in Germany at the same time, the interests of the industrialists often coincided with those of the workers, provided that their energies were usefully directed. Dharmapala's crude, assertive and intolerant discourse created a road map for the relatively vague and disordered world view of the capital's growing proletariat (and more distantly for the lower middle classes of the provinces, where the newspapers also reached), hitherto preoccupied by soft syncretic Buddhism and distinctive Ceylonese beliefs in astrology, spirit worlds and superstitions. Dharmapala regarded strikes by Sri Lankan workers 'as a manifestation of a spirit of nationalism'.[34] Other newspapers would follow suit, with the worst excesses mimicking the admiration of many Europeans for fascism; Sinhalese pretensions to Aryanism were a perfect fit. The Ceylon labour party's Sinhalese-language newspaper, *Viraya*, exalted Hitler's example of racial intolerance, and exhorted workers to avoid mixed marriages with non-Sinhalese.[35]

In 1927, forced to accept the inevitability of self-rule in India, the

British government appointed a commission to overhaul Ceylon's constitution. Delegations queued to present a bewildering array of sentiments to the Donoughmore Commission. The Ceylon National Congress, by now dominated by Sinhalese interests despite the various groups represented within, succeeded only in convincing the commission of their anti-democratic credentials and pretensions to oligarchic rule on behalf of the masses. One subset delegation from the congress rejected self-rule on the basis that the Ceylonese were not up to the task, whilst another delegation representing the radical wing argued for universal franchise. The Sinhalese Kandyan delegation, asserting their minority status in the face of southern Sinhalese dominance, vetoed self-rule, as did other delegations representing minorities.[36] It was a sign of the shape of politics to come.

The commission, in a remark that reverberates today from the pages of its final report, recognised that Western parliamentary government was a model not necessarily suited to Ceylon. The report noted: '. . . we can detect few signs . . . to make us confident that parties, if and when formed, would owe their origin to economic or political differences in national policy rather than to racial or caste divisions'.[37] Nevertheless, it recommended universal suffrage (including for the Plantation Tamils), the abolition of communal representation, endorsed under British rule for a century, and a system of seven executive councils combined under the roof of a state council, with significant powers retained by the governor. The aim was explicitly to prepare Ceylon for self-rule, cut from the cloth of British parliamentary democracy.

Ceylon, unified by Britain in the nineteenth century, was on the cusp of self-rule as a modern democratic nation state. The state council recommended by the Donoughmore Commission was designed to be a step beyond the communal bloc representation of the legislative council years, but still a step short of full independence. The hope was that in the intervening years, a kind of political maturation would take place. Communalism would loosen its hold, and in its place new blocs would distil around competing political ideas, much as happened in Britain. But minority appeals for fixed representation in the state council only sharpened the focus of a communalist lens through which all policies were suspiciously scrutinised. As it chugged along to the next elections in 1936, the state council gave the overall impression of an establishment club for gentlemen. It unhurriedly argued out the complexities of majority rule, while minority representatives tried in vain to fend off Sinhalese demands for further constitutional changes that would outwardly embrace parliamentary democracy while strengthening their political dominance.

The board of ministers in the state council was dominated by the figure of D.S. Senanayake, Ceylon's future first prime minister, who had cut his teeth on organised politics in the temperance movement three decades before. Senanayake symbolised the oligarchy of families who had capitalised on British rule, whose interests lay in protecting their own wealth, status and position and who saw themselves as the heirs presumptive once Britain relinquished power. As minister of agriculture, D.S. Senanayake had overseen a huge growth in agricultural settler schemes. The forest lands that had engulfed Anuradhapura and Polonnaruwa for centuries, and which divided Tamil northern Sri Lanka from the Sinhalese south, were being cut down. One study estimated that in less than twenty-five years, one quarter of the island's population moved from the Sinhalese-dominated 'wet zone' into the Tamil majority 'dry zone'.[38] Senanayake's programme in the so-called dry zone was grounded in practical exigencies, for Ceylon imported rice to feed its booming population. Land reclamation helped the growing class of landless Sinhalese peasants, many of whom had been ejected generations before by British regulations from lands that were subsequently purchased by capitalist families such as the Senanayakes.

However this sensible plan to feed and employ people was also pregnant with significance for Dharmapalan nationalists. Senanayake himself was wont to espouse crude communalist slogans, and seems to have believed that the Sinhalese were a 'chosen people' who, as the custodians of Buddhism, were destined to survive for 5,500 years.[39] Like the crumbled viaducts of Italy, the thousands of ancient abandoned dams throughout the dry zone recalled a magnificent city-based 'hydraulic civilisation'. Sinhalese peasant colonisation centred on the galaxy of tanks that would irrigate not just the arable land that Ceylon needed in order to feed itself, but also the political programme of Sinhalese chauvinists, a confluence in which they delighted. Tamils learned to regard the creeping land reclamation of huge projects such as the famous Gal Oya, Allai and Kantalai schemes in Tamil-dominated eastern Sri Lanka as an invasion by stealth on to territory they considered to be theirs. Sensible state policy became a manifestation of Tamil powerlessness, the reaction to which was the increasingly strident and expansive Tamil claim to a 'traditional' Tamil homeland, known as Tamil Eelam.[40]

Full independence was delayed by the outbreak of the Second World War. A cabinet of ministers dominated by Senanayake lent its unstinting support to the war effort, with the understanding that independence would follow victory. The war provided a singular if deceptive economic boost to the strategically vital island – the Clapham Junction of the Indian Ocean[41] – with Lord Louis Mountbatten's Asia Theatre Command located there. Crucially, in a period during which evolving party politics were learning to play to the gallery, the foundations were laid for Ceylon's costly welfare state for an expanding population. Yet despite occasional lapses into communalist rhetoric, Senanayake signalled his determination to see Ceylon emerge as a secular and multiracial polity and was careful to make the distinction that while Buddhists would inevitably govern the country, it should never be a Buddhist government. In contrast, future prime minister S.W.R.D. Bandaranaike and young guns like the future president J.R. Jayawardene understood the full potential of communalist politics, and agitated for policies explicitly favouring the Sinhalese majority.

In 1948, D.S. Senanayake became the first prime minister of independent Ceylon. Just six months after India and Pakistan so bloodily achieved their independence following years of painful struggle, Ceylon's own independence came about in a process 'so bland as to be virtually imperceptible to those not directly involved'.[42] Senanayake ushered in a peaceful nation redolent with promise, with a ready-made constitution and a glittering industrial and transport infrastructure. It was regarded with envy and admiration by its neighbours, as the very model of propriety. Its British-bequeathed Soulbury Constitution, drawn from a formula devised by the state council's cabinet of ministers in 1944 and incorporating explicit guarantees for the protection of minorities, self-consciously imitated British-style parliamentary democracy.

Ceylon was the second wealthiest Asian nation after Japan (a slightly misleading comparison, given Japan's post-war poverty). With almost 60 per cent of the budget devoted to social welfare, the burden of expectation created by an electorate increasingly aware of its rights would come to tragic fruition in the decades ahead. Senanayake's newly formed United National Party (UNP) incorporated a diverse cabinet of interests: from S.W.R.D. Bandaranaike's Sinhalese Maha Sabha [43] political base to the Tamils, Burghers and Muslims. All seemed to fit beneath the generous, if crowded, umbrella of inclusion, bar the Tamils of the tea plantations.

To many Ceylonese, however, the facile transfer of power from the discomforting grasp of British colonial government to Senanayake's national unity government was barely discernible and left them uneasy. Strung between the urbane, educated English-speaking Colombo elites and the equally urbane left-wing parties forming something of an opposition, the vast and influential rural lower-middle-class Sinhalese – *bhikkhus*, Ayurvedic practitioners, [44] notaries, teachers and community leaders – were dismayed by the lack of the linguistic, religious and cultural expression that had been promised with the dawn of a new era. To people fed for decades on a newspaper diet of Dharmapalan nationalism, the outwardly cosmopolitan liberal parliamentary state bore little relation to their expectations. Self-rule seemed like a cheat.

Instead, power remained a family affair, mimicking the heyday of the legislative council. D.S. Senanayake was prime minister, with the portfolios for defence and foreign affairs; his son Dudley Senanayake, a future prime minister, was minister of agriculture; his nephew John Kotelawala, another future prime minister, was minister of commerce; while his cousin J.R. Jayawardene, a future president, was minister of finance and another nephew became minister of trade. Frustrated by this family oligarchy, the majority waited for a leader to come knocking at their door. Throughout the 1940s, a new generation of Dharmapalan nationalists stoked the fires of Sinhalese chauvinism. Through his books and essays, the brilliant Sorbonne-educated *bhikkhu* Walpola Rahula provided intellectual rigour to a political Buddhism that he asserted had been the foundation of the Sinhalese state since time immemorial. [45] Capitalising on this thirst, in 1951 S.W.R.D. Bandaranaike left the government to found the Sri Lanka Freedom Party (SLFP). [46]

Nineteen fifty-six marked the 2,500th anniversary of the death of Buddha, and the year in which Prince Vijaya landed on the shores of Ceylon with his 700 men to found the Sinhalese nation. Ceylon thrilled with incipient millenarianism. During the years leading up to the anniversary, the vernacular press carried the yearnings of the Sinhalese masses along. The population had boomed, the post-war economy was buoyant and expectations were being driven by access to free education, a generous if ruinous social welfare system and a sense of political change. The issue of language and nation was by now inextricably entwined with the frustrations of the Sinhalese Buddhist constituency. The Tamil domination of many parts of the bureaucracy and places at university was an easy target.

On a visit to Jaffna in late 1955, UNP Prime Minister John Kotelawala made a rash promise to a gathering of Tamils that he would institute a series of additional guarantees for minorities. Considering the epoch, it was a foolish miscalculation. The UNP had grossly underestimated the grass-roots support for the Sinhalese Buddhist nationalist demand that absolute linguistic dominance be delivered. Bandaranaike seized the moment he had been waiting for: 'I have never found anything to excite the people quite the way this language issue does,' he remarked (in English, because his Sinhalese was halting). He announced that the SLFP was the party of change. At an election rally in ancient Polonnaruwa, he addressed the crowd with a cry of 'Sinhala in twenty-four hours!' When asked by an adviser whether he had meant it, Bandaranaike replied that he would cross that bridge when he came to it. It was an act of supreme political imprudence that has haunted the island ever since. A panicked UNP cynically followed suit. In a move that fell utterly flat with the electorate, it attempted to trump the SLFP with an even more assertively chauvinist language policy. Bandaranaike was elected in 1956, along with the burden of managing the creature that he had unleashed.

Within months of his election to office, and to great popular acclaim, Prime Minister Bandaranaike had steered the passage of the 1956 Sinhala Only Act through parliament.[47] Thereafter, the Act served as an enduring reference point for the rising pitch of Tamil nationalism. Despite efforts by successive governments to reverse or moderate this tragic opportunistic mistake, for Tamils the law was immutable proof of the innate racism of the majority. The Sinhala Only Act unleashed mob violence that killed hundreds of Tamils in 1956 and 1958. In everyday life, powerless Tamils experienced bureaucratic exclusion in a multitude of laws, ordinances and casual encounters. Just as damaging, the Act further cemented into the Sinhalese mass psyche the notion of a Dharmapala-inspired linguistic nationalism. Incredibly, in the 1970s, the sentiment embodied by the Act was enhanced under the government of Bandaranaike's wife, Sirimavo. Consequently, radicalised Tamil students and teenagers, stymied by an official discrimination already endured by their parents, founded the Tamil Tigers.

One last episode will connect Bandaranaike's linguistic nationalism with the present. Before he was assassinated by a *bhikkhu* in his front garden in 1959,[48] the prime minister recollected the scene eight years earlier when he had crossed the floor of parliament from the government of D.S. Senanayake to begin establishing his own bid for power. Looking over his shoulder, he noticed what he described as a fleeting shadow, and turned to see the figure of a stout but insignificant southern parliamentarian from the Hambantota district following behind him. It was D.A. Rajapaksa,* casting his lot in with a man he believed was destined to lead Sri Lanka. The Rajapaksas remained in the shadows of Sri Lankan politics until the twenty-first century, but when they eventually emerged, it was in a manner that their father could not have dreamed of that day: his four sons achieving a great military victory over the Tamils and amassing a fortune that would make the simple mud-floor home in which they were raised seem very distant indeed.

---

* He was the only MP who followed Bandaranaike across the floor that day.

CHAPTER THREE

Paradise Lost

Late one night in October 1988, a group of medical students gathered around the body of one of their friends in a damp, humid breeze-block room at the medical faculty in Colombo. The battered corpse of twenty-two-year-old Padmasiri Thrimawithana lay stretched across a wooden bench ordinarily used during anatomy classes. The students traced their inexpert fingers gently across his torso in an attempt to discover something of his last hours through the hieroglyphics of his wounds. The body was covered in bruises, cuts and cigarette burns, several of his limbs were fractured and almost all of his ribs had been broken. Savage blows had distorted his handsome face and half a dozen of his teeth had been knocked out. His attackers had torn clumps of his hair out by the roots and his brow remained furrowed by the terrible pain he had endured until the point of death. A nail had been driven into his head.

Earlier that day, a telephone call to the students had heralded the discovery of the bodies of the young medical student and two of his friends, dumped in a field several hours from the city. The four students who volunteered to drive from Colombo to collect the bodies would themselves become death-squad victims in the prolonged violence that lay ahead. Padmasiri had been distributing posters and meeting with local officials in the famous gemstone mining town of Ratnapura, as part of a protest by state medical students against degrees awarded by a private college to the children of wealthy and privileged families. The study of medicine at a state university was a path for only the very brightest of pupils and a rare guarantee of a prestigious career that was open to even the most impoverished. Padmasiri came from a poor Sinhalese family; his alcoholic father was a low-level provincial official.

The solemn, studious boy had excelled at school and won a place at the University of Colombo's medical college, where he was noted for his intelligent, kind and even-tempered demeanour. Three days before the discovery of the bodies, witnesses in Ratnapura had seen the young men forced into a green Pajero jeep at gunpoint before being driven away.

The sheer scale of the public outcry over the murder of a bright medical student eventually led to an arrest. The accused, the son of a local politician, was traced from the vehicle he used in the abduction. The legal convolutions of the trial guaranteed, however, that he was eventually acquitted – an all too common occurrence in Sri Lanka's judiciary. Padmasiri's murder faded from public memory – despite the 100,000 people who attended his funeral – his name disappearing into the mire of homicides, terrorist outrages and officially sanctioned mass murders that have characterised the island's history since 1956. Some of the men and women who gathered around his body that night, and who later took his ashes back to his parents' home and comforted his grieving young siblings, are today among the top physicians and health officials in Sri Lanka; others have left the country in despair over its future. Padmasiri's alleged killer now holds a portfolio in Mahinda Rajapaksa's government, along with a motley crew of other ministers with reputations for routine thuggery, murder and even mass killings.

If Padmasiri's case is remembered at all today, those asked might hazily recall that he was an activist in the JVP, the violent young Marxist revolutionary organisation that almost bludgeoned the state to its knees. As such, they might say, he deserved, at least in part, a death he had courted. With hindsight, Padmasiri's murder was a harbinger of perhaps the most gruesome and frightening period of 'crimes against humanity' bred by Sri Lanka's independence. Today, the Sinhalese know the JVP insurrection of 1987–90 as the *beeshana kalaya*, or the 'time of great fear'. This exceptionally bloody epoch, during which teenagers were tortured, 'necklaced' and strung up en masse in public squares, was a direct consequence of the clash between Dharmapala's barefoot activism and the interests of an entrenched governing elite.

The insurrection was in fact the second of two such uprisings by Sinhalese youth against the government under the banner of the JVP. The first, in 1971, led to the death or disappearance of perhaps 10,000 people before its scorching revolutionary fire was brutally extinguished by the army. The vast majority of the victims killed then, in a series of appalling extra-judicial murders, were between fifteen and twenty-five years old. The better planned and executed, and far bloodier second JVP insurrection is perhaps history's only instance of a militant challenge from one generation to another that brought a state to the very brink of implosion. Perhaps inevitably, this mortal threat to government provoked a terrible backlash. The 1987–90 uprising led to the deaths of more than 40,000 (and possibly tens of thousands more) Sinhalese youths at the hands of the police, army and paramilitary death squads.

The insurrections are just as extraordinary when measured alongside other modern mass crimes against humanity committed in states that had, or later developed, access to institutions of democracy and which later achieved some measure of reconciliation or 'closure'. Unlike in Argentina, Chile or South Africa, in the Sri Lankan polity – the government, society, the courts and the families of the victims – the terrible crimes committed, by Sinhalese against Sinhalese, remain frustratingly unaccounted for. Despite numerous government-appointed inquiries over the years, there have been virtually no prosecutions of murderers. No leader or decision-maker has been held to account, and there has been no full or frank reckoning with the past that might have given a modicum of satisfaction to the victims and their families.

Indeed, the JVP uprisings reveal an abiding dark truth about modern Sri Lanka, which strikes the observer powerfully and casts a detectable pall over the country: the business of state and the social fabric of Sri Lankan affairs in general are shrouded in a tension of unresolved violence belying the island's peaceful exterior and its natural beauty.[1] Instead, there is a pervasive sense of guilt coated by a collective apathy born of the effort to forget. Unpunished murderers in palm-fringed villages share the streets with the families of their victims, and have done so for decades. Parliament is studded with a rogues' gallery of perpetrators and those who know but dare not reveal. Furthermore, the residual trauma from the JVP insurrections continues to numb a majority of Sri Lankans to the government's violent practices, for if the Sinhalese-dominated state could consume the children of its own people, why not those of others? The true story of the quelling of the Tamil Tigers, the mass killings of civilians in 2009 and the pretence by the government that its victory was bloodless was in effect chronicled and foretold by earlier events written in the blood of the Sinhalese youths killed two decades before. The propensity of the state for extreme violence was a known quantity and was, in a word, predictable.

After the assassination of her husband in 1959, Sirimavo Bandaranaike assumed the leadership of the SLFP – a role she would grip tightly through political ascendancy and misfortune until her death forty years later. Having demonstrated throughout the 1960s a determination to carry on the socialist and Sinhalese nationalist policies of her late husband, the formidable Mrs Bandaranaike returned to the role of prime minister in 1970 in a resounding landslide victory. She promised to reverse the liberal economic programmes of the previous UNP government – a manifesto that appealed to a population suffering from an economic downturn and a steady rise in food prices – and was backed by a broad spectrum of leftist parties with voter bases in both urban and rural areas.

Despite repeated promises from all parties since the 1950s to improve the lot of struggling rural families, none had yet delivered. The peasants, who routinely suffered from landlessness and debt, as well as devastating cycles of drought and floods, felt excluded from the potential that independent Ceylon offered. The population had almost doubled between independence in 1948 and 1970 to 12.5 million, two thirds of whom were under the age of thirty-five. Sri Lanka now had more people who were better educated and politically informed, but fewer jobs, a national income failing to keep pace with population, a faltering welfare system and a costly reliance on imports of basic foodstuffs. The countryside was awash with hundreds of thousands of unemployed school leavers whose futures rang with the dull echo of dispossession and poverty. 'Our poor parents having a thousand and one hopes spent the fruits of the sweat of their labour on education . . . We studied hard . . . sat for examinations. We passed examinations. We obtained degrees . . . Finally, as a punishment we were forced to loiter in the streets and face the laughter and insults of the capitalists.'[2]

Mrs Bandaranaike had fashioned her return to power on an incendiary foundation of promises that fused a strengthened Sinhalese hegemony with economic renewal. Meanwhile, a young communist leader and modern-day Dharmapala was forging his own political identity in a series of fiery lectures to lower-caste and largely unemployed youths. Once a student of medicine at the USSR's Patrice Lumumba University, the young Rohana Wijeweera had been expelled for 'Maoist tendencies' that ran contrary to the prevailing conservative ideology in Russia, but which he would harness for insurrection in Ceylon. In the mid-1960s, he split from the Communist Party (and from his mentor, a Tamil called N. Sanmugathasan) and founded an early version of the JVP.*

Wijeweera was a tireless campaigner whose aura of simplicity held great appeal for the rural Sinhalese youth. He had changed his name to evoke the ancient southern Sinhalese kingdom of Ruhan, and modelled himself on that icon of the 1960s Che Guevara, wearing a red star on his jaunty black beret and sporting the same ill-kempt beard. Born of the lower fisherman caste in 1943 in the village of Kottegoda, in the heartland of the southern Sinhalese, Wijeweera personified a Sinhalese Buddhist tradition of yearning for *dharmista samajaya*, or a just society. His notoriously long lecture sessions, conducted at his chicken farm, in coconut groves, on the banks of paddy fields, close to bus stops or in rural schoolhouses, would last from early morning until late at night, and were as much exercises in ruthless self-discipline as they were for recruitment and indoctrination. By the time of the 1970 elections, the JVP had extended its reach into the universities, and as such reflects a rather typical picture of university radicalism that erupted around the globe in the late 1960s and early 1970s. The JVP, however, remained notable among the main Sri Lankan political movements for the humble origins of its leaders and its solid rural base. It not only espoused the Maoist doctrine of a rural-based revolution, but vigorously pursued it.

Armed with impeccable credentials and a demonstrated commitment to the woes of rural youths and their parents, the JVP subtly appropriated the nationalist tradition promoted first by Dharmapala and later by Sinhalese political chauvinism. The Mahavamsa's powerful tale of a heroic southern Sinhalese leader rising to right wrongs, repel invaders and return Ceylon to a state of pristine rule was a nationalist epic by now familiar to every schoolchild. Blended with Maoist

---

* It was initially known as the New Left.

doctrine, it provided Sinhalese youths with a compelling alternative narrative to explain their economic exclusion in independent Ceylon. The reformulated Marxist version cast as the oppressor elite oligarchs like Mrs Bandaranaike, who had inherited political power, with international imperialism and the free-market economic order as her accomplices.

Wijeweera's political programme, delivered in five distinct lectures,[3] cut through the tangle of religious, ethnic, linguistic, regional, caste and class ties that both enveloped and divided Ceylonese society, even as his message remained embedded in Sinhalese dominance. It promised a solution for the large number of students emerging from universities who were unable to find jobs that met their expectations, and promoted change through violent revolution. It was a thrilling message for discontented youths, in perfect synchronicity with the global temperature and turmoil of the times while at the same time retaining Sinhalese authenticity.

At first, the JVP ostensibly threw its weight behind the election of Sirimavo Bandaranaike. More furtively, however, they planned for an insurrection. The newly elected prime minister promised relief for the rural masses in the form of fundamental structural reforms that included increased rice subsidies, the nationalisation of local and foreign banks and land redistribution.[4] While a nascent JVP supported her reform programme, it was with an implicit threat of action, which was either not understood, or not taken seriously. Mrs Bandaranaike was convinced that the JVP and the rural masses supported her because her politics played to the gallery of Sinhalese nationalism. The JVP, however, calculated that her leftist coalition would safely disappoint.

The JVP continued to publicly press the government to institute the promised reforms. By 1971, it had amassed support from tens of thousands of workers, students, peasants and intelligentsia. Large numbers of young *bhikkhus*, fed up with the corruption and bickering of the established clerical orders, backed the movement for its platform of social equality. The revolutionary ideal of reckless self-sacrifice found enthusiastic support among schoolchildren on the verge of entering the adult world, where their futures seemed so uncertain. Sympathetic members of the armed forces added a sense of incipient action to Wijeweera's lectures by supplying rudimentary military training for the cadres. On the eve of the outbreak of fighting, and in a sign of the tactical pragmatism of its leader, the JVP had even managed to reach out to certain Tamil trade union leaders in Colombo.

The 1971 JVP insurrection smacked of an amateurism that haunts revolutions and denies them the surprise that is their principal military advantage. On 27 February, a confident Wijeweera announced to a mass rally in Colombo, 'Let the revolution of the workers, farmers and soldiers be triumphant!' But the uprising was almost triggered by accident, when several bomb-making units blew themselves up in separate incidents across the country. In one, a cache of detonators hidden in a university ceiling set off a series of explosions that lasted for five days. Ensuing police raids on JVP hideouts uncovered more weapons and bomb-making facilities that indicated an imminent insurrection. In March, Rohana Wijeweera was arrested and imprisoned in a naval base in Jaffna. After conferring at the Buddhist university at Vidyodaya, the remaining leaders, having debated the merits of a protracted guerrilla campaign, decided to press ahead with a mass insurrection, and on 5 April the revolt was launched with a series of attacks on civil administration centres, police stations and army installations.

Confusingly, the start of the uprising was pre-empted by at least one cell that misunderstood or ignored its orders and struck a police station a day early. When the main attack did come, thousands of armed youths launched themselves at almost a hundred police stations, armed with no more than knives, bombs fashioned from cans of condensed milk, and revolutionary enthusiasm. They attacked the prison where Wijeweera was being held, as well as army bases in an effort to obtain the weapons they lacked. The security forces at first fell back in disarray, barely attuned to the scale and violence of the attacks. Five police stations were overrun completely, and sixty-three policemen and soldiers were killed. Prime Minister Bandaranaike darkly stated in a broadcast that 'big money, diabolical minds and criminal organisers' intent on destroying the Ceylonese way of life were behind the insurrection.

Despite the woeful preparations, after five days of fighting the sheer courage and determination of the rebels had been rewarded with swathes of territory in the south and the control of a number of towns and villages. But while they had a shaky hold on some areas of the country, they had failed to take Colombo, to breach military installations and obtain arms, or to free their leader Wijeweera. They had also

failed to kill Prime Minister Bandaranaike, one of their main objectives. They were hamstrung by poor communications and by a
fragmentary and confused command structure. In the areas that they
did control, they proved unable to insert an alternative administration.
Cadres manned roadblocks and occupied the swivel chairs of civil
administrators, but seemed dazed by the initial success of their putsch.

Bandaranaike's government was saved by an embarrassment of
riches. The Indian government responded to appeals with troops, helicopters and frigates, whose grey forms shadowed the southern
coastline. Within days, Colombo's main airport was brimful with military cargo planes, as Cold War countries fell over themselves to shore
up a non-aligned regime. The US and Czechoslovakia supplied Ceylon
with weapons at short notice. Even Australia and Yugoslavia sent help,
the latter supplying mountain artillery that was particularly effective in
the Kegalle region, where some of the heaviest fighting took place.
The Chinese rejected the 'Guevarists' without blinking and advanced a
loan to the Bandaranaike government.

In tacit recognition of the parlous state of its relations with a large
segment of the population, the government specified that only those
over thirty-five years of age should respond to a call-up of reservists.
Using emergency regulations framed by her husband in 1959, Mrs
Bandaranaike licensed the police and army to put down the insurrection with lethal force and arbitrary arrest. The government unearthed
from the statute books an extraordinary legal indulgence granted to
British troops that had been used to suppress the 1848 Sinhalese
uprising. The army and police were given the right to dispose of bodies
without inquest or the obligation to inform families that their rebel-
lious children had been arrested or killed. It was nothing less than a
licence to 'disappear' the rebels.

On 25 April, the *New York Times* reported that the bodies of hundreds
of young men and women were floating down a river near Colombo.
The corpses were collected and burned by soldiers on the banks. Renée
Dumont, a French woman who was living in Ceylon at the time, wrote:
'From the Victoria Bridge on 13 April I saw corpses floating down the
river which flows through the north of the capital, watched by hundreds
of motionless people. The police, who had killed them, let them float
downstream in order to terrorise the population.'

Within six weeks, the revolution had fizzled out except for pockets of resistance in distant locations. While the bodies of teenage revolutionaries floated downriver, the ditches dug by JVP cadres to hold the cadavers of those included on their ambitious death list remained just empty gouges in the earth. The government denied that atrocities had been committed by the armed forces, setting a precedent for official denials that would be continued through each of the country's subsequent violent convulsions. Barely aware of events in Ceylon, global public attention was distracted by the Pakistani army's operations in East Pakistan, where hundreds of thousands of people were being killed, and by the threat of open war between India and Pakistan.

Between 35,000 and 40,000 young men and women were held in Ceylon without trial for more than a year while the government dithered about how it should handle them. In April 1972, a Criminal Justice Commission was established to try the revolutionaries. The commission was authorised to accept confessions obtained under torture. A handful of leaders were eventually tried and convicted, and Wijeweera was sentenced to life imprisonment. The fallout from the failed JVP insurrection was profound, and the effect on the country's system of government equally so. In an early model for events that would follow the SLA's victory over the Tamil Tigers in May 2009, the JVP insurrection gave the Bandaranaike government the licence to extend its grip on power. Bandaranaike rushed through new flagship laws in an effort to deal with the economic crisis that gripped the country and to resolve grievances that had spurred the crisis. The tea estates, which were still largely in the hands of British multinational companies, were nationalised. Austerity measures targeted the ownership of houses and apartments and limited high incomes.

If the 1956 language laws are today seen as disastrous political brinkmanship and the beginning of Ceylon's demise, Sirimavo Bandaranaike's constitutional and legal innovations immersed the country deeper in the murky pool of communalist strife. She set about recapturing the Dharmapalan narrative of social revolution that the JVP had usurped, but with none of the pragmatic cross-communalism that the younger revolutionaries had envisioned. The 1972 constitution declared Ceylon a republic, with Buddhism as the state religion and Sinhala as the official language.[5] Ceylon was rebranded Sri Lanka, and Bo leaves, a Buddhist symbol, were inserted into the flag. Protective measures for minorities provided for under the country's first constitution were discarded.

The new constitution reflected a sharp lurch towards authoritarianism. In the context of the times in south Asia, Bandaranaike was in step with India and Pakistan and with the birth pangs of many of the non-aligned countries.[6] It concentrated considerable powers in the hands of the prime minister and her governing oligarchy, even as it weakened the judiciary as the principal check on the untrammelled power of the executive and legislators. The new National State Assembly, dominated in its first convocation by Bandaranaike's SLFP, voted to extend her government's mandate for a further two years beyond the five it had won at the election. Another piece of legislation destroyed the process of administrative appeal that hitherto had resided with the courts, and provided the government with a menu of refined persecutions to deploy for private vendettas, to silence dissenters and to penalise the political opposition.

Next, Bandaranaike turned her attention to the troublesome free press. The government already controlled the limited broadcasters, so now it nationalised the Lakehouse Press, the largest private newspaper conglomerate in a country whose varied and vigorous press had ably served a large literate population for a century. It used emergency regulations invoked for the JVP insurrection to shutter the island's other great newspaper group, Independent Newspapers, for three years. Other newspapers were effectively stifled by measures that included the withholding of government advertising, threatening businesses that placed advertisements with disfavoured newspapers and throttling paper and ink supplies. The government began another long tradition in Sri Lankan politics by extending from month to month the emergency regulations that had proven so effective in limiting dissent. By 2009, half of Sri Lanka's years of independence had been spent under emergency regulations.

The mood of the country soured. Unemployment was rapidly rising, and by the mid 1970s, a quarter of the labour force was out of work. A downturn in the world economy and a balance of payments crisis left the government strapped for cash. It was forced to reduce one of the staples of the welfare system, the rice subsidy. Investment in industrialisation was declared to be the key to Sri Lanka's emergence from crisis, while at the same time the administrative machinery charged with promoting increased rice production was dismantled. The government seemed to bungle its way from one error of judgement to another, in an intemperate manner that smacked of the caprice of Mrs Bandaranaike herself.

When the UNP opposition leader Dudley Senanayake died in April 1973, almost half the population filed past his funeral bier in a manifestation of popular discontent against a government that had eroded other means of political expression. As national unease grew, the government introduced even more stringent emergency regulations outlawing political meetings and imposing curfews. At the same time it allocated huge government resources to the staging of mass trumped-up rallies, with crowds bussed in to beef up numbers. State employees were shanghaied into demonstrations of support under threat of dismissal or transfer to rural posts, a practice that forever politicised the civil administration.

The JVP revolt had revealed to the Tamils the potential of insurrection. Now the chauvinist constitution of 1972 sent a message to millions of Tamil citizens that their expectations in Sri Lanka could be comprised of nothing more than an entrenched status as second-class citizens. In addition to the humiliations of the constitution, Bandaranaike introduced changes to the university admissions process. Tamil applicants were required to achieve higher marks than their Sinhalese peers in order to enter prestigious university courses such as medicine and engineering, with a net effect that, albeit slightly, favoured the Sinhalese majority. Tamils regarded the university admissions policy as 'a crucial test of their equal rights as citizens of Sri Lanka'.[7] In their eyes, the move was designed to reduce their dominance in the professions and state bureaucracy. In 1956, Tamils, who accounted for about one fifth of the population, held about 30 per cent of the administrative positions. Within twenty years, that figure had fallen to just 5 per cent.

In the mid 1970s, fed up with legalised discrimination and a string of broken political promises,[8] a new Tamil umbrella party, the Tamil United Liberation Front (TULF), began to agitate for an autonomous Tamil homeland that would cover Sri Lanka's northern, eastern and western coastlines. In this imagining, the lines of Tamil Eelam were somewhat spuriously delineated by reference to historical documents purporting to represent areas that were or had once been dominated by Tamils.[9] Like the independent state itself, it was an attempt to impose modern conceptions of social and political organisation on hazy historical reckonings. In time, it would be backed by Tamil Tiger attacks on Sinhalese and Muslim communities in an effort to ethnically cleanse the claimed territory. However dubious in its broad geographical conception, the Tamil homeland provided a physical locus for a powerful idea that was both a logical riposte to decades of Sinhalese chauvinism and a refuge for a Tamil community threatened by increasing discrimination that eroded their capacity to earn a living.

Jaffna's restive youth movement, however, now rejected the non-violent Gandhian policies of its elders in the established Tamil political parties. Peaceful opposition had, after all, proven fruitless. They took the lessons of the JVP uprising and its rapid suppression to the very heart of their own liberation struggle. Between 1972 and 1976, many of these lessons were learned directly from the JVP themselves: the anxious Sri Lankan authorities committed the cardinal error of imprisoning Tamil agitators within the same walls as the JVP revolutionaries who had been incarcerated for their botched insurrection. One such revolutionary was Lionel Bopage, an early member and a general secretary of the JVP. His long path from student to ardent revolutionary sympathetic to the Tamil plight had been inspired by scenes of injustice from his youth in Matara, deep in the Sinhalese heartland: 'When I was fourteen during the 1956 riots, a Tamil delivery boy ran to us for sanctuary. We knew him well because he delivered betel leaves to our shop. My father protected him from a crowd who wanted to lynch him. Later, I was mentored by a Tamil chemistry teacher at Rahula College who simply vanished when the 1958 riots broke out. And again in the early 1960s when I was at Richmond College, I had another Tamil chemistry teacher similarly driven from his home and town by mindless violence.'[10]

Imprisoned in 1972 for his JVP role, Bopage listened to Tamil youths recounting stories of repression at the hands of the state. He became convinced that the majority of Sinhalese and Tamils shared the same fate of domination at the hands of a small, entrenched political elite. 'The stories of Duttugemenu and Elara that I had been taught as historical fact at school, as a part of the curriculum, were folk tales, irrelevant to the requirements of a modern just society. The Dharmapala tradition was alcohol for the masses, pitting Sinhalese triumphantly against Tamils, each riot a symptom of

learned and institutionalised confrontation.' This common purpose
between the JVP and Tamil revolutionary groups, which transcended
ethnicity and came as a surprise to both, would not last. However, the
fact that it existed for years up until the 1980s supports the view of those
who place economic issues at the centre of Sri Lanka's troubled history.

In July 1977, forced to the polls by left-wing parties that had withdrawn
from her coalition, Sirimavo Bandaranaike was trounced in elections that
revealed the depth of popular disgust at the anti-democratic excesses of
her government. Rule was handed back to the Senanayake family with
the election of J.R. Jayawardene, the first prime minister's nephew.
Bandaranaike's defeat was so complete that for the first time, a Tamil
party, the TULF, held the balance of power in opposition. Using the
excuse of the illegal extension of her mandate from 1975–77, the government stripped Bandaranaike of her civil rights. The surviving JVP
revolutionaries were released and inducted into electoral politics, and
became the only non-Tamil political group to develop a platform that
fully addressed language and educational equality and supported the
Tamil call for self-determination.

J.R. Jayawardene reversed the nationalisation of industries, cancelled
the nationalisation of land and liberalised the economy. In a largely
empty gesture, the new constitution of 1978 repositioned Tamil as a
'national' language of Sri Lanka, whilst preserving Sinhalese as the sole
official language. Jayawardene's constitutional makeover further
concentrated his power by transforming the existing role of president
into a strong executive. He now used that power to extend his rule with
the same deft autocratic touch as that of Mrs Bandaranaike. Whatever
the changes introduced by Jayawardene, and the restraint he exhibited
when faced with communal violence in the serious anti-Tamil riots of
1977,[11] the shadow of the Bandaranaike years had left an indelible pall
over the Sri Lankan polity in the form of extreme revolutionary violence, and the propensity of the state for comparable
counter-violence.

By the late 1970s, Velupillai Prabakharan had established himself as the
leader of one of several militant Tamil groups on the Jaffna peninsula.
The Tamil Tigers and the JVP shared a number of characteristics apart
from the promotion of liberation for their constituents. Although
both were anti-elitist, the two charismatic leaders were thoroughly

anti-democratic. Neither Prabakharan nor Wijeweera brooked opposition, and both men hand-picked their sub-commanders and political cadres right up until their own deaths. Tamil revolutionary violence was aimed both at the strictures imposed by government decree to disadvantage the Tamils, and at the traditional bonds of the caste system. While for the Sinhalese, caste is a more fluid system of social ordering, capable of considerable metamorphosis over time, Tamil caste restrictions are far less forgiving. As such, the challenge to caste and sexual roles – a signature recruitment device for the Tamil Tigers – equated with a generational break from the past.

The violence was also aimed at rival groups, upon whom the Tamil Tigers, in what was an already bloody environment, honed their reputation for cold brutality. The bloodshed in the Jaffna peninsula became akin to a gangland war, with rival Tamil groups eradicating each other's members. Bank robberies were used to finance radical groups, assassinations, demonstrations, *hartals*,* arson attacks and the sabotage of installations. Under Prabakharan's leadership, the Tigers killed moderate alternative leaders, executed 'informants', attacked police and army targets and cudgelled other radical groups into submission. By the mid 1980s, they were the dominant revolutionary force in the peninsula.

The government responded with alternate strategies of moderation and clumsy blind force. Through the use of poorly trained recruits, the vast majority of whom were Sinhalese, the security forces gradually became an army of occupation in northern and eastern Tamil areas. In June 1981, apparently provoked by the killing of two of their number, a detachment of Sinhalese policemen under the control of Cyril Mathew, the outspoken and racist minister for industries,[12] torched the magnificent Jaffna library and destroyed irreplaceable archives and rare manuscripts. It was a piece of wanton destruction regarded by many Tamils as cultural genocide – a calculated act by the state to erase the records of Tamil culture and history in Sri Lanka. Two years later, while the building was being restored, government troops attacked the partially constructed shell again and destroyed the new collection that was being assembled.[13]

On 24 July 1983, the Sri Lankan government flew the bodies of thirteen

---

* A popular strike in the form of a total shutdown of official and private business.

soldiers killed by a land mine in Jaffna back to Colombo for a public burial. The troops, who had only only arrived in Jaffna the previous day, had been targeted by a Tamil Tiger attack led by Prabakharan, an apparent act of revenge for a rumoured assault on three Tamil women at an army camp. In Jaffna, soldiers went on a rampage, dragging Tamils from their homes and killing forty-one people. In Colombo, when the arrival of the bodies at the main Borella cemetery was delayed, a restive crowd pelted the police with stones. Sinhalese mobs fanned out across the city armed with sticks, clubs, tyres and petrol. Colombo burned while its citizens were paralysed with terror.

Every Tamil family who lived in Colombo during what is known as Black July has a story of survival. Many Sinhalese took terrible risks to hide Tamil friends or neighbours, while gangs roamed around burning shops and houses, dragging Tamils from their cars and murdering them in their gardens or in the streets. Plumes of smoke pitted the blue skies above the city and mob violence broke out across the island. The capital's main thoroughfare was gap-toothed, with Tamil shops in flames. Gangs at roadblocks, including members of the security forces, checked identification cards, or tested the occupants of vehicles with difficult Sinhalese words. London's *Daily Express* reported one eyewitness version:

> A tourist told yesterday how she watched in horror as a Sinhala mob deliberately burned alive a bus load of Tamils . . . Mrs Eli Skarstein, back home in Stavanger, Norway, told how she and her 15-year-old daughter, Kristin, witnessed one massacre. 'A mini bus full of Tamils were forced to stop in front of us in Colombo,' she said. A Sinhalese mob poured petrol over the bus and set it on fire. They blocked the car door and prevented the Tamils from leaving the vehicle. 'Hundreds of spectators watched as about 20 Tamils were burned to death.' Mrs Skarstein added: 'We can't believe the official casualty figures. Hundreds, maybe thousands must have been killed already.'[14]

Helen Manuelpillai,* a Tamil and now a French teacher in Melbourne, was seventeen years old in July 1983. As she prepared for school on Monday, 25 July, her family received a phone call alerting

---

* Not her real name.

them to the riots that had spread throughout the city. Despite a night of murderous rampaging, the government had broadcast no news of the destruction, nor issued any warnings. Recalling earlier bouts of rioting, Helen's father, a retired government official, gathered the family's passports and birth certificates and buried them in a biscuit tin in the back garden. Wijitha W., a Sinhalese family friend, took Helen to his own house. As they drove through the streets, they saw mobs burning down a Tamil cinema, chanting nationalist slogans and waving clubs and knives in the air. At Wijitha's house, his wife was distraught. She had seen the houses of their Tamil neighbours set alight, and had screamed as she ran through the streets that she was ashamed to be Sinhalese. That night, Helen hid under a bed as her hosts confronted a mob trying to wrest her from sanctuary.

Helen's neighbourhood had been pillaged and many houses burned. The authorities appeared unwilling, or unable, to control the gangs. The fact that mob leaders carried voter registration lists indicating the location of Tamil houses is seen by many as evidence of official complicity. Fleeing their house, Helen's extended family had joined tens of thousands of other Tamils in a camp at a large Hindu school. By Tuesday, 26 July, the first great bloodletting had quieted. Word of the pogrom had filtered out of the country and was headline news across the world. An embarrassed government moved to rein in the violence and a curfew was imposed that evening.

Helen joined her family the following day, Wednesday. Sporadic violence continued to ebb and surge until Friday, 29 July, when fifteen rioters were shot dead, the curfew was lifted and public transport began to flow again. Helen's father's Sinhalese colleagues brought food to the camp for the family, and as dusk fell, her father and brother and several other men set off with the Sinhalese colleagues to check on their houses. At an army checkpoint, soldiers asked if there were any Tamils in the vehicle and directed them to take a route supposedly away from mobs. Three times they were directed along this route, until they were trapped in a jam of cars in an area of Colombo called Athidiya. Armed men moved up and down the line of traffic, hauling people from the vehicles. The bodies of Tamils wrenched from cars burned like torches in the street, car tyres aflame around their necks. A mob surrounded the vehicle Helen's father and brother were travelling in and separated the Tamils from the Sinhalese. They screamed at the Sinhalese to run for their lives as Helen's brother and father were set upon.

It took the police more than a week to restore order. They seemed helpless to stop the violence. Some stood idly by, while others participated actively in the bloodshed. More than 100,000 Tamils poured into refugee camps. For days, the government remained silent, as though nothing had happened. The *Daily Telegraph* described a Tamil cyclist being hauled from his bike by a mob, drenched with petrol, set alight and then hacked with knives as he ran down the street – the very same street in which President Jayawardene lived.[15]

The government's weak condemnation of the atrocities seemed tantamount to complicity in the pogrom. The Tamil anthropologist Stanley Tambiah says that President Jayawardene was 'crushed and pressured by a massive tide of collective aggression'.[16] When he finally appeared on television on Thursday, 28 July, far from condemning the riots, he apparently felt constrained to characterise the disturbances as 'not a product of urban mobs but a mass movement of the generality of the Sinhalese people', and added that 'The time has come to accede to the clamour and national respect of the Sinhalese people.' His cabinet colleague Cyril Mathew – of Jaffna library burning notoriety – declaimed in parliament on 4 August, 'If the Sinhalese are the majority race, why can't they be the majority?' The culpability of some government ministers and senior political figures is well recorded. Ministers like Gamini Dissanayake, the ultra-chauvinist Mathew, and UNP figure Aloysius Mudalali directed violence, managed gangs and assisted with the logistics of the attacks. In a solid tradition of denial, the government put the death toll at around 300, while competing estimates place the number between 1,000 and 3,000.[17] Thousands more were wounded and raped, and many thousands of homes and shops looted and burned.

The 1983 pogrom has left a searing wound in the collective Tamil memory and is a mark of intense shame for many Sinhalese. The state had proved itself incapable of fulfilling its two fundamental duties to one distinct segment of the population: the provision of security and of justice. At worst, it had instigated a bloody pogrom at the behest of its ruling class. Two weeks before the riots, President Jayawardene had stated publicly that he didn't care if the Tamils of Jaffna starved, and asserted that the Sinhalese people would be happy if they did. India understood this statement as an incitement against the Tamils, as did many Sri Lankan Tamils who recalled earlier race riots and sensed the impending violence. When Helen's father heard that the leader of the country had publicly incited violence against the Tamils, he decided that the time had come to leave their country for ever. Hundreds of thousands of Tamils who could afford to – many of them the brightest and best – fled, never to return. Helen and what was left of her family left Sri Lanka less than a week after the riots began, never having recovered the remains of her father and brother.

Sri Lanka's civil war was sparked by the 1983 riots. The unintended consequence of Black July was that many of the Sri Lankan Tamils who quit the country amassed great fortunes in their new homelands and started funding the only organisation that could stand up to the chauvinist whims of the state – the Tamil Tigers. For over twenty-five years, the Liberation Tigers of Tamil Eelam mounted daring, destructive and horrifically brutal attacks on the Sinhalese and Muslim populations of Sri Lanka, while the Tamil diaspora looked on from afar, its collective memory branded by the embers of that month, its sympathies and sense of vengeance at one with those Tamils who remained.

In the wake of the 1983 riots, the threat of Indian intervention loomed. Tens of thousands of Tamil refugees had fled to India, mostly to Tamil Nadu, whose citizens considered Black July an atrocity committed against all Tamils, and Jaffna a beloved repository of Tamil culture. India had demonstrated its will and capacity to confront neighbouring states in its 1962 border war with China, and had brought about the independence of Bangladesh in 1971 from Pakistan.[18] Already dealing with a brace of internal conflicts, Indian prime minister Indira Gandhi, with an eye and ear on the unpredictable separatist pan-Tamil movement in southern India, was sympathetic to the political aspirations of Sri Lanka's Tamils, so long as they were confined to a solution within established sovereign borders. Sri Lanka was proving incapable of delivering a settlement, and the Sri Lankan Tamil cause was emerging from Tamil Nadu's state political scene as a factor in federal politics.[19]

India's vital interests were at stake. The chief minister of Tamil Nadu pressured Gandhi to raise the issue of the large-scale killing of Tamils at the United Nations. Long-held Sinhalese insecurities about the latent military threat that India posed to the island nation, fed by the ossified battles of the Mahavamsa, rose rapidly.[20] President Jaya-wardene harboured a well-founded fear of Indian intervention. The Research and Analysis Wing (RAW), India's foreign intelligence service, opened training camps in Tamil Nadu and other parts of the sub-continent in which the Indian military trained Tamil separatist groups in guerrilla warfare and urban tactics. Thousands of Tamil refugees joined these groups. Between 1983 and 1987, Tamil militants returned to Sri Lanka, and fighting between separatist groups and the SLA and police ebbed and flowed on the Jaffna peninsula. The Sri Lankan government became bogged down in a protracted, vicious and costly campaign fought by an army ill prepared to meet the challenge.

As India and Sri Lanka inched towards an accord in mid 1987 that would formalise India's peacekeeping role, the Sri Lankan army was suddenly emboldened to press forward, whereupon it succeeded in penning the militant fighters inside Jaffna city. With the guerrillas on the verge of defeat and the Indian pretext for intervention slipping away, the Indian government sent a flotilla of ships to break the SLA siege of the city. When the Sri Lankan navy stopped the Indian ships from reaching the the peninsula, Indian cargo planes dropped supplies to the beleaguered Tamil fighters, with Indian Air Force MiG fighters providing cover against Sri Lankan interference. The SLA's best chance so far of eliminating the militant threat had been lost.

On 29 July 1987, India's prime minister Rajiv Gandhi* flew to Colombo. Under the agreement signed that day between Gandhi and President Jayawardene, Sri Lanka agreed to an Indian intervention force to disarm the Tamil Tigers. The Sri Lankan government also agreed to the 13th amendment to their constitution, a provision that would devolve certain powers to Tamil areas. As he prepared to leave the country, Gandhi attended an honour guard of seventy-two Sri Lankan naval ratings. One nineteen-year-old-rating, Wijayamunige Rohana de Silva, swung his rifle with full force at the prime minister's head.

Gandhi dodged the blow. Whether or not it was a JVP-inspired assas-sination attempt, the attack was emblematic of the deep distress the

---

* His mother Indira had been assassinated in 1984 by two Sikh bodyguards after she had ordered a military assault on Sikhism's holiest shrine, the Golden Temple at Amritsar.

Indo-Sri Lanka Accord inspired in the broader Sinhalese public. The agreement forced on the island by India reflected the prescient lectures that the JVP's Rohana Wijeweera had delivered about Indian imperialist designs on Sri Lanka. Riots erupted across the country, and forty people were killed as they protested against the accord. Less than three weeks later, a white-jacketed parliamentary caterer threw two hand grenades into a cabinet meeting of President Jayawardene and his prime minister (and soon to be president) Premadasa, killing two people but leaving the main targets unscathed. Jayawardene described the attack as an 'attempt to destroy the parliamentary democratic system of the country'. The JVP's second insurrection had begun.

Two decades on, the dossiers of the murdered and disappeared from this second insurrection are painfully thin and yellowed. The appended school photos stare back with a brooding passion, a dignity, an ebullient smile or an inscrutable blank stare, as if the girls and boys pictured had caught a barely credible glimpse of the horror that lay ahead. The fate of each one was untimely and dreadful. Some suffered long interrogations and lingering deaths. For others, the end was relatively quick and came by gun, knife, metal bar or the flaming 'necklace' of a rubber tyre, their bodies dumped in the street, strung up on a lamppost with a sign around their neck, or burned on the same white beaches advertised in the tourist brochures. Most notorious of all were those who were beheaded, their skulls stuck atop poles alongside their friends, neighbours or perfect strangers in a public square. The stories of what happened to tens of thousands of Sinhalese youths in the second JVP uprising tell of a bloodlust more easily attributed to the rampages of the Mongols or the pillages of the Norsemen.

Throughout the winter of 1987–8, reports arrived at the Amnesty offices in London from nervous Sri Lankans who had travelled to London to visit relatives, from tourists who had fled the island, from diplomats, aid workers and Sri Lankan human rights activists. Through spring and into summer and for the next three summers until the killings in the south began to tail off, Amnesty issued stony statements noting the mounting toll of reported dead and missing. Alarm bells rang, but fell on deaf ears. The crumbling walls of the Eastern Bloc distracted the world, along with perestroika and the Soviet withdrawal from Afghanistan. The first Palestinian intifada was under way, and the race between George H.W. Bush and Michael Dukakis for the US presidency was in full swing. When attention turned to tiny Sri Lanka at all, it was to remark on the Indian Peace Keeping Force in the north of the island, whose mission had deteriorated into a blundering military occupation complete with savage reprisals as it tried to stamp out the ferocious resistance of the Tamil Tigers.

The Sri Lankan dossiers that were smuggled to London, fragile notes in childishly careful loops and tails as the student activists transcribed the Sinhala originals into English, recorded the factual scraps relating to each death. Copies were also sent to the standing UN Working Group on Enforced or Involuntary Disappearances. In the corridors of the UN's Palais des Nations in Geneva during those years and months, staffers recall a stout, nervous Sinhalese parliamentarian and lawyer called Mahinda Rajapaksa, who had acquired a reputation as a human rights activist among his people. During occasional bouts of self-exile, in order to escape the wrath of the Sri Lankan government, Rajapaksa made numerous appearances before the UN's Human Rights Council to plead the case for urgent UN intervention to stop the bloodshed wrought on his constituents in the south of Sri Lanka.

This time, the JVP cadres were better prepared to rise against the state. The signing of the Indo-Sri Lanka accord was merely the ignition for an insurrection that had been planned for years. After his release from prison in 1977, and the legalisation once more of the JVP as a political party, Rohana Wijeweera had renounced violence and declared his intention to build a party of the true left. He threw his hat in the ring for the 1982 presidential elections, but drew only a paltry and humiliating 279,000 votes, a shock so deep that he retired to bed for three days. Convinced that his secular, multi-ethnic political platform had led to his electoral defeat, Wijeweera refused to countenance continued support for Tamil self-determination. But Jayawardene's induction of the JVP into the political process had been based on the cold calculation that they would undermine the strength of the opposition SLFP. The movement served just as well again when, in 1983, the government placed blame for the anti-Tamil riots squarely at its feet, and it was banned once more.

Throughout the 1980s, Wijeweera rebuilt the JVP into a clandestine network of between three and six member cells across the south and centre of the island. The movement aquired funds through a series of robberies, made great headway into university politics and gained military expertise from jungle training exercises conducted by army deserters. It acquired a base of activists resentful of the authoritarianism of Jayawardene's UNP government, which had prolonged its grip on power through mass dismissals (70,000 teachers and public servants in 1981), restrictions on the press and judiciary and the manipulation of the electorate. It also attracted hundreds of young monks fed up with the corruption and in-fighting of senior monks. For the young JVP supporters of the 1980s, *pavathina kramaya varadiy* – everything about the prevailing order was wrong – and all had to be swept away.

In early 1987, the JVP signalled their potential with a series of daring weapons raids on army camps. The government's consent to the presence of Indian troops on Sri Lankan soil in July was as good as a starting gun. Between the signing of the Indo-Sri Lanka Accord and November of 1987, the JVP assassinated more than seventy members of parliament and political functionaries. They began to target administrators, policemen, soldiers, UNP supporters at the village level and even senior monks close to the ruling party. The JVP spectre inspired generalised terror, because the depth and breadth of their infiltration into the government, civil service and security forces became quickly apparent but was impossible to quantify. The movement began to declare *hartals*, enforced by the execution of ordinary shopkeepers, bus drivers and council workers who turned up for work. The *hartals* became massive, visible and costly demonstrations of the JVP's power to asphyxiate the state, and each strike seemed to bring the country closer to collapse. The movement also began to eradicate moderates and members of the old left, while both of the country's main political parties used the violence as cover to extract advantage through the killing of rivals. In 1988, Sri Lanka's biggest film star, and the leader of a progressive political party, Vijaya Kumaratunga, was gunned down at the front door of his home, in front of his children and his wife Chandrika, the future president of Sri Lanka and the daughter of Sirimavo Bandaranaike (a judicial commission later suggested that the prime minister – and future president – Premadasa had ordered his death).[21]

While the JVP battled the Sri Lankan government in the south, the Tamil Tigers fought the Indian Peace Keeping Force (IPKF) in the north. The first troops from India had landed in Jaffna on 30 July 1987, less than a day after the accord had been signed. The IPKF would build to a peak of 80,000 men, including a significant proportion of India's crack regiments. Their specially designed insignia included a dove, although few of Jaffna's people today recall much about the Indian presence that was peaceful. Jaffna retains the scars of the Indian occupation; deserted neighbourhoods of once beautiful streets whose pockmarked walls, burned-out hulks of houses and twisted corrugated-iron roofs bear witness to the folly of an agreement that excluded the Tamil Tigers as one of the signatories.

The Tigers' reaction to attempts to disarm them was swift and bitter. After the arrest and suicide of a dozen of their cadres who had been caught smuggling in the Palk Straits, they responded by killing around 200 Sinhalese civilians, many who were in the north on peace-building initiatives. By October, the IPKF had become an army of occupation, whose methods included the wholesale bombardment of civilian areas, commando seek-and-destroy missions, strafing by helicopter gunships of suburban streets, torture, summary executions and disappearances. The Indian army in effect took over from where the Sri Lankan army had left off, leaving the Sri Lankans free to deal with the JVP insurgency in the south, which by July 1987 was in full swing. The Indian air force airlifted thousands of Sri Lankan troops directly from the Jaffna penin- sula into the Sinhalese southern heartland to re-establish the writ of the state. A majority of the troops had been recruited from the very area they were sent to police, a factor that was to have a vital bearing on the course and eventual suppression of the insurrection.

The newspaper reports and the Amnesty files from the time provide insights into the complex of violence that embroiled Sri Lanka as the government foundered and lashed out at the JVP insurrection, and the IPKF to the north became mired in a spiral of costly encounters against the Tamil Tigers. In the south, the police, army and a network of government-armed paramilitary groups with names like the Hawks, the Green Tigers and the Black Cats trawled the countryside, villages and towns, looking for supposed JVP activists and sympathisers, extin- guishing the threat they posed through a combination of executions, public lynchings, disappearances and the propagation of sheer terror. The universities were shut for three full years, and while the economic and government life of the island gradually ground to a halt, the busi- ness of killing went on.

In January 1989, Prime Minister Premadasa took over as president from Jayawardene. Premadasa was a lower-caste thoroughgoing Sinhalese nationalist, who had written a popular novel lauding the Tamil-slaying King Duttugemenu of Mahavamsa fame.[22] The JVP marked the seamless transition of power with a new tactic that would prove fatal to their revolt. They declared that they would begin to kill the families of soldiers, most of whom came from the very communities from which the JVP drew the majority of their cadres. The terror reached a peak as the army's uncompromising revenge on the JVP turned the tide of the insurrection. Although the killing continued into 1990, by June 1989 the JVP threat had been largely snuffed out.

While the young Mahinda Rajapaksa walked the corridors of the Palais des Nations, his brother Gotabaya, the future mastermind behind the army's conquest of the Tamil Tigers in 2009, played a very different role. Along with his comrade-in-arms, Sarath Fonseka, like Gotabaya a southern son of the soil and a senior army officer, he was deeply involved in the day-to-day suppression of the JVP in southern Sri Lanka. Fonseka was in charge of an army camp at Gampaha, an area that became particularly notorious for mass killings. The sweep conducted by the security forces passed through government depart-ments, villages, temple complexes, peasant communes, neighbourhoods and sports events. University students were snatched from their dormi-tories and pulled off the streets by men in green Pajeros – the vehicle synonymous with death squads and disappearances. Whole classrooms of children were swept up in the tide of massacre, marched from their places of learning into fields where they were shot and hacked to death. It is thought that in one massacre alone, fifty-three pupils from the Embilipitiya high school were killed and their bodies dumped in a mass grave. Their deaths have never been satisfactorily investigated.[23]

David, a colleague of Padmasiri Thrimawithana and now a senior public servant, who helped to autopsy Padmasiri's corpse that night in 1988, also played a pivotal role in amassing files on the missing and killed during the three-year JVP insurrection. He is still at a loss to understand the depth of the hatred that fuelled the violence. 'Killing people is contrary to everything we were raised to believe in as Buddhists, the five precepts, the practice of compassion. And here we were, witnesses to Buddhists slaughtering each other without mercy, killing the children of their neighbours.'

Lana Perera,* a Sinhalese hotelier, whose husband, a JVP activist, was tortured, recalls one killing that seemed particularly symbolic to her of the cruelty with which the insurrection was suppressed. One day soldiers came to fetch the fifteen-year-old son of a village Ayurvedic doctor, a profession considered to be at the heart of every Sinhalese village in Sri Lanka, the receptacle of thousands of years of accrued wisdom and knowledge. The boy was taken to the schoolhouse library, given charcoal and made to write on the wall in the style of a popular Sinhalese newspaper column of the time called 'A Little Child's Letter', which mimicked the ungrammatical syntax of children. He wrote: 'He posted posters. He protested the government. He wrong.' When the boy's body was found in the classroom, it was no more than a blackened stump twisted like a grotesque plinth below the infantile epigraph he had been forced to write. His captors had put a tyre around his shoulders, doused him with petrol and set him alight. 'Didn't they feel for his life?' asks Lana. 'These men were from this boy's area, men old enough to be fathers and brothers to this boy. They put a ring of rubber and steel around his neck without feeling, without compassion.'

In November 1989, the army captured Rohana Wijeweera in a high hill plantation in the centre of the island near Kandy, as he was shaving off his trademark beard. He had been masquerading as a tea planter, and his family was with him. After being interrogated for a day in Colombo, he was filmed as he appealed to his JVP followers to lay down their arms. A few hours later, he was shot on the eighth tee of the Colombo Golf Club 'while attempting to escape' – killed by an army sergeant, just like his hero Che Guevara. His body was cremated at the Borella cemetery – the place where the 1983 Tamil pogrom was sparked.

Between 40,000 and 60,000 people in the south of the country had been killed, the overwhelming majority of them civilians murdered on slight and random suspicions that they were JVP members or sympathisers (or members of the opposition UNP, as many were).[24] In March 1990, the Indian Peace Keeping Force completed its withdrawal at the behest of President Premadasa, who had re-armed the Tamil Tigers in order to harry the Indian troops out of Sri Lanka. Premadasa was now free to deal with the troublemakers as he saw fit. But the Tigers had

---

* Not her real name.

evolved considerably from the days when they were a loose band of bad boys running about the streets of Jaffna in sandals. They had cut their teeth on battles with the Sri Lankan army in the early 1980s, been trained and armed by the Indians and had then turned those same guns on their patrons.

On a hot morning in May 1991, in the town of Sriperumbudur in Tamil Nadu, a young Tamil woman joined a crowd of people thronging around former Indian prime minister Rajiv Gandhi, who was on the southern leg of his campaign to be re-elected. She bent before him and touched his feet as a sign of respect. With equal grace, the young statesman, wearing a presentation garland of yellow marigolds around his neck, paused to acknowledge the gesture of the small woman at his feet. Still kneeling, she detonated a belt filled with explosives that was concealed beneath her plain white sari. The blast of steel ball bearings killed Gandhi and sixteen others and blew the head off the young assassin, known by her *nom de guerre* of 'Dhanu'. Emboldened by the growing legend of their military prowess and an unwavering commitment to their aims, the Tamil Tigers had reached beyond their tiny enclave to punish one of the leaders of the world's largest democracy. With suicide bombers, merciless attacks on civilians and acts of reckless courage, the Tamil Tigers had learned to fashion their own version of the 'propaganda of the deed'. With this exemplary assassination, they cut a pattern of insurgency and international terrorism that simultaneously laid the groundwork for other international terrorist organisations and planted the seed of their own destruction.

CHAPTER FOUR

The Tiger Revolt

Shortly after dawn on 23 October 1983, a yellow truck barrelled through a flimsy barbed-wire barricade and sped past US Marines guarding a barracks at Beirut International Airport. As the sentries fumbled to load and fire their weapons, the driver accelerated through the front doors of the four-storey cinder block building and detonated his cargo of gas canisters and high explosives. The blast lifted the structure off its huge concrete support columns and the building collapsed. As snipers fired at them from warehouses beyond the airport perimeter, rescuers dug out the charred bodies of 241 US servicemen.

It was the largest loss of life of US troops in a single day since the battle of Iwo Jima in the Second World War. A suicide attack on the US embassy in Beirut six months earlier had killed sixty people, but President Ronald Reagan had promised that US troops would remain as part of an international force in Lebanon and would 'never surrender to terrorism'. Despite the president's equally tough talk in the wake of the barracks attack, US marines were withdrawn as quickly as possible. The men were relocated to ships offshore, and within just four months the US had extracted its entire armed forces from the Lebanon. Just one dedicated man had killed 241 heavily armed troops, humiliated one of the best-equipped and trained armies in the world and, most crucially, forced a political transformation.

The effect was not lost on other radical groups. Just after nightfall on 5 July 1987, a small truck laden with explosives smashed through the gates of a school being used to quarter SLA troops in the village of Neliady, on the Jaffna peninsula. The explosion destroyed one of the school's buildings and killed a dozen soldiers. Tamil Tigers on the perimeter of the camp fired at dazed troops as they mounted a defence throughout the night, and by morning, forty soldiers had been killed. Spectacular suicidal attacks now became the signature revolutionary weapon in the Tamil Tiger armoury. The driver of the truck, Valli-puram Vasanthan, known by his *nom de guerre* of 'Captain Miller', achieved totemic status as the first of the 'Black Tigers', the elite suicidal fighters who executed the toughest Tamil Tiger attacks. Young Tamil fighters flocked to join this elite suicidal unit, who swore personal loyalty to their Supreme Leader, and dedicated their lives to the fight for a Tamil homeland.

The first known killing by the man who rose to lead the Tamil Tigers had been a more modest affair. At dawn on 27 July 1975, Velupillai Prabakharan left a friend's house in Jaffna, made his way to a nearby temple and fired a volley of home-made bullets at the mayor of Jaffna from a rusty revolver. The slain man, Alfred Duraiappah, had been appointed by Prime Minister Sirimavo Bandaranaike, and was regarded by Tamil firebrands as a traitor. Overnight, the twenty-one-year-old assassin became a figure of notoriety across the island, and a permanent fugitive. Prabakharan had prepared for this moment for years. An ability to elude capture and apparently disappear became one of the trademarks of the future guerrilla leader. The state would not lay a hand on him until the day of his death thirty-four years later.

Prabakharan's politics were driven by the same mixture of fear, fury and frustration felt by other young Tamils coming of age during Bandaranaike's rule. In 1956 and again in 1958, anti-Tamil riots had claimed hundreds of lives across the island. Confronted by 'coloniser' settlements expanding into dry-zone areas, Tamils felt the pressure of state discrimination and what they regarded as the legalised theft of historic Tamil areas. In 1957 and again in 1965, political agreements to reverse the disastrous impact of the Sinhala Only Act had been allowed to founder.[1] The language policies introduced in 1956 and given new impetus by Sirimavo Bandaranaike in 1961 were now a palpable cause for resistance amongst Tamils. By the early 1970s, and Mrs Bandaranaike's second government, English had been replaced as the language of administration by Sinhala, a language that for the vast majority of Tamils was a foreign tongue they could not under-stand and did not want to learn. The state issued land titles, passports, university degrees, tax certificates and other official documents in Sinhala. It was, however, the introduction of two overtly populist policies that now led to a tectonic shift in the Tamil collective consciousness.

In 1972 Prabakharan had joined thousands of Tamil students in Jaffna in mass protests against the introduction of 'standardisation' for universities. Under the new policy, Tamils were required to achieve higher marks than their Sinhalese peers in order to enter certain courses. The government defended the new policy as equitable discrimination to increase university access for marginal communities. Tamils regarded it as straightforward discrimination, an insidious scheme to reduce their dominance in the professions. The second major jolt that year was the new republican constitution, along with the introduction of the new flag and the assertion of Buddhism as the state religion. High unemployment, general economic distress across the island and the first JVP uprising added to a growing sense of crisis. In late 1972, the pre-eminent umbrella Tamil party, the TULF, introduced a platform that called for the first time for a separate and independent state for Tamils.

This overheating crucible of grievances provided a cause, moral justification and a magnet for frustrated Tamils who increasingly opposed both the state and, more dangerously, participation in the political system. In 1972, a group of youths formed the Tamil New Tigers. They chose as their symbol a tiger on a blood-red background, the emblem of the ancient Tamil Chola empire, which had dominated India in the first millennium and repeatedly invaded Sri Lanka. Other Tamil militant groups – angry, determined but above all amateurish at this early stage – were multiplying. Collectively, these groups were known within the Tamil community as 'the boys'. For the next decade, these outlaw bands refined their tactics, acquired coherent ideologies and gave heart to an embattled minority through low-level banditry, bank robberies and the irregular assassination of policemen (many of whom were Tamils). The tacit support of the generally law-abiding Tamil minority for the shadowy figures who flitted across the militant scene was a measure of the festering communal resentment at the cumulative effects of government policies. Their ostensible distaste for the methods used by the militants, even as they extended various levels of cover, support, encouragement and then active participation, would characterise the Tamil community's relationship with militancy until the very end of the Tamil Tigers.

As Prabakharan and other militant Tamil youths were formulating new forms of resistance in northern Sri Lanka, the Eelam Revolutionary Organisation of Students (EROS) was being founded in Manchester and London. From its earliest days, the Marxist EROS organised fund-raising drives and benefit dinners, targeting Tamil expatriates in the UK. It arranged employment for Tamils arriving in Britain, helped them with visas and recruited them as functionaries for 'the Movement' against Buddhist Sinhala nationalism. EROS lobbied parliamentarians, agitated for the boycott of Sri Lankan tea, befriended journalists and made contacts with other foreign revolutionary organisations, which gradually coalesced into an international network of contacts, resources and methods for arms purchasing and money laundering. Tamil resistance to Sinhalese 'neo-colonialism' took on the emotive hues of other international resistance and anti-colonialist movements sequestered in small, dusty London offices. The logistical and organisational experience acquired in the UK by EROS effectively internationalised and bureaucratised Tamil resistance, in a way that the Sri Lankan state would find unmatchable for decades.[2]

The Tamil movement in the UK also provided Prabakharan with the ideological foundation the movement needed, but for which he had little personal patience: he thought intellectuals 'afraid of blood'.[3] In 1979, in Madras, southern India, where he had sought temporary sanctuary from the pursuit of the Sri Lankan authorities, he met with Anton Balasingham, a Sri Lankan Tamil journalist and Marxist based in London. The meeting between the two men forged a partnership that lasted until Balasingham's death in 2006. Balasingham became the Tamil Tiger ideologue, as well as one of the principal negotiators in the tortuous political processes that lay ahead. In Balasingham, Prabakharan recognised a man who could formulate and espouse a lucid ideology to underwrite the raw energy that he himself would provide for the brewing insurgency. In Prabakharan, the older man saw conviction, physical courage and steadfast commitment.[4] A broadly socialist creed became the catalyst for the social revolution needed to break the bonds of a deeply conservative Tamil society, and to refashion those bonds towards self-determination. The rigid caste system, now disowned by official Tiger ideology, instead spawned a renewed hierarchy for the low-caste Prabakharan. Women, children and the whole of Tamil society that lay under Tiger control would be drafted into the

68

THE CAGE

fight.[5] The spectre of the child soldier and the female bomber would become the insignia of the organisation's commitment.

The apparent emancipation of women through the prism of the emerging struggle was narrow, and served the ends of the Tamil Tiger organisation. By the time of the full-blown insurgency that followed the Black July riots, between a fifth and one third of all Tiger cadres were women. They shed their saris for black trousers and checked shirts, their gold jewellery for the ubiquitous glass vial of cyanide worn about the neck, and either cut their hair short or wore it tightly braided. Like their male counterparts, they foreswore cigarettes, alcohol, drugs, sex and even relationships. The existence of female cadres, both rank-and-file and those selected to join the elite Black Tiger units, contributed to the sense of perpetual struggle, as the fundamentally conservative Tamil society consigned its homemakers and mothers to die on the battlefield. According to one Sri Lankan Tamil woman, in the Tigers' reformulation of the female role 'there [was] no sense of independent woman, empowered by her own agency, who makes decisions for her own self-realization'.[6] Women would be expected to fight, or to suffer as their children died.

A life of struggle under a national liberation revolutionary movement was the fate of each child born under the control of the Tamil Tigers, as it was in Gaza.[7] In the latter, children learned from school-books with Qassam rockets on the cover, sang songs about their struggles and the martyrdom of suicide bombers, assisted rocket launchers who assailed Israel from civilian areas and were sometimes killed in Israeli strikes targeting missile launch sites. Likewise encircled by a hostile state, the Tamil Tigers too succeeded in folding the widespread use of children into the ideology and practice of revolutionary sacrifice. In loosely ascribed children's orphanages such as Senchcholai (Red-Blossomed Garden), which would later be bombed, the offspring of dead fighters began each morning with a ceremony of homage to their martyred parents.[8]

If there is a single testament to the way that the Tamil Tigers sought to totally control those it ruled, it is the exploitation of children. Child recruitment, their use in battle and the consequent appalling levels of cruelty towards children and their families largely defy description. In the 1980s and early 1990s, the young were inspired to join for a thousand different reasons. At first, the relative glamour of the Tamil Tigers, their popular support and full coffers proved a draw for teenagers who had witnessed or heard of Sinhalese atrocities directed at their community during Black July, or whose prospects (or those of their parents) remained stunted by state chauvinism. Coca-Cola, uniforms, fighting rhetoric and guns, as well as a basic lack of opportunity, drew in children from poor families. Orphans, those driven by revenge and ideology or those from families close to 'the Movement' joined the Tiger ranks at a steady pace.

By the late 1990s, with the generally more complete control by the Tigers of all aspects of life, the drawn-out war, failed peace overtures and the Tigers' use of summary executions to underscore the point, child recruitment continued apace, but with little of its former popularity. While ancient Tamil martial tales and modern saturation propaganda combined in exhortations for parents to surrender their children to the struggle, stubborn resistance to the sacrifice of offspring grew. The rousing cry in a pamphlet of 'young men and maidens . . . rise and come to us, one from each home, to liberate the soil . . . from the enemy' was accompanied by the more menacing promise that a Tiger recruitment squad would 'call on you and speak to you directly in your home'. Such calls more often than not took this form: 'LTTE recruiters coming in a tractor and trailer stopped opposite homes. The parents were called out and asked to give a child. When they refused, they were beaten with *panaimattais* [dry palmyra fronds with serrated edges]. Usually the children came running on hearing the parents scream. The recruiters then asked a child to come along. The child on declining was beaten and forced into the trailer.'[9]

The highly regarded independent Sri Lankan NGO, the University Teachers for Human Rights (Jaffna),[10] estimated that between 2001 and 2003, the Tamil Tigers recruited around 5,000 children, the vast majority of whom were conscripted by a noxious combination of lethal force, strong-arming, threat, trickery and blackmail.[11] The growing use of pure abduction displaced the need for threat, and children were simply snatched from the roadside as they made their way to or from school. Even those conscripts who volunteered of their own free will did so due to the highly engineered spectrum of social pressures devised by the Tamil Tiger machine, geared to induct the residents of the Vanni into the vortex of sacrifice. Perhaps worst of all, there was no escape.

To be a sixteen-year-old Tamil boy in Sri Lanka was the most dismal of fates. For the Tamil Tigers, such boys were fodder for the ranks, while for the security services they were merely Tigers in the making.[12]

In August 1977, less than a month after J.R. Jayawardene's defeat of Sirimavo Bandaranaike, hundreds of Tamils were killed in more communal riots. While Tamil political consciousness embodied by the TULF scoured the horizon for concessions from Sri Lanka's leaders, 'the boys' agitated. In 1978, the Tamil Tigers and other militant organisations were officially proscribed. Even then, the response of Tamil gangs on the peninsula to communal violence hardly challenged the writ of the state. The Tamil insurrection continued apace with fragmented attacks on police and, beginning in 1981, troops. Bank and armoury robberies netted cash and weapons. But individual murders still had the capacity to shock the island's sense of propriety, and in its early years the Tamil 'insurgency' amounted to no more than a few dozen killings. Of these, Prabakharan was credited with a handful, as well as two bank robberies.* For all the agitation, between 1977 and June 1983 there were just nineteen terrorist attacks, with the loss of thirty-one police and soldiers. The management of the insurgency remained, for the moment, a police matter.

In 1979, worried by the activity of the militant groups, President J.R. Jayawardene ushered through parliament the draconian Prevention of Terrorism Act (PTA). His government had tried to remove the sting of the most overt discrimination of the Bandaranaike years with limited reforms, including the devolution of some powers to Tamil areas in the form of district development councils (albeit that this reform failed because of underfinancing), but militant attacks had continued. Meant to last for just two years, but still in force today, the PTA gave the security forces greater scope to deal with the militants on the Jaffna peninsula. The army and the police launched a clumsy anti-insurgent drive across the peninsula, and its generalised brutality confirmed Tamil distrust for the state and forced many militants to seek refuge in India. By December 1982, 'state-sanctioned violence had reached levels never before seen in Sri Lanka'.[13]

Far from being genuinely popular movements, until the early 1980s

---

* By the time of the 1983 riots, he was officially credited with responsibility for eighteen murders.

the Tamil Tigers and other groups operating on the island, such as EROS and the Tamil Eelam Liberation Organisation (TELO), as well as later organisations like the People's Liberation Organisation of Tamil Eelam (PLOTE) and the Eelam People's Revolutionary Liberation Front (EPRLF), were composed of only a few dozen men each. For more than a decade, the thirty-odd disparate groups merged, split, scattered and re-formed in a tiresome cycle of squabbling and jostling for power and prominence. Often these struggles took violent form, and the Tamil militants sharpened their teeth and blooded themselves on the killing of perceived opponents, retributive murders and the assassination of moderate Tamil politicians. In the late 1980s, many of the survivors merged with the Tamil Tigers under Prabakharan, whose brand of ruthlessness eventually trumped all opposition. Others moved into the shadow world of Colombo politics, with one foot in parliament and the other in a paramilitary power base that was used to terrorise the Tamil population and weed out Tamil Tiger operatives and sympathisers in government-controlled areas. Like so much of the Sri Lankan polity, Tamil militancy was prone to a fragmentation that the ascendancy of Prabakharan largely checked.

It was, above all, the Black July riots in 1983 that converted Tamil militancy from outlier status into an engine of popular rebellion. Instead of placating Tamil fears, the Jayawardene government enacted a 6th amendment to the constitution, requiring all parliamentarians to disavow separatism. The sixteen TULF parliamentarians vacated the parliamentary chamber. The riots seemed to be a declaration of open war by a government either unable or unwilling to protect its Tamil citizens. Around 100,000 Tamils flocked to Tamil Nadu on flotillas of boats, most in search of refuge but a significant minority intending to take up the guerrilla training that by September was being offered by India's intelligence service, RAW, in the north Indian state of Uttar Pradesh. Young Tamil recruits, many of them students, overwhelmed the various militant groups that had previously existed at the fringes of the Tamil political resistance, and that had bases in southern India. Between 1983 and 1986, the Indians trained around 15,000 Tamil militants.[14] Instruction included basic infantry tactics, jungle warfare, artillery, the use of explosives for sabotage and guerrilla combat, as well as more elaborate schooling in scuba and sea-based incursion tactics. While the Indians supplied modern armaments and munitions to the newly trained militants, the smugglers of the Palk Straits helped ferry the armaments from India to the Jaffna peninsula. The forces of insurgency were preparing to match the Sri Lankan state's commanding monopoly of violence, blow by blow.

The government made a half-hearted apology for the Black July riots that had killed so many. There was no judicial process to assuage the fears of the Tamils who continued to live in the south, seeded amidst their Sinhalese neighbours. Instead the amendment to the constitution that forbade parliamentarians from espousing separatism effectively drove the TULF and its secessionist platform from parliament and removed the final possibility of Tamil participation in Sri Lanka's democratic process. Many other Tamils began a rigorous process of assimilation within the majority community, subsuming their identity in small ways, removing, for example, their *pottu*, the small dot worn by Hindus on the forehead. For some, the act of leaving Sri Lanka for ever was a way to escape the closing pincers of the Sinhalese state on one hand, and the dangerous radical turn taken by an assertive Tamil nationalism on the other.

By the mid 1980s, the Jaffna peninsula had become a militarised zone. More and more Sinhalese police and troops were sent to maintain order in the north, and as they encountered the razor edge of Tamil militancy, they quickly assumed the posture of an occupation force. While all three armed services had experienced counter-insurgency warfare during the JVP uprisings, when even fighter jets had been used against the rebels, Sri Lanka maintained only a small army, navy and air force, partly because governments had remained wary of potential military interference after an aborted military coup in 1962.[15] The 11,000-strong army that began to escalate the counter-insurgency war against the Tamil Tigers in 1983 was ill equipped and almost entirely Sinhalese. Troops moved about the country on public transport or hitched rides. While the Bandaranaike government had purchased its arms from China, the USSR and Yugoslavia, the Jaya-wardene regime had shopped with the United States. The army suffered from low morale, corruption, poor pay, slow rearmament and supply problems and a hopelessly politicised system of promotion that kept incompetent officers in key positions and held back experienced veterans. After a conversation with President Jayawardene in December 1983, one commentator observed that 'One factor that failed to strike

[him] was that he had no army to speak of. It could be armed and trained, but had no will to fight a war.'[16] In contrast, the army faced a disciplined, well-trained, well-armed force thirsting for revenge and motivated by a will to protect their homes, families and territory.

What they lacked in skill, good intelligence and equipment, the forces of occupation made up for with a disordered brutality that set the pace for the rest of the civil war. Sinister patterns were quickly established in the months that followed Black July. In a typical scenario, a successful guerrilla strike would claim the lives of one or two soldiers or police. Troops who arrived on the scene and found no guerrillas would interrogate frightened civilians who knew that they could not speak for fear of reprisals from those who lived among them. Young Sinhalese soldiers, usually from the villages of the south and poorly paid and armed, speaking another language and alienated from their surroundings, were easily roused to anger at the unexplained sight of dead comrades, and would burn, rape and kill civilians. In the wake of explosions, soldiers and police would open fire on anyone who happened to be nearby.[17] Reprisal built on reprisal through the following years, until the mass killing of civilians once again became one of the basic anti-insurgency tools of the security forces, just as it had been during the JVP uprisings. Floundering and demoralised security personnel sank deeper into the quagmire of atrocity and illegality. The carte blanche of various emergency laws institutionalised the use of detention and disappearance.[18] Just as with the JVP insurgency, a panicked government licensed every cruelty to fight the militant menace, and in doing so ensured support for the counter-violence of the Tigers.

In July 1984, the first anniversary of the Black July riots, the TULF leadership called for a day of mourning, fasting and prayer. TULF leaders travelled to Jaffna, where they were met by just 200 supporters. Hundreds more chanted: 'The struggle has passed into the hands of the militants. The time for fasting is over.'[19] The peaceful satyagraha fast that the TULF organisers had envisioned had failed; instead, a two-day strike called by a collective of militant groups paralysed Jaffna, Kilinochchi and other towns in the north and east. That year, Prabakharan set a newly strident tone for the Tamil Tiger struggle with attacks on two Sinhalese settlements in the Mullaitivu district of northern Sri Lanka, regarded by the Tigers as traditional Tamil territory. Until 1984, the vast majority of the victims of Tamil militant violence had been Tamils, and it was not until 1984 that the first property belonging to a Sinhalese in Jaffna was targeted for destruction. On 30 November 1984, Tiger cadres raided two farms and killed sixty-two men, women and children. The attacks were no doubt at least an equal measure of what Tamil civilians had already endured in reprisals from the security forces. But the calculated killing of civilians represented the crossing of a line. There would be many more in the decades that followed, and almost invariably the security forces would counter with reprisals that only confirmed Tamil Tiger propaganda proclaiming the state's intention to exterminate its Tamil citizens.

The future Supreme Leader had been born in 1954 in the coastal village of Velvettiturai on the Jaffna peninsula, a community famous for its tough brigands, who smuggled people and goods between India and Sri Lanka across the shallow straits to the north. The lower-caste[20] son of a minor government civil servant, from his early teenage years Velu-pillai Thiruvenkadam Prabakharan set himself a regimen of physical exercise and denial that carried him through the arduous and isolated years as the revolution took shape. As a young teenager he exhibited a maverick quality expressed in violence and fantasy; slingshots, home-made bombs and a voracious consumption of *Phantom* comics and Clint Eastwood films about hero-loners committed to just ends. At one stage, the committed revolutionary claimed not to have seen his own mother and father for more than a decade, as he ranged across the Jaffna landscape making revolution for his people – 'the armed vanguard of the struggling masses', as he put it.[21]

The shrouded and inaccessible nature of the Supreme Leader never changed. It added to his mystique, and to the power of the recorded 'national' address he later gave each November when the Tamil Tiger fight had graduated to pretender statehood through the holding of territory. The question of what motivated Prabakharan, while critical to understanding the rise and fall of the Tamil Tigers, will remain obscured by the secretiveness that had become second nature since his adolescent crossing-over from boyhood to an outlaw 'proud to be indicted as a wanted man'.[22] This metamorphosis is the essence of the type of commitment displayed by many insurgent leaders, bandits, gangsters and terrorists. Unlike ordinary mortals, they turn their backs on the ordinary relationships, quotidian fears and communal safety nets that nurture and restrain others. For Prabakharan, his low-caste status made his breaking of social strictures a matter of personal logic, as well as political and military practicality.

Those who were admitted into the sanctum that protected Prabakharan in later years – Tiger political and military commanders, important members of the diaspora, foreign diplomats and Black Tigers – encountered a short, portly, quietly spoken and calmly determined man. Like his nemesis, the future defence secretary Gotabaya Rajapaksa, then a young army officer, Prabakharan was a model of persistent brutality and single-mindedness, endowed with a sense of personal historical mission. Unlike Gotabaya, his persistence derived from the repression he had witnessed by the state against the Tamil community, and an abiding suspicion of authority. He had believed since the early 1970s that the Sri Lankan state could not be trusted, and that only armed struggle for Tamil self-determination would provide Tamils with freedom, dignity and rights in their own land. This belief was the bedrock of the long, unhappy trail of failed negotiations for peace that lay ahead.

Prabakharan exuded a self-confidence and stubborn persistence born of a cold devotion to a historic cause that was inextricably bound up with his innate belief in the utility of violence. Like a diabolical alchemist, killing people, ordering their deaths or sending young men and women to die in suicidal attacks reconfigured that belief into a confessional act, with the sacred boundaries of Tamil Eelam granting absolution. Just as the ancient caste system that ordered communal identity was transmuted in the crucible of 'the Movement', so too was the Tamil community's relationship to murder and suicide. Hitherto unthinkable violence was legitimised and elevated into the poetry of national liberation by acts of self-sacrifice. In turn, this revolutionary ideology of martyrdom was figuratively sculpted on to the landscape in the form of the military cemeteries and cenotaphs that in the decades to come dotted Tamil-controlled territory in memory of the growing thousands of martyred.[23]

The exercise of de facto power over who would live and who might die – a ruthless brand of gangster paternalism – gave Prabakharan a charmed personal authority. He demanded complete and undying loyalty to the cause from the small band of men who initially joined the

Tigers. The discipline, secrecy and methodical operational planning of those early years were replicated throughout the organisation as its ranks swelled, until it had assumed many of the capabilities of a standing army. Friends and enemies spoke of Prabhakaran's supposed genius for military affairs, a quality somewhat belied by the strategic and tactical blunders that ultimately led to his own death, the extinction of the Tamil Tigers and the demise of the dream of Tamil Eelam. His rise and eventual fall were as spectacular and surprising as each other.

Radical methods such as suicide bombings, used by both Middle Eastern revolutionaries and the Tamil Tigers, had had a brief gestation in Lebanon. Between 1976 and the early 1980s the Palestine Liberation Organisation had trained probably no more than a hundred Tamils in Lebanon, drawn in small batches from the Tamil Tigers and other radical Tamil groups that were beginning to define the resistance to state oppression.[24] In many ways, their experience in the Bekaa valley and in the streets of Beirut was disappointing and even amateurish. A number of Tamils left early, or returned home disgruntled with the food, the language difficulties and the quality of the training.

It was, however, the radical methods gleaned from the Palestinians and other groups involved in the wars against the Israelis, and the capacity for endless adaptation and evolution of guerrilla tactics, that would underwrite the incontestable ferocity and tactical impact of the Tamil Tigers. Suicidal devotion to the cause of Eelam, and its potential for replication, had existed since at least 1974, when a seventeen-year-old member of a radical Tamil group, trapped by police after a failed bank robbery, bit on a vial of cyanide. In this lone act, Prabakharan recognised the transformative potential of the impotent anger of a generation of Tamil youths.

As the war between the government and the Tigers intensified in the late 1980s, the insurgents converted Tamil helplessness into a potent military force characterised by the will to die. In the conscious manufacture of a tradition of heroic self-sacrifice, reckless death in the cause of Eelam achieved a spiritual status that subverted everyday public worship of the gods of the Hindu pantheon. To young Tamils, death in battle was an extension of the martial tradition of the ancient Tamil Chola warriors, popularised in the modern Tamil historical novels that Prabakharan kept by his bed. Unlike, however, the supranational terrorist acts of the twenty-first century, which would once again raise terrorism to a new level, the Tamil Tiger war remained bounded by its territorial political ambitions, and its struggle against the Sri Lankan state.

The use of suicidal attackers is an efficient deployment of resources, the poor man's tactical weapon or smart bomb. In the age of instant communications and, later, the Internet, each attack was a 'force multi-plier'. From 1987 onwards, the Tamil Tigers successfully honed the use of tactical suicide bombing, until the attacks on New York's Twin Towers signalled that the Tigers' ascendancy in the media had been surpassed. Between the attack by 'Captain Miller' in 1987 and the defeat of the Tamil Tigers in May 2009, the Tigers dispatched 273 suicide attackers on 137 missions. The youngest is believed to have been eighteen years old. Forty-seven of the attackers were women, whose gender assisted them in reaching guarded spaces.[25]

The aim of the attackers was not to commit suicide, but rather to achieve a political or military gain. However tempting, it is misleading to think of suicide attackers as mad, bad or irrational. Far from being cowards, those who engage in suicide warfare exhibit a high degree of bravery that is difficult to match for even the most committed of regular troops. In more normal circumstances, according to psychologists who have studied the phenomenon, suicide attackers would typically be regarded as relatively balanced and with a low instance of the kinds of risk factors commonly associated with suicides.[26] When 'Captain Miller' drove his truck into the Neliady schoolhouse, he created a template for heroic action and a rational response to oppression, as well as a soundbite for news programmes, a rallying point for expatriate Tamil fund-raisers and a training module for those who would follow him.[27]

To be selected as a Black Tiger was the highest honour, since only the most important missions were entrusted to this elite group. With their training and dedication they were, to the Tamils at least, the equivalent perhaps of the British SAS or the US army's elite Rangers corps. Black Tigers wore a different uniform from other cadres and were issued with three dog tags so that their bodies could be clearly identified by the Sri Lankan authorities after an attack or suicide blast. Before a mission, usually their last, they would share a meal with the Supreme Leader, and a photograph would be taken for global distribution and endless reproduction after the attack. Once a mission had been designated, there were calls for volunteers from within the Black Tiger unit. To be selected was literally like winning the lottery, as one young female volunteer called 'Banu' described in an interview with *Time* Magazine in 2006: 'They put everyone's name in a tumbler. They swirl them around. Then the Leader pulls out two names, reads them out and the 48 who aren't chosen are all crying. But the two who are chosen, they are very happy and the people around them raise them on their shoulders and are all clapping and celebrating.'[28]

Suicide bombers were used by the Tigers to reach heavily guarded political and military leaders. In 1991, it was a Black Tiger who killed former Indian prime minister Rajiv Gandhi in Tamil Nadu. In 1992, another bomber rammed his motorbike into the staff car of Sri Lanka's senior naval officer, Vice Admiral Clancy Fernando, killing him and four other people. The following year, Sri Lanka's president Ranasinghe Premadasa became the first and only sitting president in the world to be killed by a suicide bomber. He was blown up as he attended a May Day procession in Colombo. In 1998, a Black Tiger leapt in front of the staff car of one of the army's most experienced officers, Brigadier Larry Wijeratne, killing him and two others. A year later, twenty-three people were killed when a suicide bomber attempted to kill President Chandrika Kumaratunga – she survived but lost an eye in the attack. In 2006, a female bomber seriously injured army commander General Sarath Fonseka and killed eight others. A few months later, secretary of defence Gotabaya Rajapaksa's motorcade was almost rammed by an autorickshaw that exploded, killing some of his escort. And in January 2007, former Tamil militant turned government minister Douglas Devananda escaped assassination for the thirteenth time when a woman blew herself up in his office, killing a secretary.[29] Successful suicide attacks killed dozens of politicians, functionaries and senior security personnel, while other assassinations, such as that of foreign minister Lakshman Kadirgamar (a Tamil), were carried out by sniper rifles or remotely detonated roadside bombs.

Suicide attackers were used to hit infrastructure, military hardware and personnel and high-impact civilian targets. In 1995, Black Tigers struck oil storage complexes, blowing themselves up along with twenty-two soldiers, vital storage tanks and oil products worth an estimated ten million dollars. In 1998, eight Sea Tiger boats laden with explosives ploughed into two navy ships on the Point Pedro coastline of northern Sri Lanka, killing fifty-one troops and ratings as well as twenty-eight civilians.[30] In 2001, the fourteen-man Black Tiger raid on Colombo's contiguous international and military airport destroyed twenty-five aircraft, crippled the tourist industry and cost the country hundreds of millions of dollars in hardware and lost tourist revenue. In 2006, a suicide bomber struck a convoy of buses carrying off-duty sailors, claiming 103 lives. Later that year, a five-boat Sea Tiger squadron attacked naval vessels in Galle harbour, a tourist destination for hippies and backpackers and one of the most heavily fortified government bases in the far south. The following year, in a pre-dawn raid, a twenty-one-member Black Tiger unit attacked the Anuradhapura air force base, destroying eight aircraft, damaging a further ten, and killing fourteen personnel. Dozens of Tiger cadres blew themselves up in the final months of the war in frontline attacks on advancing government troops.

The Tiger attacks combined sheer audacity with a strategic insight that elevated their violent deeds to propaganda spectaculars.[31] On New Year's Eve 1996, a three-man Black Tiger team drove a truck laden with 200 kilograms of high explosives into the seaside high-rise building housing the Central Bank in Colombo, killing ninety-one people, wounding a further 1,400 and causing extensive damage to nine downtown buildings. Two years later, in 1998, a four-member unit drove a bomb-rigged truck into the exalted Buddhist shrine of the Temple of the Tooth in Kandy, wrecking the temple complex and killing seven people just days before the country was due to celebrate its fiftieth anniversary of independence. The Tiger 'air force', which consisted of three converted Czech civilian light aircraft, caused relatively little damage, but made riveting television as searchlights lit up the Colombo skies and confused soldiers fired randomly into the night.[32]

On rare occasions, Black Tigers returned from their missions. They were suicide attackers only in the sense that the daring and destructive capacity of their attacks entailed almost certain death. The value they added was thus twofold: in the extraordinary courage they displayed during attacks, and in the actual destruction of their targets. They combined the classic 'propaganda of the deed' with the lethality of drone-fired missiles. Nevertheless, the Sri Lankan government successfully appropriated George W. Bush's sweeping mischaracterisation of the 9/11 bombers, and to the outside world the Black Tigers became suicide bombers whose attacks and killing of civilians seemed subhuman rather than supra-human. Suicidal bravery is poorly understood in today's advanced economies, couched as they are in prosperity and lulled by electronic distraction.[33]

Combined with the suicide attacks was the cold-blooded murder by Tigers of civilians in targeted attacks. Prior to the rise of the Tamil Tigers, around 10 per cent of the population of Jaffna had been Sinhalese who had peacefully coexisted with their neighbours for generations. Sinhalese and Muslim villages, many the product of government-supported settlement schemes, were scattered throughout areas deemed strictly Tamil by the resurgent Tamil nationalist ideology. In October 1990, the Tamil Tigers issued a warning in which all Muslims were given a few hours to leave Tiger-controlled territory: 75,000 people fled south into towns controlled by the government. For more than two decades, the Tamil Tigers raided Muslim and Sinhalese villages throughout Tamil-majority areas, in an effort to drive both communities out. They hacked, bludgeoned, shot, burned and hanged civilians in a long series of massacres. The majority of those killed were Sinhalese, but a disproportionate number were Muslim. Children were slaughtered alongside the elderly in dozens of small-scale incidents.

There were large-scale massacres as well. In 1985, Tiger fighters stormed the town of Anuradhapura, killing 146 civilians at the bus station, in one of the main Buddhist shrines and in a nature reserve. In 1987, guerrillas stopped a bus and butchered thirty-four people, the majority of them young boys training to be monks. In 1990, a platoon of Tigers killed 147 men and boys as they worshipped in a mosque. The following year they killed 109 Muslim men, women and children in the village of Palliyagodella. The Tamil Tigers appear to have slaughtered captured soldiers and policemen with especially terrifying ferocity. In 1990, Tiger cadres forced the surrender of dozens of police stations in eastern Sri Lanka and executed 600 police officers in and around the town of Kalmunai.[34] In 1996, when Tiger cadres overran a military camp in Mullaitivu, more than 1,200 soldiers were killed, executed or otherwise disappeared.

The Tamil Tigers planted bombs on trains, aircraft and buses. As early as 1986, they planted a bomb that exploded prematurely on an Air Lanka plane as it sat on the tarmac in Colombo, killing twenty-one people, including thirteen foreigners. In 1987, a car bomb exploded in Colombo's Pettah market, killing 113 civilians. In 1996, four briefcase bombs exploded simultaneously on a train, killing sixty-four passengers and wounding more than 400 others. In 2006, a roadside blast killed sixty civilians on a bus in Kebithigollewa. The Tigers' long list of atrocities sowed terror throughout Sri Lanka. The sense that one could be randomly killed in an attack was a palpable one for anybody living on the island.[35] It is alleged that between the 1983 riots and May 2009, there were around 200 individual Tiger attacks on civilian targets, in which between 3,700 and 4,100 civilians were killed.[36]

Conversely, the University Teachers for Human Rights calculates that in 1990, SLA retaliation in just two districts in eastern Sri Lanka for Tiger executions of soldiers and police officers led to the massacre of 3,000 Tamil civilians over only a couple of weeks. Hundreds of Tamil men were allegedly rounded up and burned alive in the course of the retribution. Again, during the Black July massacres, between 1,000 and 3,000 Tamils were killed over just a few days. In a country that has proven incapable of investigating the crimes of its own law enforcement and military officers, it is unlikely that the true scope of the government-sanctioned killing of Tamil civilians by a plethora of security forces will ever be known.[37] In contrast, Tiger atrocities against the Sinhalese were carefully counted, scrutinised and repeatedly decried by the government. In relative terms, and in the course of a long and bloody civil war, the number of civilians killed by terrorist acts attributed to the Tigers was somewhat modest compared with estimates of the overall civilian death toll inflicted on the Tamils.

Between 1984 and 1987, until the intervention of the Indian army, the Tamil Tigers waged the first phase of their guerrilla war, known as Eelam War I, and routed their rival militant groups. Fighting between the Tigers and the Sri Lankan army escalated as well-trained fighters fresh from India returned to Sri Lanka. Direct control of swathes of territory by the militants ebbed and flowed. Funds poured in from abroad as the expatriate Tamil community reacted to the impact of Black July. India sought a political solution from the Sri Lankan government, which in 1984 had convened an All Party Conference that had failed to arrive at a formula for peace. In 1985, India sponsored talks in Bhutan between the government and four major guerrilla groups – the Tigers, EROS, EPRLF and TELO – that failed either to arrive at a peace plan or to combine the guerrillas into a single organisation. The following year, hundreds of Tamil guerrillas from TELO and the EPRLF were killed in well-planned Tiger attacks, including senior activists whose credentials in 'the Movement' stretched back to the early 1970s. Prabakharan's ruthless suppression of rivals and alternative voices in the Tamil struggle, and his marshalling of Tamil resources at home and abroad, meant that by the late 1980s, the Tigers were paramount throughout the north and east, and had deployed the same grip abroad to control the Tamil diaspora network.

By 1987, the Sri Lankan army had regrouped, taking advantage of the perceived weakness in the ranks of the feuding guerrilla outfits. More than 8,000 SLA troops had fought through the jungles of the Vanni, routing the guerrillas from their camps, until they were penned up in the Jaffna peninsula and forced to retreat to the town of Jaffna itself. But the bombarding of civilian areas and the prospect of more large-scale killings of Tamils by the Sri Lankan army triggered outrage in Tamil Nadu. The opportunity to destroy the Tamil Tigers evaporated when Rajiv Gandhi's government breached Sri Lankan sovereignty with airdrops of supplies to Jaffna. The drops effectively broke the siege and signalled to the Sri Lankan government that India would not tolerate a military solution in place of a political settlement and would intervene if necessary. By the end of July, the Indo-Sri Lanka Agreement to establish Peace and Normalcy in Sri Lanka had been signed by Gandhi and President Jayawardene in Colombo. Its provisions included devolved power to the provinces, official status for the Tamil language and a merger of Tamil majority provinces that gave territorial recognition to claims over an historic Tamil homeland. Within days, Indian troops were occupying cities throughout the Tamil majority areas of the north and east.

But the Tamil Tigers were not signatories to the agreement and had not been consulted. They believed that the scope of the Sri Lankan president's powers undermined the 'devolution of powers' provision of the accord. They refused to surrender their arms and retreated from Jaffna to the jungles of the Vanni. Within eight weeks of landing, the garlands, flowers and food with which the Indian Peace Keeping Force had been greeted as liberators were just embittering memories for the Indian troops. They were compelled to turn their weapons on the Tamil Tigers in an effort to enforce the disarmament provisions of the accord. The Indians also rearmed and strengthened the other Tamil militant groups, which had accepted the accord. The Tigers struck back with ferocity.

The 80,000-man IPKF stumbled into using much the same methods as the Sri Lankan army had, with a consequent brutalising of the Tamil civilian population. While the SLA had withdrawn from the war with Tamil separatism and was concentrating on dealing with the JVP insurgency that had exploded throughout the south after the signing of the Indo-Sri Lanka Accord, the Indians battled through jungle, village and town for three long years in an attempt to crush the Tamil Tigers. In 1989, after supplying the Tigers with arms as leverage with the Indians, Sri Lanka's new president Ranasinghe Premadasa was able to position himself as peacemaker between the Tigers and the Indian army. The Indians agreed to withdraw their forces, and by March 1990 had quit the country, after losing 1,200 troops. By July, the war between the government and the Tamil Tigers – Eelam War II – had resumed.

The bloodying of the IPKF and their evacuation from Sri Lanka left the Tamil Tigers in a position of unparalleled strength. Equipped and trained by India, then resupplied by the Sri Lankan government, and hardened by years of urban and jungle warfare, the Tigers controlled most of the Jaffna peninsula for the first time. They marked this new epoch with a fifty-three-day assault codenamed 'Land, Sea and Air' on the Sri Lankan army's 600-man garrison at Elephant Pass, a fortress that controlled the narrow isthmus joining the Jaffna peninsula with the rest of the island. Armoured bulldozers were supported by full-frontal attacks of waves of fighters as the Tigers attempted to breach the defences and overwhelm the garrison. By their own reckoning, the Tigers lost 573 fighters, with more than 1,400 wounded, but the fortress held.

The SLA strategy became one of holding key fortifications. Throughout decades of campaigning, the Tamil Tigers sought to control Trincomalee, site of one of the world's most significant deep-water harbours and home to massive oil storage tanks that had been built during the Second World War by the British. The harbour, considered by India a potential threat to its security should it fall into the hands of a foreign government, would provide the rebel group with the strategic fulcrum for the state they envisaged. Prabakharan was convinced that the supply of US weapons to Sri Lanka was part of a strategy to secure access to the harbour. Despite taking much of the town, they were never able to overrun the naval and army fortifications that kept the port firmly under the control of the government.[38]

In less than three years following the IPKF withdrawal, the Tigers exercised their new power and ability to strike throughout the island and abroad. They completely exterminated dissent and other armed groups within the area of their control. Apart from the assassination of Rajiv Gandhi and Admiral Clancy Fernando, they hit Sri Lanka's foreign and defence minister Ranjan Wijeratne, and senior government minister Lalith Athulathmudali in April 1993. A week later, a suicide bomber killed President Premadasa at a May Day rally in Colombo. The Tigers continued to sink naval vessels, overrun military camps, assassinate members of parliament, bomb buses and amass armaments and finance from throughout the world. They acquired fifty tonnes of TNT and ten tonnes of the plastic explosive RDX, a considerable proportion of the funding for which originated in Canada from Tiger front organisations resorting to extortion.[39] In 1995, the newly elected president, the SLFP leader Chandrika Kumaratunga, returned to peace talks with the Tigers.

President Kumaratunga's offer of peace included an extensive devolution package and a fundamental reform of government in Sri Lanka that amounted to the end of unitary and centralised government. But without a majority in parliament, her proposal fell foul of the same political brinkmanship that parties in opposition had assumed since the 1950s. The UNP joined forces with hardline Sinhalese nationalist parties to oppose the proposals, while for their part the Tamil Tigers rejected anything short of a separate state. After a short honeymoon period, the new government resolved to bring the Tigers back to the negotiating table by force, and war resumed – Eelam War III.

In April 1996, a massive army offensive forced the Tamil Tigers to withdraw from Jaffna. They retreated into the jungle and villages of the Vanni to the south, along with between 300,000 and 400,000 civilians who in just a few hours were intimidated into leaving their houses, jobs and villages. In July 1996, in the Tigers' first 'Unceasing Wave' operation, an SLA camp in Mullaitivu was overrun in a ferocious land, air and sea battle in which around 1,200 SLA troops were killed, more than 200 of whom were allegedly executed after surrendering. In September 1998, the town of Kilinochchi fell to the Tigers after terrible hand-to-hand fighting, with thousands of SLA dead. For three and a half years the army tried to push forward against the Tigers in order to secure a route between its forces in Jaffna and those pressing up from the south. The fighting was characterised by government advances, followed by surprise counter-attacks by the Tigers that often led to the army losing half the ground it had gained. The A9 highway linking central Sri Lanka with the Jaffna peninsula was fought over at terrible cost. The Tigers continued with their terrorist campaign across the island, keeping the public in the greater part of the country that was unaffected by the fighting on tenterhooks and opinion divided as to where the solution to the civil war lay.

By April 2000, the Tigers had stormed and overrun the Elephant Pass and threatened to annihilate the SLA Jaffna garrison of 34,000 troops, now surrounded and without the ships needed to evacuate them. By mid May, the army had consolidated and the garrison had been resupplied. The nation was shaken. The Tigers had come close to dealing a blow to the sovereign state that would have been impossible to overcome.

Yet the Tigers' 2001 attack on Colombo's international airport and the steady stream of strikes at 'soft' civilian targets increasingly exposed the inherent contradictions of the fight for national liberation. With each attack, the Tigers achieved unparalleled 'propaganda by deed', even as they stoked their reputation for fanaticism. The killing of political and military leaders struck fear into the ruling political class, at the same time dismembering the voices of moderation and compromise. The daring Black Tiger attacks buoyed the Tamil diaspora and generated funding, while they drained Sri Lanka's public coffers and weakened democratic political institutions. Suicidal terrorist tactics served to support appeals to the international community – that only extreme oppression and the relentless torment of an ethnic minority could provoke such fatalistic fanaticism – even as they reinforced Prabakharan's reputation as a totalitarian thug. The elusiveness of the attackers and their ability to strike at the heart of public life distracted the army, undermined their morale and eroded the legitimacy of successive governments unable to provide basic guarantees of security to the public. The September 2001 airborne attacks on the US mainland by Islamic extremists were about to irredeemably tip international perceptions of the Tiger fight into the 'terrorist' chasm.

* * *

While Tiger guerrilla units battled the SLA and the terrorist tactics of the organisation were refined, its power and influence grew on a number of crucial fronts that internationalised 'the Movement'. From 1983 onwards, Tamil militant groups had competed to transmit their messages through journals, newspapers, pamphlets, songs, poems and plays.[40] After 1992, with the end of the Cold War, and de facto control of large swathes of territory, Prabakharan addressed a worldwide audience through his Great Heroes Day speech every 27 November. This speech, laden with references to the sacrifice of the growing number of 'martyrs', was the only public address by Prabakharan during the year, and was initially broadcast on the Voice of Tiger radio station. By 2005, the Tiger propaganda network was capable of broadcasting the speech on the National Television of Tamil Eelam (NTT) and by satellite throughout Europe, the Middle East, South-East Asia, India and southern Africa.[41] The network also made use of a range of Internet sites, whose proliferation seemed to match a similar growth in the trappings of statehood as the Tigers fought for – and achieved – growing recognition throughout the 1990s as the legitimate representatives of a repressed people.[42] The London-based Tiger press office was called Eelam House, mimicking the official locations of other former Crown colonies such as Australia House and Canada House.

Just as with Islamist terrorism in the twenty-first century, death was a spectacle deployed for political ends. The Tamil Tigers filmed their suicide and military attacks where possible and packaged them into songs and video presentations.[43] Visual imagery included burials in cemeteries filled with martyrs and families mourning their heroes. The cemeteries themselves represented a decisive break with the past in a culture that traditionally cremated their dead. No longer lost to the vagaries of private albums and brass urns, each Tiger martyr was counted, mourned, celebrated and added to the swelling pantheon of self-sacrifice.[44]

Cemeteries across Tiger-controlled territory were solemn public spaces built at enormous cost, swirling with red flags and imbued with a reverence customarily reserved for temples. The search for freedom had assumed religio-mystical proportions and Prabakharan the status of sage and guide, leading his people from captivity like a Marxist Moses. Powerful repetitive images of sacrifice reminded the expatriate

Tamil community of those who were suffering, and of their own suffering as exiles. For those who were not there, the best way to build the struggle was to ensure that fighters were equipped with communications equipment, arms and medical care. The elevation of martyrdom to the centre of public life contributed to recruitment and took the sting out of prospective death.

The end of the Cold War opened new frontiers. Borders fell, finance flowed to new regions of the world, arms markets multiplied and communications were revolutionised. There were new opportunities for multinational corporations and for criminal and terrorist networks that mimicked the corporate business model in vague, capricious and corruptly governed countries. There were new unregulated markets in blood diamonds, drugs, illegally felled timber and the trafficking of people for labour and sex. The flood of small arms opened by the availability of massive armouries in ex-Soviet Bloc nations was channelled by warlord businessmen to national liberation groups fighting 'small wars' in places like the Balkans, the Caucasus and Central Asia, or to sovereign criminal states such as Liberia and Sierra Leone. National liberation, religious fundamentalist and criminal organisations shifted seamlessly between each other's worlds. A computer model of these networks reveals clusters around organisations as diverse as the Kosovo Liberation Army, the Hells Angels, the Moro National Liberation Front, the Sendero Luminoso, the Italian 'Ndrangheta, the IRA, the PKK and Californian Vietnamese street gangs, connected by their ability to supply given markets in, or to source goods from, the geographic locations they dominated.

The Tamil Tigers maintained representative offices in at least forty countries. The expatriate Tamil community in Canada, the UK, Switzerland and a dozen other countries created new transnational networks that included legitimate businesses and investments guided by ranks of lawyers and accountants. Front companies, offshore accounts, pseudonymous charitable institutions and the exponential explosion of non-governmental organisations provided an endless sequence of filters and decoys through which funds for the purchase of arms could be disguised and channelled to the Tigers. Kumaran Pathmanathan, better known as 'KP', who had total control of the Tigers' international finance, purchasing and transport operations through the 'KP department', maintained offices in Rangoon, Paris, Bangkok, Kuala Lumpur and

Johannesburg. His operation was strictly white collar, and employees were devoid of criminal, military or political records. Their mission was to trade and to make a profit. Other forms of business – both legal and illegal – were inducted or discarded in ever-evolving business models whose profits went to support the Tamil Tiger struggle.

Most characteristic of the nature of this corporate success was the mastery of ungoverned spaces, of which the ocean was the ultimate field of operations. The merchant shipping operation built by KP was the ideal front company, capable in these early years of dexterous evolution. Ships at sea are in theory subject to a maze of competing jurisdictions, including those of the countries of the last and next ports of call, as well as the nation under which the vessel is flagged and, in theory, controlled.[45] In 2006 and 2007, the Sri Lankan navy destroyed eight Sea Pigeon merchant ships, effectively severing the organisation's line of supply, but there are thought to have been as many as twenty-two vessels at sea.[46] The ships were registered under flags of convenience in Liberia, Panama, Honduras and Syria, countries with lax regulatory systems that allowed the renaming of ships, the disguising of manifests and frequent changes of ownership as assets were passed through an exhaustive array of front companies. In addition, the Sea Pigeons maintained a pseudo-base on the Burmese island of Twante, close to the Golden Triangle with its robust trade in arms and heroin.

The KP department became adept at complex arms transactions in order to consolidate purchasing opportunities that benefited a variety of illicit organisations, the profit of which was turned to the purchase of weapons for the war in Sri Lanka. Illegal arms shipments were loaded in loosely governed states with easily subverted officials and offloaded on the high seas on to fast and well-armed light boats for transport to the Sri Lankan mainland. Most of the time, the Sea Pigeon fleet transported legitimate goods. But ships were easily diverted for the smuggling of mixed or single manifests of people, drugs, cash and arms.[47] For example, Sea Pigeon ships are alleged to have been involved in the illegal transport of arms on behalf of Harakat-al Mujahideen, a Pakistani militant group with links to al-Qaeda, to the Abu Sayyaf group in the Philippines.[48] The Tigers also developed strong links with secessionist Eritrea, on one of the key sea transport routes of the world, in a region awash with arms and radical Islamic organisations competing for influence in the Horn of Africa.[49]

It took time for Sri Lankan governments to understand the implications of the transformation of segments of the Tamil diaspora network into a corporate operation that directly challenged the reach of the state's own international network. The government resented the lack of attention brought to bear on Tamil organisations operating from foreign territories. The liberal norms of democratic countries provided cover for businesses whose activities tended to be confined to the Tamil community, and as such remained impenetrable for local law enforcement and intelligence services. But Tiger activities could also be profoundly damaging to their hosts. As early as 1984, Swiss police estimated that Tamils were transporting 20 per cent of the heroin that was coming into the country. Italian police dismantled a number of Tamil heroin rings in the 1980s and were confronted by defendants who claimed special treatment on the basis that they were 'political prisoners and revolutionary fighters'.[50] Mostly, however, police forces left the Tamil community and its obscure and mostly internecine violence to itself. The closed nature of the international Sri Lankan Tamil community provided carte blanche for the extension of Tiger control, which was exerted through intimidation, blackmail, beatings, threats against family members, both abroad and in Sri Lanka, and a number of killings. The Tigers controlled the majority of Sri Lankan Hindu temples in the UK and Canada, which became centres of command and extortion in the form of 'taxes'.[51]

It was not until after September 2001 that western governments instituted the kind of coordination and expertise needed to track flows of cash, and even then, the Tamil Tigers were accorded low priority behind al-Qaeda and its plethora of affiliated groups. Western countries gradually followed India and the US and outlawed the Tigers as a terrorist organisation, making it a crime to provide finance to the group. But it was virtually impossible for police forces in countries that were home to Tamil expatriate communities to detect and control these flows, let alone make distinctions between legitimate businesses, charities and rackets.

While there were numerous successful prosecutions of Tamils involved in the drugs trade, evidence that the trade supported the Tigers was only ever circumstantial. It was impossible for prosecutors to prove that the accused intended to support a terrorist group. By the end of the war in Sri Lanka, there had been only around sixty international prosecutions of people accused of arms trafficking, money laundering and channelling funds to the Tamil Tigers. A case brought by federal police in Australia against three defendants in 2010 was an embarrassing failure when it came to court. One of the biggest alleged funders was US billionaire Raj Rajaratnam, but even the Rajapaksa government could not decide whether he had funded the Tamil Tigers or was merely a useful benefactor in the post-war environment.

Following the September 2001 attacks on the United States, the Tamil Tigers switched into peacemaking mode. Kosovo gradually emerged from Yugoslavia, backed by European Union midwifery and offering renewed hope that the same status might be won for Tamil Eelam. The advent of a new UNP government under Ranil Wickramasinghe in December led to the interim ceasefire agreement of 22 February 2002, mediated by the Norwegian government, which had been a principal foreign donor to the country for decades. The guns were silent, the front lines held and the Tamil Tigers established 'customs' posts (and collected revenue) along the line of control. The mood of the entire country was buoyant, and people believed that a negotiated peace was at hand. Diaspora funding flowed into the Vanni, the de facto state with Kilinochchi as its capital and Prabakharan as its self-proclaimed 'president and prime minister'. The Nordic nations sent military observers, the Sri Lanka Monitoring Mission (SLMM), to oversee the peace. Thousands of Tamil Tiger fighters left the movement and started families, a peace dividend inspired in part by the sons and daughters of expatriate Tamils who returned to their homeland for the first time to see, reclaim and help rebuild it.

But peace was a restless illusion. In April 2003, the Tigers made the first of a series of fatal miscalculations and withdrew from peace talks. Instead they put forward a number of maximalist demands that weakened their UNP government partner-for-peace and strengthened the hand of Buddhist nationalists, who saw in the demands the first moves towards a formal declaration of secession. The SLMM recorded thousands of infractions of the ceasefire, the majority of them committed by the Tamil Tigers as they hustled to consolidate their position. Hundreds of dissident Tamils across the island were murdered, the majority of them by the Tigers. Internal tensions boiled over, and in March 2004 there was a decisive split, with fighting between the cadres of the Tigers' eastern sub-commander Vinayagamoorthy Muralith-aran, known as 'Colonel Karuna', and the northern cadres. Karuna had been a senior commander since 1987, and the ensuing damage to the Tigers could hardly have been greater. His defection brought an unprecedented flow of intelligence that exposed the strength, displacement, training, scenario planning and fortifications of Tiger operations, bared its international operations and brought a force of 600 fighters over to the government.

The Karuna defection coincided with the election as prime minister of Mahinda Rajapaksa, a member of the SLFP and the head of the new United People's Freedom Alliance (UPFA), and the re-emergence of a hard-line stance towards the Tamil Tigers (Chandrika Kumaratunga was still president). Again, the Tigers were central to their own demise, as they intimidated Vanni Tamils in order to prevent them voting, a move that virtually ensured the election of a party running on a platform of war. Even before the defeat of Wickramasinghe's government, which appeared to have been duped by the insincerity of the Tigers, the Sri Lankan army and intelligence services were preparing the ground for a return to war, spurred by intelligence that revealed similar Tiger preparations.[52] Rajapaksa, now in control of the Bandaranaikes' SLFP party, was backed by the JVP, which had evolved into a hard-line nationalist party, and the Jathika Hela Urumaya (JHU, or National Heritage Party), founded that same year and led by xenophobic monks advocating a violent solution to the Tamil challenge. The new administration stepped up arms purchases and began planning for a resumption of war with a commitment to destroy the Tigers.

The Tigers had taken advantage of the chaos and the extraordinary flows of foreign aid into Sri Lanka in the wake of the Christmas 2004 tsunami, which killed around 30,000 people on the island, to rearm. Over the following year, they stepped up their programme of assassinations of Tamils and attacks on the security forces.[53] Hundreds of foreign aid agencies unwittingly provided a cover for the smuggling of additional material.[54] It was probably during this period that the Tigers built up the majority of their tiny air force, with smuggled Czech recreation aircraft, overseas pilot training and the construction of half a dozen airstrips throughout the Vanni. The establishment of an airborne capability carried with it the same inherent strategic contradictions of suicide warfare. It was the world's first terrorist air force and a brilliant propaganda coup. But it was also a dangerous act of overreach. The acquisition of air power by the Tigers, itself of relatively little military significance, held an unpalatable symbolic importance that alarmed foreign governments. The rise of suicide warfare and violent terrorist attacks in the Middle East tempered the West's tolerance for plucky liberation movements. While not presenting an imminent threat to international peace and security, the ingenuity and agility of the Tigers added to the swelling handbook for terrorist movements, quickening the erosion of sympathy or toleration for the guerrilla group.

In December 2005, Mahinda Rajapaksa displaced President Chandrika Kumaratunga to achieve the leadership of the SLFP, and the party's nomination for president. The Rajapaksas came from a provincial political dynasty based around the deep south of Sinhalese Sri Lanka, the district of Hambantota. In the early twentieth century, the English writer Leonard Woolf (later husband of Virginia) had briefly been a government agent in the town, and his novel *A Village in the Jungle* was set around the rude red hills of Hambantota. It was the same heartland in which Rohana Wijeweera had been born and which had nurtured and given rise to the JVP. Mahinda's father and uncle were prominent MPs in the SLFP party. His father, D.A. Rajapaksa, had crossed the floor of parliament to found the SLFP with S.W.R.D. Bandaranaike in 1951. His uncle, G.A. Rajapaksa, elected to the state council in 1936, had been a man of the people, incorruptible and proud of his rural roots. The young Mahinda graduated as a lawyer and had worked at various jobs (including several minor parts in films) before his election to parliament in his father's old seat at the age of just twenty-four. He adopted his uncle's trademark coarse brown *kurrakan* peasant shawl as a mark of his origins. He was regarded as 'a mature politician who has inherent courage and political skill'.[55] In parliament, he rode the political fortunes of his party, until appointed as a minister in the cabinet of President Chandrika Kumaratunga in 2001.

While Mahinda followed the family trade, his younger brother Gotabaya had joined the army shortly after the crushing of the first JVP uprising in 1971. He had commanded a battalion in the 1987 operation that had pegged the Tamil Tigers into the town of Jaffna, and had experienced the bitter humiliation of Indian intervention that had robbed the SLA of its victory. By all accounts, Gotabaya was a courageous soldier whose awards for gallantry were hard won in terrible encounters with the Tigers. He displayed a brutal and single-minded determination that was ultimately frustrated by a poorly equipped, paid and led armed force. In 1992, he had retired from the army as a lieutenant colonel and moved to the United States, where, with equal determination, he retrained as an IT specialist. In 2005, his brother summoned him back to Sri Lanka, where in November that year he was appointed defence secretary. After the war, the *Indian Defence Review* published what it called 'the Rajapaksa Model' of counter-insurgency. The eight principles[56] the writer extracted from a series of interviews with Gotabaya reveal the tenor in which the war had been fought. Above all, according to one unnamed government minister, 'That there [would] be civilian casualties was a given and [Gotabaya] Rajapaksa was ready to take the blame. This gave the [SLA] tremendous confidence. It was the best morale booster the forces could have got.'

Gotabaya cut a swathe through the military, which was seized with a new sense of purpose. He appointed his military college classmate, Sarath Fonseka, to command the army, and ensured that troops on the battlefield were led by men of proven fighting and leadership ability. He had control of the entire security apparatus in the country, including the police force. A massive training and recruitment programme was undertaken, and 75,000 more men and women were recruited. Funding to re-equip the forces was boosted. Unmanned Aerial Vehicles (UAVs), or drones, monitored the conflict zone and acted as forward observers to call in shelling, monitor the movement of people and root out Tiger leaders. China and Pakistan stepped in to fulfil much of the weapons demand, and the Pakistani air force 'extended technical assistance and training'. Indian and US long-range radar and intelligence fed to the Sri Lankan navy led to the interception and sinking of eight warehouse Sea Pigeon ships, one of which was 1,700 nautical miles south of the island, close to Australian waters.[57]

While the rearming took place on both sides, the Tigers increased restrictions on civilians living in Tiger-held areas because of a concern to preserve a manpower pool for the fight ahead. People who applied for passes to travel outside those areas had to leave behind a guarantor, usually a relative, to ensure their return. The Tamil Tigers had had similar restrictions in place as early as 1995, but had relaxed them after the signing of the 2002 ceasefire agreement. By September 2008, they had effectively stopped giving passes, except for medical cases or to the elderly. They also stepped up forced recruitment, at times going beyond the long-standing 'one person per family' policy. Many Tamil families went to great lengths to hide eligible children or have them marry early to avoid conscription. There were very few volunteers in the last year of the war, and many Tamils were pressed into service and sent to the front lines.[58]

In July 2006, the Tigers seized the sluice gate of a reservoir in eastern Sri Lanka, cutting water to 15,000 villagers and thousands of hectares of rice paddy. Although the government would not formally abrogate the ceasefire until January 2008, Eelam War IV – the 'Final War' that the Tigers were promising throughout diaspora fund-raising circles – had begun.[59] By mid 2007, with the help of Karuna's forces, the Tamil-majority eastern littoral was back in government control, and 130,000 Tamil civilians were in government camps. The armed forces turned their attention to the north and to the 15,000 square kilometres of the Vanni still held by the Tamil Tigers. Pushing up and across from the south-west of the island, the army moved with caution, as in the north it pressed down from its positions on the Jaffna peninsula to squeeze the Tamil Tigers at the Elephant Pass. By mid 2008, 20,000 civilians had been displaced by fighting in the Vanni as the army moved eastwards. Its Deep Penetration Units (DPUs) – small groups of highly trained and mobile commandos – were beginning to paralyse the Tiger freedom of movement behind their own front lines. Government artillery drove civilians into the interior while drawing more and more guerrillas into the line of combat.

'It's not that we don't have problems with the Tigers – we do,' said Father James Pathinathan, a Tamil Roman Catholic priest. 'But if you look at the whole picture, people here know they have more to gain from supporting the Tigers.'[60] By December 2008, however, the Tamil Tigers showed no sign of a counter-attack against the SLA. Hundreds of thousands of people in the Vanni were now displaced by the fighting and moving into the interior away from the front lines. The Sri Lankan government appeared to be on the verge of reclaiming its sovereign territory, for the first time in almost thirty years. The Tamil diaspora was aghast at the forces now massed to strike at the heart of this huge concentration of Tamil civilians. Those who had long insisted that there was no military solution to the Tamil Tiger problem watched in disbelief. In Sri Lanka itself, SLA commanders, ordinary foot soldiers, Tiger cadres and the Tamil civilians of the Vanni waited for the master counter-stroke to be unleashed by the Supreme Leader. It never came.

CHAPTER FIVE

Convoy 11

Tucked into the north-eastern corner of the Vanni region, on the eastern shore of Sri Lanka, is a triangle of land about one third the size of London. In January 2009, within this patch of land, the majority of the 330,000 people who had lived under the control of the Tamil Tigers for much of the past fifteen years waited for the final assault they knew must come. As the SLA closed in on all fronts throughout January and the navy blockaded the sea approaches, these people and the few thousand Tamil Tiger fighters with them were driven into an even smaller sliver of coastal land about twice the size of London's Hampstead Heath. The heat was intolerable and there was little food, water or medicine, but even worse was the bloody toll exacted on them by the bombarding siege force of the Sri Lankan army.

The Tamil civilians trapped in the Cage, as it came to be called, also suffered at the hands of the Tamil Tigers, who were increasingly desperate to force an international intervention. Tiger cadres were ordered to turn on those at their mercy. They shot many hundreds who tried to cross to the safety of government lines. Caught in the middle of competing military imperatives, some 10,000 to 40,000 civilians died, and many more were seriously injured. Thousands of raw recruits were killed or injured, as Tiger squads plucked youths from their families and pressed them into the front lines. On 18 May, the fighting ended with the death of the Supreme Leader, Velupillai Prabakharan, and his top commanders. The 290,000 civilians and fighters who had survived waded across the neck-high Nandikadal lagoon, which divided the front lines, and were trucked to internment camps by government forces.[1]

The Sri Lankan civil war had always remained unusually closed to prying eyes. Stories of the 'endless wave' full-frontal assaults by the Tigers and bloody losses on both sides frequently landed on the desks of foreign news editors around the world. These could rarely be independently verified because the government had carefully sealed the island's active battle areas from humanitarian workers and foreign correspondents. Local journalists were largely forbidden to report from enemy territory. Those journalists who attempted the journey by boat from India were arrested or forced back by the Sri Lankan navy. The only regular pictures and reports came from the Tigers' own propaganda units, such as the Internet-based Tamilnet. Foreign newswire journalists in Colombo learned to treat those reports with the same caution they used for the government's version of the flow of battles. SLA casualty lists invariably played down government losses, and inflated those of the Tigers. In January 2009, however, for the first time in three decades, this blanket of obscurity was briefly lifted when a United Nations international officer trapped by fighting witnessed what he believed to be war crimes. The conflict that successive Sri Lankan governments had tried for decades to keep shrouded in a blanket of propaganda and censorship was witnessed, in part at least, by one man who was unusually well qualified to understand the force of war.

On the night of 22 January, inside the Vanni triangle, the SLA relentlessly shelled a convoy that included 132 children, women and men under the protection of two international UN officers. All were huddled in hastily built log and earthen bunkers at the edge of a 'no fire zone', demarcated by the government only days before. Civilian campfires surrounded the bunkers – people who had been drawn to this supposed sanctuary by government broadcasts claiming that it would be safe from artillery fire. As the shelling continued throughout the night, the UN officers frantically transmitted the coordinates of their position to senior Sri Lankan army commanders, as well as descriptions of the carnage being inflicted. They could do little more than listen to the screams of people dying besides their campfires as artillery blasted them. In the morning, when the shelling had subsided, the senior UN security officer on the ground, a former infantry colonel, surveyed a scene he described as 'nothing short of the intentional murder of civilians'. The bodies of entire families with whom he had been idly chatting

the night before lay scattered about him. Blood and shrapnel had spattered UN vehicles, body parts were underfoot, the corpse of a baby
hung from a tree.

The government denied any responsibility. If artillery had struck the
convey, it was certainly the Tigers, firing on their own people and then
blaming the government. UN and International Committee of the Red
Cross (ICRC) personnel caught behind the lines witnessed a small
number of incidents in a body of reported possible and alleged war
crimes.[2] The government's response to the killing of civilians witnessed
by the UN set the scene for other massacres, large and small, that would
be repeated numerous times over the next four months. Until the very
end of the war, the government and its spokespeople parroted a
so-called Zero Civilian Casualty (ZCC) policy in answer to any suggestion by journalists, statesmen, the UN Secretary General or the
president of the United States that its forces were responsible for
civilian deaths.[3] As the death toll accumulated, so too did evidence of
the army's culpability. The international jurist Louise Arbour, speaking
about societies that seek to control information as they commit crimes,
wrote: 'Perpetrators always seek to obfuscate reality, to discredit the
information that points to their culpability and those who provide it,
routinely demanding further proof. They stall or deflect action. Buying
time and spreading misinformation is, after all, in the perpetrator's
own self-interest.'[4]

Most civilians killed during these months probably died from artillery fire. Accountability under international law for conduct in war has
in theory increased since the end of the Cold War. Gone are the days
when mass slaughter or carpet-bombing can be concealed by the
blanket denial of the perpetrators. War is invariably ugly, and never
more so than when images of dead and dying civilians are broadcast
globally. Governments alert to the 'CNN effect', and the damage that
public opinion can cause to their war aims, are careful to control the
information space of a conflict. According to international journalists,
Sri Lanka was notorious as one of the toughest wars on which to
report. Verifiable information was, as one veteran reporter said, 'as rare
as hen's teeth'. This makes the first witnessed event of this war all the
more extraordinary. But in a conflict in which independent witness had
been so carefully restricted, how had it come to pass?

*   *   *

Kilinochchi sits at the obtuse corner of the Vanni triangle. It was the
administrative 'capital' of the Tiger fiefdom, and by January 2009 had
already been bombed, strafed and shelled for months by Sri Lankan
forces as they slogged steadily forward from the south and west. Most
of the heavy concrete buildings that had been constructed in the town
during the hopeful 2002 peace process had been destroyed, since the
best of them had housed the Tiger administration. A huge water tower
that dominated the centre of the town, built with World Bank money,
lay on its side, felled by an air strike.

One side of the triangle runs for some seventy kilometres from
Kilinochchi along the A35 road to the second major Tiger-controlled
hub, the town of Mullaitivu. The Tigers had been steadily building this
eastern coastal town, once a centre of fishing in the region, into both a
formidable stronghold in its own right and one of the main bases from
which the Sea Tigers regularly launched suicidal attacks on Sri Lankan
naval ships. It had manufacturing sheds that turned out light arms,
mortars, ammunition and lethal Claymore mines,[5] as well as shipyards
that built the light fibreglass and aluminium Sea Tiger surface and
submarine attack and suicide craft.

A whole series of small villages and hamlets are strung along the
line of the A35 in a fairly unbroken chain between Kilinochchi and
Mullaitivu. This road passes through the town of Puthukkudiyiruppu
(known as PTK) before it meets the coast, and then runs south a short
distance to Mullaitivu. Seen from satellite pictures or on Google
Earth, the landscape of the Vanni appears to be exactly what it is
when on the ground. The wide, arid plains sit just a few metres above
sea level, the sandy stretches and poor soil covered alternately by
dense low jungle, scrubland and village cultivation, intersected by
small waterways and ancient tanks. Tall palmyra trees, the symbol of
Tamil Nadu in India, and ubiquitous to the region, poke above the
scrubby jungle, their huge leaves spreading like a peacock's tail. Like
most of northern Sri Lanka, the Vanni is hot throughout most of the
year, relief only coming when the sun sets, as well as with the two
annual monsoons.

From Kilinochchi, the shortest side of the triangle runs directly
north for fifteen kilometres along the vital A9 highway that connects
mainland Sri Lanka with the Jaffna peninsula. The upper corner of the
triangle, and the point at which Tiger-controlled territory then ended,

is at the Elephant Pass. There, the Tamil Tigers held a sprawling fortress built around the remains of an eighteenth-century Portuguese
outpost that guarded the isthmus crossing to the peninsula. The A9 is
the key strategic road in Sri Lanka, and had been fought over by the Sri
Lankan army and the Tigers countless times. As the key to the peninsula, the Elephant Pass had been the scene of some of the most terrible
battles between the two forces over three decades of war. In 2000,
Tamil Tiger forces had finally seized the fortress. Now the positions
were about to be reversed. Gotabaya's army was poised to break the
Tiger defences in the northern corner of the triangle.

From Elephant Pass, the third side of the triangle runs across the top
of the Vanni and back down the coastline to Mullaitivu. It passes across
a twenty-kilometre-long coastal spit divided from the mainland by the
Nandikadal lagoon, a body of water about five kilometres wide by
fourteen kilometres long. The lower two thirds of this spit, just a few
hundred metres wide at its narrowest point, was where the Tamil
Tigers would make their final stand with their flank against the sea and
hundreds of thousands of civilians packed in around them. In January
2009, Tamil Tiger forces also faced the Sri Lankan Army's 53rd Division
holding the line at the northern tip of this spit, while to their south the
57th Division pushed steadily towards Mullaitivu.

More than two years of fighting had brought the army to the gates
of these three great strategic points held by the Tigers for the past ten
years, maintaining its position for now at the northern point of the spit
into which it planned to drive those left in the Vanni pocket. On 1
January, the army launched the combined might of its 50,000 front-line
troops. Soldiers pierced the Kilinochchi bund, an enormous wall of
earth thrown up by the Tigers with heavy machinery in an attempt to
stall the army's unrelenting advance, and by nightfall the next day, after
house-to-house fighting, Kilinochchi was under government control.
The Tigers fell back in disarray, with several of their toughest brigades
decimated. A week later, Tiger resistance at Elephant Pass crumbled
under a withering air, land and sea assault, and by 25 January Mullaitivu
was also in government hands.

For most of January, the Tigers held a line 500 metres south of the
A35 road as they fought a rearguard action in the west against government forces emerging from Kilinochchi. In the east, with Mullaitivu
fallen, they retreated to their last remaining fortified bunker redoubt,

near the town of PTK. From January until April this town became the focus of the most intense fighting, as the Tigers mounted a fanatical defence. The town had a large district government hospital, as well as one that had been built and equipped with private money raised from the Tamil diaspora. This second hospital was primarily intended for wounded Tiger fighters, but it treated large numbers of civilians as well. Both of these hospitals drew in vast numbers of casualties as the weeks wore on, and both would be repeatedly bombarded or attacked by air, contrary to the laws of war.

The fall of Kilinochchi was the point of no return for the Tamil Tigers. Here, their ability to wage a conventional war, which had been steadily eroded by the refreshed tactics, arms purchases, superior intelligence and massive propaganda and recruitment drive of the government in the past few years, suddenly evaporated. No longer able to hold territory, and with their heavy weapons and fortified positions open to conquest by superior government forces, the Tigers' best option at this stage would have been to bury their arms. Prabakharan and his top commanders, many of whose faces were unknown, could have attempted escape. Their command structure largely intact, the Tigers might then have blended back into the civilian population, and infiltrated the towns, jungles and cities of Sri Lanka as they prepared for a renewed campaign, in accordance with the classic Maoist stratagem in which a guerrilla force dissipates when faced with defeat by a superior conventional army. Yet Prabakharan, moving between fortified bunkers, refused to contemplate surrender or a fundamental shift in his plans. In place of a strategy in which the decade-old de facto Tamil state would be abandoned, he chose instead to play out the 'CNN effect' of a brutal and bloody siege of Tamil civilians on international public opinion.

The vast majority of those trapped inside the Cage knew that something was now terribly wrong, and began to realise, despite their hopes, that the years of suffering had been in vain. Many families had been on the move for more than two years, driven again and again into the interior by the advance of the government lines. They had seen no evidence of a successful resistance, but where the lines could not hold, the strength of Tiger propaganda and the will of the people did. Despite all evidence to the contrary, many still hoped for a master counter-stroke from the Supreme Leader. Inside the triangle, harried by bombardment, people constantly reassured one another that there would be a counter-attack and another humiliating defeat for the government, or that international leaders or the UN would intervene. Tamil Tiger vigilance ensured that few escaped the battle zone.

Indeed, before January, just a thousand or so people had managed to make their way through minefields and jungle and cross both Tiger and government lines to safety. The choice of how best to survive, and when to attempt an escape, invariably involved tremendous risk. A family had to turn their backs on their community, decide which of their members they could take and avoid the Tiger authorities learning of their plan. If they encountered a Tiger patrol, they faced punishment and the recruitment of their children into the ranks of fighters. If they survived the jungles, minefields, booby traps and shelling, and managed to cross the Tiger lines, they might be shot in error by government forces. Certainly they knew that they were destined for internment camps at the very least, and might never see their homes again. Many thousands of people tried and failed to escape when the Tiger lines were still holding in relatively good order. It was not until much later, when the odds of survival had vastly decreased, that the majority of civilians risked escape again, running for their lives.

Having lived under the Tamil Tigers for so many years, people feared that they might be killed out of hand, or 'disappeared' if they encountered the SLA. Most knew nothing or very little of the Sinhalese-dominated state, other than as an aggressor intent on their destruction. Many of the people who lived in the Vanni had fled from the oppressive occupation of the army in the Jaffna peninsula, where they had seen torture, summary execution and the random killing of civilians in 'security incidents'. This latent fear was exacerbated by the unremitting sledgehammer propaganda of the Tigers, who erected giant billboards throughout the area featuring gory mosaics of President Rajapaksa killing babies, and Sinhalese soldiers bathed in the blood of Tamil children. Just as in Israel, where Israeli children no longer speak Arabic and have never met a Palestinian, conflict had entailed a total separation of nationalities. Many of the young Tamils who filled the Tiger ranks had never met a Sinhalese.

The better choice at the time for Tamil civilians, and the one that seemed to offer the best prospects for immediate survival, was to follow the line of retreat. Most people fled before the barrage laid down by the SLA for the precise purpose of driving people away from the front lines. For the SLA, it made no tactical sense to kill civilians. Instead, the barrage cleared the ground for fighting, and drew forward increasing numbers of Tiger cadres, who attempted to hold the front against government advances. The army then concentrated fire on buildings and fortified positions before moving in with tanks and assault teams to mop up resistance. Even so, given the Tigers' reputation for tenacity and selfless sacrifice, the army up until the fall of Kilinochchi had moved tentatively, reinforcing its lines as it advanced rather than risking overextension and a disastrous counter-attack by the Tigers.

The signal for Tamil villagers to flee was unmistakable. When the shells began to explode in the surrounding fields, they gathered what they could and headed inland by foot, tractor, bullock cart and bus. They moved as civilians always have when at the mercy of warring armies: towards food, shelter, water and immediate safety for themselves and their children. Side by side with their neighbours, they trudged to the houses of friends and relatives in other villages and towns to the east, away from the fighting. For those who had no other option, shelter took the form of plastic sheeting and tents in fields and plantations, by the side of the road or in the grounds of schools and other public buildings. For now, the wholesale retreat of civilians into the interior suited the strategy of the Tamil Tigers.

In September 2008, the government had issued a carefully worded public statement noting that they were 'unable to guarantee the safety' of UN staff inside Tiger-controlled territory. This warning had been reinforced by attack jet assaults on Kilinochchi that damaged UN buildings and sent terrified staffers in flak jackets and helmets running to their fortified bunkers. The battle was drawing closer, and small arms fire could be heard to the south of the town. The UN decided to heed the warning. With its staff under fire and confined to bunkers, its operational capacity had been crippled. Spurred on by the Tiger authorities, frightened civilians tried to prevent the UN from leaving by blockading its offices and vehicles. The UN's presence in theory provided some measure of additional protection for civilians ensnared by war. After some days the Tigers allowed international UN officers to withdraw but refused the same for Tamil support staff and their families. In a portent of what lay in store for the entire population, the Tiger authorities angrily told UN representatives that this relatively privileged class of Vanni Tamils should share the common fate of their people, whatever that might be.

The UN withdrew to a new forward operating base in the town of Vavuniya, behind government lines. There, it tried to predict the effects of the flow of the battle on the huge civilian population it had left behind. The decision to evacuate from Kilinochchi has been roundly criticised. With no senior independent professional staff to formulate assessments from the heart of the crisis, the UN was compelled to rely on what reports it could gather by satellite telephone from NGOs, clergymen and the Tamil personnel trapped in the Vanni with their families. These assessments tried to take account of the movement of the refugees[6] as their number snowballed eastwards, their physical condition and the highly complex calculation of stocks of food, shelter, water and medicine available to a population frightened, harried and on the move. Occasional UN World Food Programme (WFP) convoys into the Vanni supplemented these assessments with first-hand accounts.

The government's expulsion of the UN from the battle space mirrored the absence of the independent media. It suited the army to have no witnesses to the coming assault. Having throttled UN access, the government would spend considerable energy on attacking the UN's best guesses as to what was happening to civilians as the battle space and civilian space gradually converged. Throughout the rest of 2008 and the months up to May 2009, government ministers ranted and raged at even the most cautious UN suggestions that the battle was beginning to have a lethal effect on civilians. How, they asked, could the UN possibly know with certainty what was going on, given the fact that, apart from sporadic accounts from UN international officers on occasional WFP convoys, almost all reports inevitably originated with Tamils stuck inside the battlefield?

These shrill denouncements were cloned in newspapers and on television and radio, and in the words of every minor official with whom the UN dealt in the course of its work. The government even rejected the reports of their own civil servants, such as Tamil government doctors manning the last hospitals inside the Vanni. Most insidious of all, the reports that did emerge, from priests, doctors, humanitarian workers, and teachers, as well as from the Tamil Tiger propaganda machine, were inevitably replicated on pro-Tiger websites such as Tamilnet. The government would then point to the original reports and dismiss them as Tamil propaganda. Many of the competing versions of the truth revolved around two important calculations: how many civilians were left inside the shrinking battle zone, and how many of them were being killed or injured as the final battle took hold.

Between September 2008 and mid January 2009, WFP had managed to assemble and negotiate the passage out of Vavuniya of ten convoys, laden mostly with food. These convoys, usually between forty and sixty vehicles strong, trundled across the fighting lines during brief cease-fires, and dropped food off to refugees at the shifting locations where the UN believed they had congregated. The locations of the convoys were carefully coordinated with the army and the Tigers, with almost constant radio and GPS contact maintained throughout the short jour-neys in order to forestall the mistaken bombing of the vehicles by the air force or artillery units. Inevitably, the Tigers used the convoys to cover their own force movements, secure in the knowledge that the government would have to hold its fire or face the consequences of killing humanitarian personnel.

The government consented to only a limited number of personnel aboard the convoys, despite pleas from UN agencies for time to gather information about the condition and displacement of civilians. The most that could be extracted was an overnight stay after offloading and overseeing the distribution of the cargo, during which time the few tired and fearful UN staff (the drivers were all private contractors) tried to gather information from the multitude of people milling about them in streets and fields illuminated by the lights of vehicles. Where had they come from? How many in the family? Had many been killed? Were they carrying injured? How many times had they been forced to flee? Did they have enough to eat and drink? What did they plan to do next as the fighting drew closer?

By mid January, with Kilinochchi overrun, the Elephant Pass breached and Mullaitivu poised to fall, the battle zone was shrinking rapidly. It was becoming increasingly perilous to run convoys across lines manned by desperate, exhausted Tiger fighters who could sense that they faced annihilation. Constantly refreshed and well-armed government troops were buoyed by the conquest of the supposedly impregnable Tiger fortresses, and sensed that a complete victory was close at hand. The highly detailed weekly briefings given to foreign military attachés in Colombo were upbeat. The government laid on flights over reconquered territory, and showed them videos taken from jet fighters and UAVs of bunkers being destroyed. These men sent reports back to their governments of the high morale of the SLA and the inevitable defeat of the Tigers.

The vast majority of civilians uprooted by fighting were now massed along the length of the A35 road, seeking shelter in villages from where they could reach humanitarian aid. The seizure of the A35, however, was a key military objective for the SLA. The army was pressing up from the south, intent on severing the Tigers' east–west line of defence and communications. Tiger resistance was being concentrated around PTK, in the expectation that Mullaitivu would fall. Importantly, almost the entire pocket was now within range of the heavy guns of the army, which was pressing in from all sides, as well as from naval boats offshore. The front line was just a few kilometres south of PTK, and an overconfident SLA had suffered heavy casualties in a number of attempted breakouts by small bands of Tiger fighters. Army lines, however, were too deep, and they quickly regained the upper hand over the guerrillas. The trick now was to devise a strategy to separate the bulk of civilians from the last-stand Tiger defence.

On 16 January, despite the precarious shrinking of the battle space and the evident ferocity of the fight, WFP assembled its eleventh food convoy. The fifty-three trucks and four light vehicles of Convoy 11 were carrying the basics of WFP's 'food basket', which consisted of rice, beans, sugar, cooking oil, wheat and a small number of tents: all that the Sri Lankan government would allow. After obtaining assurances from both sides that it would not be fired on, the convoy set off on the fifty-kilometre drive along rutted roads to PTK. As it crossed the front lines, tense UN officers on board monitored the continuous shelling with their eyes and ears. They could see the plumes of artillery shells falling in the distance, and hear the thud of strikes as jets attacked Tiger artillery positions and bunkers.

Leading the convoy was a veteran of the Bangladeshi army. Retired colonel Harun Khan had led brigades into battle and managed counter-insurgency operations in his own country. He had fought through mountains, jungles and open plains, and had served in UN peacekeeping contingents abroad. He had already led a majority of the food convoys into the Vanni. From Vavuniya, Harun maintained close contact with Lieutenant General Jagath Jayasuriya, commander of security forces headquarters (SFHQ-Vanni). While reporting to army commander General Sarath Fonseka, Jayasuriya held overall field command of the four Sri Lankan army divisions and the four Special Task Forces in the daily operations now deployed against the Tigers. Five other international UN officers were with Harun on the convoy.

Equally experienced in war was the UN's veteran security chief based in Colombo. Retired colonel Chris Du Toit of the South African Defence Force was a graduate of some of the toughest campaigns fought by his country in the jungles and veldts of southern Africa. He had commanded regular forces, and had also been in the unusual position of training and commanding proxy guerrilla forces in the illicit wars fought by South Africa in Angola. He had engaged guerrillas in terrain similar to that of the Vanni, and had much later been decorated by President Nelson Mandela for his efforts to prevent civil conflict in South Africa. Du Toit kept close links with senior army officers in Colombo, conferring occasionally with the overall commander of the Sri Lankan forces, Air Marshal Donald Perera, as well as with Gotabaya Rajapaksa.

Both UN security men understood the complexities of commanding large bodies of regular troops against guerrilla forces fighting from within civilian areas. They also understood the role of the international laws of war in guiding command decisions in pursuit of the protection of civilian lives. Unlikely candidates for humanitarian missions, the two men would play a key role in saving the lives of the Convoy 11 personnel, as well as in the eventual rescue of many of the Tamil UN staff and their families. In addition, Du Toit would be the driving force behind the gathering of much of the intelligence revealing that large numbers of civilians were being killed.

All over the world, the UN operates across battlefields with shifting lines of confrontation, trying to reach large bodies of civilians who rely almost entirely on humanitarian aid. For UN humanitarian staff, the drive to reach civilians stranded in conflict zones is a powerful motivating force. That morning, a decision had been taken to proceed with the convoy despite the high-risk conditions. A secondary motivation was the precipitous position of the UN Tamil staff and their families caught behind the lines. It was hoped that with the winning of the war so clearly within the army's grasp, the Tiger high command would relent and allow the 132 staff members and their families to leave with the empty convoy on its return journey to Vavuniya.

The journey to PTK took four hours on the major roads and some narrow rutted tracks. Along the way Harun saw small groups of Tiger cadres, both young men and women, grimly making their way forward to the front lines with their weapons slung across their shoulders. The women wore their hair short, a sign that they had surrendered their womanhood to the cause and might shortly give their lives away too. Some waved cheerfully at the trucks as they drove past. The presence of the UN gave a sense of reassurance to the guerrillas that at least food was reaching the families they had been forced to leave behind. Perhaps it was a signal of imminent international intervention. When the convoy reached PTK, the town seemed to be overflowing with people, with fear scrawled across their faces. Crowds of refugees were camped under trees by the side of the road, in schools and in hospitals. Tiger cadres with loudspeakers moved through the streets shouting that people should not leave the town, and that there was nothing to fear. Artillery fire and bursts of heavy-machine-gun fire could be heard to the south.

In fact, the presence of civilians served multiple purposes for the Tiger command. Primarily a civilian population was a buffer against an all-out assault by the army. Too many pictures of dead children transmitted around the world would attract outrage, and might limit the political resolve of the government's coalition and weaken its support from foreign governments. Up until the beginning of 2009, the army's tactic of driving civilians away from the front lines had been relatively successful in limiting the propaganda advantage that the Tigers might gain from images of dead civilians. To the frustration of military planners, however, bombardment continued to push people into the interior, rather than draw them across government lines and out of the path of battle. Few people made the perilous crossing, with the inevitable result that the battle space was gradually merging with civilian space as the Vanni pocket shrank. Unwilling to let people leave, the Tigers gave little thought to separating their forces from the civilians for whom they were ostensibly fighting. The government's chances of forcing a division of civilians from combatants, and thus avoiding the political risks that mass bloodshed might bring, were looking increasingly bleak.

The population also served as a recruiting pool, a practice that would become more voracious and unforgiving as the fighting progressed. Just what proportion of those in the Tiger ranks were forced to serve against their will can never be known, but it is certain that the rate of reluctant recruits increased dramatically as the last battles sucked the remaining experienced Tiger stalwarts into the fight. There were numerous accounts of brutal forced recruitment of children in the final days, including the daughter of one UN staff member, who eventually managed to desert and escape the siege. Most ominously of all, there is good evidence that at least on some occasions the Tamil Tigers fired artillery into their own people. The terrible calculation was that with enough dead Tamils, a toll would eventually be reached that would lead to international outrage and intervention.

That evening, after the exhausted and frightened UN officers from Convoy 11 had tried to make an assessment of the civilian population, they gathered at the small UN compound opposite the main hospital. As the larger and better-equipped of the hospitals in PTK, it was well staffed, and was supported by several ICRC personnel, all of whom were struggling to cope with the casualties, which had suddenly risen to several dozen admissions each day. The sound of fighting to the south had increased in intensity and volume. There were artillery exchanges between the army and the Tigers, who had stationed mobile artillery batteries in and around PTK. Harun could see the barrel flashes from a Tiger heavy artillery piece just 300 metres from the hospital, quite apart from hearing its thumping reports. As the Tiger artillery sent outgoing rounds against the army's advance, and then quickly shifted position, he could count off the seconds until an incoming barrage responded in an effort to destroy the guns.

'These rounds were killing civilians very close to our bunkers. The whole town was packed,' recalled Harun. 'There were people on foot, with their cows, streaming this way and that, unsure where to go because the Tigers had assured people that PTK was safe, and would never fall to the enemy. There was panic, and people were bringing wounded and dead to the hospital, but because the front lines were collapsing, nobody really knew where to go.' At the same time, the Tiger propaganda machine calmly informed people that the lines were secure, and that they should simply obey the directions of Tiger cadres.

Any doubt Harun might have had about the impending defeat of the Tamil Tigers evaporated when he saw the panic and chaos on the streets of PTK. The turning point of the war had arrived, and if there was any hope of extracting the UN staff and their families from the closing pincers of the Sri Lankan army, this had to be done now. There would be no more UN humanitarian convoys as the bitter conflict reached its climax, because there were no more safe places to drop food. After speaking with UN personnel in Colombo by satellite phone, it was decided that Harun would try to force the evacuation of UN staff and their families, against the refusal of the Tiger command. Just as they had done in Kilinochchi in September 2008, they would simply put an evacuation into motion.

The convoy staff spent a sleepless night, while the shelling crept closer to PTK. Rounds were falling just hundreds of metres away, as Tiger mobile artillery units played cat and mouse with SLA artillery locator devices. They would fire off a shell or two before hitching their howitzer and moving quickly to a fresh location. Within minutes the spot they had just vacated would be pummelled by incoming fire, often in the form of multi-barrel rocket strikes, whose forty rockets would tear through a large swathe of land, cutting down civilians. The following morning Harun received word that the increasingly heavy fighting had blocked the major exit road from the Vanni, and that the government had cancelled their permission to return. As he had feared, events on the battlefield had overtaken Convoy 11.

That evening, Harun left the UN bunkers, crossed the dirt road and walked into the main hospital. He moved slowly through the wards, where the injured were beginning to overflow into the corridors. Old people lay moaning with their wounded grandchildren, ignoring their own injuries as they tried to comfort the young. Fresh-faced young men, women, and children without limbs stared at the ceiling, wide-eyed and shocked. One young man wept at the loss of both his arms, and begged people to explain what would become of him. ICRC staff moved among the wounded trying to gauge injuries. In separate wards, away from civilians, doctors assigned to Tamil Tiger cadres worked to care for the gruesome wounds of war.

'I went very slowly through the wards, trying to absorb it all,' said Harun. 'Everything had changed in such a short time. The smell of death and injury was all about. And there were the children, whose young lives had been shattered . . . and those who were dying.' He spoke with the government district medical officer, Dr Satyamoorthy, whose clothes were stained with blood from non-stop surgery. The voice of this courageous doctor would later become known across the world as he resorted to making appeals by satellite telephone to the international media, begging for the drugs that would never come, and for further evacuations for the wounded and young. He would be one of the last doctors the Tigers allowed to leave the siege, lucky to escape with his life.

For three days, UN staff and their families waited for the signal to attempt to evacuate. 'We were now firmly within the combat zone,' says Harun. 'We realised we were in serious danger. People were running everywhere, terrified, uncertain where to go to escape the shelling. The Tamil Tigers were placing their guns dangerously close to our location, and were quite intentionally in my view drawing fire towards the hospital. Civilians were being killed.' The group set about digging trenches and building bunkers using sandbags, forty-four-gallon drums, coconut trees and whatever other materials they could find. They used their vehicles to form a square around the bunkers for additional cover and tried to sleep through the din of artillery fire, which struck dangerously close, with shrapnel piercing their vehicles.

On 20 January, after PTK had been under bombardment for three days, word came through from the government that the UN convoy could move. Because the battle had now enveloped the road on which they had entered the battle space, they were to go west along the A35, parallel to the advancing Sri Lankan army line pushing up towards the road from the south. In Colombo, Harun's superior Chris Du Toit hoped that somehow they would be able to flag their presence in the battle zone as the army advanced eastwards from Kilinochchi.

The long convoy rolled out from the compound, but was stopped just 500 metres beyond their bunkers by Tiger cadres manning a road-block and ordered to turn back. After days of bombardment, recriminations broke the brittle discipline of the international staff. A heated argument began over what to do, with some wanting to pass through the roadblock, leaving the Tamil UN staff and their families behind. It was now clear that the Tigers might never grant permission for the staff and their families to leave.

The UN had been trying to make contact with the Tamil Tiger leadership from Colombo and from UN headquarters in New York. Pleas from the Norwegian government, long an intermediary between the Sri Lankan government and the Tigers, were met with silence. Harun decided that he would remain to try to win the consent of the Tiger leadership on the ground. The convoy was divided in two, with one jeep and seven trucks left for the UN families. While the rest of the convoy rolled out and across the lines of conflict, Harun and a UN engineer who had volunteered to remain behind stayed to share the fate of those in their care.

That morning, the Sri Lankan government had demarcated a No Fire Zone (NFZ) extending six kilometres north and five kilometres along the A35 road.[7] The coordinates of the zone were widely broadcast, and soon the paths and fields were crowded with people in search of shelter from the fighting and shelling. Streams of refugees on foot, or struggling with bicycles piled two metres high with their belongings, or trundling along on small tractors, moved in ribbons across the landscape. PTK began to empty as people trudged westwards, in the direction of the NFZ, and toward SLA troops advancing from the fallen town of Kilinochchi.

A furious battle was enveloping PTK, and while a Tamil Tiger defeat was almost certain, it was impossible to estimate how long it would take, or the firepower that government forces would bring to bear on the town. After two more days under bombardment, Harun decided that the best hope lay in a dash westwards along the A35 to the newly declared NFZ, away from the increasingly fraught town. Once there, they could try to bunker down and hope that the approaching front line would pass over the zone. Fighting was raging along the length of the A35 as the remaining vehicles of Convoy 11, packed with families, drove towards the NFZ. Despite the fighting, people continued to head towards what government broadcasts had assured them was sanctuary.

The convoy stopped at the village of Suthanthirapuram on the A35. 'There was an open field about one kilometre square, and it was humming with thousands and thousands of people,' said Harun. 'Some food distribution was going on, and hundreds of people had lined up. I saw that the government messages over the radio had been successful in getting people to the No Fire Zone.' For the first time in almost a week, Harun felt a decreasing level of anxiety. 'The firing was still very close, but there were so many people packed into the NFZ that it felt protected just because of its clearly civilian nature.' But the shelling just south of the road was increasing in intensity as it hammered the front line being held by the Tamil Tigers just 800 metres away. Harun recognised the danger that the lines might break and fall back in disorder, drawing the battle into the NFZ. With the only other choice being to return to PTK, the fatigued convoyers settled down to wait.

Why had the military chosen to place a sanctuary for civilians so close to the fighting? The decision to unilaterally declare an NFZ in that particular location, hard up against an unpredictable and eroding front line, had little to do with protecting civilian lives, and everything to do with their removal as an obstacle to unrestrained firepower. The laws of war allow for the declaration of safe zones in order to protect civilian lives. But without an agreement between the opposing armies that preserves the tactical aims of both, the unilateral declaration of a safe zone is a relatively pointless act. It has more do with conferring a propaganda advantage on one side while denying it to the other.

Moreover, for the government it had a significant tactical benefit, in so far as it might remove the principal obstacle stalling a full assault on the dwindling Tiger forces, and drain the human pool from which the Tigers drew new recruits to buttress their lines. Finally, it placed the onus for protecting civilians back on the Tigers, who from now on would be forced to show their hand more clearly as they manipulated the population for their own purposes. If all went well, the army would simply overrun the NFZ, or at least breach a hole on one side, from where civilians could escape out of the combat zone.

Sri Lankan army commanders and senior political leaders declared at this time their intention to 'prick' the Vanni pocket and 'drain' it of its civilians. The conflation of the notion of protecting civilian lives with that of achieving a tactical advantage was a contradiction that the Sri Lankan forces were unable to resolve until almost the final day of the conflict, despite several such 'prickings' and the escape of tens of thousands of people. Their attempts to draw people out were both reckless and costly in terms of human life, and say more about the value placed by the military and political leadership on the lives of a population seen to be 'Tiger' from skin to bone.[8]

Under international law, which has increasingly come to guide battlefield decisions, a military action must be costed and evaluated in terms of civilian life and property, against the advantage expected from a particular course. The original SLA battle plan involved driving the civilian population towards the spit of land on the coast near the Nandikadal lagoon. But with pressure beginning to mount on the government, army commander General Sarath Fonseka overruled the plan, and instead ordered his ground commander, General Jagath Jayasuriya, to locate the NFZ, close to the A35 road, which was about to be stormed by the army. It was a reckless and dangerous strategy that had everything to do with political expediency and little to do with the duty of care owed by the government to civilians. It also said much about how the Sri Lankan leadership valued the lives of the 'Tiger' civilian population.[9]

Soldiers are schooled in the 'safety templates' of the armaments upon which they rely to drive the enemy back in order to create the space for their own troops to advance. Heavy artillery might be used to soften and break a defensive line, and each shell will have a large template, while progressively smaller ordnance is used to cover the advance of attacking troops, with safety templates that in theory reduce the chances of one's own troops being killed by covering fire. The choice of which ordnance to employ at varying points in the battle, and how it would be used, was now critical. The SLA and the Tiger forces were deployed so closely that it would be only by laying down fire precisely on the Tiger lines or shortly behind them that artillery would be able to successfully break the defences.

Chris Du Toit and Harun Khan both understood that the Tiger lines were so close to the A35 that the presence of the UN and civilians in the adjacent NFZ would be perilous if the SLA continued to push forward. Any thrust would necessarily involve the use of artillery. They hoped that instead, at the point of contact between the battle front and the NFZ, the Sri Lankan army would try to outflank and force the Tigers to fall back on a line beyond the NFZ and Convoy 11, leaving the concentration of civilians to be safely enveloped by the advance of the SLA front line. If that was the SLA's strategy, it was one that relied in part at least on the Tigers relinquishing control of civilians. The Tigers, however, had a history of doing precisely the opposite, as they had shown during their 1995 withdrawal from the Jaffna peninsula, when they took 400,000 Jaffna inhabitants with them. The safety of civilians always came a distant second to their political and military objectives.

The village of Suthanthirapuram, in which Convoy 11 had stopped, at the southern edge of the NFZ, was as unremarkable as all the other small villages that lay along the A35. Concrete bungalows squatted under a fringe of trees, looking over paddy fields and groves of coconuts that provided some shade. A small Hindu temple was adorned with troupes of concrete gods dancing across its façade. Thin chickens pecked at thinner pickings along the culverts and small gully erosions. The once quiet village heaved with people and with vehicles clogging the verges of the road. Refugees also clustered around hastily erected shelters in the fields, and gathered wood for their cooking fires. Drones hummed in the sky above, surveying the thousands of civilians who had been drawn to the NFZ by assurances of safety.

The weather was brutally hot. Harun hired teams of men to help him construct another set of bunkers by digging a few feet below the surface of the ground, filling forty-four-gallon drums with soil, building earthen ramparts up against the circle of drums and laying a roof of heavy coconut trunks across the top. The inside was lined with plastic against seepage from the water table just a foot below, and a couple of slanted peepholes were opened high on each side to provide a view of the surrounding field. Several of the convoy trucks were driven close to provide additional cover. It was not shell proof, and would not withstand a direct hit, but it was good against shrapnel and better protection than the thousands of milling refugees had. Harun repeated his GPS coordinates to Du Toit, who informed the Joint Operations HQ in Colombo, as well as General Jayasuriya, the battlefield commander, in Vavuniya.

An old man in his late seventies sidled up and shyly introduced himself in English. He wore thick glasses shielding bright eyes, and a broad if slightly gap-toothed smile. He was a retired bank manager, forced to flee the fighting four times in the past year, and now on the move with his family once more. Harun pulled up a chair for him, and after a while the old man called across his wife and daughter and his four grandchildren. The young family had constructed a flimsy shelter just six metres from Harun's bunkers, beneath some trees that lined the road, while the old couple's shelter was nearby. They chatted for more than an hour about the war, about the old man's once orderly existence and his hopes for a better life for his grandchildren no matter what the outcome of the conflict.

In the early afternoon, army artillery fired along the A35, apparently responding to outgoing fire from the Tamil Tigers. Although many people were killed and wounded, the firing soon subsided. By nightfall, the field glowed with a thousand tiny fires as families prepared their evening meals. It was a scene of domestic routine under the stars, with an odd backdrop of shell-fire flashes to the south and the thud of incoming shells less than a kilometre away. By midnight the bunkers had finally been completed, and Harun mustered the families under his care into the four cramped shelters, which were only just large enough to hold them all. He smiled and waved at the old man's pretty seventeen-year-old granddaughter, lying on a mat beneath a tree, and passed into the bunker in the hope of sleeping, despite the constant roar of the battle outside.

Less than an hour later, Harun woke with a start to the first of the screams. Shells and rockets crashed around the bunker and in the surrounding field. He reached for his helmet and flak jacket. The bunker trembled as the noise of warfare sounded through the earth and the high-pitched whine of incoming shells was joined by the screams of the dying outside. Shell after shell slammed into the field packed with families. People were calling out, but almost nothing else could be heard above the din of explosions, the spitting of hot metal fragments and the thud of soil and rocks raining on to the roof and the trucks outside. Inside the cramped bunker, there was little room for panic amongst people who had encountered shellfire and death so often in the past months. Instead there was the unmistakable smell of human fear, the sound of laboured breathing and the whimpers of children.

The artillery fire was coming from government lines, even though the UN's precise coordinates had been transmitted to both the army and the Tigers. Sure that for some reason the army had neglected to communicate the convoy's position to their front-line artillery units, Harun repeatedly called Colombo on his satellite phone. Du Toit contacted the Ministry of Defence Joint Operations Headquarters in a frantic effort to get them to halt their fire. The phone calls and SMS text messages went on through the night, backwards and forwards, as the shells continued to fall.

'It went on for hours, hundreds of shells, I couldn't count,' said Harun. 'It was not directed fire, but the kind of indiscriminate covering barrage that is used to shield an advance. But it was non-stop, and it was striking the field full of people who had just eaten their dinners and gone to sleep.'[10] Looking through the ventilation peepholes, he could see the shells exploding where thousands of refugees were camped. He saw one shell tear apart a small hut housing humanitarian workers who had been distributing food and water that afternoon.

About two hours after the bombardment began, a shell exploded so close that Harun thought their shelter had taken a direct hit. His head reeled and he was unable to hear for a few seconds. Something heavy had struck the entrance of the bunker. He heard moaning and cries for help, and peered outside through the ventilation peephole. 'It was a 130mm shell impact, just where the old man's family had been. The bodies were lying there, quiet and limp across each other. Embers from the scattered fire glowed. Two or three people were calling for help, but the shelling was so intense that we couldn't leave. The moaning gradually stopped as they bled to death. There was nothing we could do,' he recalled. 'It was the eerie calm after each explosion and scream. It explained everything.'

Shortly before dawn, the shelling subsided enough for Harun to peer out through the bunker entrance. He raised the hessian flap. The half torso of the seventeen-year-old girl lay across the threshold. He took a plastic mat and covered her. The old man was wandering about dazed. He did not weep. 'Here is the body of my granddaughter,' he said to Harun. 'And here is the body of my daughter. And that is the body of my granddaughter too.' The gaunt old man wandered off into the gloom and smoke.

Some seven hours after it began, the shelling stopped, and Harun emerged from the bunker. The sound of shelling and gunfire to the south continued to provide a roar that was at odds with the thin beauty of the early-morning sunlight. A film of smoke and haze covered the field, as though the whole earth had been burning and smouldering throughout the night. All around him he could see people bloodied and shocked, their clothes torn, rough bandages ripped from dresses and shirts covering a myriad of wounds. People were dragging themselves listlessly away, making for those vehicles that had not been hit, moving in a state of confusion and despair because they did not know where to go that was safe. Others dug holes in which to bury their dead, and the sound of grief seemed to fill Harun's ears.

He took pictures of the old man's family first. 'Somehow, looking at them through a lens made it more bearable. I was back to work. I had a job to do, to record it, to make sure that people knew, and that they would not deny that this had happened.' The body of the pretty eldest girl first, the plastic mat pulled away to give a clear shot. Then her mother, contorted and torn against a tree about five metres from her second daughter, and then the youngest of the granddaughters, a girl of around thirteen, on the verge of her adult life. He photographed the impact crater and the 'splash marks' of the shell that had killed them, showing distinctly that it had travelled from the direction of the government lines. A shattered tree with the corpse of an infant suspended like a broken branch, a dead man with his children lying around a fire, a mother and a young boy in a slumbering embrace, hardly roused by the blast that had destroyed their organs. He photographed a UN jeep sprinkled with a confetti of lethal shrapnel, mixed with the blood and body parts of the neighbours with whom he had briefly shared the field, the bunkers scored by hot fragmentation and the scattered steel daggers from burst artillery rounds, some with their telltale production codes, that added up to the scene of the murder of so many.

That Sunday, the New York Times reported a memo sent to UN headquarters from Colombo, describing the experience of its staff in the government's No Fire Zone: 'Our team on the ground was certain the shelling came from the Sri Lankan military, but apparently in response to a Tiger shell. All around them was the carnage from casualties from people who may have thought they were safer being near the UN. Sadly, they were wrong that night.' Harun was convinced that the fire came 'overwhelmingly from government forces'. Given the repeated messages to the armed forces about the UN's location and the presence of large numbers of civilians, he believed that the night's bombardment was nothing short of 'the intentional massacre of civilians'.

The shelling had subsided, but still there was no indication that the convoy could cross the front lines. Fighting was too intense, and no word to move had come from Colombo. Harun set about strengthening the shelters and building an additional bunker. A third of the workers he had employed the previous day were dead, but he found others who had survived and needed the money. Displacement is a quick path to poverty, so a little income was a blessing in the midst of a life on the move. Nobody had food, and there was little water. By mid-morning, the shelling had resumed and people worked hard to finish the new bunker. Shells were striking the field around them intermittently, and with each whistle everybody dived to the ground, parents shielding their children. Clods of earth spattered them, and fragments of hot metal sliced through the air.

By nightfall, no word had come of a possible pause in fighting to allow them to escape the bitterly named and contested No Fire Zone. It began to rain heavily. 'That night we felt depressed, as though we would not survive,' said Harun. 'Outside all we could hear was shelling and moaning, explosions followed by screaming and crying, and then a silence that described everything. It was terrible, and we were the fortunate ones, sheltered to some degree by our own efforts, with the mass of people left outside exposed, their survival or death a matter of chance.' In the morning the shelling subsided again, but it was still raining, compounding the misery of the people in the fields.

By the next morning, the convoy had spent two days under bombardment. Just after dawn, a call came through from Du Toit that a two-hour pause in the fighting had been negotiated with the army, and that they should prepare to leave. At 11.30 a.m., another call gave them the signal to move. Despite the fact that the shelling continued, Harun organised the group, and on a signal they made a dash for the trucks through the muddy field. Two of the trucks could not be moved, so the group crowded into the five remaining vehicles and they set off on the road back to PTK.

'We drove along a road that looked like it was a set of a war film,' said Harun. 'There were no moving vehicles except a couple with tense Tiger cadres going in the opposite direction towards Suthanthirapuram to shore up the front line. Trees were snapped in half, and some were still burning. There were burning vehicles all along the road, and bodies everywhere, torn open, lying together with farm animals.'

Later that day, army commander General Sarath Fonseka announced that the last bastion of the Tamil Tigers, the town of Mullaitivu, had fallen. On state-run television the general stated with cold confidence that the fighting was '95 per cent over'. Prabakharan and his top commanders seemed to be trapped, with no way to escape. The Tigers had failed to mount a convincing counter-attack for more than two years. Three of their last four reinforced fortresses – Kilinochchi, Elephant Pass and Mullaitivu – had fallen within three weeks of each other. With the battle so clearly won and the Tigers on the run, how would the SLA be directed to manage the remaining 5 per cent of the war? PTK was in the path of the advancing Sri Lankan army, and held the Tigers' final fortified positions, as well as the last of the Vanni hospitals. For the moment, though, it also seemed to hold the best chances of survival for those on board Convoy 11.

CHAPTER SIX

Inside the Cage

Shortly after sunrise on 14 August 2006, Sri Lankan air force Kfir jets bombed a cluster of buildings in a secluded copse of trees near the village of Vallipunam, close to Kilinochchi. The Sri Lankan army, reinvigorated under the leadership of Gotabaya Rajapaksa, had just begun a renewed thrust to regain territory long held by the Tigers, and Eelam War IV was heating up. According to the Tigers, the buildings housed an orphanage, at which around 400 schoolgirls were attending a first aid course. About sixty school-aged girls and four adults were killed by the air strike. One girl, known as Juliet, who was seventeen years old at the time, later described the attack:

> It was 7 a.m., we were by the well, when we saw the Kfir jets far away . . .
> As the bombs fell the girls ran in all directions, and took cover by lying
> on the ground face down, hoping the bombers will go away . . . with
> each round more students were wounded and more killed. In between
> air strikes the girls . . . were running to other positions to take better
> cover. During lull periods they would run out and aid the wounded.
> Many died on the spot, many were wounded. I still have memories of
> the jets and the desperate calls of the girls for help.[1]

The next day, the senior UNICEF official based in Sri Lanka drove through army and Tiger lines to reach the devastated site. JoAnna van Gerpen, a seasoned UNICEF field operative who had spent years in Sudan and Liberia, knew the complex as an orphanage for girls called Senchcholai, something the government would hotly dispute in the weeks ahead. Now she surveyed the smouldering buildings and walls pockmarked with shrapnel. The Tamil Tigers, always quick to capitalise on an outrage for propaganda, had left the site as undisturbed as possible. Only the wounded and the bodies of their dead fellow students had been removed. Severed limbs lay on the ground, amidst a dozen or so bomb craters. Shredded foliage from torn trees was mixed with the bloodied remnants of clothes and school bags. Van Gerpen was taken to local hospitals, where she counted roughly one hundred injured girls from eighteen different local schools. With a caution typical of a foreign official in Sri Lanka, she told the Agence France-Presse news agency later that day: 'We don't have any evidence that they are LTTE cadres.' On the contrary, evidence abounded that they were simply schoolgirls.

Van Gerpen's view of events matched that of the Nordic Sri Lanka Monitoring Mission (SLMM), which had been first on the site within hours of the bombing. Although the ceasefire between the Tigers and the government was still officially intact, the SLMM was on the ground in Sri Lanka, verifying the growing number of ceasefire breaches. They had counted the bodies of nineteen young women aged between seventeen and twenty. There was no evidence that the site had been used for military purposes. From its headquarters in New York, UNICEF issued a statement that condemned the mass killing. The girls, it said, were 'the innocent victims of violence'.

The government made little attempt to deny the air strike or the fact that so many girls had been killed or wounded. The defence ministry issued an initial statement: 'The Sri Lankan Air Force bombed pre-identified LTTE gun positions and LTTE camps in the Mullaitivu area this morning, Monday August 14 . . . Air Force personnel confirmed that the bombings were precise and well targeted.'[2] The government reacted with outrage to the findings of the SLMM and UNICEF. According to a defence spokesman, Keheliya Rambukwella, their view was that 'Even if it is a 17-year-old child in terms of age, they are soldiers who are prepared to kill whoever comes in front of them. Therefore the age or the gender is not what is important.' And yet the definition of who constitutes an identifiable combatant under international law, and at what point they can be attacked, is fundamental in the fighting of modern, scrutinised warfare.[3]

To the government, the victims of Senchcholai were legitimate military targets being 'trained in an LTTE training camp'. They did not deny that they were schoolgirls, drawn from the surrounding district, or dispute that they had spent most of their young lives studying, and were in essence students. The fact that they had been briefly corralled by the Tamil Tigers, and forced to attend a 'workshop' was sufficient to convert them from children into military adversaries. Was it a workshop on first aid? Or were they learning to build bunkers, or repair generators, or clean weapons? To the government, once removed for a few hours from school and placed in training, the girls were Tiger cadres who would eventually confront the army, and thus fit objects for destruction.

The government, the press and a good deal of the Sri Lankan public regarded the killing of the schoolgirls at Senchcholai as a proportionate, discriminate strike. The press was outraged – not at the killings, but at the UNICEF and SLMM statements. The dilemma of the children – that they were forcibly militarised by one party, and then legitimised as a fair target by the other – and the scale of the killing seemed irrelevant. In a long and bloody civil war, there had been many large-scale killings. But Senchcholai is indicative of an attitude that pervaded the military response to the problem of a civilian population that by the government's own admission was trapped in the Vanni and perhaps, by now, largely held against its will.[4]

As Harun drove towards PTK hospital with what remained of Convoy 11 following behind him, he pondered what he had seen the night before. To him, a professional soldier, the intensity of the artillery attack that had killed so many people appeared to be intentional, nothing short of murder. Despite the SLA being aware of the position of the UN bunkers and senior officers knowing from the frantic calls to army HQ that their shells were killing civilians, the bombardment had continued. Did the government regard all Tamil civilians as potential targets? Did it matter to them how many people were killed as they achieved their military objectives? Had the entire Tamil civilian population trapped between the two forces become a legitimate potential target?

By early afternoon of 25 August, Harun and his convoy had reached PTK hospital. ICRC staff worked side by side with government doctors to tend to the hundreds of wounded now crowding the corridors. From the few dozen admissions of several days before, the number of bloodied and bedraggled people making their way across the battle zone to get help for their wounds or those of their children or relatives was now well over a hundred each day. It was a classic battlefield casualty station, with harried and exhausted staff making quick decisions over who should be treated and who had to be left to die.

The Tigers and government forces had agreed to respect the sanctity of the hospital. The Tigers had assured the ICRC that they would not deploy their forces within a one-kilometre radius, while the government undertook not to fire into that circumference. The NFZ having proven a killing field, the hospital seemed to offer the best sanctuary along the approaching front line. The exhausted passengers on Convoy 11 camped in the garden of a house directly across the road. Harun instructed his charges, who set about digging trenches and bunkers in the garden just as they had done inside the NFZ. They took GPS coordinates of the compound, and transmitted them to Du Toit in Colombo, who in turn passed them to the SLA's central command in both Colombo and Vavuniya. Both sides knew the precise locations of the UN and ICRC personnel, and that PTK hospital was packed with wounded. The hospital, a protected humanitarian space under international law, ought to have been a guarantee of safety.

That evening, to the background noise of artillery pounding to the south of the town, the members of the Convoy gathered firewood, found water, built a fire and prepared a simple meal from the basic UN rations of rice, beans and oil, plus the same few vegetables that most other Vanni civilians were eating that night. 'My legs were swollen and I was suffering from extreme fatigue,' said Harun. 'The lack of water had affected my kidneys, and I had shooting pains in my stomach, as though the toxins were coursing through my blood. We had been under continuous fire for days, and as we settled down to sleep in the house that night I felt grateful that we had escaped, and yet guilty that we were unable to help so many who had been left behind.'

The effects of extreme hunger, thirst, fatigue, exposure and fear on large bodies of civilians forced to flee fighting are difficult to envisage. Overwhelming numbers of civilians now die in the course of modern war through cumulative fatigue. The vast majority of the millions of civilians who are thought to have died in the Congo over the past decade were killed not by gunfire but from the simple act of fleeing their homes. Once driven out, a family is continuously on the move along with thousands of others, competing for the scant food, water and shelter available en route. Unlike armies, they cannot commandeer by force of arms. Food must be available for purchase, they must have money and there must be water. The effects are particularly acute on children, who quickly waste away and die if they fall sick when supplies are scarce. Many of the families that Convoy 11 had encountered had been on the move for months or years, displaced more than two dozen times.

As Harun looked around at the faces of those in his charge, he saw their expressions of shock and exhaustion and pondered how much worse it might have been had they not constructed their sturdy shelters in that field. While Harun had been able to buy the materials he needed to construct bunkers that would withstand shellfire, there had been no such choice for the old man whose daughters and grandchildren had perished by their campfire.

Secure in the knowledge that the ICRC had negotiated sanctuary for the hospital, the convoy settled down for the night. Soon afterwards, a doctor intruded on the tired travellers. A telephone call from the SLA had warned him to evacuate the hospital, in anticipation of a massive assault in the next few days. Harun had seen the Tiger gun positions that had violated the agreed no-war zone around the hospital. Tiger vehicles were transporting ammunition and fighters towards the front, but other vehicles were roaming about the town. The SLA had detected the presence of the senior Tiger leadership in PTK, possibly close to the hospital. Completely exposed by the fall of their last three key strongholds, the Tigers appeared to have ignored the brokered agreement meant to safeguard the wounded and medical staff. The presence of United Nations and ICRC international personnel was just additional insurance for the protection of their senior command – possibly including Prabakharan – against attacks by the air force and shelling from the army. A full assault by the SLA was brewing. Regardless of the hundreds of seriously wounded at the hospital and the streams of casualties still coming, the sanctity of the hospital had in effect evaporated.

That night, despite the shelling to the south and the news of an impending attack, Harun slept soundly on a plastic mat laid across the bare concrete floor of the house. He woke to another shimmering clear morning. He could hear the roar of trucks coming and going in the streets below, a melee of Tamil Tiger vehicles bound for the front lines, and trucks, wagons and tractors pulling up to the hospital with more wounded. He washed and shaved, then, feeling refreshed, crossed the road to meet with the international ICRC workers to work out a plan to evacuate the wounded and, he hoped, the local UN staff and their families under his care. They would try to cross the front lines with the wounded should the Tiger command allow it. If not, their alternative was to retreat further back inside the Vanni triangle, away from the fighting but into a shrinking battle space becoming more dangerous by the day.

As he walked through the front door of the hospital, a chorus of cries and groans from the wounded met him. 'There were hundreds of them from the previous night of shelling. While I had slept so well, the artillery assault on civilians appeared not to have stopped at all. It was a scene of horror. Trucks were bringing in people every few minutes. The medical staff was exhausted, the skin of the international ICRC workers was grey with fatigue and shock. I moved slowly through the wards for hours, photographing all the women and children who were screaming in pain, or just crying with shock.' In PTK hospital in the last days of January, a pattern was set for a small, dedicated group of Tamil government doctors. For the next four months they would fight to keep thousands of people alive without the necessary medical equipment and drugs. Instead, aspirin, alcohol and strips of cloth torn from saris would serve as the pharmacy. Thousands of children had their wounds sutured or their shattered limbs set with only the comfort of their parents' presence as an antidote to the pain. Many hundreds of people endured amputations without anaesthetic. According to one account, the international ICRC workers plugged their ears with their fingers to avoid hearing the screams as they walked the wards during these last days of January.

Patients who would ordinarily have been shifted by the ICRC from Tiger-controlled territory to well-equipped government hospitals were dying from lack of care. There was a shortage of basic medical supplies, such as surgical bandages, plaster and anaesthetics. For more than a year, the government had obstructed deliveries of basic drugs such as ketamine, used as both a general anaesthetic and a painkiller for emergency surgery. It was ideal battlefield medicine, useful to the Tigers, but now vital for civilians caught up in the fighting, and especially for children with broken bones, burns and shrapnel wounds. Whilst this lack might have been offset just a month before with negotiated ICRC evacuations of wounded civilians to properly equipped hospitals in government territory, the Vanni was now a sealed battleground. With the lines of confrontation locked tightly against each other, civilians could expect the same denial of aid as fighters.

'They were everywhere,' says Harun. 'All injured people, covering every space, from outside the hospital, all through the hospital. Some children were being artificially resuscitated, a twelve-year-old boy died before my eyes. There were screams from the women and children. One can't fathom the extent of the pain they were going through. Chests, abdomens, arms blown off, half a chin blown off. Mothers with injured children just did not know what to do. There was nothing the doctors could do. They hoped that the hospitals would be spared.' Harun's photographs of the dead and wounded inside PTK hospital show dozens of children, bloodied bandages around their hands or feet, their faces sprinkled with shrapnel marks, a tense parent or aunt clutching them close, fanning the flies away from their wounds with a piece of cloth or paper. One photograph shows a schoolgirl with her school bag next to her, looking glumly at her wounded leg, the lower half torn away by artillery fire. Another is of a girl lying on a bed, shielding her face from a ray of sunlight coming through the broken roof. Yet another shows a bandaged baby being brought inside from a truck.

Photos like these appeared on Tamilnet at the time, and provoked the kind of hysterical denial from the government that such incidents had always inspired in this war of words, images and horrors. The Tamil doctors are there too, pictured taking careful records of the patients, names, ages, wounds, details that would be faithfully passed on to the Ministry of Health in Colombo, which to this day holds the archived records of the thousands of people who were killed or wounded in the final months of the civil war. And yet these photographs were not taken by Tamil propagandists, but by UN international staff pursuing the careful documentation of the war's impact on civilians.

On Wednesday, 28 January, the *New York Times* reported that in a sealed battle space without journalists, the experience of the UN and ICRC under fire had provided a rare glimpse into the fate of civilians being squeezed into an ever shrinking pocket of land. Unusually for an organisation that relies on discretion and moral force, the ICRC issued a statement from its Geneva headquarters, confirming that 'hundreds of people had been killed' in just a few days of shelling, and urging both sides to respect humanitarian law. An artillery attack had struck a small ICRC clinic in the village of Udayarkaddu, close to where Convoy 11 had come under fire in the NFZ. Just as the UN had provided the army with coordinates of their position, so too had the ICRC. Nevertheless, the bombardment had killed patients, and had come close to hitting the medical crew. The Sri Lankan government, through its human rights ministry, accused the ICRC of 'either willful ignorance or naïveté' for suggesting that army shells might have killed civilians.[5]

Spotlit by renewed international scrutiny, a brief window opened. The next day, 29 January, the ICRC and the UN were able to negotiate the evacuation of hundreds of seriously wounded across the front lines. The Tamil Tigers had refused the request for days. Harun now realised that the Tigers would never allow the Tamil UN staff or their families to leave. He told the staff that he had been ordered to return to government territory along with the convoy of wounded and dying. They took the news with a stunned silence; they had learned to expect the worst. A long line of trucks and jeeps pulled out from PTK hospital, and amidst a brief pause in the shelling, Harun too crossed the front lines, safely reaching Vavuniya several hours later. It was the last land evacuation of civilians from the siege zone. The only hope now for the wounded would be a place on one of the ICRC sea evacuations that had begun far to the north.

Throughout that night and into the next day, the shelling came closer to the hospital, still manned by ICRC medics and the Tamil doctors, who continued to treat a stream of wounded. On 1 February, after announcing that the Tigers had set up a forward defensive line in PTK, government shells slammed into the hospital in earnest, striking a packed women's ward and hitting a church. A text message sent by one of the UN's Tamil staff minutes later read: 'Women and kids wards shelled. God, no words. Still counting the dead bodies.' For the next four days, as a battle raged close to the town, the government repeatedly shelled the hospital, killing patients and staff.

The government's efforts to deny that the armed forces had been responsible for killing people inside the hospital were hopelessly muddled. Defence secretary Gotabaya Rajapaksa, speaking on the news networks, happily took credit for the attacks, explaining that a warning had been issued. In contradiction, and a familiar refrain, the military spokesman, Brigadier V.U.B. Nanayakkara, asserted that either international relief staff and government doctors had been forced by the Tigers to disseminate false information, or the Tigers themselves had been responsible for the shelling: 'How does the person on the receiving end [of the bombardment] say it is from the government side? They all are trying to tarnish the image of the military and stop this offensive,' he told Associated Press's Ravi Nessman. The defence secretary would have none of it. He told CNN's affiliate station in India that his forces had bombarded the hospital because they believed that the Tiger leadership was there.[6] On 2 February, on Sky TV, he attempted to clarify the government's position:

> Gotabaya: If they [reports] are referring to the [PTK] hospital, now there shouldn't be a [PTK] hospital or anything because we withdrew that. We got all the patients to Vavuniya, out of there. So nothing should exist beyond the No Fire Zone . . .
> Interviewer: So just to be clear, if this hospital is operating . . .
> Gotabaya: No hospital should, no hospital should operate now . . .
> Interviewer: If it's outside of the safe zone, it's a legitimate target.
> Gotabaya: Yes. No hospital should operate in the area, nothing should operate. That is why we clearly gave these No Fire Zones.[7]

The hospital, however, was packed with wounded civilians and medical staff. This shelling would be one of approximately sixty-five recorded attacks that ensued in the following months on hospitals and clinics. The attacks ranged from those on large hospitals such as PTK's main government hospital, to the small mobile makeshift medical shelters repeatedly established by the Tamil government doctors as the lines moved. In the ten last days of January, for example, three different hospitals sustained five strikes that killed seventeen people and wounded another sixty-eight, many of them patients and staff. In the first ten days of February, there were eight strikes on three hospitals, including multiple strikes on the same day that probably killed around a hundred people, the majority of them patients and staff, and wounded many dozens more. The US-based independent watchdog Human Rights Watch said of the attacks: 'Repeated Sri Lankan artillery attacks striking known hospitals is evidence of war crimes.'

Hospitals, whether permanent or makeshift, have a special measure of protection under international law.[8] The unavoidable corollary is that this makes them an attractive place for refuge or cover. While it is illegal to attack a hospital, the prohibition is not absolute, and a hospital can potentially be targeted if an enemy makes use of it in order to 'commit hostile acts' (providing treatment to wounded troops is not a hostile act). If a hospital is used as an artillery position, or a command bunker, then its status is potentially converted into that of a military objective that by its 'nature, location, purpose, or use make an effective contribution to military action and whose total or partial destruction, capture, or neutralization in the circumstances offers a definite military advantage'.[9] The key determinant then is whether the anticipated advantage of destroying that capability outweighs the magnitude of the wrong committed when one kills civilians and medical staff, or fighters who are *hors de combat* because of their wounds. Even then, if the value of the target has been proven to the satisfaction of the military commander, hospitals are only subject to attack after a warning has been given, along with a reasonable amount of time for people to evacuate. A hospital is, in effect, innocent until proven guilty. An attacking commander must do everything feasible in the given circumstances to correctly determine its status. Individuals who order or carry out unlawful attacks deliberately or recklessly are responsible for war crimes.[10]

In the case of PTK hospital, there was no evidence that the senior Tiger command were in the hospital, or that it was an artillery position. The government's Ministry of Health was in almost hourly contact by radiophone with the Tamil government doctors inside, who gave detailed information of the cases they were handling, along with medical records. Huge red crosses on the hospital's roof could be clearly seen by the drones that directed artillery and aerial attacks, the images from which were transmitted directly to battlefield commanders. The drones also saw the traffic of ambulances and civilian vehicles bearing the wounded. So detailed were the images and the military's ability to interpret them that the SLA were capable of releasing dramatic footage of Tamil Tiger cadres firing at the feet of civilians in an effort to prevent their escape from the battle zone.[11] The UN and the ICRC were in constant contact with the armed forces and the Ministry of Health pleading for the 'humanitarian space' they needed in order to treat the growing number of wounded civilians. When the hospitals were attacked anyway, the organisations repeatedly warned the government that its shells were striking them and killing people.

The attacks were baffling because there seemed to be no rationale behind them. On the contrary, the government risked a backlash should it emerge that they were attacking hospitals at a point when they were so incontrovertibly dominant on the battlefield. Over the next few months, however, they persistently defended the various attacks on hospitals and clinics by denying that any civilians were killed, and that if they were, it was due to deliberate Tamil Tiger shelling, or because the Tigers were using people as human shields. The government attacks, however, were not made legal simply by the illegal acts of the Tamil Tigers, who may very well have deployed on various occasions amidst or close to civilians and hospitals. The secretary to the foreign ministry, Palitha Kohona, unwittingly characterised the senselessness of the attacks when he replied to an interviewer: 'Why should we at this last stage, when the prize is about to fall into our hands, bomb a hospital? It just doesn't stand to logic.'

The sheer scale of the shelling of PTK hospital appeared to be the result of a frantic SLA push to seize the town before Sri Lanka's annual independence celebrations on 4 February. The hospital was repeatedly struck by shellfire, and staff, patients and people in the grounds were killed and wounded. The majority of the fire came from government lines, but witnesses say that a number of strikes appeared to be from Tamil Tiger positions. The army, its lines briefly overstretched in an effort to reach PTK, had been beaten back in a counter-stroke led by one of the Tigers' most seasoned fighters, an intelligence chief known by the *nom de guerre* of Pottu Amman.* More than four hundred Sinhalese soldiers were reportedly killed. In response, the army began a ferocious barrage at the Tiger lines, which were as close as half a kilometre from the hospital, while the Tigers assembled some of their toughest fighters and dug in at the village of Anandapuram, just a few kilometres from PTK, their last concrete-fortified position. On 5 February, unable to remain in the path of the battle or to cross the front lines with the wounded in their care, the ICRC evacuated. All the drugs and equipment that remained were loaded into jeeps and trucks, along

---

* Literally 'Spot [Bullet Hole] on the Forehead Uncle'.

with 300 of the most seriously wounded patients, some of whom
would die en route to Puttumatalan, on the coastal sand spit next to
Nandikadal lagoon. Tamil staff scrambled through the rubble, twisted
roofing sheets and burned mattresses to retrieve medical equipment
and drugs.

That same morning, in the type of press briefing that self-consciously
mimicked those provided by Nato during the Kosovo war, and with the
admission by defence secretary Gotabaya Rajapaksa days earlier that
the hospitals had indeed been attacked still ringing in the air, the army
showed a video to a packed Colombo press corps. Apparently taken by
an army drone, it purported to show PTK hospital intact.[12] This clumsy
attempt to mask the bombing of the hospital would be repeated two
months later upon the overrunning of PTK itself, when the government showed a lengthy video of apparently unharmed buildings, with
not a cracked window or a chip in the paintwork. No journalist was
allowed to verify the footage with a visit to the hospital, nor was an
explanation provided for the defence secretary's earlier admission to
international media, which now conflicted with concerted government
efforts to conceal the truth.

The day following the evacuation of PTK hospital, another
hospital was struck in PTK. This attack largely escaped the attention
of the world's media because of confusion over the nature of the
hospital. Ponnambalam hospital had been built largely with Tamil
diaspora money and was used to treat both injured Tamil fighters
and civilians, as well as taking much of the overflow of patients from
the larger PTK hospital. By the time the air force had completed its
bombing runs that afternoon, between sixty and seventy-five patients
and visitors at Ponnambalam had been killed, of whom just fourteen
were reported to be Tamil Tiger fighters.[13] The government had
apparently not even attempted to warn the hospital. It had based its
target selection on what it said was the presence of senior Tamil
Tiger leaders, specifically Soosai, the *nom de guerre* of the leader of
the Sea Tigers, who had a house nearby. The government appeared
to conflate two targets into one, taking the opportunity to destroy
the hospital in the course of targeting Soosai's house. Later, the
defence ministry released a video that appeared to show Ponnambalam hospital intact.

It was clear to the UN and the ICRC that civilian deaths had multiplied exponentially since 20 January. One of the two senior government-employed district doctors trapped inside the zone, Thurairajah Varatharajah, told AP by satellite telephone that more than 1,140 civilians had been treated in three medical clinics over a period of a week, almost 250 of whom were children under fifteen years of age. He estimated that there had been between 250 and 300 deaths.[14] The UN High Commissioner for Human Rights, Navanetham Pillay, said she was 'seriously alarmed' over the fate of the civilians in the north. 'It seems there may have been very grave breaches of human rights by both sides. The lack of access for independent monitors, humanitarian workers and the media only adds to concerns that the situation may be even worse than we realise.'

The SLA's strategy of driving civilians away from the front lines by issuing 'warning bombardments' (which often killed people) had limited the deaths of non-combatants for the previous two years. That tactic evidently no longer worked. The area was simply too small, both because the front lines were falling in on each other and because the Tamil Tigers were placing mobile artillery pieces in areas now inundated with tens of thousands of people. The army was packed in so tightly on the circumference of the front line that it was having difficulty deploying its 50,000-strong force. The navy had to limit using its offshore gunboats for fear of striking SLA positions. And yet the SLA seemed either unwilling or unable to change their tactical approach at a point when, by the admission of its commander General Fonseka, the majority of the fight had been won. Escape for the senior Tiger leadership was, according to the general, 'impossible'. The government deflected concerns about the impact on civilians by shrilly mischaracterising calls for restraint as 'treachery' if issued by Sri Lankans, or 'foreign interference' calculated to save the life of Prabakharan if coming from the international arena. The Tamil Tigers repeatedly pressed civilians to retreat back into the interior.

The army continued to pummel the front lines using weapons that were inherently indiscriminate, such as multi-barrel rocket launchers.[15] In effect, 'the Government was experimenting with "hostage rescue" with no concern about how many of the civilians they killed'.[16] The fact that civilians were being killed and wounded in droves by shellfire in the NFZ declared by the government seemed to be a detail lost in the overall military strategy. Did the government and its military planners believe that the failure of civilians to make the perilous crossing of the front lines in effect amounted to complicity with the tactics of the Tamil Tigers? Did this failure confirm suspicions that these civilians were incorrigibly 'Tiger' to the bone and, like the schoolgirls of Senchcholai, were therefore guilty because of their acquiescence to the orders of the Tiger command? Now, with the exclusion of UN international staff from the battlefield and a paucity of information, knowledge of exactly what lay beneath the shroud of government and Tiger fabrications, and under the fog of war, became central to efforts by the UN to protect civilian lives.

On 4 February, Sri Lanka celebrated its independence day with a military parade of Czech-, Ukrainian- and Chinese-made war machines that stretched along the seafront in Colombo. The president gave a speech in which he noted that foreigners had long held that the Tamil Tigers were indestructible. Those foreigners – diplomats from all the embassies, as well as the UN and other multilateral organisations – lined the podiums next to him. The atmosphere was charged with anticipation as tanks and armoured vehicles rolled past. The Tamil Tigers, who had found a refuge for their political and fund-raising activities in many of the countries whose diplomats now stood listening to the president's speech, were about to be vanquished.

That same day, the UN security chief in Sri Lanka, Chris Du Toit, established a small cell to monitor the progress of the battle, gather reports of casualties and weigh the information it received. Somehow the UN had to be able to quantify the impact of the war on civilians, despite the determination of the government to stifle any contradictory version of events. The dozens of UN Tamil national staff from Convoy 11 who had been left inside the combat area now joined the general flow of refugees trying to escape the fighting. In addition, there were at least ten international NGO with hundreds more Tamil staff who were similarly forbidden from leaving the combat area by the Tamil Tigers, and who were now dispersed throughout the Vanni pocket. Dozens of Catholic priests and nuns had refused to leave their congregations. All had a range of satellite and radio telephones with them that largely continued to function until the final day of battle. The Tamil government doctors who maintained the formal government writ over health in Tiger-controlled territory pleaded daily with the Ministry of Health in Colombo for drugs, medical equipment, food supplements for malnourished children, evacuations for the injured and a halt to the bombardment. Increasingly desperate as they realised that they would receive no help from the ministry, in the months ahead the doctors turned instead to the international press to make the case for them.

Du Toit's UN monitoring cell tracked the movements and deaths of the refugees by correlating the telephone reports from the trapped UN and NGO staff. Officially, this information was used to make daily assessments about the safety of those humanitarian staff still inside the battle zone. The daily admissions sheets of the district doctors were accumulated and entered into a database, as well as details from those telephone discussions. Reports of deaths due to shelling coming in from various points inside the zone were checked and cross-checked with other reports arriving from different groups scattered across the battle area, and entered into the database. Much later, commercially available satellite photography showed the movement of civilians, craters caused by shellfire, destroyed houses and columns of displaced people on the move.[17]

The UN tried to assemble a composite picture of the effect of the battle on civilians. It seemed to be the equivalent of listening outside a door to a fracas and trying to guess the events from the exclamations, sounds of splintering furniture and hoarse shouts of those inside the room. From this confusion of information, and despite the prospect that the Tamil Tigers might be forcing the Tamil doctors or the UN's own staff to give inflated figures of the dead and wounded, the accumulation of events and casualties seemed consistent. Coupled with the denials by the government of events that Harun had personally witnessed, some sort of picture began to emerge. In a confidential memo to a Western ambassador in Colombo, Human Rights Watch wrote: 'the [UN] methodology you describe for tallying casualties and [refugee] numbers is indeed imprecise. But it is also sound as a basis for making credible estimates, and usually the only way to do so in the middle of an active armed conflict.' So why did the UN and the ICRC not consistently denounce the outrages that its own staff had witnessed and almost fallen victim to, and which by late January were killing dozens of civilians each day?

To begin to answer this, it is important to understand the distinctive roles of the two organisations. The Swiss-founded and led Red Cross dates from the mid nineteenth century, and gave institutional form for the first time to the role that custom, mercy and compassion had always played in the way that wars were fought. Acting as neutral intermediaries, ICRC staff are given extraordinary access to the battlefield, in return for extraordinary discretion about what they see. Their role is apolitical, and their interest solely to reach and treat, and if possible protect, people covered under the Geneva Conventions. They work on all sides of a conflict to safeguard those considered *hors de combat*. These include not just civilians, but also wounded or sick combatants, and those who have surrendered or who are prisoners of war. Their surgeons, lawyers and nurses work in hospitals and clinics, visit prison camps, observe crossing points between front lines, effect the exchange of bodies, arrange medical evacuations, oversee basic communications between prisoners and their families and trace missing or separated family members. In the face of inevitable brutality, and with the guarantee that they will remain silent about what they see, protagonists generally respect the neutral role of the ICRC, as well as their physical presence in a conflict theatre.

The ICRC's commitment to discretion and neutrality has sometimes been controversial. The organisation has never quite recovered from a series of notorious visits to concentration camps during the Second World War, when delegates apparently detected nothing that might lead them to broadcast the horrors that lay within, or to hesitate over the possible intentions of the Nazis. The ICRC continues to doggedly insist that it is only this use of discretion that provides a lifeline to utterly defenceless people who might otherwise simply disappear, quietly consumed by the barbarism of war.[18] The decision therefore to openly accuse the government of Sri Lanka and the Tamil Tigers of the killing of civilians was an unusual one that risked the entire ICRC operation in Sri Lanka, as well as the organisation's reputation for discretion internationally.

The reasons for the UN's restrained approach lie in its very essence, and in its evolution since its first session in San Francisco on 25 April 1945. The post-war international political settlement established the UN as the principal global security body, replacing the League of Nations, which had proved to be just an ineffectual pause between the slaughter of the First World War and the genocides of the Second. Politically, the

UN took as its starting point the traditional sovereignty-centred approach of the 1648 Peace of Westphalia, which had sought to end the bloodletting of the religious conflicts of the Thirty Years War between Europe's princes. Ever since, modern relations between states have relied on the principle that one state should not interfere in the internal affairs of another. In this early conception of international relations, civilians – those whom the princes ruled – barely mattered at all, and princes within their realm were immune from sanction. Beyond their borders, the Peace of Westphalia legitimised war as a means of dispute settlement.

The sovereignty-centred character of the UN was reinforced by the Cold War. Holding back from fully fledged conflict and mutually assured nuclear annihilation, the United States and the Soviet Union engaged for four decades in small proxy wars that were an extension of their struggle for strategic security and ideological dominance. The two imperial behemoths sought to control or curry favour with the expanding number of nations gaining independence through the de-colonialisation process that followed the Second World War. Countries such as Sri Lanka, whose non-aligned character had been largely determined by the government of Sirimavo Bandaranaike, profited from this patronage.[19] When the JVP rose against her in 1971, both the US and the Soviet Union rushed to prop up her government with armaments and cash.

From its inception, the UN's list of ambitions included humanitarianism, both in pursuit of its stated ideal of a better world, and as a practical measure to protect populations that had been ravaged by war. Organisations such as UNICEF were founded in 1946 to help the millions of children in Europe and Asia left hungry in the aftermath of the Second World War. These organisations were tasked with boots-on-the-ground action in pursuit of humanitarian principles that were gradually being adopted by the UN General Assembly. Those principles include foundational agreements such as the 1948 Universal Declaration of Human Rights, with its Article 3 that postulates the basic right to life for all people. But with time, and the realities of competing state interests, the political and humanitarian polarities of the UN have given rise to some glaring instances of failure, of which Sri Lanka is just one.

The collapse of the Soviet Union, and the accompanying end of the relative stability of bipolar power, revealed an unsightly disorder. The 1990s saw a proliferation of 'new wars', characterised by the number of lethal power struggles within states that used ethnicity as a rallying cry as various factions competed for control over power and resources. Forced to flee their homes, huge refugee populations crossed borders, often creating instability in neighbouring countries. At the same time, renewed globalisation was coming to life, with vast amounts of money and people flowing across international borders with greater speed and in dizzyingly complex currents.

An unfamiliar chaos threatened the ability of states to control their borders. A new level of cooperation was required to counteract a wave of human, drug and money trafficking emanating from the badlands exposed by the new freedom, and to contain intangible threats like global warming. Nations increasingly saw a value in reputational capital, which they could invest in the resolution of problems as good, cooperative members of the international community – and use in deal-making for trade concessions or other favours. Important notions of state accountability for the treatment of their citizens emerged alongside these new forms of multilateralism. Over the past two decades, sovereign nations have increasingly become accustomed to extending the rule of law globally in pursuit of what they increasingly see as their own interests.

Released from the grip of the Cold War, the UN seemed poised to realise greater potential. The art of global politics, however, and action based on black and white principles laid down in conventions are ambitious polar opposites. The UN relies on the fiction that it is a single body whose parts hum along harmoniously. In fact, it is better likened to a fractious parent/teacher meeting. Each parent nation jealously defends its offspring, rejects notions of bad behaviour, promotes its child-rearing methods and insinuates the right of its child to do as it wishes, whilst ultimately conceding that there must be rules that all abide by if any progress in the education process is to be made.

Multilateralism operates in the small space created by these concessions. The citizens of wealthy nations, spurred on by access to better information, clamour for action to stop foreign governments committing atrocities against their people. The 1990s gave rise to humanitarian interventions in Bosnia, Somalia, Haiti and Cambodia, amongst others, and fashioned a new use of power by strong nations in support of the persecuted civilians of weakly governed states. The historian Francis Fukuyama has called this period the end of agnostic sovereignty, as the international community came together for perceived common interests, and for an end to the vast crimes against humanity of the 1970s in places like Uganda and Cambodia.[20] The litmus test for intervention was, in theory, whether or not a conflict posed a threat to international peace and security. In reality, interventions such as Kosovo have exposed the uses to which 'humanitarian' projects can be bent. Less powerful nations often regard these interventions as challenges to their sovereignty, or as a new form of colonialism (even as some small nations conversely gained reputational weight by participating in them).

By the mid 1990s, the UN was rapidly expanding to meet the new challenges. Its humanitarian agencies grew tenfold. The Security Council passed twice as many resolutions in the two decades following the fall of the Berlin Wall as in all its previous years. From being a largely deliberative or diplomatic organisation, the UN now shepherded in the majority of the most significant positive international public law in history. From the morass of the Rwandan and Bosnian genocides emerged UN-backed armed interventions, treaties, ad hoc international criminal tribunals and, as of 2002, the establishment of a permanent International Criminal Court based in the Hague to punish those who break international criminal law. All have relied on the UN Security Council imprimatur.

It is not too much to say that the UN concerns itself with almost every aspect of life on earth, through a bewildering array of organisations that fall under its always expanding mandate. Yet contrary to the ICRC, the very breadth of this mandate makes for inherent contradictions, so that the UN often finds itself at loggerheads with itself. The direct action of a UN humanitarian agency such as the World Food Programme working to protect human life in Darfur comes hard up against 'interests', be they those of Chinese oil concerns, Libya's dabbling in border manipulation, or Dutch insistence that the International Criminal Court should be allowed to indict Sudanese president Omar al-Bashir.

In Sri Lanka, the UN was confronted by a humanitarian crisis, but was hamstrung by the interests of some of its most powerful members. As the situation unfolded, the positions of China, Russia and India became clear. There would be no resolution from the UN Security

Council warning Sri Lanka to restrain its forces. China and Russia, with separatist movements of their own, would veto any motion within the council. India struck a pose of outward ambivalence, even as it discreetly encouraged the Sri Lankan onslaught, though urging it to limit civilian casualties. But of the veto-wielding 'perm five' in the Security Council, it was China, with ambitions in Sri Lanka, which was the largest stumbling block. While the UN gave with one hand in the form of humanitarian help and expressions of concern, it was forced to withhold concrete political action with the other. A year after the war, in May 2010, Louise Arbour claimed that the UN's muted approach had 'verged on complicity'.

By early February 2009, the UN Secretary General Ban Ki-moon had been told of the informal estimate of the numbers of civilians killed, and had begun a personal campaign of intervention. In regular telephone calls, Ban sought assurances from the government, and President Rajapaksa personally, that the Sri Lankan armed forces were doing what they could to prevent the unnecessary deaths of civilians and that they were abiding by international law. A point of repeated discussion was the use of heavy artillery, which the UN team trapped inside the combat zone reported had wrought an indiscriminate toll on civilians.

The Secretary General had known the president for some years. He felt that he had the kind of personal leverage that would achieve real results, and that diplomatic notification would rein in the more cavalier elements of the Sri Lankan government (the Sri Lankan press enjoyed speculating on the 'favour' that President Rajapaksa had purportedly done Ban by supporting his candidacy for the post of Secretary General). Critically, Rajapaksa gave Ban the same reassurances that the Sri Lankans repeated to the series of statespersons who came knocking on their door over the next months, such as the US Secretary of State Hillary Clinton. All were sternly informed that Sri Lanka was the best guarantor of the safety of its citizens, that it viewed the Tamil population under the control of the Tigers as victims rather than perpetrators and, crucially, that its forces were not using heavy artillery against areas of civilian concentration.

On the morning of 8 February, a delegation from the UN in Sri Lanka arrived at the home of the foreign minister Rohitha Bogollagama. They presented the UN estimate of the number of dead to a gathering of ministers and officers. An enraged defence secretary demanded to know what business the UN thought it had collecting numbers. He insisted that they should refer to the dead as 'people' rather than 'civilians', suggesting that no distinction could be made between fighters and innocent victims.[21] A shouting match ensued between one UN official and the defence secretary that subsided only with the intervention of the foreign minister. Gotabaya would later say to a journalist, in reference to information coming from Tamils within the battle zone, 'There are no independent observers, only LTTE sympathizers.'[22] Information provided by any Tamil inside the battle zone could be dismissed as Tiger propaganda. The meeting fizzled out in the face of government bullying, with a vague agreement to review the methodology used to compile the figures.

In fact, given the circumstances, the UN was under no obligation to submit its estimates to intimidating scrutiny. The government had signalled the way it would handle accusations that its Zero Civilian Casualties policy was not working. Again and again, throughout the following months, it denied using heavy or indiscriminate weapons and tactics, or that civilians were dying as a result. On the BBC's *Hardtalk* programme on 2 March, the country's minister for human rights, Mahinda Samarasinghe, repeated that the army, engaged in a 'humanitarian operation', was not using heavy weapons.[23] In answer to a question on reports of civilian casualties, he said that if civilians were dying at all, it was because the Tamil Tigers were shelling and shooting their own people in their bid to retain them as human shields. Rather than expend his energy ensuring the army's compliance with international law, Samarasinghe spent his time shuttling backwards and forward between Colombo and Geneva to defend his country's actions. If there was a single good advertisement for the straw man of Sri Lanka's rule of law, it was the minister for human rights along with his secretary, Rajiva Wijesinhe, as they performed at international human rights forums during these months.

Disturbingly, it became increasingly clear from reports emerging from the combat area that the Tamil Tigers were indeed exercising a brand of ruthless terror on their own people that defies imagination. As the combat area shrank and their desperation increased, their brutality increased exponentially. They would shoot, execute and beat to death many hundreds of people, ensure the deaths of thousands of teenagers by press-ganging them into the front lines, and kill those children and their parents who resisted. Tiger calculations that they could amplify the pressure for international intervention by intensifying the distress of their own people backfired. Instead, the government could point to the multiplying instances in which the Tigers killed their own, and shift blame for the bulk of civilian deaths. Yet whatever the sins perpetrated by the Tamil Tigers, the evidence that has emerged so far indicates that it was the SLA that wrought the bulk of deaths upon the captive population.

On 9 February, the day after the meeting at which UN officials had confronted the government with estimates of the toll on civilians, Sri Lanka's Ministry of Foreign Affairs issued a press release in which it claimed that 'the difficulty in differentiating civilians from the LTTE cadres in the conflict zone is being carefully addressed, whilst the casualty figures reported from the areas where fighting is continuing are distorted'. The first inklings of large-scale civilian deaths were beginning to seep into the international press, and the story was gaining traction. Later that same day, the ICRC publicly called on the government and the Tigers to 'spare at all times the wounded and sick people, medical personnel and medical facilities'. Samarasinghe, in a series of statements and interviews, and in meetings in Geneva, retorted that the ICRC reports were 'sensational'. There were 'no more than 70,000 people' left inside the battle zone, and the government, he said, was not using heavy weaponry.

The UN's public position appeared muted and equivocal to the outside world. The Secretary General's style of quiet diplomacy on Sri Lanka struck observers as a blow to international good order, at a time when the world seemed 'ravaged by international economic, environmental and security problems, which cry out for multilateral solutions'.[24] Newspaper headlines decried 'The UN's "Invisible Man"', and said of him, 'Whereabouts Unknown'. The most damaging assessment, perhaps, was a leaked memo from Norway's deputy UN ambassador, Mona Juul, who accused Ban of being a 'powerless observer' to the humanitarian crisis in Sri Lanka whose 'passive and not very committed appeals seem to fall on deaf ears'. She added bitterly, 'China is happy with Ban's performance.'[25]

While the UN team on the ground spoke almost daily of the deaths of civilians due to bombardment in terms of 'dozens', an institutional decision had apparently been taken not to use the far more specific and influential cumulative estimates it had compiled on the basis that they could not be verified. Without Chinese support, diplomacy had to take its course, and to attempt to embarrass the Sri Lankan government with charges that the UN could not absolutely prove would most likely be fruitless. Confrontation, it was mooted, would reduce the organisation's leverage, threaten its access to the burgeoning internment camps to which civilians were sent as they escaped from the combat zone and loosen its already feeble grip on the humanitarian operation to aid people trapped inside the zone.

But if not the UN, then who? And, given how difficult it was to obtain any information, what standard of evidence was necessary to justify publishing authoritative figures of the dead that might have compelled, or at least encouraged, the government to restrain its forces? It was true in a literal sense that the UN could not with complete independence count the dead, or verify how they had died, for the simple reason that the government had done all it could to ensure that independent information could not be gathered. Until 16 January, when Convoy 11 had set off into the battle zone, international staff could accompany food convoys into the zone, but were forbidden – for their own safety, according to the government – to remain long enough to gauge the true condition of the vast civilian population on the move. Nor, in the government view, could UN Tamil staff be relied on for information, because they were either Tiger sympathisers or forced to distort their reports.

Information coming out via Tamil Tiger organisations was easily dismissed out of hand as Tiger propaganda. Tamilnet issued a vast array of new photographs and video of civilians being subjected to bombings. The Tamil NGO, the Tamil Relief Organisation,[26] compiled convincing written and photographed reports of the effects of the war on civilians. A small body of government-approved Sri Lankan journalists covered the army as it moved forward, but their stories gave no insight into what was happening to ordinary people. A few Indian journalists had privileged access close to the front, but their reports suggested no evidence of government wrongdoing. Other international journalists, who unquestionably would have been far more impartial, were kept firmly away and refused all meaningful access, usually on the grounds of safety.[27]

The lessons of the management of information from other wars had been well learned. The government continued to forestall, deter and obscure. When asked why journalists were denied all access to the front, the then secretary of the foreign ministry Palitha Kohona replied that 'no sensible person would have wanted to go there because there were bullets flying in every direction'.[28] Instead, journalists were compelled to rely on Colombo briefings, or were told that they were being taken to the front lines, only to be flown to recently captured territory well away from any fighting. The accounts of the Tamil government-appointed doctors who tended to the thousands of wounded were dismissed, up to the point that the Associated Press was told that the doctors did not in fact exist at all.

In one darkly comic exchange, an official from the Ministry of Foreign Affairs telephoned the AP bureau's Colombo-based chief, Ravi Nessman, to ask him where he was getting his civilian casualty figures. Nessman knew the official well. He told him that he was receiving them by radiotelephone from Dr Varatharajah, the regional director for health services for the Kilinochchi district. The ministry official told Nessman that the figures were impossible, because Dr Varatharajah 'doesn't exist'. When told that Nessman knew the doctor personally and had interviewed him over a number of years, the official then asked how he knew that the man on the phone was actually Varatharajah. The ministry's attempt to sow doubt ended when Nessman asked how he himself could be sure that he was talking to the ministry official. The American press agency was too formidable an institution for the government to toy with.

The UN was the only body, besides the warring parties, capable of making an educated guess, based on the network of sources it had established, of the extent of civilian casualties in the Cage. While Tamil ICRC staff remained inside the combat zone, and international ICRC staff became involved in the sea-borne evacuation of thousands of injured civilians from a toehold on the north-eastern coast, only the UN was able to gather information from the entire area into which civilians were hemmed. The organisation was not required to meet an onerously strict evidentiary standard, because wars, and civil conflicts in particular, do not allow for the collecting of verifiable evidence until the battle is over. It is one thing to speak vaguely of 'dozens dying each day' and another to insist on robustly defended specific estimates. The

UN was the only credible institution capable of establishing a casualty benchmark, a bulwark of neutral judgement in a society riven by fear, violence and lethal intimidation. It was the only body with the heft to resist government bullying.

To the immense frustration of Sri Lanka's browbeaten civil society groups, international journalists and many of the foreign embassies in Colombo, the UN refrained from wielding its moral authority to publicly denounce the tabulated killing of civilians. Was it right to do so? The eminent international jurist Louise Arbour says that 'the [evidentiary] standard should be reasonably credible information, or reasonable grounds to believe . . . It's not unreasonable to speculate because [you] don't have access . . . you cannot let the desire to maintain humanitarian access trump any other consideration.'[29]

It will remain a moot point as to whether or not an international outcry would have restricted or moderated the army's assault tactics. The government might have reacted by expelling the UN, closing the internment camps to the outside world, shutting off external assistance and then bombing the Vanni Tamils without a shred of restraint. On the other hand, it might have halted its forces, stopped the use of heavy artillery as it had continually promised, fortified its positions around the remaining Tamil Tiger fighters and increased its use of special forces Deep Penetration Units to target key leaders and the toughest of the Tiger units, while it took its time to negotiate the full surrender of the vanquished rebels. Cut off, without ammunition or the means to resupply or manufacture it, the Tigers would have been finished as a fighting force. The Rajapaksa government would have achieved the destruction of the Tamil Tigers in Sri Lanka while garnering international credibility and saving significant numbers of its own citizens. Instead, its actions resulted unquestionably in the deaths of thousands of people innocent of involvement in the fighting.

The mass killing of Tamils in 2009 mirrored the mass killing of Sinhalese by the state during the JVP uprisings. The cover-up by the government was yet another example of a long history of fudged accountability that added to Sri Lanka's collective, and perhaps desired, historical amnesia. In an interview with the *New York Times* in May 2010 to mark the one-year anniversary of victory over the Tigers, the new Sri Lankan Foreign Minister G.L. Peiris, former Rhodes scholar and professor of law, countered the reports of large-scale deaths during the war: 'The allegations are so vague . . . and sources are not identified. Verification is impossible.'[30] When the UN declared that its casualty reports could not be verified, it was unwittingly supporting the very narrative that the government maintained.

CHAPTER SEVEN
The Struggle for Truth

On the morning of 8 January, just a week after Kilinochchi fell to the Sri Lankan army, eight gunmen on motorcycles overtook the editor of one of Colombo's only dissenting English newspapers as he drove to work. They pulled him up outside a kindergarten on a quiet suburban street in a high-security zone manned by troops, smashed the car window and, as he struggled to escape from his seat belt, pressed a gun to his head and fired. Passers-by and witnesses bundled him into a car and took him to hospital, and a team of twenty doctors fought for three hours to save him.

The wife he had married just two months before waited outside the operating theatre. By early afternoon, Lasantha Wickrematunge's punctured body had given up. Thousands mourned the man who had begun his professional life as a lawyer and private secretary to Prime Minister Sirimavo Bandaranaike. He had also known President Rajapaksa when both were barely out of their teens. The literate, intimate and moneyed classes of Colombo were left to contemplate their own vulnerability. According to the chilled whispers of upper-class Colombo that month, nobody was safe any longer. A palpable sense of danger, quotidian to the Tamils under military occupation, had reached the largely disinterested and compliant merchant and intellectual elite of the capital. Suddenly, bloodshed felt close by.

Good-looking, clever and well connected both within Sri Lanka and abroad, Wickrematunge had received international awards for his newspaper's investigative work. People would read the weekly columns and headlines and shake their heads in wonder at the courage or fool-hardiness of the man who gave such licence to his writers. With a small English-only readership, the newspaper had always been a thorn in the side of governments, but there had never been a time when control of the courts, media, politicians and public opinion had been as complete as it was under the determined Rajapaksa family.

Through successive governments and the mire of Sri Lankan press laws, the *Sunday Leader* had ploughed on as its presses were raided and burned by gangs of masked gunmen, its paper stocks seized and its staff intimidated. Despite the weight of violence that hung over each of Wickrematunge's editorial decisions, the avowedly liberal, secular and outspoken weekly had managed to remain a critical point of dissent during one of Sri Lanka's most repressive periods. Its editor had been threatened with death, twice beaten by hooded men, and detained by the police. His house had been sprayed with machine-gun fire and his family terrified. He had endured all the strangleholds on liberty that oppressive governments wield – arbitrary arrest, the abuse of the legal system, the stifling of speech and threats to his safety – until just one more remained to bring him to heel.

Finally, he had fallen foul of the most powerful and ruthless man in Sri Lanka, the defence secretary Gotabaya Rajapaksa. The *Sunday Leader* had promised to expose the rampant corruption swirling around the awarding of no-bid defence contracts. Wickrematunge became embroiled in a court case with Gotabaya. He knew the danger he was in, and had tried to mitigate it by meeting with the president on several occasions. But he was aware of the fragility of the web of protective relationships in a country where power is wielded so personally. Wise to the brewing threat, he had carefully anticipated his fate in a society accustomed to decades of unrestrained state violence, to disappearance as a tool of state repression and to the impunity of those in power. The days following the fall of Kilinochchi and the triumphalist thrill that ran down the spine of the Sinhalese community left him frightened. One morning he told his brother, 'If there was ever a time for them to kill me, it will be now.'

In democratic states at times of war, governments often give as much attention to domestic challengers as they do to their military opponents, and the media is brought under control to the extent that the electorate will bear. According to al-Qaeda, more than half of the insurgent struggle is fought 'in the battlefield of the media',[1] which makes efforts to control the narrative of the war vital for governments, who guard their version of the truth with dozens of lies. The natural disposition of governments to control speech and direct thought is counter-balanced in theory by a watchful press, a vigorous parliament and an independent judiciary, all of which are protected by a police force guided by the rule of law. But even the strongest of democracies is strained by the demands of exercising armed violence within the boundaries of morality, law and accountability when the security of the state and its people is at risk.

The 'war on terror' declared by the Bush administration after 9/11 strengthened certain forces of repression throughout the world. Those who were present in the US during the years after the 9/11 attacks might recall that dissenters to the war in Iraq were afraid of being shrieked down as traitors intent on undermining the men and women who were doing the fighting abroad. War is instant power, as the lone Congressional voice that voted against the war discovered. George W. Bush's government distorted the causes for going to war, refused to allow coffins being airlifted back to the United States from Iraq and Afghanistan to be filmed by the media and concealed the terrible effect of these expeditions on the lives of ordinary Iraqi civilians. When the *NewsHour* Programme on PBS, one of the great free-to-air US broadcasters, began a nightly silent roll call of dead servicemen and women, it provoked a wave of jingoism and aroused indignant cries of treachery.

Beyond the US follies, and throughout the world, the war on terror 'created a political environment in which the rule of law was being constantly eroded [and] where the power of the executive was constantly affirmed over any other form of oversight'.[2] The pendulum of the contradiction encapsulated in the notion of armed resistance to tyranny – the 'terrorist or freedom fighter?' conundrum – swung against liberation groups who used violence. In the case of the Tamil Tigers, the extreme disciplined violence of their struggle put them hopelessly behind the times. When they returned to the fight following the breakdown of the 2002 peace process, their customary tactics worked against their bid for universal recognition. Nobody wanted to know about suicide bombers and child soldiers. The Tigers faced a world that recoiled from the very factors that had made them so formidable – the cult of self-sacrifice principal amongst them.[3]

The permissive space for greater control by state security services created by 9/11 found full voice in the repeated public pronouncements of defence secretary Gotabaya Rajapaksa. To him, the role of the media during the civil war was devoid of ambivalence. Journalists who criticised the war effort were 'traitors', who should be treated as such. Attacks on journalists and media organisations were almost invariably preceded by a public 'outing' on the Ministry of Defence website, Defence.lk. The defence secretary made personal editorial decisions over the portal, and decided which journalists, lawyers, civil dissenters and organisations should be revealed as 'Tiger sympathisers'. The frenzied national media would then seize on the information, holding up those outed for derision, exclusion and targeting by death squads.

By extension, anybody who criticised Mahinda Rajapaksa, the personification of the new era that would dawn in Sri Lanka following the defeat of the Tamil Tigers, also was a traitor. So too those who suggested that anything was rotten in the republic on the verge of its 'historic victory': arms deals linked to the ruling clan, the corruption and brutality of the police, the sprawling employment of hundreds of Rajapaksa relatives and cronies in government service. This virtually propagated viral terror as the state publicly named people and blackened their names throughout a network of information outlets, constituted a general warning to dissenters and was backed up by the beating, death or disappearance of those proscribed online and in the press.

One example of a monthly report by Sri Lanka's Free Media Movement provides a snapshot of attacks on journalists during the war. The month opens with a veiled incitement by the head of the country's public broadcasting system for journalist Jayantha Poddala, the general secretary of the Sri Lanka Working Journalists Association, to be killed.[4] The next day, the Ministry of Defence website publishes accusations of treachery against a number of newspapers and journalists. Two days later, a journalist is assaulted in Batticaloa, the fourth attacked in that town in recent weeks. The next week, an alleged government hit list of twenty-seven journalists begins to circulate in Colombo. On the thirteenth day, journalist Vetrivel Jasiharan, in the custody of the Terrorist Investigation Division, describes to a court his torture at the hands of police. The following day, the well-known journalist and editor Frederica Jansz receives a death threat (after two attempts to intimidate her the previous month). Three days later, a journalist is 'visited' twice at home by a gang of men. On the eighteenth day of that month, the Ministry of Defence website publishes 'Guidelines for Media Self-Censorship', which

caution that journalists should not analyse or be critical of military strategies, comment on promotions or transfers in the army, scrutinise
military procurements or tenders or oppose the war. Two days later, the
Criminal Investigation Department questions two journalists over war-
related stories and their sources. On the twenty-second day, a freelance
Sinhalese journalist, Prageeth Ekneligoda, is abducted from his home by
men in a white van, tied to a metal bar and terrorised, but later released.
A week later, armed men stop a car carrying the news director of the
TNL television station, Namal Perera, and savagely beat him and a friend
in an attempt to abduct him.[5]

The terror directed at journalists barely paused at the death of
Wickrematunge. A week after his funeral, four men on motorcycles
hauled over the editor of the Sinhalese weekly *Rivira* in his car. With
the government's smooth assurances that it respected freedom of the
press and was committed to a full investigation of Wickrematunge's
murder still echoing, Upali Tennakoon and his wife were set upon
with iron bars and knives. It was back to business as usual. According
to one Sinhalese media commentator, the most recent attack was yet
another sinister attempt 'to turn Sri Lanka into a sterile zombieland
where there is no discussion and debate'.[6] The drip effect was self-
censorship, the waning of criticism of any policy or personality
belonging to the government, and the impunity of the regime, whose
rule was increasingly personalised as dissent receded and the army's
victories mounted.

Oddly, it was the minister for human rights, Mahinda Samarasinghe,
who provided a coherent, if disturbing, justification for the crackdown
on the press. 'Human rights violations during war operations and the
humanitarian crisis that engulfs civilians caught in the cross fire have
always been the trigger points to order a military pull-back. The LTTE
would always play this card in the past.'[7] Thus the government candidly
equated objections to human rights violations with undermining the
war effort and providing support for the Tamil Tigers. With democratic civil society under attack in the cities, the room for concern over
the distant fate of Tamil civilians trapped by fighting in the dusky
nether regions of the country shrank along with the siege zone.

Lasantha Wickrematunge's assassination was just one in a substantial list of journalist deaths. By January 2009, Amnesty International
had recorded at least fourteen media employees who had been

murdered in Sri Lanka since the advent of the Rajapaksa regime (some of them almost certainly killed by the Tamil Tigers).[8] On 24 January 2006, Subramaniyam Sugitharajah, a Tamil journalist who was investigating the brutal killing by security forces of five Tamil students three weeks earlier, and the ensuing intimidation of witnesses, was shot dead in Trincomallee. The killings were sometimes preceded by torture. In July 2006, for example, the Sinhalese journalist Sampath Lakmal de Silva was found shot, his brutalised corpse discarded in the Colombo suburb of Dehiwela. The presence of the security forces made no difference. On 20 August 2006, Sinnathamby Sivamaharajah, the managing editor of the Tamil-language *Namadu Eelanadu*, was shot dead outside his home, located inside the perimeter of a high-security zone in Jaffna. On 29 April 2007, Selvarajah Rajeewarnam, a reporter for the Tamil-language daily *Uthayan* in Jaffna, was killed by gunmen as he rode his bicycle 180 metres from a military checkpoint. In May 2008, Paranirupasingam Devakumar, a Tamil journalist working for Maharaja Television in the tightly controlled Jaffna peninsula, was hacked to death in broad daylight together with his friend, having just passed through one of the hundreds of SLA checkpoints.

These killings, however, were just the rudimentary pinnacle of a campaign of terror and intimidation against journalists and those who employed them. The Rajapaksas might not have pioneered press intimidation or the killing of journalists in Sri Lanka,[9] but they took the practice to renewed levels. A spectrum of methods was used: from personal telephone calls from the defence secretary in the middle of the night to capricious tax levies designed to cripple sales, from beatings, arrests and abductions to the vandalism of printing presses, the choking-off of paper and print supplies, and the use of the moribund judicial system to bankrupt publishers.[10] Dozens of Sri Lankan journalists fled abroad and the government's confidence in its methods grew.

Government ministers like the thuggish minister for labour relations and foreign employment, Mervyn Silva (who would later be given a senior media portfolio), felt perfectly at home bursting into the newsrooms of a broadcaster with a posse of armed men to assault the news director. Silva later characterised the beating of the journalist (an incident that was caught on camera) as 'an official visit'. In July 2009, in a sign of the total impunity flaunted by those in power, and an invidious disdain for the rule of law, the same minister was recorded apparently bragging of the murder of Lasantha Wickrematunge: 'Lasantha from the [Sunday] Leader paper went overboard. I took care of him. Now a fellow in my electorate is trying to stand [for election] against me . . . I will send him to the place where I sent Lasantha.'[11]

As the war effort mounted and the prospect of snuffing out the Tamil Tiger threat seemed more and more likely, so too did the effort to stifle persistent dissent that irked those with power. After two senior Tamil Tiger apparatchiks were arrested when they managed to escape with an outflow of Tamil civilians from the battlefield in April 2009, rumours emerged from the government about what they were quarrying from the interrogations. General Sarath Fonseka publicly accused some Sinhalese journalists who continued to agitate for press freedom of being bankrolled by the Tigers. There were dark mutterings about a list of journalists being compiled from the revelations of the two apparatchiks, and panic spread. More journalists fled abroad.[12]

If scribes were no longer safe, nor were soothsayers. In a country whose president manages his affairs on the advice of a personal astrologer, horoscopes are considered the entrails of politics. In June 2009, police arrested one of the country's popular astrologers, Chandrasiri Bandara, who had predicted (incorrectly as it happens) that President Rajapaksa would be ejected from office by the end of that year and (more accurately) that the cost of living would rise. A police spokesman confirmed that the Criminal Investigation Department was questioning the star reader in an effort to discover the basis of his prediction, while a spokesman for the president said: 'We have to wonder why an astrologer would say such a thing. In Sri Lanka, astrologers are not just for fun. They play powerful roles in steering outcomes. Saying it can make it so.'[13]

In the early evening of 1 June 2009, just weeks after the end of the war, journalist Jayantha Poddala was bundled into a white van on a busy Colombo street in front of bystanders. A year earlier, the Sinhalese Poddala had been threatened with death. He worked for the government-run press but had constantly led protests against the government's attempts to throttle free expression. He had already been summoned to face the defence secretary months earlier, and told that there would be consequences if he did not stop. In a television broadcast a week before his abduction, a senior police officer had accused some journalists of being in the pay of the Tamil Tigers, while an image of Poddala was flashed across the screen. The following day, in a clear reference to the bearded Poddala, a government newspaper editorial called for the stoning and expulsion of journalists with beards. The Sinhala-language newspaper *Divaina* called for the execution of treacherous Sinhalese journalists. While Poddala was being bundled into the van, President Rajapaksa was meeting with a delegation of professional media associations to discuss their concerns about the safety of journalists.

Poddala's captors stamped, kicked, punched and beat him with sticks and iron bars. They hacked away at his trademark beard and hair, shearing it off with knives as if he were a goat, stuffing the hair down his throat. They singled out his fingers and smashed the bones with wooden logs, pounding them against the floor of the van. All the while, as the van drove about Colombo and out into the country, they told him he was going to die. Instead, hours later, they dumped him in a muddy ditch by the side of a road.

One bystander who had witnessed the abduction knew Poddala, and had quickly telephoned a journalist, who had spread the word through an emergency media network created to forestall or halt the abduction of fellow journalists. In a common twist to law enforcement, the first reaction of the police was to arrest several of the journalists who had alerted the emergency network on suspicion of having committed the abduction. What almost certainly saved Poddala's life was the immense pressure brought to bear on the Sri Lankan government by foreign embassies, who intervened while the abduction was in progress.

Journalist and cartoonist Prageeth Ekneligoda is the most recent Sri Lankan journalist to have disappeared since the war. Six months before his second and final disappearance, he had already been kidnapped and terrorised by men driving a white van. On 24 December 2009, days after writing several articles criticising election malpractices by the government, he vanished again. Local residents told journalists that they had seen a white van near his house without number plates around the time that he disappeared. When his wife went to lodge a missing persons application with the police, she was promptly arrested. Ekneligoda had written extensively about the nature of dictatorship in societies and had warned in his articles that the government was usurping power from the electorate by degrees.[14]

What made matters worse was a poisonous concoction that by this stage lay at the heart of Sri Lankan journalism.[15] In earlier times, the peculiarly rancorous and fanciful story-telling of many of the major press organs might have passed as gritty jousting or vitriolic pamphleteering. But in a country already defiled by war, ethnic strife, caste and class divisions, deadly personal rivalries, death squads, authoritarian government, a shaky judiciary and a police force inducted into the struggle against terror, the press were yet another facet of the crisis. Incendiary speeches by Tamil or Sinhalese leaders on sensitive issues would be seized on and milked by chauvinist editors on all sides, propagating odious racial stereotypes, and often accompanied by inflammatory editorial comment and salacious cartoons.

The very worst of the press outlets combined with relish in campaigns such as that against Poddala, in which they intended to do actual harm. The nationalist press fed off spurious information provided by a brace of websites that cloaked themselves in an official mantle and were run out of government institutions, yet claimed to be independent. Functionaries such as the secretary of the human rights ministry ran their own websites in which they broadcast tirades and manufactured cant and opinion as fact. It was breathtaking for foreign observers, but must have been a matter of pure terror for those who were targeted.[16]

The atmosphere of incipient violence intimidated those international journalists granted visas to report from Sri Lanka during the war. Sri Lanka was one of the great underreported war stories of the past thirty, years, its theatre sealed off and quarantined like a plague quarter. The island was long notorious amongst foreign news desks for the shrewd impediments the authorities deployed against meddling foreign correspondents. Hapless visiting reporters were drawn into a dizzying cycle of permissions followed by obstructions, official comments that were then retracted or later denied, and promised meaningful access to stories stymied by exhausting delays, outright refusal or 'bait and switch' excursions. Without substantive access to the story, news directors shied from sending costly news teams to cover the war, knowing that they would never get the vital visual evidence to justify the news value of the reports. In addition, correspondents were unwilling to file stories that were overly critical of the government while they were in Sri Lanka because they felt at physical risk.

Major international news organisations such as the Associated Press

and Reuters spirited out of the country local staff whose safety they felt
was not assured. On at least one occasion in early 2009, the BBC withdrew an international news team after a direct threat from the defence
secretary, while Reuters abandoned a text message news service partnership with one of Sri Lanka's major mobile operators in the face of
the same sort of interference. The operator was told that their licence
would be cancelled if they continued the contractual arrangement (the
company that took over the contract delivered a steady diet of cricket
scores and comments from the government). The BBC's Sinhala and
Tamil services, perhaps the news sources held in the highest regard by
all communities for their relatively balanced presentation, and unen-
cumbered by security risks because they were compiled and broadcast
from London, were targeted in the local press and in the UK's expatriate Sinhalese community with accusations of 'sympathy' for the
Tiger cause. On 9 February 2009, the BBC's relayed service was
suspended from the Sri Lankan state broadcaster (SLBC) when the
corporation refused to accede to the government editing its
programmes.[17]

Newly arrived foreign reporters who sought their accreditation
from the Ministry of Defence were confronted by a government func-
tionary who grimly led them through a file of their stories written
abroad. He would draw their attention to highlighted passages with
which the government disagreed, suggesting that they 'do better while
in Sri Lanka'. A guileless foretaste of the government's approach was
displayed on the wall of the military media centre in the form of an
inspirational slogan reading: 'It is the soldier, not the reporter, who has
given us freedom of the press. It is the soldier, not the poet, who has
given us freedom of speech.' The Independent's Andy Buncombe, fresh
from Myanmar and the news management ministrations of that country's ruling junta, was struck by the gall of the Sri Lankan effort to
influence the writing of news stories by international journalists. The
AP's Colombo bureau chief, Ravi Nessman, whose scrupulously accurate and well-researched stories were a source of constant irritation to
the government, was finally expelled. Dozens of international
journalists who wrote unfavourable articles abroad were denied
visas. Those who made it past customs spent much of their time
fidgeting in their Colombo hotel bedrooms, unable to compile
substantive reports.[18]

As the war effort mounted between 2006 and 2009, media independence and the ability to 'bear witness' was cudgelled to its knees. Yet comparatively, Sri Lanka's journalists were a privileged group. The vast majority of ordinary Sri Lankans have no access to media outlets that will expose their abuse at the hands of police, or 'bear witness' when they are snatched from the streets. At least 4,000 people disappeared from villages and towns, even from their own homes, during this period, although the real figure is probably much higher.[19] Generally unreported by the local or international press, most, if they were ever seen again, were found dead in paddy fields. Often parking an unmarked vehicle outside a target's house was sufficient to cow them into silence. The 'white van' syndrome pervaded the steadily reducing circles of dissent, spreading fear of the 'abyss without bottom'.[20]

The Rajapaksa regime inherited a method of terror broadly used by Sri Lanka's governments since the JVP uprising, and exercised it with ruthless abandon.[21] The UN's Working Group on Enforced and Involuntary Disappearances was inundated with reports of the disappeared, the vast majority of them young Tamil men. Police arrests morphed seamlessly into abductions, and vice versa. Not even the UN or ICRC Tamil staffs were safe. On several occasions UN staffers were abducted (or arrested) in circumstances uncannily like the white van abductions, but eventually located – beaten, bedraggled but alive – in police custody. In April 2007, however, men who identified themselves as police officers approached two young Tamil Red Cross workers in broad daylight in Colombo's main railway station as they waited for a train. Led through barriers manned by security personnel, they were driven away in a white van through police and army checkpoints. Their bodies were found dumped beside a dirt road after they had been tortured and then shot.

Gotabaya Rajapaksa regularly railed against NGO workers, the UN humanitarian agencies and other civil society organisations, accusing them of undermining the war effort. His attacks fuelled an atmosphere of suspicion and intimidation that could only encourage attacks on them. Using the government-controlled press and the Ministry of Defence website, he painted the UN and NGOs as being riddled with Tamil Tiger supporters who used their positions to funnel war materiel to the increasingly beleaguered Tiger forces. He played on public fears that NGOs were both the public defenders of the Tamil Tiger cause internationally, and dedicated fifth columnists inside Sri Lanka whose actions threatened the lives of Sinhalese soldiers already dying on the front lines.[22]

Among the most ludicrous examples of these attacks was the government-orchestrated campaign against the United Nations children's agency, UNICEF. Since 1946, the agency that had begun by supplying milk and blankets to massive populations of child refugees had grown into one of the great exemplars of humanitarian action. By the turn of the twenty-first century it was vaccinating almost half the world's children, and counted dozens of world leaders among its earliest beneficiaries. With staff in more than one hundred countries, often at great personal risk, the agency was among the first on the ground after the Indian Ocean tsunami, and its staff were occasionally killed in the course of action. The clarity of its mandate to protect children on behalf of the UN General Assembly made it a favourite cause for glamorous Hollywood stars.

Not, however, in Sri Lanka. The agency was already the target of particular opprobrium for its relatively mild expression of 'concern' over the deaths and maiming of the schoolgirls of Senchcholai. In the atmosphere of mounting paranoia induced by the renewed war, Sinhalese nationalists across the board convinced themselves that UNICEF was plagued with Tamil Tiger sympathisers. In late 2007, the government-controlled media began a campaign against the agency. Local employees scattered throughout the UN system in Sri Lanka, through official intimidation or a misplaced sense of patriotism, supplied the government and press with supposedly incriminating information that suited the paranoia of a society deranged by war psychosis.

The equating of humanitarian aid with the provision of succour to the enemy was a deliberate ploy that titillated the Sri Lankan public's taste for conspiracies. In the hands of the nationalist press and in the halls of government, UNICEF field jeeps equipped with anti-blast shields to protect staff against landmines as they drove throughout the conflict zone became covert Tamil Tiger war vehicles. Humanitarian and development programmes that had been devised in partnership with and agreed on by the previous Sri Lankan government became covert finance conduits for Tiger operations. Most damaging of all, a health programme to supply severely malnourished children with high-nutrition biscuits in Kilinochchi ground to a halt in the face of shrill accusations that the biscuits were ideal field rations for Tiger forces. Cabals of UNICEF staff members were 'exposed' and excoriated in the media, along with lengthy and fantastic accounts of their exotic plots.[23]

The UN considered the inflammatory language of the government and media a threat to the security of its staff. Over the preceding years, the organisation had been devastated by attacks on its personnel in Baghdad, Algiers and Kabul, in which many dozens had been killed. The deaths of NGO workers in Sri Lanka prompted the UN's highest humanitarian official, John Holmes, to remark in 2008 that the country was one of the most dangerous places in the world in which to be employed in humanitarian work. By the middle of 2009, well over sixty Sri Lankan humanitarian workers employed by a variety of national and international agencies had been killed or 'disappeared'. Dozens more were to be killed and injured in the final months of the war. A single incident in the opening stages of Eelam War IV illustrates the lethal dangers to which humanitarian workers were exposed.

On the evening of 6 August 2006, humanitarian workers following on the heels of the SLA entered the eastern town of Muttur, which had been wrested from the Tamil Tigers in heavy fighting over the previous two days. They went to the offices of the international French NGO Action Contre la Faim (ACF), where they found the bodies of fifteen humanitarian workers lying on the front lawn of the compound. They were wearing the organisation's distinctive white T-shirts, bearing an emblem that marked them as non-combatants. All had been killed by a bullet to the back of the head, including a young woman and her father who were both employed at the same office. Two more bodies were found several days later in a car close by, apparently shot as they tried to escape the mass execution. The killing of the ACF seventeen was one of the bloodiest acts ever against humanitarian workers anywhere in the world.

The government quickly accused the Tigers of the atrocity, and would later blame ACF for stationing workers in the path of danger.[24] The question of just who was responsible revolved around the issue of which side had held the territory when the workers were presumed to have been killed. When ACF officials arrived at the compound they found that police had not sealed the crime scene. An attempt had been made to burn the bodies. A number of international organisations, including the Nordic SLMM, which had been barred by government troops from reaching the site of the massacre, voiced strong suspicions that the killings were the work of government forces. The UTHR(J) would eventually issue a report detailing a precise timetable of the military engagement, which showed that government forces had held the area at the time of the killings. The report named three security personnel as the murderers.[25]

An official government inquiry was quickly announced. Just as the horrific nature of the crime exposed a level of profound disdain for humanitarian workers, so too did the inquiry expose the nature of justice in Sri Lanka, even when conducted under the light of international scrutiny. The Tamil magistrate in the town of Muttur was poised to conclude that the police investigation and post-mortem were inadequate, when the ministry of justice removed the case from his jurisdiction and placed it in the hands of a Sinhalese magistrate in the distant town of Anuradhapura. The inquiry would now be held in Sinhala. Frightened Tamil witnesses who already knew that their lives were likely to be in danger if they spoke were required to travel far from their homes, without protection, to testify in a court whose proceedings were held in another tongue.

Amnesty International produced a report on the ACF massacre and the subsequent merry-go-round of inquiries. *Twenty Years of Make Believe: Sri Lanka's Commissions of Inquiry* notes that transferring cases is just one of numerous ploys used to obstruct the course of justice. Other routine methods include threats to witnesses, threats to defence counsel, the 'misplacing' of evidence, the alteration of crime scenes and bribery. So readily observable is intimidation that lawyers representing the state begin their cross-examination by exposing the names, addresses, occupations and connection to the witness of close relatives and friends. Testimonies are toggled between three languages, with central facts either missing or deliberately altered, or small discrepancies used as reasons to suppress, delay, extend or annul legal proceedings.[26]

Yet an impatient world pressed for answers to a crime whose import affected the safety and management of humanitarian operations globally. Under pressure, in February 2007 President Rajapaksa agreed to invite a group of internationally renowned jurists and specialists to convene in Sri Lanka as the International Independent

Group of Eminent Persons (the IIGEP). These jurists were tasked to observe and assist a larger Sri Lankan inquiry into a number of high-profile human rights cases, including that of the ACF seventeen massacre. Berated and belittled in the press, mocked and accused of partiality by the government over the course of the nine months they were observing, the IIGEP eventually abandoned its mission. As they left the country in March 2008, its members denounced Sri Lanka's showcase inquiry into its most public human rights abuses as systematically undercut by official obstruction, a lack of independence, a failure to protect witnesses, obscure and glacially slow proceedings and a lack of appropriate financing. There was, they said 'an absence of political and institutional will on the part of the government to pursue with vigour the cases under review'.[27]

Sri Lanka's judicial system, the purported backbone of its democracy, is currently a sham. While the government sanctioned or directed grave violations of international law in 2009 against besieged women and children in the country's north, eloquent government officials solemnly sold Sri Lanka's democratic and judicial credentials at international forums. The country's minister for human rights, Mahinda Samarasinghe, his secretary Rajiva Wijesinge, and the secretary of the foreign ministry, Palitha Kohona (now the country's ambassador to the UN in New York), sustained the elegant conceit that a system of meaningful accountability exists in Sri Lanka. Sadly, these men, along with a number of Sri Lanka's diplomats throughout the world, smoothly and successfully promoted the notion that a 'mature and democratic Sri Lanka', in possession of a robust and independent judicial and legislative machinery, was fully capable of investigating any wrongdoing.[28]

Their rationale was a simple one, and rang true to the outside observer armed with only a superficial knowledge of Sri Lanka. In a democracy, the argument ran, justice is rarely swift and cannot reasonably be expedited merely to satisfy political or public tastes. Indeed, it is axiomatic that to hurry due process is to undermine the procedure that sits at the heart of a legal system and would erode the rule of law itself. Given this, the government was always quick to appoint commissions of inquiry or other investigative bodies that served as fig leaves, cloaking the intention to do nothing at all and to delay further inquiry. The IIGEP experienced first hand the drip effect of official obstruction before they abandoned all hope that constructive and sincere engagement with Sri Lanka's institutions would lead to justice for the murdered ACF workers. For the thousands of disappeared who were truly defenceless and whose abductions would never be noted, the concept of justice delivered belonged in the realm of astrology.

A 2009 International Bar Association fact-finding mission to Sri Lanka found that officials at multiple levels mimicked this 'due process' deception that the government projected.[29] Officials throughout the administrative, judicial and enforcement bureaucracies invariably noted that there was a police investigation into a particular crime or a pending legal case that was *sub judice*. They patiently explained that they could not possibly do anything further until the legal process had concluded, because it would undermine justice. Senior Rajapaksa government ministers, as well as the president himself, provided the same neat answer in the case of foreign envoys enquiring about judicial investigations.

The more successful the track record of this decoy, the more reflexive the posture became, and the more brazen the presumption by the government that the outside world would be duped. Another shameless example concerned the issue of battlefield executions. Months after the end of the war, a video surfaced of Sri Lankan soldiers brutalising and then executing blindfolded men who were presumably captive Tiger fighters. To the experienced observer, the video was redolent with authenticity. War is savage; it hardens the young men and women who are called upon to fight, and summary executions and the torture of the vanquished are not uncommon. Within days, however, deaf to the hollow ring of its own indignant protestations, the government decided again to test the credulity of observers.[30]

Using a hastily gathered group of purported 'experts', including serving army officers and expatriate Sinhalese telecommunications engineers, the government unveiled the conclusion of its investigation: the video was nothing less than a fake conjured by Tamil Tiger propagandists to discredit the SLA. The government would immediately sue Britain's Channel 4, which had aired it. Unfortunately, after months of measured forensic analysis, the UN's Special Rapporteur for Extra-Judicial, Summary, or Arbitrary Killings found to the contrary that the video was in all probability genuine. 'If there is evidence, it can be brought to the notice of the established Sri Lankan judicial system,'

Girls perform a harvest dance. A scene of rural serenity in the mid-twentieth century that belied the brewing troubles facing the newly independent Sri Lanka.

Anagarika Dharmapala, in perfect repose. He 'commandeered the history and culture of the Sinhalese and ritualised numerous aspects of their ordinary life'.

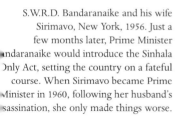

S.W.R.D. Bandaranaike and his wife Sirimavo, New York, 1956. Just a few months later, Prime Minister Bandaranaike would introduce the Sinhala Only Act, setting the country on a fateful course. When Sirimavo became Prime Minister in 1960, following her husband's assassination, she only made things worse.

Rohana Wijeweera, in Guevarist garb. The Sinhalese Marxist nationalist led tens of thousands of Sinhalese youths to their deaths. He met his own end on a Colombo golf course.

Sun God, and Supreme Leader of the Tamil Tigers, Velupillai Prabakharan, 25 November 2004. Like Wijeweera, his body would be incinerated by the Sri Lankan army and the remains scattered.

Dumped in the street, strung up on a lamp-post with signs around their necks,
or burned on the same white beaches advertised in the tourist brochures.
Bodies of alleged JVP supporters, 2 December 1989, in Tihagoda, southern Sri Lanka.
There were tens of thousands of other victims of the violence.

A crowd prepares to set upon a Tamil man trapped in the streets of Colombo during
'Black July' 1983. Helen Manuelpillai's father and brother, along with an estimated
1,000 to 3,000 other Tamils, were murdered in similar circumstances during the riots.

Young Tamil women who flocked to
join the Tamil Tiger ranks practice
a drill on the Jaffna Peninsula in 1987.
'Women would be expected to fight,
or to suffer as their children died.'

Tamil boys play against a background
of dead 'heroes' that perhaps portends
their own martyrdom. The see-saw
is painted in Tiger camouflage, and
the boys cling to wooden AK-47s.
Point Pedro, Jaffna Peninsula, 1989.

A mother mourns her
daughter, a young Tamil
Tiger cadre, on 9 September
2007. Her body was not
given back to her family,
only a headstone to mark
the grave. As the SLA
lines advanced, cemeteries
containing thousands
of dead Tamil fighters
were destroyed by
army bulldozers.

Airports were a favourite target for the Tigers. In 2001, a fourteen-man Black Tiger suicidal unit raid on Colombo's international and military airport destroyed twenty-five aircraft, crippled the tourist industry and cost the country hundreds of millions of dollars in hardware and lost tourist revenue. (*Left*) Buses and trains were also regularly struck. This one on 23 February 2008 in Colombo injured 18, and was attributed to the Tigers. Thousands of Sinhalese civilians died in attacks.

Tamil school girls in Vallipuram, in the Vanni, practice sheltering from government bombing raids, 10 September 2007. The following day the area suffered air attacks. The schoolgirls of Senchcholai would have sought slit trenches much like these.

Buddhist monk supporters of the JVP protest in Colombo in support of war, 2005. Political monks were few, but vocal and influential. Some sat in parliament.

Defence Secretary Gotabaya Rajapaksa is embraced by his brother President Mahinda Rajapaksa. The former had just survived a suicide bomb attack on his motorcade on 1 December 2006.

Sri Lankan Army special forces preparing to take on the enemy, 28 December 2006.

Tents burning inside the second No Fire Zone, 2009.

A photo of a picture drawn in the Manik Farm internment camp by a Tamil child. The caption reads 'maranaththin pinnum valvu', or 'life after death', and the picture appears to portray life under bombardment.

One of a series of photos, video, and testimony from Sinhalese soldiers that gradually emerged after the war. This one shows a man thought to be a captured Tamil Tiger fighter being tortured. Other photos in the sequence show him being bludgeoned to death.

Lasantha Wickrematunge, the outspoken editor of the *Sunday Leader*, had told his brother, 'If there was ever a time for them to kill me, it will be now'. On the morning of 8 January 2009, he was assassinated in a suburban Colombo street.

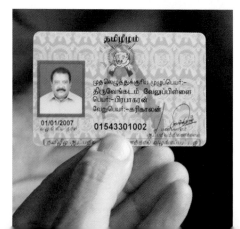

The Tamil government doctors 'confes[s] at a press conference in July 2009 th[at] they exaggerated the numbers of civilia[ns] killed during the siege of the Cag[e].

Prabhakaran's ID card, June 2009. It is all that remains of the Supreme Leader of the Tamil Tigers.

Gotabaya Rajapaksa told the Sinhalese-language *Lankadeepa* news-paper. 'They can even go through lawyers and inform the police. We have an established legal system. Use it.'[31]

After the war, the UN Secretary General demonstrated a determin-ation to pursue an international inquiry into persistent allegations of war crimes in Sri Lanka. The government response was to hastily convene its own commission of inquiry. 'The government has just appointed a Commission of Inquiry to go into this type of allegation,' said Sri Lanka's ambassador to the UN, Palitha Kohona. 'It will have a wide mandate, and I think it's appropriate for us to let that Commis-sion of Inquiry do its job, rather than to preempt . . . the evidence that it's going to call before it. Sri Lanka has a history of a very highly respected judicial system. To suggest that anybody from outside can do a better job is simply . . . colonialist.'[32] It was a statement calculated, once more, to invoke Sri Lanka's well-tested 'due process' device to delay a just reckoning.

The obstruction of bureaucrats and functionaries, however, is just one of many corrosive aspects of Sri Lanka's justice system. Contrary to the very nature of a court of justice, and according to the Inter-national Crisis Group, Sri Lanka's courts 'abet human rights violations on a daily basis', have 'corroded the rule of law and worsened ethnic tensions', and 'provide no effective checks on endemic torture in police custody'.[33] Supreme Court Chief Justice Silva had presided over the legal system during the final stages of the war and for the preceding decade. Like all chief justices since President J.R. Jayawardene's 1978 reforms, he was a direct appointment of the president. He ruled his judges with a grip that ensured complete subservience to his own polit-ical, judicial and religious prejudices. He intimidated legal practitioners, both inside and outside the courtroom, who tried to assert the political and human rights of individual Sri Lankan citizens over political prudence or popular demands, and effectively established a system of patronage that rivalled (albeit on a more modest scale) the president's own.[34]

The intimidation of lawyers almost mirrors that of journalists and humanitarian workers, though without the same deadly effect.[35] Defence lawyers have been beaten, threatened, had their houses bombed and been detained and tortured in custody when they asserted the statutory rights of their clients in a way that fell beyond the

unspoken boundaries of accepted legal theatre. Unmarked white vans
parked outside the houses of defence lawyers are an unmistakable indication of imminent physical threat in present-day Sri Lanka. In 2008, a
group styling itself 'The Battalion of the Ghost of Death' declared that
'traitors' who provided legal representation in court for suspected
terrorists would be killed. The threat specified the names of human
rights lawyers as well as the court registrars responsible for accepting
human rights petitions. The threat was backed up by an article on the
defence ministry website entitled 'Who are the human rights violators'
that 'outed' lawyers defending humans rights cases in courts, along
with their photographs. Aside from the physical risks, in a system so
obviously reliant on personal patronage, taking on the status quo
simply spells the end of a lawyer's career.

The decade-long reign of Chief Justice Silva resulted in an astonishing tally of just five dissenting decisions (that is, judicial opinions
from judges that differ from the majority decision of their fellow
judges) and a steep decline in the number of fundamental rights cases
being lodged with the Supreme Court.[34] The vast majority of those
cases that did make it to court through the multiple levels of bureaucratic deterrence and intimidation were dismissed with a peremptory
'leave to proceed is refused'. Once in court, contempt of court rules
were wielded like sticks to keep counsel and litigants in order. In 2003
Chief Justice Silva summarily sentenced one lay litigant to a year of
imprisonment with hard labour for raising his voice in court and filing
repeated petitions. The UN Human Rights Committee described this
decision as arbitrary, draconian and imposed 'without adequate explanation and without independent procedural safeguards'.[36] (A less subtle
response was the physical intimidation of complainants, or even their
killing by the police. Gerald Mervin Perera sought damages after he
was tortured by police and pursued his legal claim until the defendant
policeman killed him in 2004. The accused continues to work to this
day as a sub-inspector.)[37]

Despite the tens of thousands of people who have been extra-
judicially murdered in Sri Lanka by the security forces since the 1970s,
and the hundreds of policemen and soldiers who have been prosecuted,
a mere handful have done gaol time. While one commission of inquiry
in the wake of the disappearances perpetrated by both sides during the
JVP uprising in the later 1980s concluded that the government was

responsible for as many as three quarters of the killings, only nine security personnel were ever convicted. Just a handful of members of the security forces have been punished for murder since 1994.[38] Murders by the security forces are almost invariably conducted discreetly (which made it all the more unusual when in November 2009, a gang of four policemen were filmed as they used metal poles to beat to death a mentally ill Tamil at a beach in Colombo in broad daylight. The victim had been throwing stones at a train). Rather than increase his vigilance at a time of national crisis when the mechanism of an independent court was critical, the chief justice disparaged the importance of cases concerning torture and illegal detention. A highly centralised, politicised and unpredictable judiciary with authoritarian tendencies was hardly likely to restrain the abuses of a police force notorious for the widespread use of torture, illegal detention and 'disappearance' as a method of state control.

In Sri Lanka, illegal detention, which too often morphed into abduction, had become a part of the lifeblood of law enforcement. It was easy to detain people and deal with them at a later date. As far back as the 1990s, police had begun to avoid compliance with court orders to produce arrestees by simply denying that they had ever been arrested. Even when the courts asserted that simple denial was insufficient if there was evidence that somebody was detained, many cases took five or six years, with upwards of thirty hearings, while the prisoner faded away in custody without a single charge being laid against them. Judicial oversight was powerless against police obfuscation, and the police increasingly took the form of a private militia for the use of whichever government held power.[39]

Basil Fernando, a lawyer and the executive director of the Asian Human Rights Commission, fled Sri Lanka in 1989 after being targeted by a government death squad. He now calls Sri Lanka 'one of the most violent places on earth'. According to Fernando, 'the vast majority of police abuses never come to light'. He marks the 1983 riots as the moment of irretrievable degradation for the police force – 'The law enforcement agencies can do whatever they like – arrest people without reason, torture people for as long as they wish and fabricate charges which can land people in prison without bail' – and highlights the routine use of torture by police as the 'entry point' for the corrosion of a system of policing that was once reasonably respected.[40] But according to Fernando, the use of torture as punishment has a logic that must be understood.

In a 2009 report called 'The Phantom Limb', the Asian Human Rights Commission explored the role of caste in abusive law enforcement in Sri Lanka, and a corresponding logic 'based in deep-rooted social systems and attitudes'. The British had incorporated into their administration pre-existing social divisions based on caste, class, region and ethnicity. These divisions were used as a means of social control, a reflection of Britain's own caste and tribal practices and dominant nineteenth-century notions of social Darwinism. The colonial administration elevated some categories of people and diminished others, but on the whole strengthened the very notion of separateness based on birth. Prior to the British, caste and ethnicity in Sri Lankan society had sustained a degree of fluidity, but colonial rule encouraged rigid interpretations of social hierarchy. The introduction of the census formalised social categories into fixed and administrated facts of life.

Today, while caste is not an element of judicial reasoning and all Sri Lankans are ostensibly equal under law, it is present in the administration of the law, and most particularly in punishment. Caste, according to Fernando, 'does not recognise the equality of human beings and is based on the legal premise of disproportionate punishment for different categories of persons'. Police act as enforcers of a hierarchy that finds no expression in statutory law. The logic of caste is enforced through the use of torture and police brutality, while the 'make believe' of a recognisable Western system of law and order prevails as a smoke screen. A transgression by a lower-caste person against one of higher caste is treated as a slight by one entire caste against another, and punishment assumes a corresponding magnitude. For the Tamils of the Vanni, their besiegement would take the form of a kind of mass punishment.

The Rajapaksa government did not instigate the weakening and compliance of the judiciary in Sri Lanka, or the steady reduction of the police to a crude enforcement device. In 1948, the country had possessed a healthy and well-respected legal fraternity with clear separation between the legislative, executive and administrative arms of government. But successive Sri Lankan constitutions and governments had whittled away at the independence of the judiciary in the pursuit of centralised power. The 1956 Sinhala Only Act had led to the exclusion of large numbers of Tamil lawyers and judges from the legal system. The 1978 constitution of J.R. Jayawardene had further emasculated judicial independence by making the chief justice a political appointee, directly answerable to the president.[41] Under a 2001 reform of the government of Ranil Wickramasinghe, a constitutional amendment had sought to restore the independence of the judiciary by re-establishing an independent and transparent system for appointing judges, civil servants and independent commissions. The amendment was allowed to lapse upon the election of Mahinda Rajapaksa.

Four reports stretching back to 1946 show that poor resources, a lack of investigative capacity and the institutionalised abuse of authority have long been latent features of Sri Lankan policing.[42] A public security ordinance had been enacted in 1947 in anticipation of the possible need to suspend civil liberties during troubled times. The government of Dudley Senanayake had used this during a general strike in 1953. Additional emergency regulations had been set in place since the time of the first JVP uprising in 1971, and the 1979 Prevention of Terrorism Act (PTA) underwrote many of the extraordinary measures used by the authorities to protect the lives of citizens, without which many more people would almost certainly have perished. It has since proved impossible to loosen the grip of the PTA, and the extraordinary powers therein, on the lives of ordinary Sri Lankans.

The International Covenant on Civil and Political Rights recognises the duty of a state to protect its citizens. But civil libertarians are attuned to the distinction between a state enacting emergency laws in order to protect the fundamental right to life of its people and a state dismantling the rule of law in an effort to cope with threat to the state. In under three years, Mahinda Rajapaksa's government introduced more than twenty new emergency regulations that weakened the rule of law and deepened the existing human rights crisis in Sri Lanka. These regulations fuelled the complicity of the security services in the killing of journalists, humanitarian workers and civil society activists. The government supported the aberrant rule of a judicial chief whose rulings and personal behaviour were considered by the International Bar Association to be deleterious to the actual practice and rule of law in Sri Lanka.

Rajapaksa's emergency laws weakened the rights of individuals against arbitrary treatment by expanding the notion of who would be considered a terrorist and what would constitute terrorism; or where, for how long, by whom, and under what circumstances the person in the street could be detained without anybody ever knowing what had happened to them. Some provisions promulgated in 2006 made it an offence to engage in transactions with terrorists – regardless of knowledge or intent. It was thus theoretically possible for humanitarian workers delivering aid to areas under the control of the Tamil Tigers, lawyers defending terrorism suspects, or civil society activists attempting to safeguard ebbing rights, to be imprisoned indefinitely. The decision of the president to declare an emergency is not subject to oversight by the courts, and parliament has no meaningful restricting authority. It is merely required to rubber-stamp extensions. In the case of the death of a person due to the actions of the security forces, the police are authorised to deny relatives access to the body, and to dispose of corpses at will.

In 2009, the International Commission of Jurists (ICJ) scrutinised the emergency laws in Sri Lanka. In its opinion, the Rajapaksa government had expanded impunity for officials who commit human rights violations, granted 'sweeping powers to military personnel' to carry out police functions and largely done away with the legal circumscription of arrest and detention procedures. They had also quashed freedom of expression and assembly, reversed the burden of proof on to suspects and allowed confessions obtained under torture. And for an extra measure of latitude in enforcing the regulations, the ICJ pointed out that these were all 'couched in ambiguous language'.[43]

But for civilians who fell foul of those in power, much worse lay beyond the legal minefield. By the middle of 2009, there were allegedly at least three 'official' death squads at work run by various sections of the security services. A former foreign affairs minister in the Rajapaksa Cabinet, Mangala Samaraweera, alleged that one death squad was known as 'Gota's Sinha Mafia.'[44] The UN had experience of the way that these units operated, since at least two members of its staff were snatched from the streets of Vavuniya by murky security units who had been specially sent from Colombo and who operated from the ubiquitous white vans (in these instances, the process of disappearance was reversed when the rapid UN response resulted in its staff reappearing in the system as formal arrestees).

With the senior echelons of the government providing the model, it is extremely unlikely that there was a monopoly on death squads. There must have been a proliferation of imitations run by police at a provincial level, as well as the unpoliced activities of the pro-government Tamil paramilitaries, the Home Guards,* the Special Task Forces, individual army units and the various intelligence services. Government ministers and officials had posses of bodyguards, a number of whom were involved in high-profile assaults and intimidations of private citizens who got in their way, or who came up against their offspring in Colombo's nightclubs and bars.[45] Moreover, the ease with which people could be killed exacerbated the worst existing tendencies of the police. The newspapers regularly reported cases of people who had died in custody. A part of the stock-in-trade of the police was to label each defenestrated or 'shot while attempting to escape' arrestee a gangster. Police used their powers to carry out vendettas that were either on behalf of businessmen and politicians, or were personal.

After the war, the government finally reacted to several police killings of Sinhalese that triggered mass protests. Two young men had been arrested after a young woman said that they had touched her hand. They were arrested and brought before the station commander (who was allegedly having an affair with the woman). An eyewitness said, 'I could see more than five police officers kicking, punching and throwing things at them . . . I heard them being beaten. The OIC [officer in charge] shouted to another police officer to bring him fire and then he was burning and beating them from time to time. In the early hours of the following morning the police team took them in the police jeep to the railway crossing and shot them dead. Both bodies had multiple bullet wounds to the chest and legs. One had a bullet wound to the face and contusions.' The government paid hush money to the families of the dead victims. [46]

At the lower end of the scale, Sri Lanka's vibrant underworld played the part of private bodyguards to government ministers, and terrorised the public in nightclub and sidewalk encounters. In the pursuit of opportunity, the underworld had generally transcended the muddying

---

* Officially known as the Sri Lanka Civil Security Service, the Home Guards was an armed militia established by statute in 1986 to serve as a first line of village defence against attacks by Tamil militants. The all-volunteer militia fell under the authority of the police and hence by extension enjoyed certain police powers. During the war they numbered around 40,000 personnel.

business of politics and ethnicity, and Sinhalese gangsters had a ground-level intelligence network throughout the country that rivalled that of the intelligence services. After the war, to its shock, the underworld was not rewarded by the government for its patriotic fervour. In November 2009, one Sri Lankan barrister bemoaned the fact that his clientele of underworld thugs was disappearing.[47] The police had initiated a programme of extra-judicial killings, and the gangster ranks were being rapidly thinned. In a series of copycat police killings, detainees were 'shot while attempting to escape' or, more bizarrely, while 'trying to throw a grenade at police'. The slayings were in part a demonstration of the government's promise to get tough on crime, and in part a useful way to cover up the involvement of organised crime with government. By June 2010, the *Sunday Leader* was reporting a spate of murders of street beggars, a phenomenon resembling the solution of a number of Latin American states to visible poverty and crime.[48]

In the absence of an overly inquisitive press, a vital civil society, an effective investigative police force, an independent judiciary or the meaningful scrutiny of parliament, the war and its aftermath provided an ideal opportunity to loot the country's coffers. It was a time when a victory-obsessed parliament was enthusiastically voting increases to the defence budget while the defence ministry was publicly warning journalists not to report on defence purchases. Large percentages could be scooped off billion-dollar defence contracts, as well as programmes for the reconstruction of the war-torn east and north. There were huge development projects funded by the Asian Development Bank and other bilateral donors, and major infrastructure improvements such as the billion-dollar Chinese-built port complex in the president's home-town of Hambantota.

By 2007, with Mahinda holding the finance portfolio, Gotabaya in charge of defence, another Rajapaksa brother, Chamal, responsible for ports and airports, and a fourth, Basil (known as 'Mr Ten Per Cent'),[49] tasked with redeveloping the dilapidated east, which had just been wrested from the Tamil Tigers, financial reporters estimated that the Rajapaksa clan directly controlled ninety-four government departments and approximately 70 per cent of Sri Lanka's finances. Any big investment decision now required what the Reuters bureau chief called a 'Rajapaksa blessing'.[50]

Just as the decision-making process of the war effort was micro-managed by the defence secretary and his brother Basil, so too were decisions over who would make money in the renewed Sri Lanka. One businessman, a gem merchant who ran a high street shop and also traded some of Sri Lanka's beautiful stones throughout the world, described the situation thus: 'You cannot imagine that these people who are running a country could concern themselves with the tiniest matters of business, but their fingers are in everything: Timber, the garment trade, construction, banking. You name it, and they are taking a cut. And it is a model for the entire country now, where everybody is on the take, and the remaining honest police and judges can't fight the tide. There are too many Rajapaksas to feed.'[51]

A foreign businessman who was establishing a flower plantation abandoned his effort upon learning that the final step involved a meeting with a member of the Rajapaksa family, during which he would be expected to hand over 10 per cent of the purchase price of the 200-hectare parcel of government land. Companies coveted by the Rajapaksas or those close to them could apparently, on occasion, be simply snatched in a manner that, as missing journalist Prageeth Ekneligoda had written, recalled to mind Caligula's Rome. The Rivira newspaper group, for example, had been taken over a year earlier in a business model described by the noted columnist D.B.S. Jeyaraj as 'in mafia jargon, an offer that could not be refused'. Both of the two new owners were related and close to the Rajapaksas, as well as to the military establishment.[52]

But between 2006 and 2010, international donors continued to beat a path to the brothers' door. They were anxious to see 'progress' in the reconstruction of the war-torn fringes of the country and enthusiastic about big-ticket reconstruction programmes that laid down roads, dams, bridges and power stations. Nevertheless, reconstruction, however well or blindly intentioned, left unaddressed the basic problems of equity, justice, the right to life and a share for minorities in the destiny of the country. With China and India competing for favour from tiny Sri Lanka, it seemed as though in order to receive, all the government had to do was ask.

In July 2009, despite pressure from France, Britain and the US, the International Monetary Fund (IMF) voted to approve a $2.6 billion loan to Sri Lanka. Critics saw the loan as crucial to shoring up an authoritarian regime that had ridden roughshod over its humanitarian obligations and which ought not to benefit from the fruits of international cooperation. Human Rights Watch called it 'a reward for bad behaviour, not an incentive to improve'.[53] The Sri Lankan nationalist press saw the IMF loan as yet another triumph for the plucky little nation. The government *Daily News* newspaper characterised it as a victory over the US-led colonialist 'henchmen of the West', who were no longer able to dictate terms to weaker countries. 'The centre of gravity . . . is shifting away from Europe and the United States to Asia . . . Sri Lanka, today, stands taller among the nations of the world because as a small country it stood up to bullying by big countries.'[54] Canada quickly tripled its aid to Sri Lanka, and Australia became one of the largest international bilateral donors.

The earnest post-war development and reconstruction of the country provided lucrative opportunities for corrupt politicians and officials. Not surprisingly, Basil Rajapaksa has been the prime mover behind reconstruction in the east and north of the country in the wake of the war waged by his brothers. He chaired the Presidential Task Force on Reconstruction, with another eighteen members who were largely ex-servicemen. The principal role of the task force, forcefully sold to donors as a 'coordinating mechanism', is to ensure that as much work and funds as possible are channelled through the government. Since the berating of NGOs for their corruption, mismanagement and support of the Tamil Tigers is actively promoted by the government – and is one of the favourite discussion topics in the columns and letter pages of Colombo newspapers – NGOs and UN agencies are meekly corralled into dealing with the task force. Ironically, the relatives and wives of government ministers have established NGOs in order to participate in development and reconstruction activities. There were allegations of official corruption on a massive scale related to Sri Lanka's national airline; a huge oil-hedging deal; a private airline deal; arms purchases; the creation of a wildlife park; government IT acquisitions; the purchase of cranes; the construction of reservoirs; the building of power plants; and the bilking of VAT schemes.[55]

The concerted personal deal-making and deal-reaping approach to government that characterised the Rajapaksa brothers is reflected in the biggest deal of them all: the 130-member cabinet consisting entirely of ministers of their United People's Freedom Alliance Party. Here the

Rajapaksas could genuinely claim world-beating notoriety. From just twenty-six ministers at the accession of Rajapaksa to the presidency in 2005, the brothers cajoled, bribed and flattered members of the main UNP opposition party to cross the floor in a parade of what Transparency International called 'unquestioning loyalty to the government'. The engorged cabinet, struck by palace fever, was accompanied by perks and privileges that subjected the capital city to a circus of competing convoys of ministers replete with carloads of machine-gun-wielding, lollipop-waving bodyguards. These protection squads harassed and threatened ordinary citizens, blocked roads and occasionally provided a frisson of *Schadenfreude* when they collided with each other.

While politicians competed for the crumbs, and an emasculated opposition tried to find some purchase on the slippery slope down which Sri Lanka's democracy was sliding, power and decision-making became more and more centralised. It was striking how often, in the telling of stories of bureaucratic stasis and government obstruction, the source of authority boiled down to one or another of the Rajapaksa brothers. When President Rajapaksa changed his travel plans and decided to return early from a trip to England to see his son's Dartmouth Naval College passing-out ceremony, he requested, and finally ordered that an outgoing Sri Lanka Airlines flight make thirty-five seats immediately available. When the general manager of the airline refused, Rajapaksa's response was to break the joint Emirates/Sri Lanka Airlines management deal that had made the formerly failing carrier a going concern. The British general manager was given seven days to leave the country.[56] As Alan Keenan from the International Crisis Group told *The Times*: 'There's always been corruption, but it's got to the point where you have to know a Rajapaksa to get something done. That's unprecedented.'

In April 2010, the newly elected President Rajapaksa, boosted by a huge majority in the recent parliamentary elections, appointed his henchman Mervyn Silva deputy media minister. The man who had boasted of killing Lasantha Wickrematunghe would now be in part responsible for the supervision, control and support of the very community he had been responsible for terrorising. The international media watchdog Reporters Without Borders posed the question: 'In what country do you appoint an arsonist to put out fires?' In his first

press conference, Silva confirmed that he would work to protect journalists, and urged them to provide balanced coverage with the homely
reminder: 'When I watch some channels they always show the holes in
the roads but never show the repaired ones – please show the repaired
roads.'

A week after Lasantha Wickrematunge's assassination, a posthu-
mous editorial was published in the *Sunday Leader*.[57] It pointed a
Claudius-like finger at his alleged killers. As his wife and children
grieved, his letter from the grave accused the government of wielding
terror as liberally as the Tamil Tigers, of using murder as a principal
tool of state control, of being 'the only country in the world routinely
to bomb its own citizens' and of hushing up the extent of its atrocities
against Tamil civilians through the use of censorship by terror. He said
that Mahinda Rajapaksa's government had betrayed the ideals of
Buddhism and in the name of patriotism had fostered corruption,
trampled on the rights of citizens and squandered public money in the
pursuit of power. He mocked the futility of the government-appointed
inquiry that he said would inevitably be called for to investigate his
death, and which was predictably established by presidential decree.
Long and chequered though the history of the media industry in Sri
Lanka was, with successive thin-skinned governments using their legislative powers to limit the power of critics, the Rajapaksa government
had cast what Wickrematunge called 'a shadow of death' across the
country, leading directly to the murder, exile and intimidation of
dozens of his journalistic colleagues. And Mahinda Rajapaksa, said
Lasantha, had been a friend.[58]

CHAPTER EIGHT

Managing the Siege

In early February 2009, north of the bombed and smoking wards of PTK hospital, a fifty-five-year-old grandmother heard and saw the signs of war as they pressed upon her home in the small village of Kombavil. Sri Lankan navy vessels swept the nearby shoreline, bottling up the remnants of the Sea Tiger boats and loosing off salvoes at Tiger targets. Kfir jets swept low over the beaches and scrub and occasionally struck targets presumed to be Tiger bunkers or vehicles. People were dying all around the district and they were mostly civilians. Krishna T, the wife of a fisherman who took his catch from the Nandikadal Lagoon on the country's north-east coast, did not know it then, but her village of tiny thatched houses with bare dirt floors would be one of the last to be overrun by the Sri Lankan army before its total victory over the Tigers.

Since the beginning of 2009, a trickle of refugees from the other side of the Vanni had begun to arrive in the village. Each day the number increased along with the boom and thunder of artillery guns, until Krishna's yard and those of her neighbours, the dirt roads between their houses and the paddy fields and coconut groves that surrounded them were teeming with tired, hungry, wounded and grieving refugees. Some had been driven from their homes almost two years before and had fled the fighting dozens of times. They had lost their houses and land, family members, their savings, and they were fast running out of options for refuge from the fighting.

A teacher from Mannar on Sri Lanka's west coast sat weeping in a corner of Krishna's home, stroking his small son. The boy's cheek was covered with a rough cloth bandage protecting the wound suffered when he had been dropped by his mother in an artillery barrage. She had been killed during the attack as they ran for shelter. Still Krishna swept the road around her home each day, marking the dust with cross-hatch patterns. Within days the swell of people would become so great that she would be carried with them from her home, across the shallow lagoon and on to the barren sand spit that would form the final frontier of the Tiger resistance, and the graveyard for some of the people who huddled in her yard.

With its defences collapsing, its manpower depleted, its lines of escape largely cut by a naval blockade and the jungles around their shrinking pocket of land awash with SLA troops, the Tamil Tigers knew that their chances of victory or decisive counter-stroke were slim. They hoped and began to count on international intervention, an intervention that could only be provoked by the plight of the hundreds of thousands of civilians trapped in a classic siege. Their last line of defence increasingly included the story being projected to the outside world of the sheer misery and perilous conditions of the civilians being pounded and driven back by the government advance.

Like the sieges of Sarajevo or Grozny, the government knew that the plight of more than 330,000 people on a tiny piece of barren land, defended by a small army of courageous fighters, was perfect stuff to ignite an international outcry. But between the claims and counter-claims of adversaries locked in a struggle for survival, misery can only be an effective tool of propaganda if recorded and widely distributed. While the government limited independent reporting on one hand, it managed to produce and disseminate a flow of reports to the national press, and to those international journalists who had obtained visas and who now sat frustrated in Colombo. In the government account, its management of the war was just fine.

The government was happy to publish evidence of Tiger atrocities. Each desperate act provided more evidence of the cultish, nihilistic, irrational and incontestable violence of the enemy. Occasional urban bus bombs in early 2009, the testimony taken from hospitalised Tamils who had been shot by the Tigers as they fled the siege, and the few attacks by Tamil light aircraft on Colombo only served to underscore the desperate nature of the rebels. Apart from its hold on the national media, the government controlled numerous official and unofficial websites located within Sri Lanka and in countries such as Sweden, Singapore and Canada. Roving self-styled Sri Lankan 'terrorism experts' eloquently explained the workings of the Tamil Tigers in international

TV studios, and backed up Sri Lanka's diplomats abroad. Carefully manufactured information converged to support the government's narrative of events.

The state-controlled press faithfully milled the statements of government ministers claiming that the violent incipient destruction of the Tamil Tigers was being pursued with very little cost to civilian life. Spokesmen touted their Zero Civilian Casualties policy, which contrived to be a guarantee that the Sri Lankan army was carefully weighing the proportions of its attacks in favour of the preservation of the lives of the hundreds of thousands of civilians trapped between the army onslaught and the desperate retreating defence thrown up by the Tamil Tigers.

On 1 February, Gotabaya Rajapaksa, in an open threat to aid workers, journalists and diplomats, told *The Island* newspaper that those undermining the war effort would 'be chased away'. He singled out CNN, the BBC and Al-Jazeera for particular mention. All of them had suggested that the government was not telling the truth, was concealing the numbers of people being killed and was using heavy weaponry in areas of civilian concentration. On 6 February, angered by the statement from the ICRC that hundreds of civilians had been killed in the fighting, an orchestrated mob of around 150 people passed through army-manned checkpoints in Colombo and stoned the organisation's main office in the country.

Foreign journalists inside Sri Lanka, and those trying to report the story from outside the borders, began to sense that no statement coming from the Sri Lankan government could be trusted, whether it was a public undertaking that the government was not shelling hospitals and health centres, or an assurance from the president to the UN Secretary General that his forces were not using heavy weapons. The exasperated *New York Times* correspondent Somini Sengupta, prevented by the government from actually entering the country, took to inserting as a matter of course into her copy that 'it is impossible to know what is happening behind the frontline because the government bars journalists from travelling to the war zone, except on guided tours of areas seized by the army'.

The actual number of civilians caught in the zone was a matter of considerable contention between the UN, the Tamil Tigers and the government, and yet it is central to a complete understanding of the proportions and impact of this war. Population figures in Sri Lanka are heartily political, and there had been no reliable census conducted in the areas under Tamil Tiger control for almost three decades.* In 2008, Tamil Tiger functionaries claimed that 450,000 people were inside the Vanni. A higher population figure strengthened the Tiger claim on the international political stage and amongst the Tamil diaspora to a Tamil homeland.[1] It also meant that they could claim greater benefits from the Sri Lankan government, which had continued to exercise its writ over Tiger-controlled territory by supplying a full range of government health and education services.

An inflated figure obliged the various NGOs and UN agencies to allocate more funds and programmes to Tamil Tiger areas. This raised the hackles of the government and strengthened the legitimacy of their complaint – as well as the attendant conspiracy theory fed to the Sri Lankan public by government officials and absorbed by a largely compliant press – that the international community was supporting the Tigers. The dark plot included suggestions that a divided Sri Lanka suited those powers interested in the island's strategic Indian Ocean position, and the imminent discovery of oil reserves in the Palk Straits.

In early 2008, the World Food Programme (WFP) had, with the agreement of the government, been using a figure of 350,000 people in order to plan its food distributions. By early 2009, that number had been whittled down: the government insisted that many people had left the battle zone because of the war. The UN had half-heartedly agreed to an estimate of some 230,000 people, a figure that it had negotiated with the most important social service ministries in Colombo, such as the health ministry and the Ministry of Education. It would transpire that this figure was a gross underestimate.[2] Nevertheless, in January, the government publicly scoffed, and denounced what it called 'the UN figures' as fabrications. President Rajapaksa opined that there were 'no more than 50,000' civilians inside the steadily diminishing battle zone. Increasingly, the notion of any people at all left in the area who were not fighters seemed a chimera.

In February, after the first significant numbers of civilians had escaped the fighting and been transported to military internment

---

* The last island-wide census was held in 1981.

camps around the town of Vavuniya, the foreign minister Rohita Bolla-gallama asserted that a total of just 70,000 civilians remained trapped. His deputy, the current Sri Lankan ambassador to the UN, Palitha Kohona, insisted that the figure of 230,000 people still being used by the UN was 'an exaggeration'.[3] But logic, credibility, and the accuracy of their statements regarding the conduct of war were rarely issues for the government. Their aim remained the shrouding of any clear under-standing of the fate of civilians, an interest well served by the growing frustration of the international press at their inability to establish just how many people were actually caught up in the siege.

In the heady days following the end of the war in May 2009, a senior government official gleefully admitted that the government's insist-ence on lower population figures had been a ploy. A confused figure allowed the government a great deal of latitude, and created doubt and confusion. Accuracy and reliable figures, or at least reliable estimates from authoritative sources, are vital as journalists seek to construct stories that bring home to their publics tales of suffering in distant lands in what are often extremely complex political and social settings. Without a concrete number, the siege of the Cage remained abstract and remote, the population of Tamils a ghostly figment. Journalists were unable to confidently quantify the magnitude of the suffering being inflicted.

A lower population figure also created leverage for the govern-ment as it sought to restrict the flow of UN convoys carrying food, vital medical supplies and plastic sheeting into the siege zone. Finally, and most ominously of all, without an accurate figure it would be impossible to tell how many people had been killed at the war's end merely from those who finally made it out alive. As the government 'rescued' tens of thousands of civilians in several batches between January and May, but did not mention the dead, it left an impression that those who came out accounted for all those who had been besieged. The government could claim, as it did, the successful and bloodless rescue of the captive population, as well as vindication of its methods.

One man, however, a senior Tamil civil servant employed by the government but living in Tiger-controlled territory, sounded a consistent note of warning that the figure was far closer to the actual number of around 300,000 people who eventually emerged from the conflict zone. Throughout the final year of the conflict, he had continued to insist to the UN by telephone from the Vanni that there were 330,000 people living in Tiger-controlled territory, a figure that may or may not have included official and unofficial estimates of the active-service Tiger cadres who were thought to be under arms – anywhere between 2,000 and 3,000 men and women.

The very notion of who and what constituted a 'Tiger' eludes definition. Reported in *The Island* on 19 August 2006, the army chief of staff General Sarath Fonseka had estimated Tiger strength at 8,000 to 10,000, of which just 2,000 were considered 'battle-hardened cadres'. In the same article, the Senior Army Coordinator for Military Operations, Major Upali Rajapaksa, said that of the Tiger forces, half were made up of child soldiers. By November 2008, the estimate of surviving cadres was just 4,000.[4] And yet in October 2009, General Fonseka said that a total of 22,000 Tiger cadres had been killed in the final phase of the war. Taking the army chief at his word (and Fonseka was not a man noted for playing to the gallery), a majority of people who could be conceived of as bearing arms and thus as legitimate military targets, were pressed into service in the latter stage of the war. A vast number of these were probably teenagers and novice fighters.

Extensive professional investigations conducted by the International Crisis Group since the end of the war concluded that tens of thousands of civilians probably perished during these final months. Shortly after the war, one of the most vocal Sri Lankan civil servants, and now a member of parliament, Rajiva Wijesinha, rejected the then current UN figure of 7,000 civilians dead. He estimated instead 3,000 to 5,000, and said 'the figures went up very badly'.[5] While the basis of his estimate is not clear, nevertheless, it was the first such admission by the government that the battle had exacted a terrible toll on civilians.

Then, in June 2010, an Indian army doctor who had been in charge of the field hospital that had been the primary care centre for civilians as they emerged from the siege zone broke his silence. In an interview with the *Hindustan Times*, the unnamed doctor said that the true death toll had been 'brushed under the carpet'. His teams had treated thousands of Tamils, 80 per cent of whom had said that they, or somebody they knew, had reported an injury or death of a relative or friend. In addition, 80 per cent of children the Indians had treated had been malnourished, and thousands of children had been treated for battle-field injuries. [6]

The Sri Lankan army had failed to prick a hole in the first so-called No Fire Zone that ideally would have drained the battlefield of most civilians. The battle continued to force civilians in a headlong retreat away from the front lines. But in early February, the first serious indications emerged of the brittleness of the Tamil Tiger lines and the willingness of individual Tiger commanders to allow civilians to escape. Barely two weeks after the bombardment of Convoy 11, 58th Division troops overran 20,000 civilians crouching in bunkers inside the No Fire Zone. Using loudspeakers as they inched forward through the jungles and across the rice paddy fields, troops summoned people towards their lines, despite the ferocious fighting and shelling all around.

It was a fraught experience. Ordinary soldiers had to determine if there were Tiger fighters among the desperate people who had heard the summons and were waiting for the battle to pass over them. After crouching for days on end without cooked food or water in shallow trenches, bodily shielding their children, people rose abruptly and dashed through the underbrush to what they hoped was safety. Sometimes nervous soldiers shot them. Sometimes they were caught in crossfire. For the first time, reports began to reach the UN that Tiger cadres were shooting at people to prevent them from escaping.[7] On the whole, however, the vast majority of people who escaped seem to have been received with relative restraint and care by the front-line SLA troops, who quickly passed them up the line for tea, rice and first aid. The faceless enemy, such a source of terror for the young peasant men and women of southern Sri Lanka who made up the majority of the troops, were suddenly given a human aspect, as thin, bedraggled women clutching children to their breasts and pleading in a foreign tongue fell at their feet.

Around another 300,000 people had decided that their best chances lay to the north-east. On 12 February, unaffected by the failure of the first No Fire Zone, the government declared a second, this time on the twelve-kilometre-long sliver of coastal land next to the Nandikadal lagoon.[8] From this point on, the army plan was to drive people into a single corner of the Vanni from where nobody could escape, and attempt to whittle down the Tiger resistance through attrition. Great streams of people packed the dirt lanes and tiny paths of the Vanni pocket as people fled on foot, bicycle, tractor and bullock cart to escape the onslaught and headed to the new NFZ. The refugees discarded whatever they could no longer afford to carry, balancing their worldly goods against the need for speed and their depleting physical reserves. Incoming shellfire from the army and the report of outgoing shells from the few dozen Tiger artillery pieces whistled and thundered across the landscape. At impact, many sought safety by throwing themselves to the ground to escape the deadly fusillade of shrapnel, but others died on their feet, too fatigued to repeat the exercise. Still the streams of refugees trudged north towards Krishna's village, knowing that the end was near, yet still hoping for a counter-stroke from their Supreme Leader.

By mid-February, the overwhelming government forces were pressing down from the north, up from the south, and from the west along the A35 road. The army had a total of some 50,000 front-line troops ringing the Tamil Tigers. They were met by an astounding level of resistance from the guerrillas, who now had virtually no line of retreat left to them and certainly no means of escape. A last fortified position lay in the hamlet of Anandapuram, less than two kilometres from PTK. This final redoubt frustrated the SLA advance for almost two months, despite the Tiger positions being pounded daily by multi-barrel rocket fire, artillery and up to a hundred sorties a day flown by the air force. It is thought that some 600 cadres held out, and that several hundred actually managed to survive. These, including almost the entire senior leadership, retreated across the lagoon into the second No Fire Zone. It was a fanatical resistance, which says much about the core fighting capabilities of the Tigers.

In 2002, many of the best fighters had left 'the Movement' in the expectation that the peace agreement would last. Four years later, when the Tigers began to recruit once more in readiness for a return to the fight, few of the 5,000 battle-tested demobbed fighters could be induced back into the ranks. The Tigers introduced a policy of enforced conscription. There was mass discontent as families were compelled to surrender one member to do service. As the war gathered momentum, more and more untested cadres were thrust into front-line positions. By the time the Nandikadal lagoon had been cut off and surrounded, the army of thousands was a straw man, with each unit of fifteen usually including just two or three experienced Tigers, whose own will to fight was increasingly tested by the chaotic retreat, massive losses and concern about the fate of their families. In effect, the conscription policies of the Tamil Tigers soured popular morale, robbed them of vital support and ultimately contributed directly to their defeat.

Krishna T, whose village had been overwhelmed by distraught refugees, says that she had become disenchanted with the Tamil Tigers. With her two daughters, two sons and five small grandchildren, she finally fled her home and crossed the lagoon on 16 February to the long sand spit that formed the second No Fire Zone at the coastal edge of the Cage. There they sat in a rough shelter of plastic sheeting and palm fronds tied down over a frame of coconut planks and twine that had been built over a circular hollow dug in the ground to protect them from shrapnel. Thousands of other families sat in their own dugouts all around. Each day they supplemented the food they had saved with handouts of humanitarian aid that was still being distributed by the dedicated government agents, who continued to ostensibly provide social services, and by workers from the Tigers' own Tamil Relief Organisation.[9]

They avoided leaving the hollow. Shells intermittently thudded into the zone, sometimes intentionally lobbed, sometimes overshots or ricochets from the pitched battles being fought across the lagoon. One shell landed in front of their shelter, but failed to explode. People who had experienced bombardment over the years were expert at anticipating the shells from the initial report to the whistle overhead seconds before it found its mark. By Krishna's reckoning, and from what the people who were camped all around her said, government shellfire had caused most of the deaths in the first NFZ and the areas around it. Inside the second, the picture was a more complex one. The Tiger recruitment drives among the young, a paucity of medicine and food, sheer exhaustion and fear, constant small-arms overshots, rocket-propelled grenades, air attacks on Tiger targets, the shooting of people when they tried to escape and a growing hunger all took their toll.

Krishna's eldest son, a man of thirty, had been injured in the shoulder and leg by a shell blast. She had helped to carry him a kilometre to one of the primitive health points now being run by the Tamil government since the evacuation of the last hospitals around PTK. He was given a Panadol because drugs were in short supply. What shrapnel that could

be seen was removed, his wound was dressed and he was sent back to
the family dugout to make way for more serious injuries. Hundreds of
badly wounded lay around the health points, sheltered from the baking
sun and monsoonal rains only by rough lean-tos. The unnecessary
suffering of the wounded was, according to one battle-seasoned ICRC
official who helped to evacuate wounded civilians by ship from the
beaches throughout the three-month siege, 'the most terrible thing I
have ever seen or imagined that I might see'.

The government had apparently calculated that it was better to let
civilians die through lack of medicine rather than risk supplying the
Tigers with drugs. The UN and ICRC repeatedly purchased, imported
and supervised the transport to the Vanni of these vital basic drugs 'in
partnership' with the Ministry of Health, only to have those shipments
delayed, returned or otherwise stymied by government employees and
the SLA. Just as with visas or food convoys or with hundreds of other
requests made to the government, nothing was ever directly denied.
Instead, permission was given when it must have been known that the
majority of aid would be prevented from ever arriving.

Nor in these last months was there enough food to go around.
Children who eventually emerged from the zone were malnourished,
and hungry. Because of the mass displacement of civilians over the
preceding two years, the government knew that supplies of humanitarian food aid were vital for this fragile population on the move.
With hundreds of thousands of people away from their land and
homes, without the capacity to earn money or cultivate crops,
humanitarian supplies of food and medicine were their only option.
Since the government knew that its own persistent reductions of
population estimates were untrue, it must be assumed that the restric-
tion of the quantity of food going into the siege zone during the final
four months was a tactic of deliberate starvation. The words of
Palitha Kohona in a radio interview on 11 March sound rather sinister
in hindsight: 'Don't forget that these are our people, and it is our
responsibility to feed them.'[10]

On the coastal sand spit to which Krishna and hundreds of thousands of others had retreated, the daily life of besiegement swung from
boredom and discomfort to sheer terror and grief. People were
randomly killed and injured as they walked, chatted, played and
queued. The villages on the sand spit had been badly hit by the tsunami

in 2004, but international aid groups had restored a number of wells for the inhabitants. People lined up for water or food for hours in the open, and many dozens were killed or injured as they waited. It was hot, and in April, heavy monsoonal showers flooded almost a third of the land occupied by the refugees, adding to the general misery and squalor, spoiling food supplies and spreading human refuse throughout the area. People mostly spent their time huddled inside their shelters, trying to prevent their children from going out to play, and during some of the most intense shelling not emerging for three days.

Despite the presence of death, fear and grief, life quickly assumed another kind of normality. 'People still greeted each other in the morning with big smiles, and enquired after each other's health, and told jokes,' said Krishna. 'They tried to beautify their surroundings.' There was a shortage of material for everything, and people were compelled to use their colourful, expensive wedding saris, which are usually handed down from mother to daughter. Bandages were made from a rainbow of materials, and tailors stitched these glorious garments into sandbags so that shelters resembled the bright confusion of Hindu temples. 'You couldn't stop kids flying their kites. You would trip over the twine as you walked around. And they were ingenious, figuring out kites from the skeletons of palm fronds and plastic bags. It was all such a game for them. Many kids died because their parents couldn't keep them inside.'

People supplemented their diet from the sea, and families spent mornings collecting cockles along the seashore and casting nets for shrimps and small fish. Whole families were destroyed by single shells along the beaches or in their bunkers, and covered over with sand by neighbours, their deaths unrecorded. 'When you see so much death,' said Krishna, 'life becomes cheap, and your own life becomes cheap.' When forced to search for food or water, or to go to the toilet, or to take an injured or sick relative to one of the makeshift medical points, they faced exposure to shellfire and overhead small-arms fire, since the whole area was well within range of the army assault rifles, quite apart from heavier armaments. Children lay dead on the beach, felled where they played. When people were injured, they avoided the trek to the health point if possible, having learned that there were no anaesthetics, and that harried doctors would at best bandage them and send them on their way. Nevertheless, a serious injury meant a certain kind of luck, in so far as a person and some of their family might qualify for evacuation on one of the ICRC ships.

Between February and May, government officials continued to insist that 'not a single drop of civilian blood' was being spilt. As the injured evacuated by the ICRC ships began to overwhelm the hospitals in government territory, hundreds of Sinhalese doctors and nurses were drafted in from the south. Doctors who had met the first seaborne evacuations had expected to find that the Tigers would be easy to distinguish from civilians, in accordance with government propaganda: those suffering illness and disease would be civilians, while those with wounds would be fighters. Instead, they were confronted by dozens of children who had been blinded, burned, maimed and crippled. Sri Lankan doctors are formidably professional and their care of the wounded was excellent. As they worked long hours in well-guarded hospitals where policemen stood sentinel even in children's wards, the medical personnel began to join the dots. Soon their accounts began to supplant the official reports and spread to the broader public.

During the course of research for this book, dozens of Tamils described the Sinhalese as inherently kind and gentle people. The front-line soldiers who received the first civilians as they escaped to government lines, those who guarded them in the camps and the civilian and military doctors who provided vital treatment distinguished themselves most commonly through their mercy and care. In Colombo, as television images appeared of those civilians who had escaped and were now in internment camps, many dozens of private individuals, schools, banks, religious institutions, department stores and newspapers began drives to raise money, food and clothing for the bedraggled 'enemy', to the considerable credit of a population that had lived in fear of random Tamil Tiger terrorism for three decades. They had also been subjected to constant government propaganda that scarcely made a distinction between the Tiger war machine and ordinary Tamils.

One source of information that constantly defied the government version of events was the small group of Tamil government doctors trapped inside the siege zone. These men,* and the nursing staff with

---

* The particular group of doctors who occupied senior government positions and spoke with the press were all men. There were many female doctors, nurses and volunteers at the hospitals and the makeshift medical points inside the battle zone.

them, bravely continued their work almost until the final day of the siege. They stitched, bandaged, administered and, perhaps most importantly of all, maintained careful records of their patients, even amidst the chaos of war and the deaths of their staff and volunteers. Instinctively they understood better than most that the only gravestone that those who died would receive would be in the form of the ticks and marks on a hospital casualty form. The compilation of memory, as well as a cumulative systematic record of the scale of deaths, came largely from their hands. Often the UN would speak to the doctors calling from their radiotelephones, listening to their pleas for help and intervention while the dull sound of exploding shells crackled up the line as a curious backdrop to the disembodied conversations.

With most civilians on the sand spit, and surrounded in a small area, Tiger recruitment parties now swept the Cage. Families engaged in cat-and-mouse games to hide their children. The squad leaders were motivated by self-preservation as much as anything else, filling quotas that helped them and their own families to evade recruitment to the front lines. Open confrontations increased, with squads dealing out summary executions when people resisted, and dozens of families ganging up to disarm and shoot or beat to death recruitment squads attempting to take their children.

In early March 2009, a Tiger recruitment party surrounded Krishna's family dugout and called for her twenty-seven-year-old younger son to come out. Krishna hurled chilli powder into the squad leader's eyes while her son dashed to escape. He was caught and dragged away, while Krishna was thrashed and taken as well. For two weeks she was chained to a tree in an enclosure, where she watched teenage conscripts being brought in all day and throughout the night. Many wept for their mothers for the first few days they were there. Hundreds of interviews conducted by UNICEF after the war reveal that a majority of those recruited in the final weeks were probably teenage children. This account was given to UNICEF by one young survivor whose sixteen-year-old sister had been recruited:

On that morning when she was recruited my aunt heard about it and came to tell my mother. We knew the rule about each family contributing [a member to the Tigers] and so we thought to ask for them to swap – her for me. We thought it would be difficult for her if

she were recruited to run away. I told my mother I could go with them
and then I would escape later. So we went to the LTTE camp but at the
gate a cadre told my mother not to take me inside or I'd be recruited,
so I turned back home. The next day the cadres came to the hut – my
mother argued and told them they had already taken my sister, but they
insisted. I was taken to dig trenches and after we moved around and
were sent to the [front line]. After two weeks on the [front line], my
friend and I were put on the checkpoints together with a cadre who
wanted to escape. So one evening we threw our weapons away and
ran. I ran back to my hut but my family was gone and some female
cadres were there. They told me not to stay or someone would recruit
me. They told me the civilians were all moving in a big group and to
join them and [cross to the government lines]. I ran with those people
and met a relative who said my mother was near the front, so I went
forward and found her and my sister (who had escaped after 3 days) and
we crossed out together.

The revolution was literally consuming its children. This nihilistic
final phase was perhaps the logical outcome of a cult of sacrifice developed in the pursuit of national liberation by Sri Lanka's Tamils. The
tactic of forced recruitment reached younger and younger children,
who were as incapable of fighting as they were juvenile. Merciless
though this forced recruitment was, there is also compelling evidence
of commanders and cadres who helped people to escape across the
lagoon by turning their backs, showing them paths to the SLA or
fighting back other cadres who fired on those fleeing. When pressed to
choose, many opted for survival for themselves and others as army
shells shredded the dream of Tamil Eelam.

After the first week in April, the small fortified redoubt of Anandapuram had fallen. The UN's humanitarian affairs chief, John Holmes,
had warned of a possible bloodbath should civilians and fighters be
pressed together inside the Cage, with no room for the innocent to
escape. Those Tiger fighters left from Anandapuram now fell back on
the sand spit to mount a final stand. The SLA moved up to the perimeter of the Cage, with one division facing a line of Tiger defences
across the north of the strip, one division facing the Tigers across the
small sea channel that let into the lagoon at the spit's southern end, and
the majority of troops massed along the western shoreline separated

from the Tiger lines by the shallow lagoon in between. For the next few weeks, the army probed the Tiger defences, and calculated how to separate civilians from cadres. It was feared that the elusive Praba-kharan would escape, or that an internationally brokered peace deal would see him left to live.

But the war was far from finished for well over 200,000 civilians. Sieges are as old as warfare, and certainly pre-date walled cities, as bands of hunter-gatherers encountered each other in the open field and sought to protect their hunting grounds and water sources. They can be entirely military confrontations, where one adversary has fallen back to a defen-sive position and resists until their food, weapons, water or defences are spent, or until the attacker can afford to maintain the siege no further. At the other extreme, they can be mostly civilian affairs, with men, women and children sheltering behind a line of defence manned by fighters drawn substantially from the besieged population.

In the series of rearguard actions after the fall of Kilinochchi, the numbers of legendary and lesser fighters had been considerably whit-tled down, and the command structure of the Tigers hollowed out. In the battle around Anandapuram, the Tigers lost hundreds of their finest men and women. There were probably no more than 1,500 core fighters by the middle of February when the final stage of the siege began at the Nandikadal lagoon. There were thousands of other conscripts, but they were no match for the front-line units of the SLA. Yet the government still could not resolve the dilemma of how to detach civilians from the battle zone. Although the government gener-ally dominated information coming from the battlefield, enough was known through the UN's network, through satellite imagery and through the Indian intelligence network to rule out an onslaught that took no regard of civilian life. But what was the solution?

Customs of war that guide and restrain the behaviour of armies and the use of weapons have ancient antecedents. One can delve into the canon of a number of civilisations to find examples of kings and commanders restricting the anticipated bloodthirstiness of their troops. In the Old Testament's Deuteronomy, there are injunctions against the cutting of enemy fruit trees and the mistreatment of women. In the seventh century, the first caliph and friend of the Prophet Muhammad, Abu Bakr, instructs his troops thus: 'Do no betray or misappropriate any part of the booty; do not practise treachery or mutilation. Do not kill a young child, an old man, or a woman. Do not uproot or burn palms or cut down fruitful trees. Do not slaughter a sheep or a cow or a camel, except for food.' Islamic legal treatises from the ninth century explored the application of military jurisprudence to what would come to be called 'humanitarian' aspects of conflict, including conduct on the battlefield, the protection of non-combatants and prisoners, and even the use of poisonous weapons. Interestingly, Islamic jurisprudence, concerned with a burgeoning multi-ethnic caliphate around the rim of the Mediterranean, recognised the differences between wars between empires, involving people of different creeds, and wars within empires, when co-religionists and those of a common identity would face each other. These treatises were like guidebooks of moral philosophy for leaders at war. They were not legal codes in the narrowest sense, and made no suggestion of legal sanction if the suggested rules of conduct were broken. Rather, the individual actions of men engaged in war were scrutinised for what those actions said about the commanders – for the moral health of the commanders as much as anything. To what extent, in the course of achieving a victory, were they wise, just, proportionate, merciful or excessively homicidal?

Today, legal restrictions on a commander that are meant to prevent the deliberate or reckless killing of civilians and those *hors de combat* are increasingly severe. The industrialisation of warfare, whereby the Gatling machine gun had multiplied the capacity for one soldier to destroy many, worried nineteenth-century military theorists and commanders. The US Civil War forever changed notions of what is considered acceptable in the waging of war. In 1863, two years into the conflict, President Lincoln signed General Order No. 100. Under what is now better known as the Lieber Code, the wholesale slaughter of the enemy, the unjustified killing of prisoners of war, the use of torture, summary reprisals, the use of hostages and the inhumane treatment of an occupied population were prohibited, or prescribed and limited. Without effective sanctions, these prescriptions had before been left solely to the judgement, discretion and personal morality of a commander in the field.

The Lieber Code later formed the basis for the first multilateral effort at codifying customary law.[11] The Hague Conventions of 1899 and 1907 recognised restrictions on battlefield behaviour and codified the rights and obligations of belligerents, as well as occupied popula-tions. With this positive legal recognition, the notions that internationally recognised crimes can be committed in the course of war and that commanders are legally responsible for the actions of their troops entered into force in the modern world. While the Hague Conventions were primarily designed to govern the waging of war, the later Geneva Conventions of 1925, 1949 and 1977 were more narrowly tailored to deal with humanitarian concepts, such as the treatment of the wounded, prisoners of war, civilians and populations under occu-pation. Somewhere in between the Hague and Geneva Conventions was a restrictive line defining how commanders must account for people in the path of battle, but who were not participants in the combat.

Civilians have almost always been a tactical element in warfare, and as such a part of a battle plan. For example, the withholding of food and water, along with the attrition of the fighting itself, is elemental to siege warfare. A weak army retreats to a place of strong defence and ample supplies, which is often a city brimming with sympathetic civilians. It is the natural place for the last stand of an exhausted or outnumbered force. Typically, the more civilians there are confined within the bound-aries of a siege, the more the military advantage accrues to the attacking force, because the burden of maintaining that population falls on the shoulders of the defender. Civilians will naturally resist an invader at first, because they value their freedom and will defend their families. The panic and fear that arrives with an encroaching enemy morphs into a defiant mood that is vital to the defending army. A besieged population will tolerate terrible hardships and physical losses.

Hunger, however, is a great leveller, and erodes at notions of freedom, turning a resistant mood. In *The Art of War*, Machiavelli approvingly quotes the tactics of Alexander the Great when he drives people from outlying towns into the besieged city of Leucadia in order to force starvation. Inflicting hunger on a population enclosed and surrounded is a sure way to force a positive result for the encircling force, because, as when enduring incessant bombardment, people will eventually seek their survival and that of their families by either risking death to break out or rebelling against the prevailing authority. Starva-tion is a way to break the collective will to resist, and to divide people as each person individually re-evaluates their priorities and loyalties.

It was a long way from the early efforts in The Hague to limit 'total war' to the comparatively recent recognition of what we know as crimes against humanity, or concepts like the crime of genocide. For example, during the Nuremberg trials after the Second World War, Allied judges acquitted the German field marshal von Leeb for ordering his troops to fire on civilians who were trying to leave the city of Leningrad. More afraid of the German guns than they were of starvation, men, women and children trying to flee across the frozen wastes were forced back inside the besieged city. A million civilians eventually died from starvation, but the judges could not find a positive precedent in customary or treaty law to suggest that the field marshal should have created a military disadvantage for himself by letting the fleeing Russians pass through his lines.

Today, armies engaged in battle are guided by the concept of military necessity weighed against the actual costs of an attack in the course of the shortest path to victory. Those costs include money, time and the lives of soldiers under command as well as the consequences for civilians who are in the line of fire because of unavoidable circumstances. Wholesale and militarily unjustifiable slaughter is clearly prohibited under international laws that guide the conduct of war. In a battle, a commander is obliged to take account of the cost to civilians, to weigh that cost against the value of his objective and to decide if, proportionally, the chosen path of attack can be justified. Modern armies, particularly those of democracies, are at pains to demonstrate the discrimination with which they weigh the proportions of an attack, involving careful video presentations, descriptions of the value of the target and legal justification in the form of military lawyers who have vetted the targets and objectives.

The SLA was equally at pains to demonstrate its mastery of the battle space. The defence secretary was never slow to show the diplomatic corps that the SLA possessed and used to great effect the constant stream of footage from a number of Israeli-supplied drones. It served up relatively slick presentations of the progress of its battles to a press corps that had no real battlefield access whatsoever, save the versions presented by the protagonists. The army's repeated demonstrations of its mastery of the intelligence it obtained from drones was also proof that its command decisions could rely on real-time close-observation imagery from the battlefield. Even for a relatively poor military, the old

adage about 'the fog of war' had been largely dissipated by modern
battlefield communications.[12]

The commander of a well-equipped modern army can, in theory,
survey a target, choose the appropriate (and possibly 'smart') weaponry available and weigh the cost of his or her strike against the number
of civilians likely to be killed. Sri Lanka, however, was relatively poor
in terms of smart weaponry, and relied overwhelmingly on basic high-
explosive ordnance fired at a distance by its 300-odd artillery pieces,
albeit with sophisticated radar targeting equipment. Yet as the wholesale bombardment of Convoy 11 showed, something was clearly amiss.
Somewhere between the army's state-of-the-art drone intelligence, the
battlefield supremacy it held after the fall of Mullaitivu on 26 January,
its apparently blunderbuss use of artillery and the most credible current
estimates of the final death toll of civilians, lies the point at which the
legality of individual command decisions broke down.

In April 2009, the UN Human Rights Council voted for an inquiry into
whether or not crimes had been committed by Israel in the course of
its invasion of Gaza between late December 2008 and 18 January 2009.[13]
The Israel Defence Force had invaded in order to quell the barrage of
rockets being fired into Israel by Hamas guerrillas (or 'terrorists', as the
Israelis would have it). The short conflict had killed somewhere
between 295 and 926 civilians (according to the Israelis and Palestinians
respectively), a third to a quarter of whom were children. Richard
Goldstone, a South African judge, was appointed to lead the investigating panel, and in October 2009 its findings were made public. The
Goldstone commissioners asserted that both sides had, prima facie,
committed war crimes and possible crimes against humanity. They
recommended that if the protagonists failed to credibly investigate the
allegations, then the matter should be referred to the International
Criminal Court.

In Gaza, an invasion force consisting of 176,000 Israeli men and
women with tanks, aircraft and gunboats faced a force of 20,000 Palestinian fighters seeded amongst a civilian population of one and a half
million people. The three-week battle resulted in the deaths of possibly
close to a thousand civilians, a tragedy deemed worthy of international
judicial investigation according to the United Nations Human Rights
Council. In the case of Sri Lanka during the first five months of 2009,

roughly 160,000 soldiers, sailors and airmen faced off against a core force of perhaps 2,000 to 5,000 Tamil Tiger fighters, seeded amidst a civilian population of some 330,000. The sixteen-week siege led to the deaths of between 10,000 and 40,000 people. If the Sri Lankan example is compared with Gaza, and the figures extrapolated to make the point, the comparable death toll in the Palestinian population would have been between 50,000 and 200,000 people killed.

Although all wars are profoundly different in the eyes of the protagonists, there are often methodological similarities that underpin each, thus making them worthy of, and wide open to, comparison. In both the instances above, one side was significantly stronger militarily than the other, with that side wielding a mytho-historical document that purported to trump the claims of the other to the land under contest. Both the Gaza invasion and Eelam War IV were fought between two distinct ethnic groups who heatedly argued their differences, but who were umbilically joined by claims to the same land, by proximity, by strong cultural affinities, by the assertion of religious righteousness and by the shared blind bitterness of their struggle. Such conflicts spawn harrowing identity wars that numb men to their own instincts for empathy, and propel them irresistibly to infanticide.

The Israeli invasion was carried out against a force of tough and dedicated fighters who drew their defence from the sanctuary of the urban battleground, surrounded by civilians. The bulwark of civilian Palestinian men, women and children was key to the military strategy of the Hamas fighters, just as it was to the Tamil Tigers in their defence of the shrinking Vanni pocket. In both Gaza and the Vanni, children were raised from an early age with a vehemently nationalistic political consciousness. In Gaza, six-year-old children sang liberation songs in school, learned from exercise books with photos of Quassam rockets on the cover and played with replica assault rifles with a very different resonance from the games of children in most other countries. So too in Kilinochchi, where young children sang liberation songs, venerated photos of the Supreme Leader and knew of fathers, sisters, brothers, uncles and neighbours who played some part in the Tamil Tiger movement. When an invader is charged with extracting an enemy force from a civilian population under these circumstances, the line between civilians and lethal foe can seem elusive.

And yet, as the Goldstone Report made clear, it is the job of military commanders and the soldiers under their command to define and tread the line that exists. International law provides the prescriptions with which a commander can locate that line. The burden is even more onerous for the forces of a sovereign government engaged in a civil war, which derives its authority and the very reason for its existence from the laws that it extends to protect its citizens – those that it proclaims to be 'rescuing'.[14] The Goldstone Report found that in the case of the Gaza invasion, breaches of international law had resulted in the death or injury of many of the civilians who found themselves in the line of fire. What standards was the UN Human Rights Council applying to the Israel Defence Force's conduct during its invasion of Gaza, and what standards was it using for Sri Lanka's conduct as it eradicated the Tamil Tigers?[15]

The Geneva Conventions of 1949 had made only passing reference to civil war, a mode of conflict that would come to dominate the late twentieth century. In the mid twentieth century, in a throwback to a strictly Westphalian conception of sovereignty, civil wars were still seen as the sole business of individual governments. The primacy of sovereignty in modern international relations was somewhat challenged by the Additional Protocols to the Geneva Conventions of 1977. These protocols sought to restrict the actions of nations as they prosecuted wars within their borders, but relatively few nations took to them in the way they had in 1949. Sri Lanka, for one, has never acceded to the protocols. The dozens of mostly small nations that had achieved independence since the end of the Second World War, many of them struggling with issues of development and governance that kept them in a permanent state of frailty relative to more developed countries, tended to view the protocols as unwelcome interference in their policing of internal affairs.

Just days after the end of the war in Sri Lanka in May 2009, the UN Human Rights Council issued a resolution that lauded the Sri Lankan defeat of the Tamil Tigers, criticised alleged Tamil Tiger war crimes, but made no mention of any allegations regarding the SLA's conduct of the war. It was a bare-faced assertion of the rights of sovereignty trumping the right to life, and an example of the inherent double standards of the Council. It ignored altogether the plight of the hundreds of thousands of civilians then interned in camps. It did not address the manner in which the SLA had wrested the civilian population from the control of the Tamil Tigers through massive bombardment. Nor did it mention the bombing of hospitals, the withholding of medicine and drugs or the denial of food.

In the wake of the ethnic conflicts of the 1990s in places such as Yugoslavia and Rwanda, efforts were made to define the circumstances under which joint international forces, acting with legal authority, might intervene to prevent crimes against humanity. Professor Alex Bellamy has written extensively on the uncertainly developing international doctrine of R2P: the notion that nations have a positive 'responsibility to protect' their civilian population, failing which, and provided that a crisis meets certain criteria, that responsibility falls by default to the international collective. He notes that whereas in the 1990s the discussion was about infringing sovereignty, 'nobody today seriously posits that a government can do what it wants with its citizens, or that the international community doesn't have an intrinsic interest in internal conflicts with potential grave crimes'. Regardless, and whilst the concept of R2P remains highly controversial, it is now generally accepted that The Hague and Geneva Conventions and Protocols, whether acceded to or not by individual nations, have assumed the weight of customary law because they have been broadly accepted by a majority of nations as good law. Whether war crimes are committed between nations or during a civil war, they are considered so heinous that they are an affront to all humanity.

Aware of this emerging primacy of responsibility, the Rajapaksa government peppered its pronouncements with references to the responsibility it held for its besieged Tamil citizens, even as it was bombarding them and withholding food and medicine. They could do so because of their domination of the narrative emerging from inside the battle zone. While the Tamil Tigers preserved the Vanni Tamils as a human shield against attack, the Sri Lankan government deliberately denied the besieged population food, medicine, shelter and medical and aid personnel. When impartial and neutral aid organisations such as the UN humanitarian agencies and the Red Cross persistently attempted to gain access to the Vanni Tamils with land- and seaborne convoys, the government found many ways to obstruct them, whether by declaring that they could not guarantee the safety of aid personnel, by outright refusal to allow certain kinds of aid or by finding ways to slow, delay or spoil humanitarian operations. The numbers who died from hunger were probably negligible, and certainly inconsiderable when compared with those who died by shot and shell. The figure for those who died because they did not have access to medical personnel, or because the necessary medicines were not available, was probably significantly higher, and both the Tamil Tigers and the government bear varying degrees of responsibility for this shortage. Considering that they had played a part in driving them from their homes and into the second NFZ, the government bears considerable moral and legal responsibility for the predicament in which the besieged 330,000 found themselves, and for the resulting deaths.[16]

It is not that the SLA should have ceded its right to conquer its Tamil Tiger enemy, and to extinguish the practice of terrorism from its sovereign soil, but at the point at which it arrived on the shores of the lagoon, with soldiers and armaments outnumbering its enemy by a factor of at least thirty to one, did those in command correctly weigh the advantages of an SLA assault versus the cost to civilian lives? With an effective land and sea blockade, and escape virtually impossible for the Tiger leadership (an assertion borne out by the eventual death or capture of the entire core of the Tiger command), was there a less costly alternative to the wholesale bombardment undertaken by the armed forces? Did those with command responsibility scorn the efforts of the Tiger leadership to surrender, a fact that inevitably resulted in further unnecessary civilian casualties? Or were the deaths of between 10,000 and 40,000 people an inescapable fact of war, and thus forgivable in the ultimate search for a just and stable Sri Lanka?

CHAPTER NINE

The Watching World

The Sri Lankan government continued to proclaim the care they were taking to avoid civilian casualties. Whether it was in Colombo, or at the numerous diplomatic meetings from Tokyo to Washington, or at the various human rights assemblies in Geneva, or at the UN headquarters in New York, the line remained the same: the government was fully conscious of its responsibilities towards its citizens, and if there were civilian casualties at all, they were due to the Tamil Tigers. Nevertheless, it roundly rejected calls for a ceasefire, or what came to be called 'a pause in fighting', which might have given civilians the chance to flee, or for the UN to help evacuate the zone.

On 17 February 2009, a little more than a week after the heated confrontation between UN and government officials in Colombo, Matthew Lee, a blog journalist based at the UN in New York, posed a question to the UN Secretary General's spokesperson. He asked whether in the UN's estimation the number of civilians killed thus far was higher or lower than those killed in the Gaza war a month earlier. Lee, often well briefed by UN and diplomatic sources, had raised the prospect for the first time that the UN actually possessed an estimate of the dead. By now, around 35,000 men, women and children had managed to escape in batches from the battleground and were being held in the internment camps around Vavuniya. The ICRC had just finished its second seaborne evacuation of hundreds of seriously wounded from the beaches of the government's second No Fire Zone on the coastal sand spit, and more than a thousand patients were being treated in government facilities in Trincomallee, Vavuniya and Colombo. The Secretary General's spokesperson replied that the UN 'was trying to save people, not count bodies'.[1]

While the UN was unwilling to release any estimate of the number of dead, its chief humanitarian official, John Holmes, declined to play dumb. Shuttling regularly now between briefings at the Security Council in New York and meetings with the government in Colombo, he had been eating dinner the previous night in the seafront Galle Face Hotel in Colombo when a Tamil Tiger squad of two light aircraft mounted an attack on the city. As the Tigers tried to bomb Colombo, Holmes suspected that the SLA was heavily bombarding the Vanni. He told journalists that 'significant numbers of people' were being killed and injured every day, and that 'the government at every level assured me that they have virtually stopped using heavy weapons because of their recognition of the need to spare civilian lives. It remains unclear how far this is the case in reality.' It was vital, he said, that both sides should avoid an end observers suspected was likely given the prevailing tactics of both sides, a 'final bloodbath', as he put it, as the army stormed Tamil Tiger positions with both sides oblivious to the cost.

Nobody now was in much doubt as to what was taking place. The European Union called upon both sides to comply with the laws of war and noted that the Tamil Tigers were preventing people from getting out of the path of the battle. Foreign ministries throughout Europe were abuzz with discussion over tiny Sri Lanka. Spurred by massive street demonstrations by the Tamil diaspora, the British foreign secretary was spending as much as three quarters of his time on the plight of the trapped civilians. From February onwards, the UN Secretary General would repeat his calls for a temporary halt to the fighting so that humanitarian aid, by now reduced to a nominal trickle, could be transported into the battle zone, and so those civilians who were able might be permitted by both sides to leave the area. He reminded 'both parties' of their responsibilities to protect civilian lives, and not to use the heavy weapons that were inherently indiscriminate when fired into such a small area.

To the UN, and those countries that felt they had a stake in encouraging Sri Lanka to be a good member of the international community and magnanimous in the victory that was at hand, the issue of the SLA using heavy weapons when it had such an overwhelming tactical advantage was critical. Were they backing a universally recognised sovereign government exercising its right under international law to reclaim its territory from an armed group determined to illegally divide that territory? Or were they dealing with a government that was exercising that right and at the same time flouting some of the most basic precepts of modern international law?

On 24 February, the Sri Lankan government announced that they would no longer use heavy weapons. However, as February rolled into March, a succession of supplicant diplomats found it necessary to persist in entreating them to keep their word. Point blank, they were reassured that the government had ordered a halt to the use of the weapons. Dispirited or incensed envoys felt compelled by diplomatic protocol to accept the vapid assurances of the government, despite suspecting otherwise. India sent statesmen who made it clear that with an approaching national election in May, the political costs in the southern Indian state of Tamil Nadu could be disastrous. When *Time* magazine accused President Obama of failing the first great human rights test of his term, his Secretary of State Hillary Clinton sought and received a personal assurance from President Rajapaksa that his army was not using heavy weapons.

Sweden attempted to send an envoy, the former prime minister Carl Bildt, to intercede. But in an astonishing piece of bloody-mindedness, the Sri Lankan authorities refused him entry into the country.[2] They seemed unable to resist a flying visit from Bernard Kouchner, the humanitarian activist and co-founder of the famous medical NGO Médecins sans Frontières, who, days before he arrived, stated boldly that, 'group massacres aren't internal matters'. In his role as France's foreign minister, Kouchner flew in on a French military cargo plane carrying a fully equipped French field hospital, accompanied by his British counterpart, David Miliband. Both men sought and received assurances from the president that the Sri Lankans were not using heavy weaponry. Their choice was to accuse him of lying, or accept his word. They unloaded the French hospital and departed from the island.

Sri Lanka was undeterred and unimpressed by imploring diplomacy, and President Rajapaksa avoided taking phone calls from international leaders. The government's stubborn concealment of its use of heavy weapons led to increasing pressure for the Security Council to tackle Sri Lanka. In the halls of the UN in New York, Mexico, which held one of the rotating Security Council seats, tried to have Sri Lanka formally placed on the agenda. While Western and democratic nations broadly lined up in support, it quickly became clear that China would block moves to have the council consider Sri Lanka's actions.

Instead, to the frustration of some member states, the Security Council agreed only to briefings in basement meeting rooms that seemed to signify the paralysis regarding Sri Lanka. After all, the business of the Security Council was properly that of threats to international peace and security. If Sri Lanka was discussed at all, it was considered under 'other matters', which resulted in routine condemnation of the Tamil Tigers for their use of civilians as shields, whilst reserving 'concern' for the reports of government use of heavy weapons. The possibility of an influential Security Council resolution remained distant, and Sri Lanka's government felt confident enough to persist with their heavy artillery assaults. Sri Lanka had deftly played its China card, and had trumped.

Sri Lanka's unassailable confidence stemmed from the radical shift in China's interests in just a few short years. The Chinese relationship with Sri Lanka is an ancient one. For two millennia, the Buddhist Chinese had regarded Sri Lanka as a principal staging post for Asian trade. In the twentieth century, after Mao Zedong's victory over the Kuomintang in 1949, Sri Lanka had been among the first nations to recognise the new government. Throughout the 1960s and 1970s, as China consolidated and gradually built its industrial base, it concentrated on strengthening its ties with non-aligned countries such as Sri Lanka, and reinforcing its security interests close to home, in its far western Muslim territories and Tibet, and in various wrangles with India, Russia and Vietnam.

Since the early 1980s, the succession of Sri Lankan governments had been repeatedly rebuffed each time they sought Chinese military assistance to deal with the Tamil Tiger insurgency. Premier Deng Xiaoping, just then embarking on an ambitious domestic reform agenda, told President J.R. Jayawardene's government that China regarded the insurgency as a strictly internal affair requiring a political solution. In 1986, the Sri Lankans had looked for China's help to establish factories for the manufacture of light arms and the patrol boats they needed to stem the flow of arms being smuggled across the Palk Straits from India. Again it was refused in light of a thaw in China's testy relationship with India.

Two decades later, the world was very different. Whereas China and India had sustained trade parity throughout south Asia in the 1990s, China's trade with India's neighbours doubled in the decade preceding

2006, with a parallel rise in influence. The sudden surge in its economic clout gave it leverage in areas that India considered lay within the Indian sphere of influence. India, however, had squandered a part of its clout in its disastrous 1987–90 intervention in Sri Lanka's domestic affairs. Again, when Sri Lanka's government had approached India in 2006 with a shopping list of armaments it needed to crush the Tigers, the Indian government had refused, in the belief that significant support would be detrimental to their domestic political base in unpredictable Tamil Nadu. Remarkably, when India was approached to build a billion-dollar port for Sri Lanka, they refused 'first bite' yet again.

In 2007, following a trip by Mahinda Rajapaksa to China, a joint statement was issued: 'The two sides resolved to fight tirelessly against the three evil forces of terrorism, separatism and extremism, and would step up consultation and coordination on regional and international counter-terrorism action.' China agreed to fill a void left by India's refusal to supply arms for the suppression of the Tigers. According to army commander Sarath Fonseka, 'India had told us they were not in a position to sell or send offensive weapons or even equipment like radars and basic communication equipment to meet our requirements.' In April 2007, a $37.6 million deal was signed for Chinese artillery guns, armoured personnel carriers and light weapons, and there were additional agreements for specialist weapons to destroy deep concrete bunkers and airstrips and to counter ambushes. The Chinese also supplied the bread-and-butter ordnance used on the front lines, such as the mortar shells that killed so many civilians.

China's new military support reflected the significant shift in Chinese power globally. A month after Rajapaksa's 2007 trip to China, the two countries signed a billion-dollar agreement for the development of infrastructure and the deep-sea port in the president's hometown of Hambantota, a sleepy and once impoverished fishing village in the southern part of the country. Similar to the Chinese port project in Gwadar, Pakistan, the Hambantota scheme provides potential anchorage and port facilities for Chinese merchant ships, container vessels, oil and gas tankers, and military vessels including nuclear submarines operating in the Indian Ocean or transiting through the western approaches of the Straits of Malacca, one of the world's principal maritime routes linking the major Asian economies.

Hambantota port might enable China to monitor not only Indian military traffic and India's proposed nuclear facility at Rambilli in the Bay of Bengal, but also electronic traffic from the US base on the island of Diego Garcia in the Indian Ocean. It follows China's building of other ports, in Chittagong in Bangladesh; Laem Chabang in Myanmar; and Sihanoukville in Cambodia. One month after the war ended in May 2009, the Hambantota deal was followed with an $891 million finance deal for a coal power station, raising the total Chinese investment in Sri Lanka from just a few million dollars in the early 1980s to some six billion dollars. As Kanwal Sibal, a former Indian foreign secretary and a member of India's National Security Advisory Board, noted, 'This kind of effort is aimed at counterbalancing and undermining India's natural influence in these areas.'[3]

What motivates China? And is the rise of China and its so-called 'string of pearls' strategy of port-building around the Indian Ocean rim the looming threat it appears to be? Robert Kaplan has likened China's current policy of establishing ports in the Indian Ocean to Britain's network of coaling stations in the nineteenth century. China's vital interests lie in the supply of raw materials and power to sustain the massive economic growth that now underpins its internal stability and security. Ocean-borne oil is inherently more secure than pipelines, which can be easily and repeatedly destroyed at any point. Just as with any nation, China is cutting the pragmatic deals it needs in order to secure order and to fulfil the transforming expectations of its people. Two thousand years of Chinese hegemony in east Asia suggests that China is essentially an inward-looking nation, intent on maintaining a harmonious and coherent internal structure, and with little interest in an aggressive expansion into territories that are culturally distinct. Abroad does not matter very much, except in so far as it should sustain the integrity of the Chinese state.[4] As Deng Xiaoping noted, whether a black cat or a white cat, 'it's a good cat so long as it catches mice'.

China is engaged in a process of foreign policy 'subversion . . . rather than confrontation and contest', probing the limits of tolerance to its expanding strategic and economic interests.[5] The rise of the so-called new 'Beijing consensus' (as opposed to the 'Washington consensus' that dominated the international economic–political nexus of the 1990s) is exemplified in Sri Lanka. Sri Lankan officials liked to boast of the new market in 'aid competition', familiar in the US–Soviet struggle for influence, and resurgent in the emerging dominance of China. As

Christopher Walker from Freedom House noted in the *New York Times*, China's economic influence has seen the expulsion of ethnic Uighur political refugees from Cambodia, the suppression of pro-Tibetan demonstrations in Nepal and the barring of the Dalai Lama from a peace conference in South Africa in 2009. In October 2010, after Chinese dissident Lui Xiaobo won the Nobel Peace Prize, China took the extraordinary step of threatening dozens of nations with unspecified retaliation should their representatives attend the award ceremony.

After the war, Sri Lankan diplomats boasted of the strategies that had kept at bay Western diplomatic interventions on behalf of the trapped civilians. Sri Lanka's ties with China, Myanmar, Iran, Venezuela and Libya had bloomed, and officials expressed delight at the shifting of economic power to the Asian region during the global economic crisis.[6] The US Senate Committee on Foreign Relations issued a report that encouraged the Obama administration to adjust its human rights approach to post-war Sri Lanka, and to inject more economic, political and security aid into the relationship. 'While humanitarian concerns remain important, US policy cannot be dominated by a single agenda. It is not effective at delivering real reform, and it shortchanges US geostrategic interests in the region.' The report went on to warn of a scenario of an isolated and rogue Sri Lanka, hobnobbing with unsavoury patron-nations, and concluded, 'The United States cannot afford to "lose" Sri Lanka.'[7]

On 4 March 2009, the minister for human rights, Mahinda Samarasinghe, reassured a meeting of humanitarian agencies in Geneva that the government was giving its human rights and international legal obligations the utmost priority. The very next day, Human Rights Watch condemned the government's firing of heavy weapons into civilian areas and at hospitals. It said that government statements suggesting that 'all ethnic Tamils who remain in LTTE-controlled territory are combatants, effectively [give] a go-ahead for unlawful attacks'. A steady stream of photos and videos on the Internet of long columns of refugees trying to escape the fighting, and of the injured, dead and dying crammed into makeshift medical points, were denounced by the government as 'Tamil propaganda'. In contrast, the Associated Press described the pictures as a glimpse of the agony of civilians caught inside the zone.

On 13 March, a senior UN official broke ranks with the UN's discreet and hopeful approach to the Sri Lankan conflict. One month after the first questions about an estimate of the dead had been put to the UN in New York, the High Commissioner for Human Rights, Navanetham Pillay, an ethnic Indian Tamil of South African origin, decided that it was no longer conscionable to ignore the consistent leaked figures, as well as the reports piling up in the press. In a press release that day she noted that as many as 2,800 civilians, including hundreds of children, 'may have been killed'. She urged the government and the Tamil Tigers to suspend hostilities to allow for the delivery of humanitarian supplies and for the full evacuation of the entire civilian population by land or sea.

The government response was to draw a link between the death toll used by the high commissioner 'and those on Tamilnet'. It was a sly reference to her Tamil ethnicity (although her family had lived in South Africa for more than a century). In fact, the reverse was true, and the figures on Tamilnet had been drawn from those put out by the high commissioner herself. The indefatigable minister for human rights, Mahinda Samarasinghe, repeated that the government 'would never target civilians', and that the army would no longer (once again) use 'long-range heavy weapons'. It was, if anything, an admission that the government had been lying about its use of heavy weapons, and that it had continued to bombard the NFZ despite its public commitments to the contrary.

Critically, the civilian death toll Pillay quoted finally established a baseline that had some sort of official imprimatur, and weakened government efforts to confine solid numbers to the realm of speculation and confusion. To the frustration of the government, journalists now had a tangible figure to which they persistently referred in their reporting. From this point onwards, the death toll could only grow. The Sri Lankan defence spokesman Keheliya Rambukwella took the government attack on Pillay a step further, and accused international organisations of being seeded with Tamil Tiger sympathisers and of giving out false information. By this time, in mid-March, 45,000 people had managed to flee across the front line into government-controlled territory, while the government continued to insist that just 70,000 remained – between a quarter and a third of the true tally.

Then there was satellite. Whereas in the first NFZ it was difficult to detect flows of people as they moved backwards and forwards across the zone, occasionally getting caught up in large clusters on roads or in fields, and with their tents and shelters pitched beneath trees, the much smaller sand spit into which people had been pressed by March made understanding satellite images easier. Hemmed in by the physical barriers of the sea, the lagoon and the front lines, people were largely static and confined to a fixed perimeter. Their physical presence was flagged to the eye-in-the-sky by the shelters they erected to shield themselves from the sun and rain. At least a quarter of a million people were trapped on the sand spit in a vast tent city. Plastic sheets covered the landscape, looking like white pinheads from above. They could be counted.

Satellite technology has come a long way since the Srebrenica massacre of 1995 in Bosnia, when US satellites observed the shifting of bodies into mass graves by the Bosnian Serb army as it attempted to cover up their murder of some 8,000 Muslim men and boys. Any organisation that has access to commercial satellite imagery of Google quality (let alone of military precision) possesses graphic evidence of what was taking place inside the second NFZ. It was much like a cartoon, with each subtle change in the images of the landscape denoting a shift in the circumstances of the hundreds of thousands of people who were being bombarded daily. From one day to the next (assuming that there was no cloud cover to interrupt the satellite), it was possible to detect each destroyed house or vehicle, but more pertinently, any abrupt shift or vanishing of a section of the vast tent city, or the appearance of fresh circular dimples in the landscape, which indicated the places where shellfire had fallen.*

While the UN counted the thousands of white dots from above using satellite images, the Tamil UN staff stuck inside the Cage with their families did a sectional estimate to arrive at a rough minimum average figure for the number of people under each shelter. Incredibly, the government had vastly downplayed how many people were still trapped. It was a huge refugee camp, the largest in the world, and the second largest concentration of people in Sri Lanka after the capital city. This huge population was almost completely cut off from humanitarian aid, except for the irregular ICRC-flagged ships that were ferrying

---

* The government argued that these dimples denoted shallow shelters dug by the refugees.

out the thousands of wounded and their families. Despite being an obvious way to supply the most critically needed medical supplies, the ICRC was permitted to transport next to nothing to the makeshift medical points inside the siege zone.

In April, images obtained by the US National Geo-spatial Intelligence Agency (NGA), based in Bethesda, Maryland, a part of the US Department of Defense, were released to the media, and buttressed claims that the Sri Lankan government was understating the true number of civilians trapped inside the Cage. A spokesman for the NGA told the *New York Times*: 'It's a safe assumption that we didn't release everything that we have.' The US images spurred American congressmen to request from the US Office for the Investigation of War Crimes in late 2009 an influential report that listed day by day the terrible toll of artillery on civilians.[8] But the public reporting of the death toll had no discernible impact on the progress of the fight, and the Sri Lankan army continued to use heavy weapons.[9]

After the fall of the last fortified Tiger redoubt of Anandapuram in mid-April, the Tiger lines had fallen back and were now stretched around the entire periphery of the sand spit. These lines were in many places just yards from the places where civilians had erected their shelters. As Krishna T says, 'It was all the same wherever we wanted to go [within the second NFZ], because there were shells and bullets everywhere, and it was difficult to find a place to put our tent. We needed to be close to where we could get food, and close to a place to find water.' The less that civilians had to move around, the higher their chances of surviving, so they congregated together, where the food distributions still being managed by government and Tiger functionaries could reach them, and where they continued to serve their tactical function for the Tigers as a bulwark against attack. Tragically, this clustering also meant that when an artillery shell struck, the toll on life was high.

Why did the government continue to use heavy artillery, giving little or no thought to the possible criminality of their actions or to the potential political cost? Certainly the army possessed sophisticated radar targeting equipment that allowed it to detect hostile fire, and then to counter-fire from a distance of ten kilometres with deadly accuracy. Its numerous drones gave it real-time visual information that communicated directly back to the computer desktop of the defence secretary and to command posts, allowing correction in the case of a miss or if artillery was landing in heavily populated areas. And with the chaos of displacement and people constantly on the move, the civilians were seeded with infiltrators from the Sri Lankan forces, as well as Indian intelligence agents keeping tabs on the real impact of the war on civilians.

When Harun Khan and Convoy 11 had been under fire in the first NFZ at the end of January, the position of UN bunkers had been transmitted back to army headquarters and field commanders, but failed to stop the fierce bombardment that killed so many. Hospitals and medical points were struck so often during these months, and with such repeated accuracy, that the Tamil government doctors busy stemming the loss of life asked the ICRC to conceal the coordinates of the makeshift medical tents from the government. They suspected that they were being actively targeted, possibly because of their increasingly frank appeals to the media for relief. In the second NFZ, people learned to expect the daily pounding from familiar SLA artillery positions, even shifting the low sand mounds that lined the edges of their dugouts to account for the direction of incoming fire.

One factor in the decision to bombard so wantonly, or at least without the sufficient duty of care demanded under international law, was to save manpower. For all the steady progress they made against increasingly inexperienced and youthful Tamil fighters, the army was also constantly battling a high rate of desertion, and a very high death and injury toll.[10] While forcibly recruited Tiger conscripts held most of the front, the Tamil Tigers threw some of their most seasoned and courageous cadres into intensely fought confrontations and small-scale lightning counter-strikes that stalled the advance of the SLA and exacted a terrible toll on the troops.

One distinct advantage the Tigers retained was the capacity for fanatical suicidal attacks. Despite their own unquestionable valour and dogged fighting skills, such levels of dedication generally eluded most of the Sinhalese troops, and remained a source of terror to them. Elite cadres from the Black Tiger units, who had already been wounded, hid in bunkers until surrounded by army troops, before blowing themselves up. Army officers who fought on the front line admitted to an incessant terror of suicide cadres in the battle to crush the Tigers and the quest to locate and kill Prabakharan. Suicide bombers retained an almost mythic quality, just as the Supreme Leader did up until the moment his corpse was finally recovered.

The most obvious explanation, however, for the government's reckless use of artillery was that they were using it to 'smoke out' civilians. A UTHR(J) report, compiled after speaking with many witnesses to the shelling, says that 'the most charitable interpretation was to see shelling by the army as intended to mentally harass [civilians] to break out from the LTTE's control and flee into the army's control no matter how many were killed or maimed – a matter of counterbalancing the LTTE's threat to shoot those who escaped'.[11] Foolishly the army allowed the intransigence and cynical brutality of the Tamil Tigers to lure the SLA's tactical artillery decisions on to illegal territory.

The government energetically propagated the notion that the Tamil Tigers were shooting their own people in an effort to prevent them from leaving the battle zone. For two years, the army had been using one tactic – bombardment – to drive people from their homes with relatively little harm to civilians, so that they could conquer territory and compress the Tamil Tigers into a contained space. The inevitable endgame was a combining of battle space with civilian space. Many civilians, against great odds, had somehow managed to escape. To attempt to do so, however, risked incurring the dangerous wrath of the Tamil Tigers, who did all they could to preserve a civilian shield against attack. It also meant abandoning extended family and communities, and any family members stuck fighting with the Tigers. If a civilian survived the crossing, they faced an uncertain future in government internment camps (of the existence of which they were well aware).

As the space compressed, and more and more people were killed, the narrowing odds of survival were obvious. The bombardment induced each individual family to weigh up their survival decisions, and to run the risk of fleeing the battle zone. In a confidential note to a Western senior envoy to Sri Lanka, Human Rights Watch wrote: 'A cynical but unfortunately plausible interpretation of the government's strategy is that it plans to continue shelling to pressure as many IDPs [internally displaced persons] as possible to escape.'

Unrestrained by any independent organ to oversee the actions of military strategists – no independent press, no credible challenge from the judiciary, no supervisory bodies to speak of and no political challenge to the Rajapaksa clan – the Sri Lankan government adopted a charade. Its diplomats, politicians and generals began to sell to the public and world at large the notion of a 'hostage rescue'. This fresh approach to the problem was revealed in an exclusive interview with army commander General Sarath Fonseka on 6 April in Sri Lanka's *Sunday Observer* newspaper. He promised that no foreign force would obstruct the army from 'marching forward to liberate the innocent civilians' in what would be 'the world's largest hostage rescue operation'.

Indeed, just six months before, the world had been gripped by a terrorist attack on hotels and tourist haunts in Mumbai. Dramatic twenty-four-hour television news coverage showed Indian troops and police battling their way through luxury hotels to flush out terrorists and rescue hostages (many of whom were killed). With the kind of vaunting ambition that presaged his post-war challenge to the Rajapaksas, General Fonseka confidently asserted that Sri Lanka would do it even better. Defence secretary Gotabaya Rajapaksa suggested that the SLA would undertake an operation that would emulate the legendary – and virtually bloodless – Israeli rescue of hostages at Uganda's Entebbe airport in 1976.

The notion of rescue morphed seamlessly with the government's primary military and political ends. Despite satellite pictures that revealed the extent of the government deception, if not its intentions, the true numbers of people trapped inside the Cage remained uncertain. For this reason alone, nobody would ever know how many were killed in the attempt to 'rescue' them. After all, who would see the dead, what evidence would be left for people to discover, who could possibly mount an investigation, and when was the last time that an independent investigation or inquiry had succeeded in Sri Lanka? When asked in January 2010 about the numbers of civilians killed in the war, Sri Lanka's newly appointed ambassador to the UN, Palitha Kohona, scoffed at suggestions of between 10,000 and 40,000 dead and said, apparently without a note of irony, that Sri Lanka would have 'needed an army' to tidy away all those bodies.

The large-scale 'hostage rescue' began on 16 April. The army fired barrage after barrage of shellfire into the Cage in an attempt to pummel Tiger positions and shatter their lines. The plan was to pierce the zone at a place called Pokkanai in the upper third of the zone, after an earlier attempt to cut across further south at the narrowest point in the lagoon had been beaten back by the Tigers. Had the first attempt succeeded, the majority of civilians inside the zone would have been cut off from where the main remaining body of Tiger forces was massing, on the southern tip of the Cage's sand spit. For three days shellfire pounded the selected incursion area, killing civilians and cadres alike.

On 19 April, under cover of a pitch-black night and heavy rain, army commandos waded forward through shallow water and nestled against the high earthen bund that had been built by the Tigers the previous month along the foreshore of the lagoon, and which shielded the Cage from the eyes of soldiers on the opposing bank. For some reason, the Tigers had failed to shore up the defences at Pokkanai, and the few defenders were quickly overcome in hand-to-hand fighting. The pocket had finally been pricked, and while some Tiger units frantically battled the incursion, others concentrated on forcing civilians south along the spit to a place called Mullivaikal. The last remaining health post also moved hurriedly south at the order of Tiger cadres.

By the afternoon of the following day, the army had secured a patch of the eastern shore of the lagoon about two kilometres long. Two SLA pincers struck out from the extreme northern and southern edges of the breach in an effort to reach the sea on the other side of the sand spit. Tens of thousands of tightly packed civilians were now hemmed in on three sides, with the army battling the Tigers at close quarters, artillery providing covering barrages, white phosphorus shells exploding and Tiger units trying to drive hundreds of thousands of civilians south. It was a bloody affair and there must have been a huge toll exacted on civilians, who were overwhelmed, running haphazardly in confused bids to escape, or cowering in dugouts while the battle swirled about them. Commandos were fighting their way through a tent city, hurling grenades, trying to distinguish Tiger fighters from civilians, with smoke covering the battlefield, tents ablaze and army vehicles crashing over the landscape of flimsy shelters and shallow bunkers.

Thousands of people streamed across the lagoon to the safety of army lines as soldiers urged them on. Tiger cadres fired at both soldiers and civilians. Krishna T, who had been told just two days before that her conscripted son had been killed, waded with her family, stepping over the bodies of hundreds of dead, watching as civilians struck by bullets or rocket-propelled grenades slipped beneath the water or triggered landmines. Other witnesses describe apocalyptic scenes of children being dropped into the muddy water while their parents moved on, of mothers dying and their infants being scooped up, of an infant suckling on the breast of her dead mother, and of people being trampled underfoot in the stampede to escape the ghastly Cage inside which so many had already perished. One aid worker later recorded this account in the internment camps:

> A young father told us that as his family was coming across the bund, the army opened fire on civilians (he estimated a group of around a thousand people had crossed ahead of them and more than 10,000 were behind them and moving in the same direction). His wife was carrying their four-day-old baby – she was shot in the chest and he shouted at the army who were ten metres away, 'That's a baby, she's carrying a baby!' She was shot a second time in the head and died on the spot. The baby was injured.

Over the next three days, about 100,000 people were able to flee across the lagoon. The army had, according to the triumphant headlines in the capital, successfully executed the world's largest hostage rescue.[12] But far from being a bloodless affair, witnesses who crossed the lagoon reported seeing between 600 and 1,000 bodies, and nobody was able to hazard a guess at just how many had been killed in the jumbled and scorched tent city. Government propaganda simply asserted that the army had killed nobody. By most accounts, despite isolated cases of looting by soldiers, the army did their best to retrieve the wounded and transport them to hospitals. One old man, left alone and with a wounded leg in the burning tent city, was retrieved by soldiers and was then able to notify his family that he was alive because he could recall his son's telephone number in Germany. There were many acts of mercy that emerged from the inferno of civil war.

The bedraggled columns of civilians were massed and counted, fed as well as possible and then transported by truck and bus to waiting internment camps in Vavuniya. Front-line soldiers gave their own rations to the terrified civilians, who fully expected to be brutalised by the victorious Sinhalese troops. General Jagath Jayasuriya, then the battlefield commander based in Vavuniya, confessed that the scale of the breakout had overwhelmed his men. It is certain that dozens if not hundreds of civilians died because of the failure of the government to adequately prepare to meet the huge numbers who emerged, despite constant warnings from the UN of an impending humanitarian crisis. By the general's own account, at least sixty people died at the Oman-thai checkpoint* from fatigue, hunger, wounds and thirst.

Many more must have died in the first days and weeks of their confinement as the army, which had primary responsibility for the security of the camps, struggled to shelter, feed and clothe people, to provide them with water and to care for the considerable numbers of sick and badly wounded. The government resisted UN requests for full access to the camps, and stubbornly refused the help of any of the highly experienced national and international non-governmental organisations, which would have considerably lowered the death toll in those early weeks.

One glimpse of the chaos came from a British surgeon working for Médecins sans Frontières, who told AFP that his team in a state-run hospital near the conflict zone had been overwhelmed by the influx of injured civilians, with more than 320 patients in a forty-five-bed ward. 'It's so crowded that the nurses cannot physically walk around,' he said. 'We are not able to save some people . . . There are simply not enough nurses.'[13] Alarmed at the reports of the large numbers of people dying, the Indian government sent envoys to Sri Lanka. A spokesman for the Indian external affairs Ministry said: 'We are very unhappy at the continued killing in Sri Lanka. All killing must stop. There must be an immediate cessation of all hostilities.'[14]

After the 20 April breakout, the internment camps, or 'welfare villages' as the government called them, were overflowing. It took weeks for enough tents to arrive to house all the people who had survived the SLA 'rescue'. Thousands of people slept on bare earth, and broiled beneath the sun during the day. People queued for up to eight hours each day for enough water to drink and cook with, and went without washing. Tents made for six people held up to three times that number. Rough pit latrines were too few, exposed and quickly overflowing, and the gutters of the roads hastily carved through the scrubby jungle by the army were filled with waste. Soldiers set to guard the camps continued to give their own rations in sympathy at the plight of starving children.

---

* The major crossing and choke point between government-held territory and the first – and by 2009 long since overrun – fortified Tiger positions in the Vanni.

Thousands of people who had been separated from their families during the frantic stampede to escape, including children from their parents, were haphazardly allocated to different camps. They remained apart for months, often ignorant of whether or not their loved ones had survived. Thousands of wounded were in hospitals, their families unable to visit them and often not even aware of whether they were alive or dead. Parents who were interviewed by aid personnel said that before food and water, they wanted word of their children and relatives. The elderly slept on the barren earth alongside the newborn, who slumbered beside the maimed, the sick, the deranged and the dying. While the UN and the ICRC were held back, full access was granted to pro-government Tamil paramilitary groups and the intelligence services, which moved among the sea of exhausted humanity at night-time, shining torches in their faces and leading people away.[15]

The UN was only gradually and grudgingly allowed full access to the bedraggled survivors in the camps. Even then, the government continued to impose severe conditions, such as prohibiting humanitarian workers from entering tents where people lay. The ICRC was forbidden from instituting a tracing and reunification programme for people separated from their relatives by war, one of the standard activities of the Red Cross throughout the world. The government was wary of aid agencies having access to the camps for fear of what they might discover, and for good reason.

Andy Brooks, a widely respected psychologist who ran a part of the huge UNICEF operation in Sri Lanka, wryly observed, 'We began discovering what we already knew.'[16] Children began to talk about what had happened to them and their families. When schools and recreational activities started up in the camps, children expressed in their stories and their artwork what they had been through. Some of the paintings and drawings by children, illustrated in the picture section of this book, clearly show the close proximity of the terrors of war. Rendered in crayon with a childish simplicity, these starkly emotive scenes overwhelm the officially concocted record of events.

Other simple testimonies formed a rudimentary alternative tableau to the 'hostage rescue' narrative. Natalie Grove, a young Australian UNICEF aid worker, spoke with hundreds of the detainees and compiled their information. Grove lived and worked in Vavuniya for nine months until July 2009, and visited the camps and hospitals almost every day. She was compelled to gather her data like an undercover agent, concealing her discoveries from the government and the army. An academic researcher by training, she had already served stints in East Timor, Uganda and the Philippines, working with children who had often experienced terrible violence. She understood the value of carefully acquired individual stories, and of the patterns they collectively form.

Armed with only notebooks and pens, Grove and a team of other aid workers shuttled between Menik Farm, the largest of the camps, the smaller camps around Vavuniya town and the main hospital in Vavuniya. To disguise their task, they sometimes accompanied truckloads of clothes or cooking utensils that were being distributed to the exhausted camp inhabitants. There Grove would begin casual conversations with inmates, who would lead her from tent to tent, where the stories of individual ordeals unfolded, told by parents and grandparents whose children or grandchildren had been killed or maimed. Often people recounted their tales in the simple hope that their missing children might be found.

The result was a randomly obtained but detailed account of the fate of hundreds of children during the worst phase of fighting, when the government persistently denied that it was mounting bombardments or aerial attacks that killed civilians. Grove says that the numbers of people who wanted to recount their stories overwhelmed her. The body of evidence that she was able to amass 'was the tip of a very large iceberg, just a snapshot'. The accounts of some 300 cases of children who had been killed or injured during the fighting are a fragile firsthand collective testimony that effectively sketches in faint form, like the pictures of the children themselves, the final six months of battle, and the incontrovertibly lethal impact on civilians.

Following the major breach on 20 April, government forces had been storming three high earthen bunds that stretched across the width of what remained of the Cage. The Tamil Tigers had built these futile mounds at night-time with earth-moving machinery. The bloody series of encounters saw heavy losses on both sides. Tamil Tiger fighters defending the bunds ran into government lines with bombs strapped to their bodies, or tried to drive vehicles rigged with explosives as ramming engines against army tanks and artillery. Untested Tiger cadres press-ganged from civilian tents nearby died pointlessly in droves. At the end of the war, SLA generals Jagath Jayasuriya and Shavendra Silva admitted that after the middle of April, most of the cadres their troops had encountered were teenagers, many of them children, and some as young as eleven.

The fighting was tooth and nail. The army used massive artillery fire and air sorties against the bunds with an inevitable impact on civilians tightly massed on the other side. About 100,000 or so civilians who still remained trapped had been forced south by the Tigers. Thousands more managed to cross the lines by wading across the lagoon, waiting in their bunkers until the fighting passed over them, or slipping past Tiger patrols on fishing boats on the seaward shore. Each story of escape seems remarkable in its recounting because of the intensity of the fighting, the volume of firepower and the chances of being shot at either by SLA troops searching through their rifle sights for hostile opponents among a confusion of rather indistinguishable civilians, or by the more deliberately murderous fire of the Tamil Tiger cadres trying to prevent people from escaping.

It remains a credit to many of the front-line SLA soldiers that, despite odd cruel exceptions, they so often seem to have made the effort to draw civilians out from the morass of fighting ahead of them in an attempt to save lives. Soldiers yelled out to civilians, left gaps in their lines while they waved white flags to attract people forward and bodily plucked the wounded from foxholes and bunkers. Troops bravely waded into the lagoon under fire to rescue wounded people threading their way out of the battlefield or to help parents with their children, and gave their rations to civilians as they lay in fields, exhausted in their first moments of safety after years of living under the roar and threat of gunfire.

This does not mean that soldiers did not directly kill thousands of civilians in the heat of combat. Once ordered to advance into a packed battlefield the split-second decisions they were compelled to make in order to preserve their own lives were weighed against the survival of those civilians who still hugged the bottoms of their bunkers, hoping that the battle would pass over them. In hand-to-hand fighting with Tamil Tigers, soldiers increasingly chose to close off the field of war pocket by pocket. Survivors testify that advancing soldiers lobbed grenades methodically into bunkers that often held civilians. This account of the final days was given by an unnamed child recruited by the Tigers:

> In February my mother was killed when a shell hit our tent during the day. The fighting got worse and worse until 13 May when we couldn't come out from the bunker for any reason. The shelling from the SLA was continuous, day and night for three days ... some people were killed in the trenches they had dug ... We had finished our water and we didn't know what to do because there was no break in the firing ... We had to try to run because we were going to die if we stayed where we were. When we came out of the bunker, there were vehicles burning and civilian bodies everywhere, some of them were killed and others we could see were lying there, injured but they couldn't move. The shelling was going on, even people in our group were falling down, but no one could stop or go back to check on them. I was holding my crutches and people were helping to carry me. We could see the SLA soldiers about three hundred metres away and they were waving their hands at us to come ... as the people ran away the LTTE shot at them ... Some people were hit but we just kept going ...

From February 2009, the Tigers had put out feelers for a negotiated surrender. These moves seem to have been ploys rather than a genuine recognition of the hopelessness of their position. It was classic Tiger strategy, using the offices of the Norwegian government, the UN, the ICRC, the Indian and American governments and individual intermediaries who seemed to have earned the trust of the Tiger leadership. Their demands and positions were evasive, unstable and inscrutable, and reflected divided assessments within the leadership about what their next moves should be. That there was any dispute about the futility of resistance indicates a certain divorce from the reality of their position. All the time, and as the battlefield was squeezed, the implicit threat was the control that the Tigers maintained over so many civilian lives. Gotabaya Rajapaksa dismissed as 'a joke' an offer in late April from the Tigers of a ceasefire. He called upon them to surrender without conditions. By the government's own estimate, there were only 500 or so fighters left inside the Cage.

With nationwide elections looming in India, the jockeying of local

politicians in Tamil Nadu reached farcical proportions. The main opposition leader, a former movie star, had long been a strident critic of the
Tamil Tigers and their murky presence in the southern state. Now she
suddenly announced her support for the establishment of a separate
homeland for Sri Lanka's Tamils. The incumbent chief minister of Tamil
Nadu met this volte face by starting a hunger strike 'to call attention to
the plight of Tamil civilians'. Seizing on a fresh announcement from Sri
Lanka's president that once again he had ordered an end to the use of
heavy weapons, the minister was able to return to his customary diet
after just five hours of striking in sympathy with the besieged civilians
across the Palk Straits. The UN's chief humanitarian official John Holmes,
leaving Sri Lanka after another meeting with the country's leaders,
sounded a jaded note: 'I hope the idea of not using heavy weapons will
be genuinely respected this time.'[17]

By now, around 100,000 people were trapped, packed into an area
of a few square kilometres. On Saturday, 9 May, having breached the
third and final bund, the SLA started fighting southwards to the small
village of Mullivaikal, about two and a half kilometres away. That
same afternoon, the ICRC managed to land by ship its final small load
of medical supplies and food on the beaches where thousands of
terrified people gathered, knowing now that any escape would have
to be through the confused fighting erupting all around them. While
small boats ferried the supplies from the ICRC ships to the beach,
shells exploded in the water and bullets winged across the heads of
the fishermen manning the craft. Under fire, the ICRC managed to
evacuate the final batch of more than 500 wounded and their accompanying relatives.*

The conflagration of shelling now erupted all across the densely
packed siege area, exploding with such rapidity that the blasts could
not be counted. Through Saturday and Sunday, with the offshore ICRC
ship gone and no independent witnesses, the army pounded the area.
By the end of Sunday, the bodies of more than 400 people, a quarter of
them children, had been dragged to the final dressing station still run
by Tamil doctors. More than 1,300 others who were wounded made it
to the hospital. Many hundreds more must have been buried where
they fell, and one doctor estimated that at least a thousand civilians had

---

* The ICRC evacuated a total of approximately 18,000 wounded and accompanying
family members from the beaches of the Cage.

died. The sheer apparent scale of the death toll emboldened the UN to decry the impact on civilians as 'a bloodbath' that had eventuated as it had warned it might.[18] One Tamil parliamentarian called the day's death toll 'the deadliest attack on civilians since the 1983 anti-Tamil riots'.[19] Pits were dug close to the nearby marshes and fifty or sixty corpses buried in each one.

Just days earlier, the UN Secretary General had spoken with President Rajapaksa and implored him once more to stop using heavy weapons and mortars, and to grant a pause in the fighting to allow civilians to escape. On Monday morning, Ban Ki-moon condemned the killing without equivocation, as well as the heavy weapons that had been used despite the repeated assurances from President Rajapaksa that now seemed hollow. 'No one can be in any doubt that this is an issue that deserves the international community's attention,' Britain's foreign secretary David Miliband told reporters at UN headquarters in New York. A statement from the president of the Security Council, Vitaly Churkin of Russia, blandly denounced the Tamil Tigers for continuing to hold civilians as human shields, demanded that the Tigers lay down their arms and allow people to leave the Cage and noted the council's 'deep concern at the reports of continued use of heavy calibre weapons in areas with high concentrations of civilians'. With this final statement, and no small relief, the UN Security Council seemed to have finally washed its hands of Sri Lanka.

The Tamil Tigers had fallen back from the third and final bund. They fought a minor Stalingrad defence from a cluster of some dozens of sturdy houses that had been built with international donations following the 2004 tsunami. Remarkably, even at this late stage, they continued to hold off their attackers, who were constantly reinforced by freshly rested and well-fed troops. But the toughest of the Tiger cadres knew very well that their chances of survival were slim. Neither side had much of a record of taking prisoners. In the heat of this bitter battle it was unlikely that any quarter would be given to the insurgents whose fight had killed so many Sinhalese soldiers.

For four days the Tigers put up a desperate defence amidst the warren of houses before succumbing to overwhelming firepower from air sorties, artillery and multi-barrel rockets. It is difficult to imagine what the confusion of the final days and hours of this terrible siege must have been like. The Tiger command and control chain had largely crumbled, and individual groups made their plans for escape or for a final stand. On the front lines, some Tiger commanders put up stiff resistance, while others concentrated on filtering civilians across to government lines. On 15 May, many of the Tiger cadres began to burn their weapons in a huge bonfire in the centre of the zone, in preparation for surrender. The leader of the fearsome Sea Tigers, known by the *nom de guerre* Soosai, dispatched his family to safety in a boat; the Sri Lankan navy later picked them up offshore. Seven captive Sinhalese soldiers and sailors who escaped summary execution were released by their Tiger guards, and made their way to safety with their gaolers in tow.

Tens of thousands of civilians attempted a breakout at the lagoon, but even at this late stage they were driven back by the Tamil Tigers firing artillery rounds at them. Still thousands managed to wade, swim, or paddle across the lagoon on floats of plastic bottles or bicycle and car tubes. The army's 59th Division crossed the small outlet to the sea that separated the Cage from Mullaitivu in the south, while just a few kilometres to the north, the 53rd and 58th Divisions moved down along the edges of the sea and the lagoon. As the army chiselled out territory and the fighting passed over them, thousands of civilians emerged from bunkers to escape from the battle zone, and the two army thrusts converging from the north and the south seized the final stretch of beachfront, controlling the entire coastline of Sri Lanka for the first time in decades.

The SLA troops picked their way forward, slowly closing in on a cluster of tens of thousands of people who cowered in the pitted and now burning landscape, not having eaten or drunk anything for days for fear of being killed by the fighting if they came out. Bodies lay strewn throughout the zone where bullets or explosions had felled them. Since nobody could move to the medical points still manned by the courageous Tamil government doctors, people lay moaning and dying all around. The doctors had not left their own bunkers for days. For the next two days, the battlefield would alternate between deadly exchanges between troops and Tiger fighters, and extraordinary lulls in the fighting when an eerie silence would descend, punctuated by the explosions of Tiger cadres committing suicide with hand grenades or rushing troops in final acts of annihilation.

*   *   *

It was not until May that reality seemed to finally dawn for Prabakharan, despite the earlier misgivings of his senior front-line commanders. On the 16th, Balasingham Nadesan, the head of the Tigers' political wing, spoke to *The Times* newspaper by satellite telephone and said, 'We are ready to lay down our arms if the Americans or British can guarantee our safety. There will be a tragedy if no one helps us.' The real tragedy had long since happened, and the betrayal of the people for whom the Tigers had fought so long seemed complete with this final statement, still couched in illusory terms of defiance. 'Any agreement must be attached to a commitment to a political process that will guarantee the human and political rights of the Tamil people.'

Another of the UN Secretary General's envoys, the Indian Vijay Nambiar, had just met with the government. 'I think there is an unwillingness of the Sri Lankan government to accept a surrender,' he said, with great understatement. Nevertheless, by burning their weapons, releasing their captives and allowing thousands of civilians to stream out of the zone, elements of the Tiger leadership attempted to comply with the terms of a negotiated surrender that they believed was in place, and which had been, at the very least, tacitly agreed by some members of the government. Witnesses testify that senior Tiger commanders seemed remarkably unperturbed as the conflagration consumed the innocent all about them, and several referred to a deal that was being worked out.

Throughout the confusion of 16 May, fierce battles continued to rage, with civilians being killed and wounded while thousands more slipped away to safety. The main group of courageous Tamil government doctors, finally allowed by the Tigers to leave, crossed over into government territory. Doctors Shanmugarajah, Varatharajah and Sathiyamoorthy blended in with the thousands of other anonymous civilians flowing out of the Cage, but were quickly spotted at the Omanthai crossing by alert UN staff, who observed as they were arrested and led away. Days later, after numerous enquiries as to their whereabouts by the UN, the diplomatic community and the international press, the government admitted that the doctors were being held pending an inquiry and possible charges for 'giving out false information and speaking with the media'. Dr Varatharajah, with a shrapnel wound to his chest, lay untreated in a police cell for a week before he was moved to a hospital.

At around the same time as the doctors were crossing Omanthai, 'KP' Kumaran Pathmanathan, the Tamil Tigers' chief arms procurer and one of the architects and managers of their worldwide financing operation, spoke from abroad on behalf of the leadership and said, 'our people are now at the mercy of the international community'. Later that day, speaking from Amman in Jordan, where he was attending a GII summit, President Rajapaksa announced that he would be returning 'to Sri Lanka as a leader of a nation that vanquished terrorism'. The next day, an army spokesman announced that the last of 50,000 people had been 'rescued', and there were no more people left inside the Cage. The battle still raged, however, and civilians continued to stream out, but with the communications systems of the Tigers by now almost completely destroyed, confusion was inevitable.*

That morning, it dawned on the senior leadership of the Tigers that there would be no surrender. Instead they made a final bid to escape after issuing instructions to the remaining Tiger fighters to continue the battle to the bitter end. At noon on 17 May, KP issued another statement in which he declared, 'This battle has reached its bitter end . . . we have appealed to the countries of the world and called on them to halt the unrelenting massacre of our people by the Sri Lankan armed machinery. We are extremely saddened that this plea has fallen on deaf ears. We have decided to silence our guns.' But by this time, the battle had reached its primary objective, and his long-time leader Prabakharan was probably already dead.

In November 2009, a few young army officers who had been present at the final battles described to me in detail on a map the last stand of Prabakharan, his high command and his sons. As troops closed in from all sides, the area controlled by the Tigers had dwindled to a mere square half-kilometre. Tens of thousands of civilians remained hemmed in by the confusion, the sheer brutality of the Tigers and the advancing fire of the army. By dawn on 17 May, the senior leadership, including Prabakharan, Pottu Amman and Soosai, were gone, having apparently made an attempt to cross the lagoon under cover of dark and break through the army's western lines to the jungles beyond.

* One senior UN official did not help matters by rashly announcing to the BBC that all civilians had been rescued.

All the next day, according to civilians who miraculously survived, the army fought a terrible battle as it tried to flush out the last of the Tigers from amidst their civilian cover, with the result that by the morning of 18 May the battle was over.[20] But what had happened to Prabakharan and the senior leadership, who had all been alive at least until the early hours of 17 May? Had they committed suicide through devotion to the cause of liberation, as hundreds of devoted fighters and bombers had elected to do down the years? Had they bitten on cyanide capsules or blown themselves up, as dozens of wounded fighters were doing inside the battle zone, rather than face capture?

The government propaganda machine was confused. On the afternoon of 17 May, as the president flew back from Jordan, it was announced that he would give a speech on the morning of the 19th, thus setting in stone a political timetable. Presumably he was aware that the army had already accounted for the senior Tiger leadership. Later that day, Reuters and an Internet site known to be close to the government both issued reports of the death of Prabakharan, along with his wife Mathivathani and sons Charles Anthony and twelve-year-old Balachandran. The first official word on the whereabouts of senior leaders came on 18 May from the Gotabaya-run Defence.lk, which announced that the bodies of senior Tigers Nadesan, Pulidevan and Ramesh had been discovered during mopping-up operations, while a few hours later the same site issued another statement in which it said that the body of Prabakharan's elder son Charles Anthony had been found in a separate location. But there was no official word on Prabakharan.

The following day, the 19th, a story appeared in Colombo's *Daily Mirror* quoting army sources that described a madcap attempted escape by Prabakharan along with Pottu Amman and Soosai in an ambulance. They had apparently managed to make it through government lines before the vehicle and around 250 cadres who were somehow keeping pace with it were obliterated after what the paper reported was 'a fierce gun battle lasting over an hour'. According to this version, the ambulance was totally destroyed and the charred bodies (which the army was certain were that of Prabakharan and his chiefs) were being examined for DNA identification. This story places three remaining key Tiger figures together, with no mention of their families. Later that day, pictures were released to the press of Prabakharan's body in neat uniform and relatively pristine condition, apart from the enormous wound to his head. Over the next few days, the body would appear in various photographs clothed, then nude, then partially nude, then clothed again, but never giving the impression that it had not been doctored.

In yet another 'official' version of events, the one that was eventually given the greatest play (and the one carefully explained to me in November by the young officers who were fighting nearby), the senior military leadership made an attempt to escape across the lagoon early on 17 May, in part covered by the civilians who were streaming out of the battle zone wherever they could discover a gap. A small group of unarmed senior Tiger functionaries remained in the last pocket still controlled by the Tamil Tigers as a kind of decoy while Prabakharan escaped, and in the expectation that their surrender would be accepted.

Several of the senior commanders and somewhere between 70 and 150 cadres were killed in a firefight when they confronted army lines on the other side of the lagoon, while the rest, including Prabakharan, were driven back across the lagoon, where they sheltered on a tiny mangrove islet just off the edge of the NFZ. Detected and then surrounded by troops, Prabakharan and his remaining men were cut down by rocket-propelled grenades and gunfire (with the leader killed by a 12.7 millimetre bullet, according to the army officers who briefed me).[21] Charles Anthony, separated from his father's group, was gunned down on the sand spit. No mention was made of the fate of the political leadership or their families.

What is certain, and has been reported in some detail by *The Times* and *The Independent*, is that negotiations for the surrender of the remaining leadership, their families and perhaps another 300 people with them were well advanced, and included the president's personal guarantee of safe passage. Right up until they met their deaths, the final group of Tiger leaders around Nadesan and Pulidevan, who had been left behind as the military leadership made their break across the lagoon, believed that they had a surrender deal, a belief encouraged by the survival of several other senior leaders, who had escaped earlier in April and were alive in Colombo. The negotiations involved a flurry of complex exchanges between senior Colombo-based Tamil politicians, the Tigers' international representatives, the UN, the ICRC, the government of Norway, Basil Rajapaksa and the secretary of the foreign ministry, Palitha Kohona.

With their lives at stake, the surrender timetable was detailed. It was agreed that the remaining Tiger leadership should walk at a precise time and location under a white flag towards army lines. The UN Secretary General's envoy, Vijay Nambiar, confirmed the president's guarantee in answer to questions from *The Times*, an assurance repeated by the Tamil parliamentarian Chandra Nehru, who had also spoken with the president. Basil Rajapaksa had prescribed the precise route that the group should follow. Shortly after dawn on 18 May, with Prabakharan having left to make his escape the day before, and after Nadesan had spoken to Chandra Nehru by satellite telephone to confirm the surrender agreement once more, the party went forward across no man's land with a white flag in a group of about a dozen men and women.[22] The story of what followed next varies greatly between the accounts from the army grapevine and the confused and contradictory official versions. With unimpeachable regularity, and with multiple confirmations from different army sources, senior and lower-ranking officers and enlisted men alike recounted the cold-blooded massacre of Pulidevan, Nadesan, their families and accompanying civilians and cadres.

The Times quoted a source who heard Nadesan's wife, who was Sinhalese, shout at the soldiers: 'He is trying to surrender and you are shooting him!' before she too was killed along with everybody else in the group. And in the most damning statement of all, in December 2009 the newly civilian Sarath Fonseka told the *Sunday Leader* newspaper that he had been completely unaware of the surrender negotiations. 'Later, I learnt that Basil had conveyed this information to the Defence Secretary Gotabaya Rajapaksa – who in turn spoke with Brigadier Shavendra Silva, Commander of the Army's 58th Division, giving orders not to accommodate any LTTE leaders attempting surrender and that they must all be killed.' In May 2010, Britain's Channel 4 aired a programme in which more Sinhalese soldiers confirmed the battlefield executions, and linked the army's 53rd Division, under the command of Major General Kemal Gunaratne, with the alleged crime.[23]

As for the end of Prabakharan, one version has his twelve-year-old son being executed in front of him in the course of his torture, before

he too was shot. In keeping with the vast majority of official communications from Sri Lanka's government, there is no reason to trust their
version of events. The government's explanations were confused,
ambivalent, disconnected from the flow of events and contrary to
perhaps the best measure of truth in Sri Lanka relating to the events of
these days: the mill of rumours fed by the personal communications to
family and friends from front-line troops. The *Daily Mirror* quoted the
chilling words of Sri Lanka's ambassador to the UN, Palitha Kohona:
'The LTTE wanted to surrender their arms a little too late.' Whatever
the precise form of his death, the Supreme Leader, the self-anointed
'Sooriyathevan' (Sun God) was dead, and in imitation of the summary
killing of the leader of the JVP, Rohana Wijeweera, two decades earlier,
his body was quickly incinerated without inquest or post-mortem, and
his remains scattered.[24]

In parliament, an exuberant President Rajapaksa declared that
henceforth there would be 'no more minorities'. There would be only
two kinds of people, those who loved their country, and those who
'have no love for the country of their birth'. It was not a promising
embrace of the diversity of Sri Lanka. Rather, as the *Sunday Leader* said
of the celebrations that week, 'the posters, the chants . . . the pagodas,
the floats, the flags, the media coverage, the symbolism of the Buddhist
flag entwined with the Lion flag . . . the deification of the President, the
blessings for violence and veneration of the armed forces by the
Buddhist sangha clearly flag an underlying Sinhala Buddhist nationalism very much alive and pulsating with triumphalism'.[25]

CHAPTER TEN

Aftermath

On 22 May, just three days after the announcement of Prabakharan's death, two army helicopters swooped low over the Cage. Peering from within, a group of journalists who had flown from New York with the UN Secretary General jostled for room. Their cameras zoomed in on the scene below as they passed over the second NFZ, the last stand of the Tamil Tigers.[1] Ban Ki-moon had politely insisted on the fly-over, and since the New York press pack was a part of the official delegation of the leader of the world's peace and security body, it would have looked bad had the request been refused. After all, a country that was basking in the warm light of victory had nothing to hide.

The trajectory of modern politics in Sri Lanka had altered with the extinction of the Tamil Tiger leadership. The Rajapaksa clan now had full control over the way the story that mattered to their grip on power was portrayed. Despite expecting a dismal and war-blighted scene, the wasteland awaiting the journalists and Ban Ki-moon shocked those in the helicopters. Empty of people and corpses, the landscape below revealed a confetti of shredded plastic sheeting across a vast sandy expanse of bomb craters, fire-blackened smudges, lines of earthen bunds, knots of hasty graves, smashed houses, burned-out vehicles, broken coconut trees, gun emplacement positions, trenches and the detritus of human habitation.

That night, a victorious President Rajapaksa insisted that the Secretary General meet him in the city of Kandy, where he was preoccupied cementing his rule and legacy in a ritual symbolising the Sinhalese triumphalism that the *Sunday Leader* had decried. While Ban Ki-moon wended his way for two hours along a one-lane road to the old mountain kingdom, a convocation of the high Buddhist priesthood blessed the president's power and the pre-eminence of political Buddhism. Over the following weeks, Rajapaksa would be variously dubbed Vishvakeerthi Sinhaladheeswara (Universally Glorious Overlord of the Sinhalese), Shree Wickrema Lankadheeswara (Heroic Warrior Overlord of Lanka) and Sri Lanka Raajavamsa Vibhooshana Dharamadveepa Chakravarti (Monarchical Emperor of the Glorious Land of Buddhism) by the leading Buddhist chapters. Ban Ki-moon waited in a Kandy hotel for the ceremony to finish. After a brief meeting with the president, the Secretary General signed an agreed 'joint statement' with Sri Lanka's foreign minister, followed by a press conference at which the statement was read. Then he drove back to Colombo in a long convoy, and flew out of the country that same night.

The extinction of Tamil hopes for political and social equality were accompanied by scenes in Colombo of people falling to their knees and bowing in supplication as the presidential motorcade glided along the troop-lined avenues. A campaign was launched to make Mahinda Rajapaksa president for life. Government ministers lauded his 'foresight, patience, and bravery'. As crude effigies of Prabakharan were burned in fiery nocturnal street parties and pictures of his bloated body played across television screens and in public photographic exhibitions, two-storey-high silhouette billboards of a gaily smiling and waving president were erected in Colombo. The same billboards were raised in the centre of the camps in Vavuniya, surrounded by the numbed and grieving Tamil masses of the Vanni, who still had barely adequate supplies of food, water, shelter and medical care for their range of horrific wounds.

The Secretary General's entreaties to the president that evening in Kandy for the quick release of the internees from the camps, for a commitment to political reconciliation and a lasting peace and for an investigation into any 'credible allegation' of war crimes were indulged by the president and his aides in the joint statement agreed between the two leaders. Earnest vague statements of intent had proven their worth in the preceding months, and yet the president was still being asked to provide additional guarantees of his good intentions and magnanimity in the flush of high victory. I stood near the Secretary General at a press conference that night at the Queens Hotel in Kandy, and wondered what was passing through his mind as he strained every tether of civility to deliver on his duty as the senior international arbiter of peace and security.

On 27 May, at the Palais des Nations in Geneva, the UN High Commissioner for Human Rights, Navanetham Pillay, addressed the Human Rights Council and called for an international inquiry into the conduct of both parties to the war. While the EU and a brace of other countries formulated and then moved a resolution in support of Pillay's call, a majority of countries on the council rejected it out of hand. Instead, they adopted an alternative motion framed by Sri Lanka's representatives praising the Sri Lankan government for its victory over the Tigers. It was a tribute to the skill of the diplomats and politicians who had raced from Colombo to lobby member states. Attuned to the peculiarly rancorous and intimate double-deals of their country's political scene, these men seemed well equipped to parry the earnest outrage of those countries that were pressing for a condemnation of Sri Lanka's violent military solution.[2]

Billboards were erected in the streets of Colombo in praise of yet another giddy Sri Lankan victory – this time over the dismal attempt to have international dissent at the government's methods publicly noted in Geneva. The billboards featured the smiling faces of the men who had worked the corridors of Geneva to bring about the resolution in Sri Lanka's favour, including the minister for human rights, Mahinda Samarasinghe.[3] Flushed with success on the diplomatic and military fronts, the government held a massive victory parade along the shore-front Galle Face promenade in Colombo. Columns of troops, naval personnel and air force officers marched alongside Chinese- and Czech-made armoured vehicles and artillery guns, Ukrainian multiple rocket launchers, Indian mobile radars and anti-aircraft guns. US, Indian, Israeli and Chinese gunboats hovered off shore, while Ukrainian MiG 27 fighters, Chinese F-7s, Israeli Kfir C7s and Russian helicopters flew overhead.

On 4 June, India's ambassador to the UN in Geneva, Gopinathan Achamkulangare, rebuked the independent office of the High Commissioner for Human Rights for a second attempt to have Sri Lanka's human rights record raised in the Human Rights Council. The ambassador accused Pillay of going beyond her brief and said, 'the independence of the High Commissioner cannot be presumed to exceed that of the UN Secretary General'. It was a grim assessment of

Ban Ki-moon's role in Sri Lanka, as well as an effort by India to gain favour with the Rajapaksa regime in the face of the considerable political leverage that India had already lost to China. Countries intent on asserting a respect for human rights as fundamental to international cooperation, peace and security regarded the Sri Lankan resolution as a disaster. African countries that had encouraged or led accountability moves in Liberia, Congo, Sudan and Guinea, wondered that the same kinds of crimes might be condemned in Africa but ignored in Asia.[4]

The next day in New York the UN Security Council listened to a briefing from the Secretary General on the three principles that had been agreed with President Rajapaksa in Kandy. While Russia and China congratulated Sri Lanka on extinguishing its terrorist problem, other council members – France, the UK, the US, Austria, Japan and Costa Rica – were more critical. In the press briefing that followed the Security Council session, one journalist asked why it was that the UN had been 'continually going to Sri Lanka as a petitioner'.

> Journalist: Mr Secretary General. . . there doesn't seem to be any 'right to protect' being asserted here – you are coming late to the conflict – there are allegations that there may be excesses of 20,000 people who died . . . what is the lesson about the United Nations that we have learned from your experience in Sri Lanka?
>
> Ban Ki-moon: First of all, I do not agree with your point that the United Nations came late. From the beginning of this crisis, I have been constantly in contact with the Sri Lankan government leadership. I have been making many telephone calls, all the time, even until just right before and after this conflict . . . It is crucially important that the Sri Lankan government follow up on all the promises that they have made. Any inquiry, to be meaningful, should be supported by the members of the United Nations, and also should be very impartial and objective. I have been urging the Sri Lankan president on this matter. He assured me that he will institute the necessary procedures to ensure the transparency and accountability of this [process].

Sri Lanka's UN representative in New York told one journalist that President Rajapaksa was 'deeply committed to political process and against triumphalism'.

*   *   *

The Tamil government doctors who had done so much to bring the war's impact on civilians to the world's attention had been held in army custody since the end of the war. On 8 July, they were brought before a press conference held at the defence ministry press centre in Colombo. The doctors announced that they had lied throughout the conflict and had been forced by the Tamil Tigers to exaggerate civilian casualty figures. Still wearing a sling after being treated for his injury, Dr Varatharajah, the top government health official during the siege, told the crowded room: 'It's difficult for you to believe, but it's true,' while his associates nodded in agreement. They related woodenly how the Tamil Tigers had taken food and medical shipments sent by the government and then forced the doctors to tell the media that there were shortages. According to Varatharajah, only some 650–750 civilians had been killed in the five months up to May 2009, and some 600–650 injured. The Associated Press drily noted in its subsequent report that the statements by the doctors 'contradicted other evidence from the battlefront'.[5]

While the ICRC and UN international staff had witnessed government artillery strikes on the paediatric and women's wards of PTK hospital and the deaths of patients and staff, Varatharajah denied the veracity of his own desperate telephone appeals to the Associated Press during those days. 'That was the clincher,' said the AP's Colombo bureau chief Ravi Nessman, who had posed the question in the midst of a largely complaisant Colombo press corps. 'There was no credibility to their testimony. They looked scared, nervous, and rehearsed. They were taking directions from two guys in white shirts who sat off stage. It made me physically sick to watch, knowing what they had been through already.' It was later alleged that one of Sri Lanka's better-known journalists had spent a full month coaching the doctors on their answers, and playing the results back to them on videotape until the government thought them plausible. Two weeks later, Nessman was expelled from Sri Lanka after the government refused to renew his visa.

July was a busy month for coining history. While MSF performed more than 5,000 surgical operations on camp inmates recovering from their bloodless 'hostage rescue', Indian army doctors now operating a field hospital inside the camp continued to fill buckets with shrapnel fragments extracted from civilians.[6] On the 14th, the chairman of the

Sri Lankan government-appointed presidential commission charged with investigating the killing of the ACF seventeen in 2006 announced that the SLA had not been near the town at the time of the mass execution. He said that the Muslim paramilitary Home Guards might have been, and speculated that the Tamil Tigers could have been responsible as well. Despite the chairman's complaint that his investigations were at best half finished, and that he had been hampered by the lack of a witness protection programme, President Rajapaksa had demanded an expedited report and a Bastille Day release.

A little more than a week later, the BBC reported that the relatives of the seventeen slain humanitarian workers had been given three letters to sign by the Sri Lankan government, two of which demanded increased compensation from ACF and a third addressed to President Rajapaksa that read in part, 'we are extremely grateful to Your Excellency for appointing a commission of inquiry and ensuring that justice prevailed . . . We agree with the findings of the commission that the deaths were caused by the LTTE and the compensation as determined must be paid by ACF.' Human Rights Watch called upon the international community to stop being dazzled by the 'elaborate song and dance' of the government of Sri Lanka, and to initiate a credible international inquiry into the killings.[7]

The judicial make-believe continued with the same commission's findings on the August 2006 bombing of the schoolgirls at Senchcholai, which declared them a 'justifiable military target'. The report detailed that the Tamil Tigers had taken the girls by force from their schools, over the objections of their parents, and had driven them on buses to the camp site, where they were guarded by female cadres and compelled to watch propaganda films about the struggle for a Tamil homeland, led by the Tamil Tigers. They were then, according to the report, taught to dismantle a gun and clean and reassemble it, before an afternoon of drills with sticks in place of rifles. The commission acknowledged the immensity of the tragedy, but exonerated the air force, which had given evidence of the assiduous due diligence of its intelligence analyses prior to the air strike. Reporting the commission's findings, *The Island* newspaper recalled UNICEF's characterisation of the girls as innocent victims, and denounced again the 'blatant lie' of the aid agency.

The government's command of the narrative continued. At the end of the war, some of the first people given access to the north were archaeologists. In Kilinochchi, a whitewashed Buddhist shrine appeared from the ruins. It had been renovated by the army and was 'an ancient site' according to the military spokesman. The archaeologists fanned out across the reconquered north, reportedly identifying and interpreting sixty sites that coincided with the dates of known Sinhalese habitation. 'For three decades we haven't been able to do anything in the north,' said Senarath Dissanayake, the head of the government's archaeology department. 'Now we can find out about how ancient people lived here – their culture, economy, social background, living conditions and religion.[8]

Tamils saw things differently. 'The government is putting up new Buddhist shrines and building permanent housing for soldiers,' said Tamil parliamentarian Suresh Premachandran. 'They are trying to colonise the area, to show it belongs to the Sinhalese.' Champika Ranawaka, minister for the environment and natural resources, leader of the extremist JHU party and an enthusiastic amateur archaeologist, had also been tasked with dispensing the government licences for archaeological excavation. At the same time, under the direction of defence secretary Gotabaya Rajapaksa, the army methodically razed the Tiger cemeteries dotting the Vanni, destroying the gravestones and statues dedicated to thousands of dead Tamil Tiger fighters. Prabakharan's childhood home on the Jaffna peninsula was demolished by SLA bulldozers.

The army was in a confident mood, and even felt qualified to offer its anti-insurgency expertise and training, backed by a 'written doctrine', to the US and India. The newspapers said that Sri Lanka had done what 'no other country in the world' had managed to achieve and had 'defeated terrorism'. In a country that had decisively crushed its only significant security challenge, and in which an estimated two fifths of its Sinhalese population was a member of either the defence or the security establishment, or directly related to a member, the announcement that the army was set to expand in order to fulfil its peacetime role came as something of a surprise.

The army was boosted by a 20 per cent increase in a defence budget that already accounted for almost one fifth of the national budget.[9] The army's newly appointed chief, Lieutenant General Jagath Jayasuriya, said that the military would 'consolidate what is captured and ensure

this type of thing won't arise again. Then help in government, development, and reconstruction.' He asked for 50,000 additional troops for
the 300,000-strong army, and a recruitment drive across the country
called for 'more heroes'.[10] On independence in 1948, Sri Lanka had had
no army, and only a small and reasonably well-trained and disciplined
police force. It now had the seventeenth largest army in the world,
more than thirty times its strength in 1983.[11]

Throughout June and July, there were reports of low-level clashes
as troops swept the jungles of the Vanni for small groups of insurgents who had managed to evade capture. Arms caches, many of
them dating back a decade or more, were uncovered by the armed
forces as interrogations of captured cadres led to more and more
disclosures. Gotabaya Rajapaksa continued to warn of active Tamil
Tiger elements, and urged Sri Lankans to remain vigilant. Each
month the parliament renewed the extension of the country's emergency laws, under which people could be arrested and detained
almost indefinitely. The parliamentary opposition, enfeebled more
than ever by the military victory, claimed that the emergency regulations were being used to stifle their campaigning in the run-up to the
April 2010 elections.[12]

The government gazetted the permanent status of 147 army camps
spread across the largely Tamil northern and eastern provinces, and
fortified its main new military bases in Kilinochchi and Mullaitivu. In
addition to the army camps, large swathes of land in Tamil-majority
areas have been converted into High Security Zones (HSZs), to which
it is forbidden for the former landowners and residents to return. By
mid-2010, the Jaffna peninsula had fifteen HSZs, totalling 160 square
kilometres, or about one fifth of the peninsula's land mass, displacing
130,000 people. In Sampur, in the Tamil-majority east of the island, a
portion of an HSZ was declared a Special Economic Zone in preparation for the establishment of industrial investment. One Tamil
parliamentarian said that the army was building housing for 40,000
soldiers and their families in the north, even before it had resettled the
300,000 Tamils being held in internment camps.

In July, an 'executive committee' of the Tamil Tigers released a statement purporting to appoint the Tigers' finance mastermind, the
permanent exile 'KP' Pathmanathan, as the organisation's new leader.
KP, whose role in surrender negotiations to save the senior leadership

had foundered so badly, would continue to lead the organisation in a campaign for an independent homeland. In the same statement, the Tigers renounced the use of violence to attain their goals. Instead they would reconstitute themselves according to democratic principles, as opposed to the authoritarian practices of Prabakharan. 'Like all liberation struggles,' said KP, 'we will modify the form and strategies of our struggles according to times and demands.' In an interview with Britain's Channel 4, however, he rattled a sabre, suggesting rather fantastically that he still controlled as many as 2,000 guerrilla fighters in the jungles of the Vanni. It was a claim of a desperate and rudderless organisation. Without the Supreme Leader, the Tamil Tiger international finance, crime, transport and business network was crumbling. In a sign that the diaspora was at least split if not in total disarray, the long-time mouthpiece of the Tigers, Tamilnet, refused to carry the statement. Just days later, KP Pathmanathan – number one fugitive from Sri Lankan justice, arms merchant, smuggler and finance mastermind – turned up in Sri Lanka, a captive.

The circumstances of KP's 'extraordinary rendition' to Sri Lanka on 6 August have not been explained. The Sri Lankan government said that it would respect the wishes of the country from which he had been snatched to remain anonymous. KP had maintained an operational base in Thailand, but a detailed description of an abduction conducted in a Malaysian hotel emanated from Tamil diaspora sources. Quite possibly, in the Byzantine world of Sri Lankan politics, rival claimants to the fertile commercial remnants of the Tiger corporation had betrayed him to the Sri Lankans. In a world into which the Bush administration had introduced the widespread practice of extraordinary rendition, the arrival of KP in Sri Lanka was lifted straight from the user's manual of the 'global war on terror'.

Brimming with confidence, a government spokesman said, 'We are quite capable of demolishing LTTE activities anywhere in the world.' Gotabaya Rajapaksa gloated about the information that was being extracted from KP, and in late 2009 the Sri Lankan authorities began claiming former Tamil Tiger shipping assets from a variety of countries. In Colombo, people flocked to the docks to wander about one of the notorious seized Sea Pigeon arms transportation ships that had been identified in a foreign port, seized and then sailed to Sri Lanka. In the government's opulent reckoning, the Tamil Tigers had stashed between one and five billion dollars in bank accounts throughout the world, but there was scant mention of what, if any, money had actually been recovered.

In November 2009, gossip that had festered for months about a rift between the Rajapaksas and army commander General Sarath Fonseka finally burst into public view. Some suggested that Gotabaya had taken to circumventing the army chief in the last months of the war while Fonseka had been distracted by arms purchasing missions in China. The defence secretary had even issued orders directly to battlefield commanders, to the chagrin of his old army classmate. One newspaper detailed how Fonseka had been infuriated by an offer made to him by the president of a peacetime role as secretary of the ministry of sports.* In July, as rumours began to circulate of a planned coup by the army commander, Fonseka was promoted to the purpose-made job of chief of defence staff, reporting to Gotabaya Rajapaksa and leaving the defence secretary in direct control of the armed forces. Fonseka, in a mood of palpable rising anger, gave a series of public speeches in which he made brooding references to people degrading the value of the army's contribution to the victory over the Tigers.

In November, Fonseka declared his candidacy for the January 2010 presidential elections, backed by an unlikely coalition of political parties and with the promise that he would defeat what he called 'the corrupt and despotic Rajapaksa family regime'. He promised to 'expose the Rajapaksa regime of its misdeeds and rampant corruption'.[13] The JVP, which had reinvented itself as a Marxist nationalist party and had been vital to the war effort, quit the government and teamed up with the floundering opposition UNP to back the Fonseka candidacy. The Tamil National Alliance (TNA),† reluctantly punting on a frontman they disliked and distrusted, and whom they held to be responsible for, at the very least, a large proportion of the brutality inflicted on the Vanni

---

* The editor of the newspaper was arrested. Fonseka was nothing if not prickly and vengeful: his long-time cook had been unmasked as a Tamil Tiger sleeper, and was found hanged a week later in his cell.
† A coalition of Tamil parties that had fought elections since 2001, and is the largest Tamil party in Sri Lanka. In 2010 it gave up its long-standing commitment to an autonomous Tamil state, opting instead for regional self-rule.

Tamils, joined the team. Acknowledging the paucity of alternatives and its forlorn political gambit, the TNA party leader Mano Ganesan said, 'In this case, it's better the devil we don't know.'[14] With Fonseka once having told an interviewer that in his opinion 'Sri Lanka belongs to the Sinhalese', it was an intriguing prospect that the Tamil minority vote might decide the election should the general split the Sinhalese electorate. One leading Buddhist organisation warned him that he should not 'fall prey to national and international conspirators'.[15] It seemed that nobody was above betraying the Sinhalese.[16]

With a bare head and unbraided shoulders, however, Fonseka was never anything more than a flailing political ingénu, who struggled to break out from his frigid, unsmiling military mould, and who continued to make intemperate remarks that entangled him in a series of recriminations and counter-recriminations with the government. As he launched his Facebook page, Fonseka improbably declared, 'there is no clear policy to win the hearts and minds of the Tamil people . . . paving the way for another uprising in the future'. He also accused the government of corruption, waste, running death squads and crushing media and personal freedoms. In one interview, he said that he knew about 'certain crimes', and would reveal all; after a furious reaction from Gotabaya Rajapaksa, who accused him of treason and betraying the army, Fonseka hastily claimed that he had been misquoted.[17]

The presidential election of January 2010 was a decisive victory for Mahinda Rajapaksa, and Fonseka's bid to rid Sri Lanka of the violence, corruption and political decay of the Rajapaksas an unhappy and abject failure. Incredibly, on the day of the elections, Fonseka had announced that he would cooperate with any international inquiry into war crimes in Sri Lanka. The alliance of political convenience swiftly crumbled post-election, and unified political opposition to the Rajapaksas seemed utterly discredited. Within days of the result, troops stormed Fonseka's political headquarters and dragged the protesting veteran general away. The government announced vague and incoherent charges of treason, later parsed into seven charges of illegally engaging in politics and corruption. The disgraced war hero began his own voyage through the system of judicial make-believe in Sri Lanka, with his wife filing human rights petitions with the courts in a futile effort to win his release. It was a neat if unfortunate irony that when denied access to the fallen general with urgent medicine, she appealed to the ICRC to reach him in prison. The editor of the *Sunday Leader* wrote: 'Fonseka's rise and fall from hero to villain reflects a lot about our society. Our heroes do not know when to quit gracefully and we as a people are left desperately looking for a credible, committed leader who at the minimum can keep his hands off the till. What this whole episode has made clear is that we are destined to be governed by a bunch of thieves for some time to come.'[18]

In 2009, the international media watchdog Reporters Without Borders rated Sri Lanka number 162 out of 175 countries for media freedom. Physical assaults, disappearances and the demonising of journalists, the media and academics continued after the war. Paikiasothy Saravan-muttu, the only prominent Sri Lankan civil society figure to have spoken out on international TV networks against the government for its treatment of civilians, was threatened with death by an anonymous Sinhalese vigilante group. In March 2010, the BBC reported that his name was reputedly on a secret list of activists compiled by sectors of the Sri Lankan government. In Sri Lanka, such lists amount to proscription.

In June, the government reactivated the defunct Press Council. This hand-picked watchdog had been first constituted by Sirimavo Bandara-naike's government in 1973, with the express purpose of controlling the media. The rejuvenated council had the power to fine and imprison journalists for writing about 'internal communications of the govern-ment and the decisions of the Cabinet; matters relating to the armed services that may be deemed prejudicial to national security; and matters of economic policy that could lead to artificial shortages and speculative price rises'. The *Sunday Leader* said in an editorial that 'the reactivation of the Press Council is a blunt statement to the effect that anything resembling a free press is both unwelcome and out of order . . . the independent media is already weak having been terror-ised through months of killing and abductions . . . and reveal the government's determination to stifle conclusively any and all avenues for dissent'.[19] Two journalists from the *Sunday Leader*, whose editor had been slain just nine months before, were threatened with death in anonymous letters.

In August 2009, the Tamil J.S. Tissainayagam, cited by President Barack Obama as a symbol for all persecuted journalists, was sentenced to twenty years' imprisonment for his supposed links to the Tigers, and for violating the all-encompassing Prevention of Terrorism Act. The High Court, in passing sentence, said that the journalist had sown communal hatred by writing and publishing articles that criticised the government's treatment of Sri Lankan Tamil civilians affected by the war. While the world reacted with indignation, and a number of international awards were given to Tissainayagam, one government official pointed to the presence of a defence lawyer, a properly constituted court and the possibility of an appeal. 'He faced a proper trial,' said Sri Lanka's secretary of the foreign ministry, Palitha Kohona. 'If there is still a doubt about the conviction he has the option of appealing to a higher court.' The US ambassador to the Human Rights Council said that Sri Lankan legislation equated 'disagreement over government policy with treason'.[20]

The government continued to expel international journalists, and also turned its attention to UN officials. It accused one of the two UN international officers who had witnessed the bombing of the first NFZ of acting against Sri Lanka's interests, and ordered him out of the country. In September, he was followed by James Elder, a UNICEF official who had remarked that children in the siege zone were going through 'unimaginable hell'. Palitha Kohona, who by now had been appointed to his ambassadorial post representing Sri Lanka at the UN in New York – and who once told an interviewer that he had joined the UN in order to make a difference for children – explained that Elder had been 'doing propaganda in support of the LTTE', and that UN officials ought to act neutrally. Kohona, an expatriate Sri Lankan who enjoys Australian citizenship, would later accuse the author of being part of an Australian human rights conspiracy, a cabal that apparently included Philip Alston, the UN's Special Rapporteur on Extrajudicial, Summary or Arbitrary Executions, who is a prominent international law scholar and human rights expert.[21]

Alston had long been a thorn in the government's side. He had insisted that the Sri Lankan government investigate the thousands of disappearances taking place under the Rajapaksa security regime. Unwilling to accept the government's findings on the killing of the ACF seventeen, he also rejected its impetuous verdict on the video that had surfaced in August apparently showing Sri Lankan troops brutalising and then executing prisoners of war. In a letter to the government,

Alston wrote, '. . . an authoritative study of customary international humanitarian law finds that attacking and killing persons who are recognized as *hors de combat* is prohibited. Persons declared as *hors de combat* include anyone who clearly expresses an intention to surrender, provided he or she abstains from any hostile act and does not attempt to escape.'

For several months, an independent body of forensic experts convened by Alston scrutinised the video. Sadly, the investigative group concluded that the video, apparently shot as a 'trophy' by the executioners, was in all probability exactly what it purported to be.[22] The International Criminal Court's chief prosecutor, Luis Moreno-Ocampo, said that in the view of the ICC's prosecutions office, Sri Lanka was a place where 'crimes have been committed'.[23] In October 2009, after a request from US senator Patrick Leahy, a sixty-eight-page blow-by-blow preliminary State Department report detailing alleged war crimes in Sri Lanka was tabled in the US Congress. The Sri Lankan government dismissed the report as 'baseless'.[24] President Rajapaksa issued a statement claiming that 'conspiracy after conspiracy' was degrading the victory of the army.

The issue of illegal executions and other alleged war crimes, however, just would not go away. Throughout 2010, more evidence of brutality emerged, including a series of graphic photos (one of which is included in the picture section of this book) of a captured prisoner being mutilated with knives and then beaten to death. On 8 December 2010, Britain's Channel 4 broadcast a report and photographs confirming the identity and non-combatant status of a twenty-seven-year-old female Tiger apparatchik known by the pseudonym of Isaipriya. A news presenter, dancer and singer for the Tiger propaganda wing, she appeared to have been executed by members of the SLA's 53rd Division in the final hours of the war.[25]

Despite the stubborn impenitence of the Sri Lankan government, and its insistence on cloaking its victory in a Potemkin-like pretence at bloodlessness, a quarter of a million people had witnessed the death and destruction inflicted by both the army and the Tigers. Although around 80,000 of these were still in internment camps more than a year after the end of the war, most had been returned to their homes. Thousands more, however, were leaving Sri Lanka for Malaysia, Singapore, Thailand, Australia, the US, Canada and dozens of other countries that held Sri Lankan Tamil communities. In early 2010, the Australian chapter of the International Commission of Jurists began taking testimony from Tamil survivors in a low-budget evidence-gathering project, in the first moves to compile a legal brief that might eventually serve as the basis for prosecutions.

In the past two decades, since the end of the Cold War, there has been a dramatic evolution in the role of international justice mechanisms being used to punish crimes against humanity, and in the view taken of the role justice ought to play in healing the wounds of civil conflict. Various judicial processes have laid down incontrovertible drafts of history, carefully detailing the motivations and crimes of perpetrators. If there is a lesson that has been drawn from the prosecutions of war crimes in The Hague, in the expansion of the doctrine of 'universal jurisdiction'* and even in the establishment of an International Criminal Court in 2002, it is that the yearning for justice often runs directly counter to the demands of peace and diplomacy, and to the currents of history.

In the statement of principles thrashed out between the UN Secretary General and President Rajapaksa following the helicopter sweep over the Cage on 22 May 2009, Sri Lanka had agreed to investigate any credible allegations of war crimes. Its reaction to the allegations that have arisen since the end of the war – claims of thousands of unexplained civilian dead, mass battlefield executions, the torture and rape of captives – as well as the island's long-established record of impunity for those who have committed atrocities in the defence of the state, gives little hope that Sri Lanka will attempt to come to terms with its past.

Shortly after the war, the Attorney General of Sri Lanka, Mohan Peiris, spoke to an audience of government officials, ministers and diplomats, arguing for 'restorative' rather than 'retributive' post-conflict justice and for a generous amnesty for those Tiger combatants who had survived.[26] It was a nuanced description of the challenges facing Sri Lanka as it wrestles with the competing demands of justice, peace and memory, after decades of bloody civil strife. As Peiris quoted

---

* This doctrine holds that certain crimes are so heinous and such a moral affront to humanity that they rise above jurisdictional limitations, and that countries are morally and legally obliged to prosecute these crimes when they can.

with approval from the South African constitutional court on the subject of amnesty, he might well have been describing the past three decades, and sounding a warning for Sri Lanka's future:

> Most of the acts of brutality and torture which have taken place have occurred during an era in which neither the laws which permitted the incarceration of persons or the investigation of crimes, nor the methods and the culture which informed such investigations, were easily open to public investigation, verification and correction. Much of what transpired in this shameful period is shrouded in secrecy and not easily capable of objective demonstration and proof. Loved ones have disappeared, sometimes mysteriously and most of them no longer survive to tell their tales. Secrecy and authoritarianism have concealed the truth in little crevices of obscurity in our history. Records are not easily accessible, witnesses are often unknown, dead, unavailable or unwilling. All that often effectively remains is the truth of wounded memories of loved ones sharing instinctive suspicions, deep and traumatizing to the survivors but otherwise incapable of translating themselves into objective and corroborative evidence which could survive the rigours of the law.

What had happened to all those survivors, with their 'wounded memories'? More than 290,000 people were crammed into enclosures in Vavuniya, surrounded by razor wire and guarded by the Sri Lankan army. The government disputed that they were detention camps at all. International law provides for the internment of people for a limited period of time in the interests of national security, so long as they are informed of the specific basis for their detention and have an opportunity to challenge it before an impartial authority. Thousands of those in the camps were deeply compromised by their involvement with the Tamil Tigers. But instead of describing clear guidelines for the identification and prosecution of those accused of crimes, the government preferred secrecy. Intelligence agents and pro-government Tamil paramilitary groups had a free hand to root out insurgents. It is unclear how many of those who were removed from the camps were 'disappeared'. There were many scores to settle between the Tigers and those Tamil paramilitary groups who represented political parties targeted by the Tigers for destruction, or the Karuna group that had split with the Tigers in 2004.

Almost as soon as people began to enter the camps, however, they discovered that they were able to leave them. Some simply escaped through gaps in the hastily unrolled razor-wire fences, slipped past guards or were smuggled out in the many vehicles that moved in and out of the camps each day. The Sri Lankan military that maintained the cordon sanitaire around the camps, manned the gates, patrolled the perimeters, monitored the handing over of food parcels from worried relatives and managed the thin trickle of visitors allowed into the camps now began to allow people to slip away. It quickly became apparent to senior commanders that lower-ranking soldiers were taking bribes to let people go, or sympathetically turning a blind eye to bedraggled and worn civilians escaping the heat, filth and confinement of the enclosures.

When the government realised what was happening in the weeks after the end of the war, it closed the camps to the humanitarian operation for the second time. From scores of trucks and jeeps entering the camps each day with relief supplies, the operation to ease the suffering of hundreds of thousands of people came to a virtual halt overnight. It was the worst of all possible times, with 290,000 people almost totally reliant on a complex array of aid to take care of their needs. Thousands of people were badly wounded, or were suffering a variety of ailments exacerbated by the appalling fatigue and hunger that they had been subjected to inside the battle zone. It will never be known how many died as a result of this closure, but it quickly became apparent to senior officers that they would be unable to deal with the most basic needs of the internees. Within days, aid agencies were allowed to resume services.

By late June 2009, somewhere between 20,000 and 30,000 camp inmates – or around 10 per cent of the captive population – had escaped. According to aid workers and government officials, there was a menu to choose from, varying from the 5,000 rupee option to have a guard avert his eyes, to the 400,000 rupee option for a passport, a car and permission to cross the tightly controlled Medawachchiya checkpoint that lay between Vavuniya and Colombo, plus a ticket to Singapore and the expunging of one's name from the camp registry.[27] In the estimation of one senior civil servant involved in the camp operations, most senior Tiger leaders who had not been killed or identified earlier were able to escape. The government had unwittingly helped by establishing a branch of Western Union inside the camps, even before it had arranged sufficient places for inmates to purchase additional food.[28]

One notable measure of the success of the smuggling racket concerned the UN. Within six weeks of the end of the war, of its 131 staff members and family who had been interned, only thirty-five were left inside. While the UN Secretary General had personally been requesting President Mahinda Rajapaksa to authorise the release of UN staff, and had received successive assurances that they would be let go, desperation, the burgeoning smuggling racket and market forces had combined to win their release regardless of the political snubs delivered by the government. One army officer, nicknamed 'Schindler' by aid workers, fed up with the extortionate schemes of his comrades, simply opened the gates of the small compound he was in charge of and allowed people to escape en masse.

President Rajapaksa publicly thanked China, India and Pakistan for their help with the victory. Notably excluded were Western countries that had also sold arms or offered training to Sri Lanka over the years. It was Rajapaksa's way of noting a simple new calculation in international affairs that had been useful in extracting concessions from three key regional Asian rivals. By playing off the Indo-Pakistan antipathy, and the mutual suspicions inherent in the Sino-Indian relationship, the Sri Lankan government achieved three critical things. First, it had access to a competitive and sophisticated arms market in Pakistan and China, with loans provided on generous terms. Second, it was provided with Indian intelligence that strangled traditional smuggling routes across the Palk Straits and culminated in interceptions at sea that sank the majority of the Sea Pigeon fleet and smashed the rearmament pipeline to the beleaguered Tiger forces. Finally, it had the political support from China that was necessary to forestall action in the Security Council, the only body potentially capable of slowing the army's rush to extinguish the Tamil Tigers.

The Tigers contributed three significant elements to their own downfall. The first was that their ability to wage war had changed substantially since the signing of the ceasefire agreement in 2002. The population they governed expected stability and a lasting peace as a result of the CFA pact. With fighting suspended, the Tamils of the Vanni first celebrated, then began to enjoy and finally expected the fruits of peace. Expatriate Tamils began to invest in the homeland, as did development agencies. Buildings sprang up in the nominal capital of Kilinochchi, along with supermarkets. Thousands of fighters once wedded solely to the cause of a Tamil homeland married other fighters, or took spouses outside 'the Movement'. With young families, the personal calculations of these former fighters diverged from their commitment to armed struggle. When called to arms again in 2006, much of the will to fight had simply dissipated. Widespread discontent grew as families were called upon to give one and then two members. Despair increased as more and more children were drawn into the threshing machine of war.

The second error was to fight as a conventional army despite the unprecedented range of forces amassed by the renewed Sri Lankan army, and to attempt to hold territory. The Tigers could have revolutionised their battle plan and switched to the guerrilla tactics that were their core capability. Had they dispensed with their territorial gains, buried their caches, folded the majority of their fighters back into the civilian population and recommenced a strategy of hit-and-run attacks on installations, army patrols and urban targets, the government might well have quickly spent their political and financial capital. The base of their supporters would have disconsolately recognised business as usual in the ineptitude and failure of the SLA to master a foe whose essence and advantage was not only its legendary resilience, but also its elusiveness. There would have been no 'final victory'. In 1990, Prabakharan himself had noted the dangers of what he called 'over-confidence'.[29] In a war where the myth of indomitability had been key to battlefield success for the Tigers, Prabakharan allowed an overweening sense of superiority to dominate his strategic judgement. Despite the numerical, political and material advantages that had developed in the Sri Lankan government and army, he believed that he could preserve his hold on territory. He failed to recognise that his enemy had metamorphosed in both mind and body.

Finally, the Tamil Tiger leadership was simply out of touch with the way the rest of the world had changed since the September 2001 terrorist attacks on US cities. The political advantage stoked by al-Qaeda's blitz – the atmosphere of generalised terror – accrued decisively to the government. By May 2006, the European Union and more than thirty other countries had proscribed the Tamil Tigers as a terrorist group. They were also included on the United Nations list of terrorist organisations. The political costs of providing support to murky national liberation movements were too high. While public opinion abroad might have sympathised with the vaguely understood plight of civilians trapped by two armies in an obscure war, liberation groups had become conceptually too confused with the terrorist causes that continued to lead to bomb plots and attacks in New York, London, Sydney, Bali, Baghdad, Stockholm and Algiers, and the proliferation of apparent threats. The international narrative had converged neatly with the story told by the Sri Lankan government: that the malevolent and ingenious Tamil Tigers, spawned by opaque or even metaphysical imaginings, was a terrorist group that had to be eradicated as surely as al-Qaeda.[30]

With a succession of post-war local, presidential and parliamentary elections, the Rajapaksas could claim that Asia's oldest democracy was in good shape, despite the turbulence of the Tiger years. The presidential election in January 2010 was fought amidst widespread claims that the government intimidated candidates, flouted electoral rulings and stuffed ballot boxes. According to elections commissioner Dayananda Dissanayake, he 'could not even ensure the safety of one ballot box', and had done his duty only 'under great duress and mental agony'. Just half of Jaffna's registered voters were able to vote, and only a sixth of those detained in the camps. While Sarath Fonseka languished under house arrest and the government tried to define coherent charges against him, the April parliamentary elections began to take form. An unprecedented 7,520 contestants – the highest number in the country's history – vied for just 225 seats, and the number of people registered to vote had risen steeply.

So healthy was the competition that in one district alone, voters faced a ballot paper a metre long listing 660 candidates who were contesting just seven parliamentary seats. One newspaper editor called the elections 'a big joke', while Rohana Hettiarachchi, the head of an election monitoring group, complained that the huge number of candidates was essentially a bait-and-switch tactic by the government, bamboozling the electorate with phantom candidates who closer to the election would withdraw their candidacy in favour of genuine party nominees. The opposition alliance, hopelessly weakened by the dismal performance of Fonseka in the January presidential contest, and with the errant general now locked up, predictably splintered into a powerless array that stood no chance against the government's juggernaut.

With a thoroughly refreshed mandate (and widespread genuine popularity), President Rajapaksa now added the planning, ports, aviation and highways portfolios to his finance and defence* chest. His brother Basil was appointed minister of economic development, and entrusted with the tourism and investment boards, as well as with economic regeneration of the newly devastated north. Brother Gotabaya retained his humble post as defence secretary, with close to half a million security personnel under his authority, although he expanded the mandate of that post to absorb the Urban Development Authority and the Land Reclamation and Development Corporation. Brother Chamal was elected, unopposed, speaker of the parliament, a position from where he could scupper any move to impeach the president. One cousin was handed a cabinet portfolio, while cousin Jaliya Wickramasurya was appointed ambassador to the United States, and cousin Udayanga Weeratunga was given the ambassadorship to Russia.[31] 'Unprecedented,' said Kishali Pinto-Jayawardene, a prominent legal scholar. 'Placing all this power in the hands of one individual has never happened before in Sri Lanka. What was *de facto*, is now *de jure*.'

And lest anybody challenge the legality of the power concentrated in so few hands, the president for the first time added the office of the Attorney General to the seventy-eight institutions he already directly controlled. Reforms considered by the Rajapaksas included doing away with the constitutional limit to the number of terms a president could serve, and revising the 17th constitutional amendment to empower the president to directly appoint members to important commissions such as human rights, elections, corruption and public service (the 17th constitutional amendment had been originally conceived as a way to check presidential power by ensuring the independence of such commissions). Finally, a proposal was mooted to allow the president to take part in parliamentary proceedings. One

---

* The president formally holds the defence portfolio, with his brother Gotabaya holding the post of secretary to the defence ministry.

newspaper noted that 'every aspect of our lives from the registry of our births, to the taxes we pay . . . and the documents we must carry in order to move freely is under the control of Rajapaksas. Their domination is absolute.'[32]

CHAPTER ELEVEN

Post-Mortem

The conquest of the Tigers was a resounding military success. Despite the overblown rhetoric of the government suggesting a singular and prescient strategic formula, victory was due to a timely confluence of factors. The simple geographic isolation of the island, together with a well-defined theatre of operations and the easily delineated population within which the guerrillas operated were the most significant elements. The emergence of a China willing to supply weapons and easy credit triggered more generous support from an array of other nations competing for spoils of influence at a time of unusual international uncertainty. Sri Lanka was in the enviable position, for a tiny country, of being able to pick and choose favours from an array of powerful or nettlesome countries. The country's readiness to play the 'rogue nation' card and to court support from Iran, amongst others, provoked timidity from a group of influential nations traditionally far more assertive regarding morality in foreign policy. Not least among the ingredients of victory, the personal ruthlessness of Gotabaya Rajapaksa and Sarath Fonseka, and their good management of the political and military assets at hand, combined to produce a well-led, enthusiastic and effective armed force. Finally, with critical Indian intelligence locating Sea Pigeon merchant ships as they attempted to reach the embattled guerrillas, the Sri Lankan navy were able to cut the Tigers' vital supply chain. Defeat was then a matter of time.

Just a few months after the end of the war, Reuters hawked the small but surging Sri Lankan stock market as one of the best performing in the world. By late 2010, the economy was growing at 8 per cent, sales of Sri Lankan bonds were over subscribed and some predicted that the island would overtake Vietnam's economic performance. The IMF, which had just released a loan to Sri Lanka over the objections of Britain and the US, proclaimed the 'fundamental stability' of the country.[1] Hired by the Sri Lankan government, the London-based international public relations firm Bell Pottinger worked to gloss over the nasty business of war.[2] The *New York Times* gave Sri Lanka top billing as the best holiday destination for 2010. Colombo hosted the International Indian Film Academy awards (although a number of senior Indian entertainers declined to attend). As tourists flowed back to Sri Lanka in large numbers, the tourism authority rebranded its flagship slogan from 'A land like no other', to 'A land of small miracles'. Even as tens of thousands of Tamils continued their lives behind barbed wire, European tourists flocked to the island's beaches, and almost 300,000 people – the vast majority of them Sinhalese – visited the north of their country for the first time.[3] Sri Lanka was at a kind of peace.

But there was another side to this apparent stability. The European Union withdrew a valuable trade preference scheme from Sri Lanka in exasperation that the country continued to flout basic human rights agreements, such as the torture convention.[4] Many Sri Lankans – Tamils in particular, but thousands of Sinhalese also – live in daily fear of their government. The death squad threat enforces the government's writ. Opposition media and public opinion remain full of trepidation in the atmosphere of a Sinhalese supremacist ideology vindicated by the conquest of the Tamil Tigers. Even as this book goes to publication, newsrooms are being wrecked and burned by gangs of thugs and journalists forced into exile.[5] In August 2010, a group of global leaders including former UN Secretary General Kofi Annan, Archbishop Desmond Tutu and former US president Jimmy Carter characterised the ongoing persecution and disappearances of human rights activists, journalists and government opponents in Sri Lanka as 'truly terrifying'.[6]

In what Tutu called a 'deafening global silence', the international community – or what passes for such – took an effete collective stand over the final bout of bloodletting in Sri Lanka. In doing so, it failed all Sri Lankans who yearn for a modern, inclusive, progressive and well-regarded democracy that abides by the rule of law rather than the rule of the jungle. The United States was notable for its articulate ineffectiveness; the government of India for its ubiquitous but ambivalent presence; and the government of China for its highly visible development role on the island, even as it quietly blocked formal debate on the war in the chamber of the Security Council.

It had suited all Indian political factions to sit on the fence. With a national election in May 2009, a dislike for the troublesome Tigers and an eye on the swinging voters of Tamil Nadu, India's interests were best served by hushed military assistance, protecting Sri Lanka in global forums and holding the outrage of Tamil Nadu in check through that front for diplomatic inaction: regular expressions of 'concern'. Prabakharan's death brought personal satisfaction to India's Congress party and Rajiv Gandhi's widow, and avenged India's military humiliation at the hands of the Tigers. By playing along, India managed to limit its loss to China and Pakistan of influence in Sri Lanka, and will profit from stabilised borders, cooperation with the island, increased trade across the Palk Straits,[7] and the disappearance of a locus in northern Sri Lanka for pan-Tamil separatism. Other members of the international fraternity of nations who professed to care about Sri Lanka watched India's vacillations and double-dealing with dismay. Without great India, how could they hope to restrain Sri Lanka from its final excess of violence?

The US, with its response to Sri Lanka stalled by the transition from the Bush to the Obama administration, by the distraction of Afghanistan and by a lack of confidence in the strength and reach of its own ethical foundations during the global financial crisis, responded fitfully. In the words of *Time* magazine, Obama failed the 'first human rights test' of his administration. China and India consistently undercut the US promptings to Sri Lanka that it ought to limit its assault on civilians, as the two Asian giants competed to protect the country from international scrutiny. China repeated in Sri Lanka its performance in Sudan, where, conscious of its strategic oil interests, it had thwarted international action against the government of Omar al-Bashir during the Darfur crisis. Then, mounting international pressure and the approach of the 2008 Beijing Olympics had eventually compelled China to agree to intervention. But, as we have seen, the war in Sri Lanka was far less visible than Darfur, and China's position in the pecking order of world affairs had changed substantially from that of 2003, and even more so from 2006, when the Sri Lankan army began to march once more. A sure-footed Sri Lanka astutely managed its interests between the purposeful rise of China and a far less certain US grip on world affairs.

The UN, in the estimation of Louise Arbour, in effect withheld information that would have forcefully alerted the world to the impact on civilians of this last chapter of war.[8] As a critical report had noted a decade before, the UN's anxiety to appear neutral, and to sustain its presence even in the midst of the mass killing of people, 'can in the best case result in ineffectiveness and in the worst case may amount to complicity with evil'.[9] However ineffective at stopping the bloodshed, the UN earnestly strove to remain engaged before, during and after the war. A week before the first anniversary of the victory over the Tamil Tigers, the Sri Lankan government announced the formation of a Lessons Learnt and Reconciliation Commission (LLRC). It was, in part, a response to the consistent engagement from the office of the UN Secretary General, which was pressing for lasting solutions to the conflict. But from the outset, the tasks of the LLRC were limited, and predicated the cause of the war on the rise of the Tamil Tigers: to 'find out the root causes of the terrorist problem' and to determine 'what happened during the last three decades which would be helpful for reforms that would go hand in hand with constitutional reforms'.[10] Louise Arbour and Philip Alston, two senior international jurists familiar with the exhausting parade of hollow Sri Lankan inquiries, dismissed the latest commission. Louise Arbour noted that in the hands of the Rajapaksas, the LLRC was 'bound to fail . . . a government [whose] entire history has been one of denial and impunity. The prospects for closure emanating from within Sri Lanka – historical, political, or judicial – seem highly unlikely.'[11]

Six decades after independence, Sri Lanka displays a characteristic common to many post-colonial states: a disconnect between the liberal democratic institutions of government imagined at its foundation and the ethnic, class, cultural and religious fissures that have instead dominated society. Minorities feel that they have a place in Sri Lanka only so long as they are 'compelled to fall in line and be slaves within a Sinhal[ese] identity and within the contours of a Sinhal[ese] nationalism'.[12] The state of democracy in Sri Lanka – ostensibly returned to good health by the defeat of terrorism – is at best an uncertain proposition. The instruments of liberal democracy have been degraded and reconfigured in the decades since independence to support the hegemony of a small clique of rulers representing the ethnic majority in an illiberal democracy.[13]

Regular elections are the legitimising front for a political racket now run by the Rajapaksa family. Instead of the 13th amendment to the constitution, which would have devolved power to the provinces, the president and his brothers engineered the passage through a compliant parliament of a novel 18th amendment. This 'constitutional reform' removed the president's term limit, wiped out some of the last vestiges of an independent judiciary, tightened his personal grip on the free press and scuttled independent oversight mechanisms, 'transforming Sri Lanka from a flawed democracy into a dynastic oligarchy'.[14] Sri Lankans who supported the war effort, in the belief that better times were ahead, are now aghast as their democracy dissolves. A new Buddhist fundamentalism – or 'era of purity', as one government minister put it – is taking hold. Officials concern themselves with banning miniskirts, billboards and music videos. Police harass young couples holding hands or kissing in public. As one Sri Lankan noted, 'too many of us backed the prosecution of a war at any cost, not realizing that it was also being used to cut away the ground from beneath our own feet'.[15]

With military defeat and the death of Prabakharan in 2009, the Tamil Tigers seemed to vanish.[16] From the last day of the war, there were no armed attacks of any substance, and no suicide bombers. The guerrilla army appeared to have been crushed completely. The population of Tamils who had lived under the Tiger writ was beaten, bewildered and mourning its dead. The vast network of legitimate businesses that underwrote the insurgency throughout the world disappeared into the pockets of individual Tamils. The Tigers' international propaganda network displayed a confusion of emotions and messages, with many reports denying for months on end that Prabakharan had died. The current debate in the Tamil diaspora appears to be a fierce one, with some resigned to working within the status quo simply to end the misery of the northern Tamils. Others remain convinced that force is the only solution, but lack any realistic vision for a renewed insurgency in a state flooded with half a million members of the security forces. No sensible observer, however, imagines an armed internal threat to the island emerging under the current security state.[17]

Aid workers and non-governmental organisations are prone to exaggerating the numbers of dead, or the numbers of women raped, or the numbers of landmines sown, in order to stir up timely attention to

conflicts. Overblown figures used by advocates to 'sell' the very genuine
humanitarian crises in Darfur and the Congo undermine the credibility
of those conflicts, and of those that follow. Nevertheless, it seems
certain that in Sri Lanka, many thousands of civilians were killed in the
final few months of a war 'conducted with unprecedented secrecy'
behind a wall of managed silence.[18] Ordinarily charged in the world's
conflicts with tracing missing relatives, the ICRC in Sri Lanka was
prevented by the government from collecting any data that would
provide an overall picture of the dead or missing. If so few had died, it
made no sense for the government to hide the dead and prolong the
misery of those who survived, wondering at the fate of their missing
relatives. If the 1983 riots and the deaths of a few thousand Tamils had
created a searing memory and rallying point that gave rise to the Tamil
Tigers, how do prospects fare now for peace and stability in Sri Lanka?

Memory, or grievance, is passed from one generation to another like
a talisman, and shapes our present.[19] Survivors or victors process these
grievances, and their children are initiated into the past in a variety of
narratives, traditions and pageants, depending on the course of history.
Germany was forcibly brought to terms with its crimes through defeat
and occupation, and universal shame helped to create the Jewish state
of Israel. Modern Spain treads the stage as one of the most socially
evolved states of Europe, but conflicting interpretations sustained by
the protagonists of its civil war seventy-five years before have never
been reconciled. In the spirit of the times, a contrite Serbia has owned
its culpability for the genocide committed by its proxies in Bosnia, in
return for political acceptance internationally. Russia recently soothed
the human and political need for closure and assumed responsibility for
the Second World War slaughter of Poland's intelligentsia and officer
corps in the Katyn massacre. It took persistent families and the passing
of almost forty years for Britain's prime minister to apologise for the
Bloody Sunday killings by British paratroopers in Ireland. However
imperfect the result, South Africa dealt with the crimes and suffering
of the apartheid years through a Truth and Reconciliation Commission. On the other hand, and against the recent tide of history, Turkey
refutes Armenian interpretations of the massacres carried out by
Turkish forces during the First World War. The Turkish intransigence
has provoked outrage, pro-Armenian motions in liberal legislatures,
and stone memorials. In the dominant liberal international order,

historical, political and judicial closure is held to be a good thing.

Even the Sri Lankan army's new commander has called for a political reconciliation to effect closure and to take the wind out of the grievances that gave rise to the insurgency. So too have many Sri Lankans – the so-called 'civil society', but also ordinary men and women – who view the latest bout of killing and the swagger of their rulers with horror. The large-scale killing of Tamils has certainly inflamed a new generation of young Tamils abroad. Helen Manuelpillai, the woman whose father and brother were killed during the 1983 riots, watched her fourteen-year-old daughter's attitude evolve during the 2009 siege. From an Australian teenager uninterested in family history, she became an ardent demonstrator for Tamil rights in Melbourne. For the first time, she asked for details of the fate of her uncle and grandfather. She skipped school, painted placards, amassed petitions and swore fealty to the recognition of Tamil rights. Like other expatriate national groups frustrated by the brutality and denial of wrongdoing of their home countries, a new generation of Tamils is unlikely to forget the latest chapter in their history. They will almost certainly continue to agitate for a Tamil homeland, for an international inquiry into the final stage of the war and for a true historical accounting *from within* Sri Lanka of the Tamil struggle against discrimination.

Unfortunately, judging by current trends on the ground, an astute soothsayer might guess that the future for Sri Lanka's Tamil citizens is bleak. The emigration of Tamils from Sri Lanka will continue, encouraged by political stagnation, a lack of rights and rule by fear. Tens of thousands of Tamils displaced by the fighting, but unable to leave, will be resettled at the government's discretion, using security as a pretext for usurping private property in key areas.[20] The hitherto relatively contiguous area that has formed the basis for a Tamil claim to a historic homeland will be broken up and interspersed with hundreds of army camps, staffed by Sinhalese soldiers. The families of the soldiers will work on agricultural lands wrought from the proliferating HSZs, or in factories established in the adjacent Special Economic Zones and awarded to Chinese or Indian interests. It is ethnic cleansing of the Israeli rather than the Yugoslav variety, but without the inquisitive eyes of an exterior world blind to Sri Lanka's machinations.

To effect these demographic changes, the government seeks the support of international donors who, perhaps in spite of themselves, scramble at the first sign of 'moderation' in the form of rousing presidential speeches that call for development, a word that carries a whiff of hopeful progress along with the march of the government's actual political intentions. Development projects, like the irrigation/ settlement schemes of D.S. Senanayake in the 1940s, are a reasonable response to poverty, but are easily distorted to support ideological ends such as ethnic cleansing, or bled to enrich those who hold absolute power. In playing along, donors are complicit in exacerbating conflict while they anxiously sustain stable relations with the government. As development ideologues, they wilfully propagate the argument that prosperity breeds political progress, despite the unfortunate historical trajectory of Sri Lanka. There is nothing new about the creeping erasure of Tamil territorial claims in the name of development, but the extinction of the Tamil Tigers has once again made possible the total domination of the narrative by the state.[21]

Archaeologists and historians, sanctioned by the government, unleashed on to conquered territory and possibly funded by UNESCO, will supply the academic legitimacy for the 're-territorialisation' of Sri Lanka. Eventually, postcards will be printed of newly minted Buddhist sites in formerly Tamil areas, and tour guides will regale sightseers with stories of their discovery and antiquity. Just two weeks after Prabhakaran's death, the president's wife unveiled a statue of Sanghamiththa, the daughter of the emperor Ashoka and the woman who – two and a half thousand years before – is said to have brought a seedling of the holy Bo tree to Sri Lanka. The statue now sits in the middle of one of the HSZs, in the heart of Tamil Jaffna. It is a kind of re-creationism that would be familiar to nineteenth-century European nationalists who in countries like France and Italy sought to erase complex regional identities and allegiances as they constructed myths about the homogeneous nature of the state.

A great many Sinhalese regard with disappointment the government's regressive pandering to the worst instincts of political Buddhism. Dayan Jayatilleka, one of the most capable diplomats appointed by the Rajapaksa regime, had outmanoeuvred Western diplomats to help Sri Lanka escape censure from the UN Human Rights Council in Geneva. He had also been one of the most trenchant advocates within the government for meaningful constitutional reform, including the devolution of power to the provinces.[22] Post-war, having been dumped as Sri

Lanka's ambassador to the UN in Geneva, he urged Tamils to rejoin the political process and forswear violence, in order to 'neutralize and outweigh the influence of the Sinhala hard-line parties and dark fantasies of settler-colonized permanently Occupied Territories'.[23] Another young academic, Sanjana Hattotuwa, wrote, 'Sri Lanka is sadly . . . not post-racial. I fear that the essential nature of the Rajapaksa regime will return Sri Lanka to violence more virulent than what we now celebrate the end of. Political will such as it exists in Sri Lanka is openly unwilling to entertain a process that could engineer its own demise.'[24] Sri Lanka, as a sovereign entity, has emerged strengthened by its conquest of the Tamil Tigers. Its critical international alliances are largely intact, its economic prospects promising, and it appears more stable than before. As a democracy, however, it has been weakened, its reputation ruined for a generation at least, its significant minority now yoked to subordinate status, its historic trajectory fixed to a familiar course.

The prospects for a majority of Sri Lanka's Tamils do not look good. However brutal and totalitarian the writ they imposed, the Tigers represented the legitimate aspirations of Sri Lanka's Tamils for two generations, and kept alive the hopes that they would achieve a degree of control over their destiny that has been denied to them by majoritarian rule. Dayan Jayatilleka acknowledged the grievances that gave rise to the Tamil Tigers, but also believed that the time had come when their violence had to be matched by the equal violence of the state. Even Jayatilleka, however, who had so earnestly committed himself to that end, eventually harboured doubts about the intentions of the Rajapaksa government, with its 'studied silence or at best an ambiguity about the shape of the political settlement or the political reconciliation between the south and the north'.[25] In the search for that most basic quality of a state – security for its people – negotiation between the protagonists, successive elections and the democratic system had proven futile. The only force capable of mustering sufficient unity of purpose to tackle the threat to the state had been Sinhala Buddhist nationalism, and victory had infused the Sinhalese public with blinding resurgent ultra-nationalism.

The young soldier who discovered Prabakharan's body, and who had grown up with the Tiger threat, no doubt thought that his children would have to live with the same menace hanging over their daily lives.

But apart from the army's efficient campaign, the Tamil Tigers had contributed to their own downfall. Terror was successful as a tactic of war, and in the Tiger estimation, the thousands of Sinhalese citizens who died represented a 'military necessity' that helped to keep the oppressive Sinhalese state at bay for more than two decades. For many years, terror was also more successful than not as a political strategy. Each national liberation group that decides to take up arms against an oppressor seeks to justify its actions as proportionate to its ends. The very extremism of the Tigers helped to sell their cause. But the choice of terror ultimately overwhelmed that cause. As the American political philosopher Michael Walzer said in his magisterial book, *Just and Unjust Wars*, 'the revolutionary reveals his freedom in the same way as he earns it, by directly confronting his enemies and refraining from attacks on anyone else'. Under the Tamil Tigers, an initially legitimate response to state violence distorted, and ultimately supplanted, the very terror that it sought to thwart.[26]

But states, too, reveal themselves in the way they are defended. The choice between strategies when fighting an insurgency is relatively straightforward. One strategy tries to win the soul of a people, with all that that entails – a demonstrated respect for their culture, their rights as citizens, their condition as human beings, and even recognition of their grievances. This 'hearts and minds' approach tries to restore the writ of that state over a contested population by fighting as decently as possible. Such a strategy knows that 'ideas cannot be shot, imprisoned, or exiled'.[27] These kinds of counter-insurgencies are fought by liberal democracies in places like Afghanistan. Their leaders and decision-makers understand that they are ultimately answerable to constituencies who might, like the French in the Algerian war of independence, withdraw support if they become too murderous. The soul of the state and its essential qualities must not be eroded as it seeks to regain control of territory and people. In such circumstances, counter-insurgency inevitably has limits.

States in which accountability is subordinate to ideology, and to oligarchs, simply do not recognise such limits or choices. Theirs is a strategy largely or sometimes completely comprised of terror. In the modern world at least, it is an approach suited to governments that elevate militant nationalism to an ideal, thereby reducing the humanity of the enemy. Armed with this ideology, the subtleties of the 'hearts and minds' approach, or obedience to the rule of law, are shunted aside. The evident brutality of the final phase of Sri Lanka's war, the treatment of the captive population, the post-war militarisation, the rejection of accountability and the political reconfiguring of the nation imply a political objective that has little interest in the hearts and minds of those who were 'rescued'. It suggests instead a commitment to the complete subjugation of the Tamil population by force, and an intention to sustain a grip over this restive group through terror and ethnic cleansing. And for those many Sinhalese who care about how they are governed, the same methods of control used on dissenters throughout the war – shooting, imprisonment, exile and disappearance – remain implicit. The state has replaced the terrorist violence that it thwarted with a new terror-backed hegemonic hold that is unlikely to be dislodged for many years to come.

Many countries – mostly Western, but also some of Sri Lanka's Asian neighbours like Japan, South Korea and Singapore – continue to press for political reconciliation, and for a meaningful and effective inquiry into allegations that the laws of war and humanity were breached by both sides during the civil war. They do not accept the view of the Sri Lankan government that the defeat of the Tigers has provided a long-term solution to Tamil grievances. Nor do they believe that social problems ought to be resolved through simple suppression. These countries – internationalist in outlook and aligned with US power – see such an inquiry as an important element of long-term peace and stability. They view adherence to international agreements such as the torture convention or the genocide convention, as elemental to the dominant international consensus that seemed to take hold after the Cold War. These agreements include accountability to fellow signatories. As historian Timothy Garton Ash has written: 'Liberal internationalism . . . means developing norms and rules by which most states will abide, preferably made explicit in international law and sustained by international organisations. It posits some basic rights that belong to every human being on this planet . . . It seeks to build peace between nations on these foundations.'[28]

This cooperative view of modern international relations maintains, by natural extension, that the deaths of tens of thousands of civilians do count, and that the way you fight a war does matter, even when your cause is just. With the Cold War out of the way, and US power paramount, the international prosecution of Balkan and Rwandan war criminals during the 1990s was evidence to liberal internationalists of the advent of a more enlightened age, with its intellectual roots in the ideals of Immanuel Kant, and its practical expression in new foreign policies informed by morality. The 2002 Treaty of Rome, which created the permanent International Criminal Court sitting in The Hague, promised a system of international jurisdiction in which all governments could be held equally accountable for the mass murders that had historically been considered the right of those who ruled.

In June 2010, the UN Secretary General formally empanelled a group of experts to advise him on accountability issues related to allegations of war crimes in Sri Lanka.[29] But if the panel's findings are adverse for the Sri Lankan government, or if there is an international judicial process, what will be achieved by holding the protagonists in Sri Lanka to account? Will an international investigation, for example, serve the interests of peace and security on the island, as well as *international* law, order and stability? To some, the social tensions stoked in the pursuit of justice after a war directly undermines long-term stability. Given the sudden irruption of China into the neat, progressive assumptions of this liberal internationalist order, is it more prudent to ignore allegations of war crimes, and to leave the nature of government in the hands of the Rajapaksa brothers? A 2010 US Senate committee report explicitly noted that the US risks 'losing' Sri Lanka to the Chinese team. Given the advent of Great Powers jostling in the Indian Ocean, does the pragmatic US interest in retaining Sri Lanka in its orbit trump the demands of justice?

Many small and powerless countries believe that liberal internationalism is another form of colonialism, in which wealthy, privileged countries tell the locals what is good for them. International agreements, like contracts, can only be considered well conceived if they are perceived to be fair. The liberal internationalist order is dominated by the wealthy, democratic West (although perhaps not for much longer). At peace for two generations, their middle classes have only a vague understanding of the kind of threat that the Sri Lankans have just vanquished. They insist that their governments should apply ethical foreign policies that are compatible with their own globalising consciousness. Yet these same countries that proselytise human rights abound in ironies and hypocrisy. In the worst of instances, the pursuit of a supposed objective moral good in foreign policy has resulted in the opposite. Under the Bush administration, both Afghanistan and Iraq were cast into years of lethal instability, for which the populations of those unfortunate lands have paid the price. The US in the twenty-first century also retarded the brief expansion of the rule of law into international affairs that had flourished in the 1990s. It refused to ratify the Treaty of Rome that brought the International Criminal Court into being: no US government could endorse Marines being tried for war crimes by foreign nationals. Sri Lanka only had to refer to US practices such as torture in secret detention facilities, mass civilian deaths in Iraq, Guantanamo's gulag, extraordinary rendition, bombings in Afghanistan, targeted drone killings in Pakistan and Yemen and the language and moral duplicity of the global war on terror in order to render dumb Western diplomats who quibbled with its methods. Who is this privileged international community, with its own dark episodes, to tell Sri Lankans how to manage their affairs?

Moreover, these liberal internationalist societies are either new states like Australia and Canada, with multiculturalism at the core of their identity, or relatively prosperous uni-ethnic states, best expressed by the unique territorial mosaic of the European Union. It was the states of the European Union, after all, that practised violent ethnic cleansing over the course of hundreds of years in order to achieve the stability that its populations derive from homogeneous communal identity. In the year of Sri Lanka's hopeful independence in 1948, for example, European states had only just concluded the forced expulsion of around three million of their German citizens, the greatest single episode of mass ethnic cleansing in history. In many countries it is the very homogeneity born of this ugly past that now anchors national identity, provides stability and ultimately underwrites the broad international system of sovereign states. The current backlash in liberal Europe against Muslim immigration is about nothing if not the threat to identity and the correlative sense of threat to a stable and familiar order.

The search for national identity in the unstable liquid of history, literature, archaeology and ethnography only provides approximate renderings of our past, ever vulnerable to manipulation. To assert that our bloodlines, or past, are in some way 'pure' is fruitless, to imagine that our societies are or have retained mono-ethnicity is a matter of

fantasy, and to link both with a current claim to the modern conceit of
a nation state is dishonest and dangerous. But in the breakdown of
great empires, and the build-up of new nations, questions of proven-
ance and identity have mattered, as elites established their claims to
rule on behalf of the constituent peoples of territories with fixed
borders. And as we have seen in the rapidity with which parties of
archaeologists have been sent forth in Sri Lanka, historical narrative
matters in the preservation of power. When Britain left Sri Lanka as a
unified country in 1948, it left fundamental communal fault lines with
which its constitutional settlement was incapable of dealing. Colonial
Britain had institutionalised ethnic-based representation and then care-
lessly conferred a liberal democratic system as it sought to detach itself
from the burden of rule. Poverty, population and poor leadership
trading in a mythologised past did the rest.

The role of identity in world affairs – personal, local and national – is
far from over. The potential power of grievance on the collective
imaginations of repressed or marginal peoples was graphically imposed
on the psyches of modern, advanced and cosseted societies by the
attacks on New York's Twin Towers. In our Age of Terror, and despite
the elusive and muddying 'terrorist or freedom fighter?' dichotomy,
well-informed publics understand that conflicts have causes that can be
traced to grievances. Each of us recognises that if we are denied the
expression of our individual, cultural, ethnic, political or religious identity by a tyrannous ideology, our reaction might be blessed with the
stoicism and wisdom of a Gandhi, or doomed by the violence and
nihilism of a Prabakharan. The grievances of the Tamils, whose identity and place on their island was eroded by the formation of the state,
in turn threatened the integrity of Sri Lanka as a stable sovereign entity.
Perhaps through the eradication of the Tamil Tigers, the dilution of
Tamil-dominated areas and the imposition of authoritarian rule, Sri
Lanka will find the stability that has eluded it since independence. For
now, its reply to grievance is more tyranny.[30]

Other insurgent groups present more potent challenges to the international order than the Tigers, who were only ever a threat to Sri Lanka.
They will continue to rise against the kinds of perceived injustices that
the Tamils have faced in Sri Lanka. These grievances are grounded in
clashing identities and competing narratives swirling around the current

heirs to history, the nation states of the United Nations. In the twenty-first century, these rebel groups are well informed, operationally fleet-footed, capable of rapid evolution, masters of propagating their cause amongst the aggrieved and, most critically, better armed than ever. People will flock to those promising them liberation from states or ideologies that erode, suppress or 're-imagine' the core identities of segments of their population. Grievances in distant corners of the earth will continue to affect global security. The allure of these groups is apparent in Afghanistan, Yemen, Myanmar, Thailand, Somalia, Indonesia, India, the Philippines, the Caucasus and places with names that we will come to know more of in the next decade, such as the troubled Ferghana Valley, which runs through former Soviet Central Asia. The operatives of al-Qaeda have demonstrated the multiplying potential of grievances harvested from people ruled in weak, autocratic, unjust and corrupt states that resemble Sri Lanka.

One of the consequences of being a Big Power in the modern world is the inevitable extension of domestic interests into the global sphere, as states identify aspects of their vital security in far-flung places (and, conversely, like the US, are held to account for their meddling). The US has been left to founder in Afghanistan in what was a poorly conceived counter-insurgency that morphed into an inept nation-building project. In time, it may be forced to withdraw, just as the Soviets were, because the alternative to the failing 'hearts and minds' strategy is to use the kind of terror and ethnic cleansing employed by Sri Lanka's military and political planners. In any vacuum created by a US withdrawal, emerging powers such as China, India and an increasingly beleaguered Russia will be left to deal with a proliferation of small 'liberation wars' that threaten their borders, their energy and trade routes, and that ignite restive ethnic groups within their countries. China has sharpened its counter-insurgency teeth on its internal separatist conflicts in Tibet and in the far western region of Muslim Xinjiang, but it has yet to be blooded by the kind of modern foreign expeditionary warfare seen in Afghanistan. In Sri Lanka, China acted in its perceived strategic interests with no eye to the long-term strategic consequences of undermining the finely honed system of international human rights agreements and the rule of law that had evolved throughout the 1990s and which, in the hands of the liberal international order, is one of the best forms of 'soft' power.[31]

Instead of confronting this test case of Chinese 'foreign policy subversion', most of the US arms of government predictably ignored Sri Lanka as too distant, too small, too insignificant and too much in the Indian and Chinese spheres of influence. The US government collectively surrendered one of the planks of its foreign policy architecture – along with the grand vision of liberal democratic hegemony – on which liberal international order has been built. The US remains both the creator and the preferred model for the edifice of current international cooperation, and yet is struggling with the leadership and responsibility that is necessary to manage global disorder. To be sure, its neo-con fantasy role as 'global policeman' has been downgraded by the reality of two decades of post-Cold War domination, but where will the ambitions and vision of a global liberal democratic order, still led by the US for decades to come, now settle? As the Sri Lanka case illustrates, just how the West, the emerging great powers of India and China and the rest of the international community choose to deal with similar insurgencies will affect the purchase of justice and the place of human rights in world affairs in the years ahead, and goes to the heart of global stability.

Individual liberty is a matter of eternal vigilance, and what happens in one tiny country to a small and insignificant people – as Lasantha Wickrematunge noted, and as Sri Lankans concerned with their own liberty are now discovering anew – reflects on our own survival. Just as the line between international and internal conflicts is less clear than in the past, so too the line 'between the state of war and the state of peace has also diminished'.[32] Along with the threat of force and sophisticated counter-insurgency methods, the grievances that underlie these insurgencies must be addressed more effectively through the evolving multilateral structures of the UN, through regional groups such as the African Union and through the international justice and arbitration mechanisms that have evolved so much since the end of the Cold War. Modern states, fashioned from the collapse of empires and left with the kinds of internal divisions seen in Sri Lanka that threaten their stability, must discern that their best interests lie with the devolution of powers within their borders into ethnic, religious or sub-regional expressions of group identity. The states of the European Union, for all their history and faults, exude an enviable *esprit de corps*. The EU is a political model that provides for the expression of identity that is fundamental to humans, even as it seeks an umbrella of moral and economic unity. The African Union, against great odds and in what has been the worst-governed continent in recent history, has shown that moral authority is both possible and regarded as beneficial in mutually cooperative unions of nations. The alternative is the Sri Lankan model: A society sliding into tyranny where myth-making, identity whitewashing and political opportunism have defeated justice and individual dignity.

Glossary

Ayurvedic medicine | A system of traditional medicine and healing that dates from India's Vedic period in the second millennium BC. It is widely practised throughout Sri Lanka today.

bhikkhu | A fully ordained Buddhist monk. The word, meaning 'beggar', is derived from ancient Pali.

Black Tigers | The Tamil Tiger unit specialising in suicidal warfare.

Bo tree | A Sinhalese word for Bodhi, a fig tree (*Ficus religiosa*), said to be the genus of the tree under which the Buddha attained enlightenment in the town of Bodh Gaya, India. The still living sacred Bo tree at Anuradhapura, in northern Sri Lanka, is said to have been brought as a sapling to the island in 288 BC by Sanghamiththa, the daughter of the Emperor Ashoka.

bodhisattva | This Pali word denotes a sentient being who is either consciously in the process of seeking or otherwise destined to encounter enlightenment. The Buddha himself referred to his life prior to his enlightenment as his bodhisattva. In Buddhism, to choose this path is considered an ideal.

cadre | The English term used in Sri Lanka to describe the foot soldiers of the Tamil Tigers. In this context it seems to have developed to denote both the military function of the individual and the politicised nature of their role.

Ceylon | According to Anagarika Dharmapala, the Mahavamsa includes the following additional names for the island: Tambapanni, Taprobane, Lanka, Rainadwipa, Sihaladwipa, Serendib, Zeylan, Mandadwipa, Ojadwipa and Varadwipa. Ceylon was renamed Sri Lanka under the 1972 constitution.

Chola | A Tamil dynasty from southern India that ruled in

varying strengths between around 300 BC and AD 1300. At its furthest reach, it was dominant throughout much of south and south-east Asia.

dagaba   A bell-shaped solid brick structure usually rendered and painted white. It is a Buddhist place of veneration, derived from the stupa, which itself is derived from ancient pre-Buddhist Indian burial mounds.

Dravidian   Describing the people, cultures and areas bound by languages with Dravidian roots. A pan-Dravidian movement was prominent in India (with reverberations in Tamil Ceylon) between the 1940s and 1960s.

drone   A generic term for all Unmanned Aerial Vehicles, light, remotely controlled aircraft used primarily by militaries for real-time video field surveillance and missile attacks.

Eelam   An ancient Tamil word denoting the island of Sri Lanka. 'Tamil Eelam' was the name used by Sri Lankan Tamil nationalist groups to denote the presumptive state to which they aspired.

Eelam War   The 'Homeland War', as Tamils called the civil war, actually consisted of four periods of conflict between uneasy periods of truce. These were Eelam War I (1983–7), Eeelam War II (1990–5), Eelam War III (1995–2002), Eelam War IV (2006–May 2009).

hartal   A Gujarati word meaning a popular strike in the form of a total shutdown of official and private business. *Hartals* were first used by the Indian independence movement. The first *hartal* in Ceylon took place in 1953, in protest against the move by the government of Dudley Senanayake to reduce the rice subsidy.

Mahavamsa   The Great Chronicle. A chronicle of Sinhalese and Buddhist history on the island, written in Pali in the fifth century AD by a *bhikkhu* called Mahanama, and believed to represent a faithful chronological historical record. It is the second of the four great *bhikkhu*-authored chronicles of the island (often collectively known as the Mahavamsa). The first was the Dipavamsa, also written in Pali around the third to fourth century AD, which deals with much the same subject matter as the Mahavamsa. The other chronicles are the Bhodivamsa, written in the tenth century AD, which records the arrival of a sapling from the Buddha's Bo tree in Sri Lanka, and

	the Culavamsa, which records Sri Lankan history between the fourth and early nineteenth centuries.
mudaliyar	A revenue collector, or a military or civil rank under the Sinhalese kings; the title was adapted for use as an honorific by Low Country Sinhalese from the mid nineteenth century.
Pali	Thought to have once been an active language, by the time the Mahavamsa was composed, Pali was akin to a canonical literary language for the Theravada school of Buddhism. It is a Middle Indo-Aryan language, and has been aligned with Magadhi, the much earlier north Indian vernacular, in which the Buddha is thought to have taught, and which was in use in the court of the Mauryan king Ashoka during the third century BC. The Mahavamsa is considered the finest of the Pali texts.
pavathina kramaya varadity	A Sinhalese phrase popularised during the JVP revolt, roughly translated as 'all is wrong'.
Sabha Maha	A political group founded by S.W.R.D. Bandaranaike in 1937, promoting the interests of Sinhalese Buddhists.
sangha	An ancient Pali word meaning 'community'; it denotes here the monastic community of ordained monks or nuns.
satyagraha	Literally 'soul force', an element of Gandhian non-violent tactics.
Sea Pigeons	The fleet of merchant ships amassed by the Tamil Tigers, and used for the shipment of regular merchandise, as well as armaments.
Theravada	The school of Buddhism practised by the overwhelming majority of Sri Lanka's Buddhists, and throughout much of South-East Asia. It is one of the oldest of the Buddhist schools, and hence regarded as relatively conservative in its practice.
Vanni	In ancient times through to the twentieth century, the vast forest of the Vanni stretched across the northern third of the island, providing a physical border between the main concentrations of Tamils and Sinhalese. It was probably inhabited by the aboriginal Vedda people. The Vanni is a loose geographical description that combines the current government districts of all of Vavuniya, Mannar and Jaffna and parts of Kilinochchi and Mullaitivu. After the Tamil

Tiger retreat from Jaffna in 1995, it became their main
base of operations.

Vedda   The hunter-gatherer aboriginal people of Sri Lanka,
            who are thought to pre-date all other racial groups
            on the island. Vedda inhabitation can be traced as far
            back as 18,000 years, and may be much older. The
            Vedda were probably forest-dwellers, and feature in
            the Mahavamsa as co-habiting with Prince Vijaya and
            his followers. Today there are thought to be around
            2,000 Vedda people, though only perhaps as few as
            several hundred who intermarry and maintain their
            traditions on government reservations.

Vesak   The second month in the Buddhist calendar (May–
            June), the day of Vesak is held to mark the birth,
            enlightenment and death of Buddha. In Sri Lanka,
            it is celebrated in part with magnificent displays of
            paper lanterns across the island.

yaksha   The original inhabitants of the island; a kind of be-
            nevolent forest spirit and keeper of earthly treasures
            common to Buddhist, Hindu and Jain mythology.

List of Acronyms

ACF	Action Contre la Faim (Action Against Hunger)
AFP	Agence France-Presse
AP	Associated Press
BBC	British Broadcasting Corporation
DPU	Deep Penetration Unit
EPDP	Eelam People's Democratic Party
EPRLF	Eelam People's Revolutionary Liberation Front
EROS	Eelam Revolutionary Organisation of Students
EU	European Union
GAA	Genocide Accountability Act
HSZ	High Security Zone
ICC	International Criminal Court
ICJ	International Commission of Jurists
ICRC	International Committee of the Red Cross
ICTY	International Criminal Tribunal for the former Yugoslavia
IIGEP	International Independent Group of Eminent Persons
IMF	International Monetary Fund
IPKF	Indian Peace Keeping Force
JHU	Jathika Hela Urumaya (National Heritage Party)
JVP	Janatha Vimukthi Peramuna (People's Liberation Front)
LLRC	Lessons Learnt and Reconciliation Commission
LRIT	Long Range Information and Tracking
LSSP	Lanka Sama Samaje Party (Ceylon Equal Society Party)
LTTE	Liberation Tigers of Tamil Eelam
MBRL	Multi-Barrel Rocket Launcher
MSF	Médecins sans Frontières
NFZ	No Fire Zone
NGA	National Geospatial Intelligence Agency
NGO	Non Governmental Organisation
NTT	National Television of Tamil Eelam
PLOTE	People's Liberation Organisation of Tamil Eelam
PTA	Prevention of Terrorism Act

PTK	Puthukkudiyiruppu, a town in eastern Sri Lanka
RAW	Research and Analysis Wing
RPG	Rocket Propelled Grenade
SLA	Sri Lankan Army
SLFP	Sri Lanka Freedom Party
SLMM	Sri Lanka Monitoring Mission
TELO	Tamil Eelam Liberation Organisation
TNA	Tamil National Alliance
TRO	Tamil Relief Organisation
TULF	Tamil United Liberation Front
UAV	Unmanned Aerial Vehicle (drone)
UN	United Nations
UNICEF	United Nations Children's Fund
UNP	United National Party
UPFA	United People's Freedom Alliance
UTHR(J)	University Teachers for Human Rights (Jaffna)
WFP	World Food Programme
ZCC	Zero Civilian Casualties policy

Timeline

589 BC   Buddha's enlightenment.

483 BC   Prince Vijaya, the mythical founder of the Sinhalese colony, lands on the island with his 700 followers after travelling from north India. The year is said to coincide with the death of the Buddha.

246 BC   Emperor Ashoka sends his son Mahinda to convert the Sinhalese king to Buddhism.

161 BC   The Tamil king Elara is slain in battle by the Sinhalese King Duttugemenu.

5thC AD   The *bhikkhu* Mahanama writes the epic Sinhalese chronicle the Mahavamsa.

13thC   After hundreds of years of Tamil invasions from south India, the Sinhalese fall back to the south-west quadrant of the island.

1293   Marco Polo visits Ceylon.

1505   The Portuguese arrive on the shores of the island.

1638   The Dutch ally with local factions to expel the Portuguese. By 1660, they control all of the island except for the kingdom of Kandy in the centre.

1796   British warships land on the coast of Ceylon during the Napoleonic wars. By 1802, Ceylon has been ceded to Britain.

1815   The last independent kingdom of Kandy falls to British forces.

1818   A year-long rebellion by the Kandyan chiefs is ruthlessly suppressed. The capture by the British of the Holy Tooth Relic helps to suppress the revolt.

1833   As an outcome of the 1829 Colebrooke-Cameron Royal Commission, a legislative council is established in Ceylon, with representatives appointed by the British governor from the Sinhalese, Tamil, Burgher and European communities. The Kandyan province is administratively joined with the rest of the island. Ceylonese are admitted into the civil service.

1837   The Mahavamsa is 'rediscovered' and translated from Pali into English.

1848   Another rebellion in the Kandyan provinces is suppressed.

1877	The Mahavamsa is translated into Sinhalese.

1877   The Mahavamsa is translated into Sinhalese.

1880   Henry Olcott lands in Ceylon with his theosophist companion Mme Blavatsky.

1921   The first legislative council elections in which a majority of members are elected by popular vote, rather than appointed by the British governor.

1931   As a result of the 1927 Donoughmore Commission, universal suffrage is introduced, along with a state council and a series of executive committees managing each aspect of government affairs. It is effectively self-rule without actual independence.

1933   Death of Anagarika Dharmapala.

1948   Ceylon becomes independent.

1950   Hundreds of thousands of 'Plantation Tamils' disenfranchised and deprived of citizenship in a bargain between the main political parties, including the Tamil parties.

1951   S.W.R.D. Bandaranaike splits from the UNP to found the SLFP, which will become Ceylon's second major party.

1956   2,500th anniversary of the death of Buddha, the same year in which Prince Vijaya is said to have landed on the shores of Ceylon with his 700 men to found the Sinhalese nation. The Sinhala Only Act is passed through parliament, making Sinhala the official language of Sri Lanka. Around a hundred Tamils killed in riots. Full provisions of Act meant to be introduced within five years.

1957   The first of the Chelvanayakam agreements. The following year, the pact fails when a UNP-led Sinhalese backlash forces Prime Minister Bandaranaike to abandon his attempts to conciliate the Tamil community with a political settlement to protect their rights.

1958   Hundreds of Tamils and some Sinhalese killed in inter-communal riots.

1959   S.W.R.D. Bandaranaike assassinated by a *bhikkhu*.

1960   The SLFP's Sirimavo Bandaranaike becomes prime minister of Ceylon for first time. Reverses her electioneering assurances to Tamils, and begins to implement provisions of 1956 Sinhala Only Act.

1965   UNP sweeps to power under Dudley Senanayake. Now in coalition with the Tamil Federal party, the PM signs new and almost identical Chelvanayakam pact. The provisions are never fulfilled.

1970   Second term in office for Sirimavo Bandaranaike (SLFP party).

1971   First JVP Marxist uprising under the leadership of Rohana Wijeweera. The uprising is crushed within weeks. Thousands of Sinhalese dead.

1972   The introduction of the republican constitution in May. The Tamil Tigers are founded that same month. New constitution replaces governor general with ceremonial president, and strengthens Sinhalese nationalist grip with new flag and central role for Buddhism. New 'positive discrimination' university entrance regulations disadvantage Tamil community.

1975   Around these years, the Eelam Revolutionary Organisation of Students (EROS) is uniting Tamil diaspora resistance to the Sinhalese hegemony. EROS makes first contacts with Palestinian resistance groups in the Middle East, with whom Tamil militant groups such as the Tigers later train.

1977   J.R. Jayawardene (UNP party) elected as prime minister, ousting the SLFP's Sirimavo Bandaranaike. The following year he introduces a new constitution that includes executive presidency. Main Tamil nationalist TULF party holds balance of Tamil vote in parliament. Riots leave around a hundred Tamils dead.

1978   Prime Minister Jayawardene becomes president, while Ranasinghe Premadasa becomes prime minister.

1981   Burning of Jaffna library by security forces.

1983   The 'Black July' riots. Between 1,000 and 3,000 Tamils are killed. The start of Eelam War I. India begins training Tamil militants in earnest in camps throughout India.

1984   The first of the large-scale killings of Sinhalese civilians by the Tamil Tigers. Sixty-two people are killed at farms in Jaffna.

1987   Sri Lankan forces trap Tamil Tigers in Jaffna city. Indo-Sri Lanka Accord is signed. The Indian Peace Keeping Force lands on the island. Second JVP insurgency begins. The Tamil Tigers turn their guns on the IPKF.

1989   Rohana Wijeweera is captured and executed. Second JVP insurgency peters out by the beginning of the following year.

1990   IPKF leaves the island. The uneasy truce between the Tamil Tigers and the government breaks down. Eelam War II begins. Around 75,000 Muslims expelled from Tamil areas by Tigers.

1991   India's former prime minister Rajiv Gandhi is killed by a suicide bomber in Tamil Nadu, southern India.

1993   Sri Lankan president Premadasa (UNP party) is killed by a suicide bomber at a May Day rally in Colombo

1994   SLFP's Chandrika Kumaratunga elected as president on peace platform.

1995   Eeelam War III begins after peace talks fail between the Tigers and the SLFP government of President Chandrika Kumaratunga. Tamil Tigers retreat from Jaffna into the Vanni jungle with half a million Tamil Jaffna residents.

1996   Suicide truck attack on downtown Colombo destroys high-rise office buildings, kills around a hundred people and injures another 1,200.

1999   President Chandrika Kumaratunga is injured in a suicide bomb at-
         tack.

2000   The Tamil Tigers overrun the Elephant Pass fortress.

2001   Tiger attack on Colombo's aiport destroys dozens of aircraft. The
         UNP wins significant proportion of power in parliamentary elec-
         tions. Ranil Wickramasinghe (UNP) appointed prime minister on
         peace platform, while Chandrika Kumaratunga (SLFP) retains role
         as president.

2002   Signing of ceasefire agreement (CFA) between Sri Lanka's govern-
         ment and Tamil Tigers.

2003   Tamil Tigers withdraw from peace talks.

2004   President Kumaratunga dismisses Wickramasinghe in April, and
         appoints Mahinda Rajapaksa as prime minister. The Karuna group,
         based in eastern Sri Lanka and headed by 'Colonel' Karuna, splits
         from the main body of the Tamil Tigers, centred around the Vanni
         and the north, bringing his 6,000 cadres over to the government side.
         Indian Ocean tsunami strikes the Sri Lankan seaboard in December,
         killing 30,000 people.

2005   Mahinda Rajapaksa is elected leader of the SLFP and becomes presi-
         dent of Sri Lanka in December that year. Foreign minister Lakshman
         Kadirgamar assassinated by sniper in August.

2006   Eelam War IV begins. The Tamil Tigers seize a sluice gate in east-
         ern Sri Lanka, and cut water to tens of thousands of people. After
         fierce fighting, the SLA wrests back control. In August, seventeen
         humanitarian workers executed. Suicide attacks increase. October
         peace talks in Geneva lead nowhere.

2007   Government successfully regains full control of eastern Sri Lanka,
         leaving only the northern Vanni region under Tamil Tiger control

2008   CFA between the government and the Tamil Tigers is formally ab-
         rogated by the government in January. Government forces steadily
         push back Tiger lines across the Vanni. UN leaves Kilinochchi in Sep-
         tember.

2009   In January, Kilinochchi, the Elephant Pass and Mullaitivu fall in quick
         succession. UN Convoy 11 is bombarded. The government forces the
         Tigers and 300,000 civilians to fall back into the Cage at Nandikadal
         lagoon. In May, Velupillai Prabakharan and almost the entire senior
         command of the Tamil Tigers are killed. Three hundred thousand
         Tamil civilians interned. Presidential and parliamentary elections
         called in October. In November, General Fonseka announces candi-
         dacy for president.

2010   Mahinda Rajapaksa re-elected president in landslide. Fonseka is
         arrested in February, accused of a variety of crimes including

treason. Landslide victory for SLFP in April parliamentary elections. In August, military court sentences Fonseka to thirty months'
imprisonment for political involvement while still in uniform. He
is also dishonourably discharged. In October, parliament approves
eighteenth constitutional amendment, allowing unlimited terms
for president. December publication by Wikileaks of a US embassy
cable in which the ambassador suggests that the Rajapaksa brothers
are responsible for alleged war crimes.

Dramatis Personae

Sirimavo Bandaranaike	Thrice prime minister of Sri Lanka (1960–5; 1970–7; 1994–2000), the first female prime minister in the world and leader of the SLFP upon her husband's death, she implemented the provisions of the 1956 Sinhala Only Act, introduced a republican constitution, renamed Ceylon as Sri Lanka, changed the flag and initiated restrictions on university entrance, with a disproportionate disadvantage for Tamils.
S.W.R.D. Bandaranaike	Solomon West Ridgeway Dias. A brilliant graduate of Oxford University and a Christian convert to Buddhism. Prime minister of Sri Lanka from 1956 until his assassination at the hand of a Buddhist monk in 1959. Founder of the opposition Sri Lanka Freedom Party (SLFP) in 1951, husband of Sirimavo, father of Chandrika Kumaratunga and the driving force behind the 1956 Sinhala Only Act.
Anagarika Dharmapala	Mystic, visionary and Sinhalese Buddhist ideologue whose ideas inspired much of the rise of Buddhist nationalism.
Sarath Fonseka	A general who was appointed army chief by Gotabaya Rajapaksa in 2006. He stood against Mahinda Rajapaksa in the 2010 presidential elections, was accused of treason and imprisoned. Fonseka alleged that the armed forces had committed war crimes at the direction of Gotabaya Rajapaksa.
J.R. Jayawardene	Junius Richard. Prime Minister (1977–8) and the first executive president of Sri Lanka (1978–89). A nephew of D.S. Senanayake and a leader of the UNP, Jayawardene converted from Christianity

	to Buddhism in his youth, and pressed hard for a political accommodation within the UNP party with the SLFP-devised Sinhala Only Act of 1951.
Chandrika Kumaratunga	Daughter of Sirimavo and S.W.R.D Bandaranaike, president of Sri Lanka (November 1994–November 2005). Husband assassinated by JVP in 1989. Upon election as president, she appointed her mother Sirimavo as prime minister. Tried to introduce a pluralist constitution, and embarked on peace talks with the Tigers. Blinded in one eye by a suicide bomber in 1999.
Vinayagamoorthy Muralitharan	Former child soldier and later the Tamil Tigers' eastern sub-commander, better known as 'Colonel Karuna'. In 2004 he defected to the government, taking with him an estimated 6,000 fighters and valuable intelligence.
Henry Olcott	America soldier and mystic, member of the Theosophical Society, and foreign sponsor of the Buddhist revival in Sri Lanka.
Kumaran Pathmanathan	Known as 'KP', the most wanted Tamil Tiger in Sri Lanka behind Velupillai Prabakharan. Pathmanathan remained in exile for decades, from where he built and then ran the complex arms, finance, transport and revenue collection network on behalf of the Tamil Tigers.
Velupillai Prabakharan	Founding member and self-styled 'Supreme Leader' of the Tamil Tigers, killed sometime between 17 and 19 May 2009.
Ranasinghe Premadasa	Prime minister under President Jayawardene (1978–89), then president of Sri Lanka from January 1989 until his assassination by a suicide bomber on 1 May 1993. He ruthlessly suppressed the second JVP insurgency and was the first lower caste to attain high political rank.
Gotabaya Rajapaksa	Brother of the president, secretary of defence, computer geek and the most powerful man in Sri Lanka. Gotabaya commands the army, police, navy, air force, intelligence services, border control and the building permits for Colombo. He was the main architect of the military defeat of the Tamil Tigers between 2006 and 2009.
Mahinda Rajapaksa	President of Sri Lanka 2005–present. A former

human rights lawyer, Mahinda has been a parliamentarian for forty years. One of four brothers who are active in Sri Lanka's political life: Chamal, Basil and Gotabaya.

D.S. Senanayake — Don Stephen (1884–1952). First prime minister of independent Ceylon, father of Dudley. Founder of the United National Party (UNP). Negotiated Ceylon's independence from Britain.

Dudley Senanayake — Dudley Shelton (1911–73). Prime minister of Ceylon on the death of his father (March 1952–October 1953), and twice more (March–July 1960 and 1965–70).

Rohana Wijeweera — Founding member and leader of the Janatha Vimukthi Peramuna (JVP, or People's Liberation Front), a Marxist youth group that twice rose violently against the state. Executed in 1989 by government forces.

Lasantha Wickrematunge — Founder and editor of the *Sunday Leader*, an independent Sri Lankan weekly newspaper. Assassinated by death squad in January 2009.

Notes

Preface

1. The Jathika Hela Urumaya (JHU, or National Heritage Party) was launched in February 2004, with a brace of leading *bhikkhus* (Buddhist monks) amongst its founding members. Many Buddhists decried the formal entry of clerics into the political fray. In the first election contested by the JHU, its candidates, all of whom were *bhikkhus*, won 6 per cent of the popular vote, and 9 out of 225 parliamentary seats. The JHU supported Mahinda Rajapaksa in his successful bid for the presidency in 2005, and in 2007 the party entered the Rajapaksa cabinet with the appointment of the lay Buddhist Champika Ranawaka to the post of minister of environment and natural resources. • 2. As in all the great religions, the sangha can assume a decidedly political form. It is one of the great Western misconceptions that Buddhism is somehow detached from worldly existence. In fact, it is not difficult to find numerous examples of political Buddhism in Asia. A good introduction to political Buddhism in Sri Lanka is given by the 2007 Al-Jazeera documentary 'Monks of War', directed by Dom Rotheroe, and reported by Juliana Ruhfus. Like all faiths, Buddhism breathes the same air as its constituents, and cannot be separated from the history, ethnicity and politics of a country's evolution. Buddhist monks were instrumental in the independence movement in Burma, and died in droves resisting the oppression of the current military rule. Militant Buddhist monks played a role in the destabilisation of South Vietnam in the early 1960s. In the nineteenth-century Tibetan theocracy, it was the Buddhist clergy who organised resistance and fought against the British invasion, and against the Chinese invasion in the twentieth. The JVP militant formations of the late 1980s included a brigade called the Bhikkhu Front. The sangha in Sri Lanka is multifaceted, and as politically diverse as any group. It ranges from those devoted to meditation, universalism and compassion for all humankind, to the narrowest and most vicious of clerics who promote war, ethnic cleansing and an exclusivist view of Sri Lanka. In 1983, a survey of the sangha in Sri Lanka by Nathan Katz, a Western student of Buddhism, suggested that three quarters of the clerics were unsympathetic to the Tamils, and considered the Sinhalese a justly aggrieved majority. Another scholar, James J. Hughes, has divided the

monks generally into 'cosmopolitans' and 'mahavamsists' (those who believe the Mahavamsa to be an accurate rendering of ancient Sri Lankan history). See his research paper 'Buddhist Monks and Politics in Sri Lanka'. • 3. Simon Gardner, 'Sri Lanka says bullied by West on rights', Reuters, 11 June 2007. For a further insight into the defence secretary's rationale, see two pieces available on YouTube: the BBC's Chris Morris interviewing Rajapaksa on 8 February 2009; and the interview on the BBC's *Hardtalk* with Stephen Sackur of 7 June 2010. • 4. International Committee of the Red Cross, *International Humanitarian Law and the Challenges of Contemporary Armed Conflicts*. • 5. Larry Diamond, 'The Democratic Rollback'. • 6. General Sir Rupert Smith's phrase, used in his seminal book *The Utility of Force*. In this work the former Nato supreme commander attempted to define the 'new' kind of war that he had encountered in Bosnia, in which 'the people in the streets and houses and fields – all the people, anywhere – are the battlefield. Military engagements can take place anywhere, with civilians around, against civilians, in defence of civilians. Civilians are the targets, objectives to be won, as much as an opposing force.' The twenty-first-century war takes place in a world where psychological warfare is fought on the internet, where the degree of recklessness leading to civilian deaths might be established in an international court, and where guerrilla forces lure armies into politically disastrous territory with full intent. • 7. In the preamble to the Universal Declaration of Human Rights, the notion of a connection between peace, an accessible system of justice, human rights and political freedom is concisely expressed thus: '*Whereas* it is essential, if man is not to be compelled to have recourse, as a last resort, to rebellion against tyranny and oppression, that human rights should be protected by the rule of law.' • 8. Philippe Bolopion, in June 2009.

Chapter One: The Lion's Victory

1. For a detailed sketch of what probably happened to 600 prisoners held by the Tamil Tigers at the so-called LTTE Reform Prison at Iranapillai until the final days of Eelam War IV, see the UTHR(J), *Let Them Speak*. • 2. This phrase was frequently used by subjects interviewed by the author. It seemed to account for all those who might have been members of the Tamil Tigers, as well as others who broadly supported the political aims of the Tamil Tigers, without necessarily having a commitment to the organisation itself, or its methods. • 3. Editorial, 'And then they came for me', the *Sunday Leader* (11 January 2009). • 4. In an opinion piece published under the heading 'Let them decide' in *The Guardian* of 8 April 2009, the UN's senior humanitarian official, John Holmes, warned of an impending 'bloodbath' should the government continue with its advance into the enclave.

Chapter Two: Paradise Found

1. The poem of an unnamed writer, drawn from the spiritualist magazine *Medium and Daybreak* of 1875, and extracted from Hoare, *England's Lost Eden*, p. 423. • 2. Wijesinha, *All Experience*, p. 70. • 3. The author was on the receiving end of this impressive tradition in Sri Lanka's 'deep south' in 2007, when a *bhikkhu* worked up to a new level of indignation a crowd of high-school students who were protesting against the slow rebuilding of a school destroyed by the tsunami of 2004. A UN agency tasked with completing the project was accused of dragging its feet. The students had blocked a highway, and a group of UN officials had been sent to defuse the tension. The political consciousness of the students left a powerful impression, as did the policemen, who stood warily on the sidelines with assault rifles, and escorted ashen-faced officials from the school at the conclusion of a long *bhikkhu*-led harangue. • 4. The eminent Sri Lankan anthropologist and historian H.L. Seneviratne has said, 'The conflict is rooted in recent developments going back to no more than a century or so.' See Seneviratne, *Buddhism, Identity, and Conflict*, p. 1. The Sinhalese social historian Nira Wickramasinghe writes, 'The debate about who came first, who was the original inhabitant, what expanse of land was under Tamil control and hence who had more claims to part or totality of the land was a late development.' See Wickramasinghe, *Sri Lanka in the Modern Age*, p. 259. • 5. The phrase originates with the Sinhalese anthropologist Gananath Obeyesekere. • 6. Arunachalam Ponnambalam also happily recommends the Mahavamsa as 'a veritable storehouse of valuable information, of which there is an excellent translation by Turnour and Wijesingha'. It is a sign that, in 1906, a literal reading of the ancient texts had not yet taken hold that would locate them as the central charter of the Sinhalese nationalist movement. See Ponnambalam, *Sketches of Ceylon History*, p. 2. • 7. The great Chinese admiral and traveller, the eunuch Zheng He, made three voyages to Ceylon in the early fifteenth century. During his second, he visited important Buddhist shrines. A contemporaneous commemorative stone called the Galle Tri-lingual Inscription sits in Colombo's National Museum. It is inscribed in three languages, Persian, Chinese and Tamil, but curiously not in Sinhala. • 8. It was not until the late 1960s, almost three decades after the opening of the country's first department of history at the University of Ceylon, that young historians began to challenge the authority of the Aryan-centric origin myth hitherto widely accepted. The ensuing studies, dialogues, monographs and academic tournaments are a story unto themselves. This story is partly told by K. Indrapala in *The Evolution of an Ethnic Identity*. The Tamil Indrapala quotes the description given by the Sinhalese Professor Leslie Gunawardena of the dogmatic distortions that pervaded the nascent history department. One example of the road down which such dogmatism leads is the conclusion by both Indrapala and Gunawardena that a series of interlinear stone inscriptions (that is, inscriptions written in between the lines of existing inscribed

stones) that had been discovered by an eminent and influential scholar were either fabrications or had been intentionally read into the stone. The inscriptions purported to reveal Ceylon's ancient foreign relations, including a connection with the court of Alexander the Great. The hijacking and promotion of a sliver of mythology by nationalists who paint a picture of a resilient Buddhist faith and of a vigilant Sinhalese people resisting Tamil invaders gives, in the words of the British historian Eric Hobsbawm, which could have been written for Sri Lanka, 'a more glorious background to a present that doesn't have much to celebrate'. More pertinent to this story, the Singaporean statesman Lee Kuan Yew blamed the nationalist narrative and myth-making by Ceylon's scholars and statesmen for the strife that was to dog the country throughout independence. In his autobiography, *From Third World To First – The Singapore Story: 1965–2000'*, Lee wrote: 'Ceylon was Britain's model Commonwealth country. During my visits over the years I watched a promising country go to waste. The majority of some 8 million Sinhalese could always outvote the 2 million Jaffna Tamils who had been disadvantaged by the switch from English to Sinhalese . . .' See Amarasuriya, 'Lee Kuan Yew's impressions of Sri Lanka'. • **9**. In the wake of the defeat of the Tamil Tigers in 2009, a cavalcade of sycophants vied to outdo each other in their comparisons of President Rajapaksa with Duttugemenu of Mahavamsa fame, casting the unlikely figure of the dead Prabakharan as his defeated foe Elara. For a sense of this excited adulation, one might view an amateur YouTube collage, 'King Mahinda Rajapaksa', of 23 September 2009. • **10**. As Indrapala notes in *The Evolution of an Ethnic Identity*, Mahanama, the author of the Mahavamsa, is full of admiration for the just rule of Elara, including his generous patronage of Buddhism. Once slain, Duttugemenu honours his fallen foe with a monument that, according to Mahanama, the princes of Lanka revered for ever after by silencing their instruments whenever their processions drew near it. The saviour of Buddhism also gives votive thanks to his patron Hindu deity, Kartikeya, in the town of Kataragama, worshipped by both Hindus and Buddhists. • **11**. De Silva, *Managing Ethnic Tensions*, p. 14. • **12**. Wickramasinghe makes the point that this first translation by the English civil servant George Turnour 'transmuted oral conceptions of history and erased in its translation notions of non-linear time and fantastic miracles [and] became the authoritative text of Ceylon'. In 1859, James Emerson Tennent made the first attempt at an authoritative history of Ceylon, and these two early efforts to reconstruct the past served as the platform for emerging proto-nationalist formulations in the theatre, novels and newspapers. 'The Mahavamsian vision of the authentic past has today become the central charter of Sinhala nationalist thought.' See Wickramasinghe, *Sri Lanka in the Modern Age*, pp. 89–90. There is a competing Sinhalese nationalist narrative that despises altogether the Vijayan myth. This alternative, known as the Hela, proposes Sinhalese inhabitation at least as far back as 2837 BC in a great empire that outweighed those in India, and bemoans the incursion by Vijaya. This school

of nationalism saw its heyday in the 1930s and 1940s, but failed to take purchase on
the popular imagination the way that the Vijayan myth did. • **13**. The Danish-
French geographer Conrad Malte-Brun, writing in the early nineteenth century,
describes how 'The Buddhists of Ceylon have numerous sacred writings, which
are extremely obscure, and are reproached for that quality even by the Brahmins
... Their books are greatly venerated. They are not touched without a preliminary obeisance: a person will not sit down where a book is present, unless it is in
a higher situation than himself.' See Malte-Brun, *A System of Universal Geography*,
Chapter XLIX. • **14**. The social historian Kumari Jayawardene deals extensively
with the rise of the arriviste merchant class during Britain's occupation. These
families, 'an important part of the emergent 19th century bourgeoisie, were landowners, whose holdings provided them with a means of accumulation and later,
a basis for expanded growth in the plantation era . . . mediating between the alien
rulers and the bulk of the indigenous population'. See Jayawardene, *Nobodies to
Somebodies*, p. 21. • **15**. The Crown Land Encroachment Ordinance of 1840 was
enacted to formalise land tenure for the new plantation economy, predominantly
coffee. Most land in the plantation areas was traditionally held by the Kandyan
aristocracy, and farmed by peasants, but years of turbulence had thinned the
ranks of the traditional landowners. The new ordinance effectively rendered any
land not clearly denoted as 'owned' as Crown lands. Informal and movable
peasant slash-and-burn cultivation was displaced, reduced and discouraged. • **16**.
There was no truly comprehensive census until the twentieth century, and the
great census of 1911 (a legacy of the civil servant Arunachalam Ponnambalam).
Portuguese tax levies had established a population of approximately 750,000,
which may have increased to around 800,000 by the nineteenth century, and the
advent of British rule. Thereafter, the population of the island grew rapidly. In
1835, the population of 'whites, free blacks, slaves, and aliens and resident strangers' was approximately 1,240,000 (Wickramasinghe, *Sri Lanka in the Modern Age*,
p. 48). Patrick Peebles notes that it is virtually impossible to know what the population of Plantation Tamils was throughout the nineteenth century (Peebles, *The
Plantation Tamils of Ceylon*, p. 43). The first attempt at a comprehensive and well-
categorised population census in 1871 recorded 2.8 million people, but divided
them into 78 nationalities and 24 races! The 1881 census reduced this to 7 races and
71 nationalities. In 1879 there were probably around 300,000 Plantation Tamils.
The 1911 census established that there were approximately 2,550,000 Sinhalese,
1,125,000 Tamils, 250,000 Muslims, 25,000 Burghers and 6,500 Europeans. Around
half a million of the Tamils were Plantation Tamils. It was not until this census
that Indian Tamils were differentiated from Ceylon Tamils, an indication of the
kind of fluidity attached to community in pre-political Ceylon. From constituting
two thirds of the population at the beginning of the twentieth century, the
Sinhalese grew to account for three quarters by the end, in part a result of the
expulsion of hundreds of thousands of Plantation Tamils after independence,

and the large-scale emigration of other Tamils following the 1983 riots. • **17**. The Tooth Relic of the Buddha is considered the holiest relic in Sri Lanka. Legend holds that it was taken to the island in the fourth century AD One of a number of similar relics located in Singapore, Japan, Taiwan and China, the Tooth Relic disappears and reappears a number of times in the course of its history in Ceylon. It was probably destroyed by the Portuguese in 1560. For Buddhists, it is also the symbolic root of sovereign power and a sign of the claim of Buddhism over Sri Lanka. The Mauryan emperor Ashoka's daughter Sanghamitta is recorded as having brought to the island a branch of the sacred Bo tree under which the Buddha attained enlightenment. According to legend, the tree that grew from this branch can be seen to this day near the ruins of the ancient city of Anuradhapura in the north of Sri Lanka. The tree is said to be the oldest living thing in the world and is the subject of great veneration. • **18**. Kaplan, 'Buddha's Savage Peace', quoting SinhaRaja Tammita-Delgoda in *Eloquence in Stone: The Lithic Saga of Sri Lanka* (Colombo, 2008). Conrad Malte-Brun has a number of observations such as this one: 'Near Weligama, in this province, is a Sinhala temple of Buddha, called Agra-boddha-ganni, with some idols and hieroglyphical paintings representing the history of their kings. The statues of Vishnu and Siva are conjoined with that of Buddha.' See Malte-Brun, *A System of Universal Geography*. • **19**. Ponnambalam, *Sketches of Ceylon History*, p. 49. • **20**. Ibid., p. 50. • **21**. V. Nithiyanandam, 'Sri Lanka: The politics of development', in Pararajasingham (ed.), *60 Years*. Conversely, the activity of Christian missionaries on the peninsula also gave rise to a form of Tamil nationalism that both preceded by half a century and provided a model for Sinhalese nationalism. In this model, the Saivite movement sought to distil identity into a form that distinguished levels of Tamil-ness, which at its extreme placed high-caste Jaffna Tamils above all others, including the Tamils of India. • **22**. De Silva, *A History of Sri Lanka*, p. 461. Much later, the deeply elitist Ramanathan opposed the broad franchise introduced by the 1931 Donoughmore Constitution, on the grounds that suffrage for women and the lower castes would lead to mob rule, and was anathema to the Hindu way of life. • **23**. Arunachalam's work belongs to a body of literature from the period that 'seems to corroborate the fact that before Sinhal[ese] nationalism rekindled its myths of origin Tamils did not feel it was vital to justify their belonging or claim to the land they lived on'. When this changed, claims to belonging became specific, with reference to demarcated boundaries. See Wickramasinghe, *Sri Lanka in the Modern Age*, p. 259. • **24**. Stephen Prothero, *Olcott and Buddhism*, the Theosophical Society, www.theosophical.org. • **25**. 'Traditional Sinhalese customs of polyandry, polygamy, easy divorce, several marriages in a life-time, and a liberal definition of legitimate heirs, conflicted with the British notion of marriage as a monogamous, lifelong union': Agrawal, *A Field of One's Own*, p. 182. Dharmapala was opposed to most foreigners, except for the British, whom he apparently admired (he lived in England for a number of years). Seneviratne (*The Work of Kings*, p. 19)

says, 'It is this new Western-derived morality that Dharmapala foisted on the
Sinhala people as their two thousand year old morality.' In 1638, Robert Knox
described at some length what he calls the 'whoredom' of the women, for
example, 'In some Cases the Men will permit their Wives and Daughters to lye
with other Men. And that is, when intimate Friends or great Men chance to
Lodge at their houses, they commonly will send their Wives or Daughters to bear
them company in their Chamber. Neither do they reckon their Wives to be
Whores for lying with them that are as good or better than themselves.' Knox had
been shipwrecked with his father in 1619 and taken hostage by the King of Kandy.
When, after 19 years, he escaped the mountain lair of the king (his father had
died), he wrote a long account of his captivity and the customs of his hosts. It
became a bestseller, one of the first, and a source for Daniel Defoe's story of a
mariner's stranding, *Robinson Crusoe*. Of the island inhabitants Knox wrote
sweepingly: 'They make no account nor conscience of lying, neither is it any
shame or disgrace to them, if they be catched in telling lyes; it is so customary.'
As one might expect, to the English mind his book (with a breathless 35-word
title) seemed a wonderfully purple tale, spun with cruel monarchs, heathen
habits, and chocolate-fleshed voluptuaries – oddly foiled by arid descriptions of
agricultural husbandry. See Robert Knox, *An Historical Relation*. • **26**. Seneviratne,
The Work of Kings, p.30. • **27**. An extract from a letter written by Dharmapala in
the wake of riots in 1915 to the British colonial secretary in London. See Jonathan
Spencer, 'A Nation Living in Different Places: Notes on the impossible work of
purification in post-colonial Sri Lanka', in Gardner and Osella (eds.), *Migration,
Modernity, and Social Transformation in South Asia*, p. 10. • **28**. There was also an
economic advantage that accrued to some of the riot leaders through the large-
scale sacking of Muslim businesses. According to Kumari Jayawardene (*Nobodies
to Somebodies*), who quotes from a debate in the legislative council that followed
the riots, 'Half a dozen misguided, designing villains . . . have been trying to pose
as leaders of Buddhists. Had it not been for this encouragement, these disturbances would never have occurred . . . the proprietary peasant villagers . . . have
been deluded into this trap for the personal aggrandizement of a few who are
nobodies, but who hope to make *somebodies* of themselves by such disgraceful
tactics.' Some of the rioters, such as the Senanayake brothers, who aspired to
political prominence in their leadership of the populist temperance movement,
had made their original fortunes through 'arrack renting', that is, control of the
brewing, sale and taxation of the powerful liquor widely drunk throughout Sri
Lanka. Ironically, the widespread problem of alcohol abuse that prevails today in
Sri Lanka is often tendentiously attributed to that ideological holdall 'colonialism'. • **29**. An outcome of the 1829 Colebrooke-Cameron Royal Commission.
The Kandyan province was administratively joined with the rest of island, probably the first time Ceylon was truly united in any meaningful nation-state sense.
Ceylonese were also admitted into the civil service, and schools established for

the education of privileged natives. • **30**. The Tamil and Sinhalese caste systems are correlative, but distinct, with the latter closer to a form of ancient north Indian caste ordering than to today's modern India. Altogether, caste amongst Tamils is a far more rigid and unforgiving structure than it is amongst the Sinhalese. In Malte-Brun's *A System of Universal Geography*, the difference between the caste system of the Tamils and that of the Sinhalese is described thus: '[The Sinhalese] are divided into castes, but they have not the ridiculous pride of caste which prevails in India. A Sinhala will not refuse to eat in company with any respectable European.' In 1638, Robert Knox made the same point. The native Tamil community on the Jaffna peninsula nurtured a chauvinistic dogma of superiority towards their mainland Indian brethren, the eastern and Plantation Tamils and, perhaps most importantly, the Sinhalese. This was especially true of the dominant Vellala Tamils. These notions of superiority were anchored in a strict observance of Hindu rituals, as opposed to the far more syncretic approach to worship of the Sinhalese, as well as in the high value placed on the chastity of Tamil women compared with the less rigorous preoccupation with the same amongst the Sinhalese (see also Wright (ed.), *Twentieth century impressions of Ceylon*). For example, in 1930, when the colonial authorities attempted to enforce 'equal seating' on the Jaffna peninsula so that lower-caste Tamils might attend school, higher-caste Tamils rioted and schools were burned. A letter at the time from the villages of Jaffna to the authorities read: 'The Jaffna Tamils are different from the Sinhalese in race, religion, language, customs, civilization, diet and personal cleanliness.' See Wickramasinghe, *Sri Lanka in the Modern Age*, p. 113. • **31**. In December 1948, partly as a way to undermine left-wing parties that had made political capital from their support for the tea-estate Tamils, Prime Minister Senanayake ushered through parliament the Citizenship Act, which excluded Ceylon's Plantation Tamils from the franchise on the basis that they were really Indian, and despite the fact that the majority had lived, worked and raised families on the island for generations. The left-wing parties – dominated by Sinhalese – opposed the bill, while the Ceylonese Tamil deputies largely colluded in its passage. One of the leading Sinhalese left-wingers, Dr. N.M. Perera, the leader of the LSSP, said in 1948, 'I thought racialism of this type died with Houston Chamberlain and Adolph Hitler. I do not believe that anyone claiming to be a Statesman would ask us to accede to a bill of this nature . . . We cannot proceed as if we were God's chosen race quite apart from the rest of the world; that we and we alone have the right to be citizens of this country.' See Thiranagama, *The Broken Palmyra*, Chapter 1. The negotiations over who would stay and who would go were long and tortuous, and lasted many years. The net result was that by the end of the twentieth century, the proportion of the population who were Plantation Tamils had fallen from close to 13 per cent at the beginning of the century to around 5.5 per cent. The lengthy negotiations, mired in political brinkmanship, are described in Wickramasinghe, *Sri Lanka in the Modern Age*, pp. 171–6. • **32**. The unwillingness of

Sinhalese politicians to counter communalist tendencies at this early stage 'cost us the friendship and benevolence of two of the most outstanding men produced in 152 years of British rule, Ponnambulam Ramanatham and Ponnambulam Arunachalam ... this unwillingness to yield gracefully from a position of strength, so that concessions have to be extorted with ever increasing suspicion, seems to be part of a congenital incapacity that continues to destroy the country'. See Wijesinha, *All Experience*, p. 107. • **33**. Wickramasinghe, *Sri Lanka in the Modern Age*, p. 122 • **34**. De Silva, *A History of Sri Lanka*, p. 496. • **35**. Wickramasinghe, *Sri Lanka in the Modern Age*, p. 131. • **36**. The following remarks were made by a Kandyan in relation to the carpetbagging low-country Sinhalese traders: 'The relation of the low-country Sinhalese man to the Kandyan is the same as that of the foreign born Tamil, Moor or Malay. He comes and goes ... The low-country man comes and sticks on. He flourishes in any soil and in any clime; he is a sort of human parasite. Given time and opportunity he will, as it were, absorb the Kandyan, leaving him neither his lands, nor his chattels, nor even his independence. Very soon the Kandyan landlord, who at first befriended the stranger, the low-country man, and lodged him, tenanted him and patronised him, owing to certain circumstances, changes place with the latter. By degrees the plot thickens till at last the low-country man becomes the landlord and the Kandyan the tenant ...' See Hoole, *The Arrogance of Power*, section 1.2; and Major Frank Modder, 'Kandy and the Kandyans', in Wright (ed.), *Twentieth Century Impressions of Ceylon*, p. 326. • **37**. See 'The Donoughmore Commission', in Edrisinha et al., *Power-Sharing in Sri Lanka*. • **38**. Manogaran, 'Colonization as Politics', p. 85. • **39**. Quoted in the *Ceylon Daily News*, 17 April 1939. • **40**. The argument that a combination of policy, administration and force was used to 're-territorialise' Tamil lands, converting them into places of Sinhalese domination, is described by de Fontgalland, 'State aided colonization', in Pararajasingham, *Sri Lanka*. In the same volume, see also Rampton, 'Colonization'. The similarities with Israeli land-acquisition policies are striking. See Murray Li, *The Will to Improve*. A comparison of populations between the 1911 and 1981 censuses shows a slight increase in the Sinhalese population in the northern province of Sri Lanka, and a marked rise in the eastern province. Manipulation of electoral boundaries served to strengthen Sinhalese electoral power. See Peebles, *The Plantation Tamils of Ceylon*, p. 38. President Jayawardene decided to accelerate the Mahaweli project in eastern Sri Lanka from its planned thirty-year completion to just six years. An unmistakable pattern emerged of grossly disproportionate favour to the Sinhalese. Government data from 1985 showed that of the 39,622 settlers given land under the Mahaweli scheme, 1,050 were Muslim and just 364 Tamil. See Richardson, *Paradise Poisoned*, pp. 406–7. In critical political parlance, 'coloniser' is used in preference to 'settler'. The terms are used interchangeably throughout this book. Work on the restoration of the great tanks that formed the basis of the ancient city-state 'hydraulic' culture had begun in around 1870 under the British, for precisely the same reasons of land relief for the peasants and agricultural self-sufficiency. These public works also conformed with British notions of a lost ancient civilisation, with scholars positing that the irrigation works, when flourishing at the height of the power of the ancient Sinhalese kings, had allowed for a population many millions more than existed at the time (Arunachalam Ponnambalam amongst others suggests that, based on the sources, there were importations of large numbers of Tamils in ancient times for the cultivation of rice, the art of which they had mastered in southern India). • 41. The phrase belongs to Arunachalam Ponnambalam. See Wright (ed.), *Twentieth Century Impressions of Ceylon*, p. 326. Today, 50,000 ships ply the seas, of which as many as one third pass through the waters of Sri Lanka. • 42. De Silva, *A History of Sri Lanka*, p. 569. • 43. The Sabha Maha was a political group founded by S.W.R.D. Bandaranaike in 1937. It cultivated a base among communal groups and around expressions of indigenous identity such as the village *bhikkhu* or Ayurvedic practitioner. It promoted the interests of the Sinhalese and of Buddhism, as well as linguistic and religious policies that were often directly at odds with the UNP, with which it allied itself in 1945. In 1951, Bandaranaike took the Sabha Maha with him when he split from the UNP to found the SLFP. • 44. Ayurvedic medicine is widely practised throughout Sri Lanka today, from primary to hospital care. Ayurvedic dispensaries are an important part of every village and urban neighbourhood. The Indian emperor Ashoka is said to have directed that medical aid be available throughout his empire, and the Mahavamsa notes the details of the medical care provided by Duttugemenu to his subjects. Imbued with a deep historic and cultural significance, Ayurvedic practitioners have sometimes, at a village level, been at the vanguard of Sinhalese nationalist consciousness. • 45. Walpola Rahula's two most famous works were *What the Buddha Taught* (1959), and *The Heritage of the Bhikkhu.* • 46. In 1996, in an interview with Peter Kloos, former president J.R. Jayawardene said that the SLFP had been a convenient device to appropriate the left-wing vote from the strengthening working-class parties. The new SLFP drained power from the 'true left' and concentrated it in the hands of a small elite, standing for very different values. 'The new UNP/SLFP rivalry, no longer class-bound, stressed Sinhala-ness.' This appropriation demolished the potential of the old left-wing parties, and laid the ground for the emergence of the radical and violent Marxist JVP. See Kloos, 'From Civil Struggle to Civil War', in Schmidt and Schröder (eds.), *Anthropology of Violence and Conflict*, p. 185. • 47. It was formally known as the Official Language Act, and replaced English with Sinhala as the language of official business. It was due to come into force in 1961. Sirimavo Bandaranaike, having assuaged Tamil fears in the 1960 general election campaign with a promise that she would moderate the impact of the language law, implemented the full provisions of the Act once she had won the election. • 48. Bandaranaike's murder was thereafter mistakenly attributed to Buddhist extremism; the actual motive was much more venal. A leading Buddhist cleric, believing that Bandaranaike had betrayed him in

a business deal, conspired to assassinate him. The prime minister was shot dead
with a revolver on the front veranda of his Colombo residence, now an upmarket
restaurant. The assassin, a Buddhist monk, converted to Christianity prior to
being hanged. Bandaranaike, as a young man, had converted from Christianity to
Buddhism.

Chapter Three: Paradise Lost

1. It is worth noting at this stage the submission of Jayantha Dhanapala, former
UN under-secretary and a Sri Lankan diplomat since 1965, provided to the post-
war Presidential Commission on Lessons Learnt and Reconciliation on 25 August
2010: 'Your mandate artificially sets a time frame from 21 February 2002 to 19 May
2009. That and its restricted mandate is also a limitation in your good faith efforts
to discharge your task. The lessons we have to learn go back to the past – certainly
from the time that we had responsibility for our own governance on 4 February
1948. Each and every Government which held office from 1948 till the present bears
culpability for the failure to achieve good governance, national unity and a framework of peace, stability and economic development in which all ethnic, religious
and other groups could live in security and equality. The political expediency of
apportioning blame will not serve the purpose of national reconciliation. A
collective apology to the people of Sri Lanka is owed by all political parties.' See
Groundviews, 'Jayantha Dhanapala responds'. • 2. The insurgents were typically
labourers, students, unemployed or cultivators. The vast majority were not
university students as such, but were rather the thousands of Ceylonese 'baby
boomers' who had been born in the years following World War II, had benefited
from the first Sirimavo Bandaranaike government's focus on primary and
secondary education (1960–5), but had been tripped up at graduation by the
faltering Ceylonese economic model. They found that their degrees (the arts
were overwhelmingly represented) were not useful, or that they simply could not
find a job befitting expectations that had often been raised to unrealistic levels by
political rhetoric. Ironically, the same education reforms had degraded the quality
of the education system, whose teacher-training and induction simply could not
keep pace with demand, and whose lack of English speakers matched the paucity
of high-quality Sinhala equivalents. In short, the JVPers were 'a clear picure of
frustrated economic aspirations'. See Richardson, *Paradise Poisoned*, pp. 342–4. • 3.
These five lectures were called 'classes', and consisted of the following topics: the
crisis of the capitalist system in Sri Lanka; the history of the left movement in Sri
Lanka; the history of socialist revolutions; Indian expansionism; and the path of
revolution in Sri Lanka, which carefully described the minutiae of the violent
overthrow of the existing system. The lecture on India seemed particularly
prescient to the masses following the Indian incursion into Sri Lanka in the form

of the 1987 Indian Peace Keeping Force (IPKF). • **4**. In an move that appeared to demonstrate a genuine personal commitment to reform, the government limited land holdings to a maximum of fifty acres per family, an act that stripped the Bandaranaike family of a considerable portion of its wealth. • **5**. For Buddhist nationalists this was simply the reassertion of the spirit of the treaty established between the chiefs of Kandy and their British conquerors in 1815 that had loosely acknowledged the 'special place' of Buddhism in the affairs of state. The application of this colonial paradigm to the late-twentieth-century independent nation state was quite another matter. The relevant article of the Kandyan Convention of 1815 reads: 'The Religion of the Boodhoo professed by the Chiefs and the Inhabitants of these Provinces, is declared inviolable, and its rites, Minister and Places of Worship are to be maintained and protected.' • **6**. The Bandaranaike family was personally close to the family of Indira Gandhi, India's prime minister: the aristocratic Sirimavo (descendant of a high Kandyan feudal family) and the equally haughty and indomitable Indira were great friends. So much so that J.R. Jayawardene's humiliation and ill treatment of Sirimavo after the 1977 elections was a cause for strained ties between India and Sri Lanka. Sirimavo possessed, by many accounts, a warm personality, and was distinguished by a genuine concern for the poor, albeit that she also persisted along the path suggested by her husband, and instituted genuinely chauvinist policies to the cost of the Tamils. • **7**. Tambiah, *Sri Lanka*, p. 29. The merits of this policy remain very much in contention today. A Sinhalese journalist friend, who is no chauvinist, believes passionately that had it not been for these policies of the Bandaranaike government, he would never have been able to enter university. In addition, the policy benefited Tamils from more peripheral and lower-caste communities, even if the Sinhalese majority gained the greatest net benefit. Writing in 1972, the Sri Lankan journalist Mervyn de Silva warned of the folly of university exclusion and of alienating Tamil youth, thereby inflaming 'a movement of militant youth rooted in the soil of Jaffna and nourished by material frustration, a feeling of humiliation and bitterness'. See Jayatilleka, 'Mervyn de Silva and the Lankan condition'. • **8**. In 1957, the first political accord between the country's two main ethnic groups had finally been reached. It was a pivotal moment, and a chance to reverse the damage to Sri Lanka's race relations and international reputation in the wake of the discriminatory 1956 Sinhala Only Act. The so-called Chelvanayakam-Bandaranaike Pact was designed to take the heat out of brewing ethnic violence and to protect the basic rights of Tamil citizens. Both Prime Minister S.W.R.D. Bandaranaike and the principal Tamil negotiator S.J.V. Chelvanayakam, leader of the Federal Party, made significant concessions. The Tamil side gave away its central policy of a separate Tamil state within a federation as a solution to Sri Lanka's ethnic deadlock, and opted instead for a set of powers that would be devolved to provincial councils and to the provision of government services in those areas in the Tamil language. There was an immediate backlash from hardliners on both sides, but with majority power on their side, it was the Sinhalese response that counted for more. A protest march to the symbolic heart of political Buddhism at Kandy, led by the UNP's two main leaders, future president J.R. Jayawardene and former prime minister Dudley Senanayake, was redolent with Sinhalese patriotic umbrage. Within a year, Bandaranaike stood on the steps of his Colombo house before a crowd of indignant *bhikkhus* and in front of their eyes tore up the signed agreement. A new and almost identical Chelvanayakam pact followed the UNP victory in 1965 that ousted the SLFP and brought the Tamil Federal Party into coalition government, this time signed with UNP prime minister Dudley Senanayake (the very same man who had marched against the first pact). But by 1970, and with the advent of the ultra-nationalist government of Sirimavo Bandaranaike, an aged and embittered Chelvanayakam had conceded that no major Sinhalese political party intended to devolve powers that would provide Tamils with a say in how they were to be governed and their lives administered. Chelvanayakam, who died in 1977, was the last Tamil leader to advocate a non-violent solution to Sri Lanka's woes. • 9. Aside from contentious archaeological evidence, these documents include, for example, a quote attributed to Sir Hugh Cleghorn, British colonial secretary to Ceylon, in June 1799: 'Two different nations, from a very ancient period, have divided between them the possession of the Island: the Sinhalese inhabiting the interior in its Southern and Western parts from the river Wallouwe to Chilaw, and the Malabars [Tamils] who possess the Northern and Eastern Districts. These two nations differ entirely in their religion, language and manners.' See Schmidt and Schröder, *Anthropology of Violence and Conflict*, p. 180. A seventeenth-century map by the English cartographer Rob Morden, called 'Three Sovereign Regions In The Island of Ceylon', which shows the island divided into three kingdoms of Kandy, Jaffna and Kotte, was also consulted. • 10. Conversation between Lionel Bopage and the author, May 2010. • 11. The 1977 anti-Tamil riots, which came just days after the 21 July general election, were triggered by a minor altercation between police and civilians in Jaffna. Rioting broke out in Colombo, Kandy and Jaffna, and left 128 people dead, of whom around a hundred were Tamil. A public inquiry, the Sansoni Commission, failed to establish conclusively the cause of the riots, but they certainly further alienated the Tamils, and left an early stain on the Jayawardene government that seemed an omen of what was to follow six years later. As with each of the riots directed at Tamils since 1956, Tamil families left villages and towns in which they had lived for generations, and moved into the Tamil-majority north, thereby exacerbating the separation between the two communities. • 12. Cyril Mathew was a malignant presence in the Jayawardene cabinet. In two books, *Diabolical Conspiracy* (1979) and *Sinhala People – Awake, Arise, and Safeguard Buddhism* (1981), he accused Tamil military and police officers and government officials of being the beneficiaries of collaboration with British colonial authorities, and of displacing Buddhism. He proposed the aggressive colonisation of Tamil areas, including the

Jaffna peninsula, and if necessary a Buddhist 'jihad'. His books prophesied his later role in the 'Black July' pogrom of 1983. See Richardson, *Paradise Poisoned*, p. 412. • **13.** According to a BBC report, in October 2010, a large group of Sinhalese tourists, disgruntled at being unable to visit a part of the refurbished library due to a conference, vandalised books, shelving and plants. It was a minor criminal infraction, but highly provocative given the context. Due to the level of security in Sri Lanka at the time, Tamils were in no position to respond other than with murmurs of dissent. Senior government officials quickly apologised. See Havilland, 'Sri Lanka's Historic Jaffna Library "Vandalised"'. • **14.** *Daily Express*, 29 July 1983. • **15.** Jayawardene set the tone for some of the excessive traits of the Rajapaksa years. 'As Executive president [Jayawardene] became the most monarchical head of state since independence, using ancient traditions to legitimize his authority. He asked Sinhala speakers to address him as "your Excellency", with a Sinhalese phrase denoting kingly, even divine status. He chose Kotte, the capital of a fifteenth and sixteenth century Sinhalese kingdom, as the site for a new parliamentary complex and resurrected the capital's traditional name. Fortuitously, that name, Sri Jayawardenepura, was the same as his own.' Generally regarded as one of Sri Lanka's most complex, intelligent and accomplished leaders, Jayawardene was a devout Buddhist who seemed genuinely to hold to Buddhist ideals of a just society – *dharmista*. As a quintessential political realist, he had been a key opponent of the 1958 Bandaranaike–Chelvanayakam pact, and was not above delivering virulently anti-Tamil speeches; what would be called today 'hate speeches'. Despite his lengthy eloquence and writings on nonviolence, he responded swiftly and forcefully to perceived threats to state security. See Richardson, *Paradise Poisoned*, pp. 395, 403 and 493. • **16.** Tambiah, *Sri Lanka*, p. 26. • **17.** Bradman Weerakoon, a Tamil-speaking Sinhalese civil servant widely regarded as one of Sri Lanka's most incorruptible and honest, was appointed Commissioner General for Essential Services by President Jayawardene in 1983 to clean up after the riots. He is quoted by Rajan Hoole, the author of *The Arrogance of Power*, as saying that he had 'no difficulty' with the figures of 2,000 or 3,000 dead. What is clear is that, as with the two JVP uprisings, an accurate accounting is virtually impossible because of the manner in which many bodies were burned, buried *in situ* or dumped into rivers. See also Wickramasinghe, *Sri Lanka in the Modern Age*, pp. 285–7. A government assessment – *Masterplan for the Rehabilitation of Persons Displaced in the Disturbances of July 1983* – calculated that 122 factories, 2,300 commercial buildings and more than 20,000 houses were destroyed during the riots. Violence was not confined to Colombo, but spread to many Sinhalese-majority towns, as well as to Trincomalee. The violence subsided, but did not end completely for a month: Feith, *Tamil and Sinhala Relations in Sri Lanka*. The number of Tamils uprooted in the wake of the 1983 violence has been put at one and a half million people. In 1995, three quarters of the Sri Lankan Tamil population had either fled abroad or had been internally displaced. By 2006, one quarter of Sri Lankan Tamils, 90 per cent of whom were from the Jaffna peninsula, lived abroad. See Wickramasinghe, op.cit., p. 265.

• **18**. Up to three million people may have been killed during the nine-month conflict, in an unending series of atrocities. Bangladesh's recent efforts to try alleged war criminals from this period under the country's International War Crimes Act of 1973 have been mired in allegations that the trials are aimed at opposition figures from the Islamist Jamaat-e-Islami party. The road to truth, let alone reconciliation, is a fraught one. • **19**. In 1981, Prabakharan had briefly fled across the Palk Straits to Tamil Nadu to escape a police dragnet (he remained in India between 1983 and 1987). There he was involved in an exchange of pistol shots with a rival Tamil militant, and arrested by the Tamil Nadu state police. Sri Lanka's Inspector General of Police flew to India with an extradition request. Protests in Tamil Nadu, and the personal intercession of Prime Minister Gandhi led to his release, leaving the inspector with no option but to fly back to Colombo without Sri Lanka's most wanted man. It was another close call for Prabakharan, whose arrest would certainly have altered the course of Sri Lankan history – and that of India, given the humiliation of the Indian army, and the assassination of Rajiv Gandhi a decade later. • **20**. Sri Lankan historian K.M. de Silva famously characterised the fears of the Sinhalese looking across the Palk Straits at the sixty million Tamils of southern India as those of a majority community with a minority complex (while for the minority Tamils of Sri Lanka, the reverse was the case: they possessed a 'majority complex' within a region dominated by Tamils). The findings of an inquiry into these 53 cases and eleven others were handed to the then President Chandrika Kamaratunga, but no further action was taken. These findings were contained in Volume 11 of the Special Report of the *1994 Western, Southern and Sabaragamuwa Disappearances Commission, 'Some Reports of Cases'* dated 31 May 1997 (unpublished). Despite evidence that the children had been rounded up and detained in the local army camp, the most senior army officer, then Lt. Col. R.P. Liyanage, was acquitted of involvement in the disappearances. • **21**. See Hoole, *The Linkages of State Terror*. • **22**. Kapferer, 'From the Crime of War to the Crime of Peace?', in Pararajasingham, *Sri Lanka*. The writing of popular novels appears to have been one of the rites of passage for Sinhalese chauvinists, if Premadasa and Cyril Mathews are any indication. • **23**. The findings of an inquiry into these 53 cases and eleven others were handed to the then President Chandrika Kamaratunga, but no further action was taken. These findings were contained in Volume 11 of the Special Report of the *1994 Western, Southern and Sabaragamuwa Disappearances Commission, 'Some Reports of Cases'* dated 31 May 1997 (unpublished). Despite evidence that the children had been rounded up and detained in the local army camp, the most senior army officer, then Lt. Col. R.P. Liyanage, was acquitted of involvement in the disappearances. • **24**. As in the first JVP uprising, the death toll is contested. One study puts the figure over two years at 65,000: 'The government unleashed a firestorm of repression which is yet to be matched proportionately: 15,000–20,000 killed in just 5 weeks. This is an average of 3,500 deaths per week – far higher than the 625 per week figure for the second insurrection which was suppressed by the UNP.' *Insurrectionary Violence in Sri Lanka: The Janatha Vimukthi Peramuna Insurgencies of 1971 and 1987–1989*, Tisaranee Gunasekara, Ethnic Studies Report, ICES, Vol. XVII, No. 1, January 1990. Renée Dumont, who witnessed the bodies floating downriver from the Victoria Bridge, estimated some 8,000 dead. Nira Wickramasinghe, in *Sri Lanka in the Modern Age*, accepts the estimate of G.H. Peiris of some 40,000 dead. The Commission of Inquiry appointed by then President Chandrika Kumaratunga in 1994 received well over 40,000 reports, but it is unlikely that this is a full accounting. Richardson (*Paradise Poisoned*, p. 524) puts the figure at 'more than 60,000'.

Chapter Four: The Tiger Revolt

1. See note 8, Chapter Three. • 2. The aggressive and superbly organised activities of Tamil political activists abroad fed into Sinhalese paranoia, and helped create a siege mentality that still reverberates today. They succeeded in having the governor of Massachusetts declare 22 May 1979 'Eelam Tamils Day', and lobbied for cutbacks to foreign aid, boycotts of Sri Lankan goods and restrictions on tourist travel to the island. Reports from the UN, the International Commission of Jurists, the World Council of Churches and Amnesty International made scant mention of the role of Tamil militant activities in provoking – to some degree – the responses from the security forces. By the time Black July arrived, a great deal of the groundwork had been effectively laid abroad to anticipate this mass atrocity by the Sri Lankan state. See Richardson, *Paradise Poisoned*, pp. 412–13. • 3. Narayan Swamy, *Tigers of Lanka*, p. 68. • 4. In an ABC Australia radio interview on 13 May 1999, the Rand Corporation analyst Peter Chalk, who had just returned from Sri Lanka, said, 'I think that there's a possibility of a political solution with the Tamil communities, I think there's a possibility of a [political] solution with the LTTE, but there is no prospect of a solution with the LTTE so long as Prabakharan is in power.' • 5. For more on the total militarisation of civilians under the control of the Tamil Tigers, see, for example, UTHR(J), *the Tragedy of Vanni Civilians and Total Militarization*. • 6. Wickramasinghe, *Sri Lanka in the Modern Age*, p. 298. • 7. There is an explicit comparison between the two in a Tamil Tiger propaganda piece on YouTube, 'LTTE Special Operations Assault Against Sri Lankan Army', 15 July 2007. • 8. On 15 January 2006, Velupillai Prabakharan opened what Tamilnation.org described as 'a children's home to care for children who had lost both parents in the war', in the village of Senchcholai near Kilinochchi. The photo of Prabakharan cutting a red ribbon and raising a flag shows a group of perhaps forty girls gathered for the obligatory applause and adoration of the Supreme Leader, some apparently as young as five or six and dressed in bright dresses. The director of Senchcholai, who the website noted was known by the *nom de guerre* of 'Sudarmahal', was a female Tamil Tiger fighter who had taken part in the first engagement fought by women against

Indian troops, in 1987 on the Jaffna peninsula. In an interview given to the main-stream Colombo weekly the *Sunday Times* in 2002, she spoke about the number of times that the home had been displaced by the various phases of the war to different locations. Apart from music, their school lessons and karate, the girls were taught what the paper called 'life survival techniques'. The director denied that the girls were being groomed for war, but admitted that there were some who had volunteered to join the revolutionary effort. Such are the subtleties of the induction of children into the social organisation of permanent revolution. • **9.** UTHR(J), *The Sun God's Children and the Big Lie.* • **10.** The University Teachers for Human Rights (Jaffna), founded in 1988, is a highly regarded civil society organisa-tion, which perhaps more than any other, against great odds, and with an even-handed condemnation of all brutality, has successfully monitored human rights abuses committed by the Tamil Tigers and government security forces. One of its founding members, Dr Rajani Thiranagama, the author of *The Broken Palmyra*, was murdered in 1989, probably by a Tamil Tiger hit squad. • **11.** UTHR(J), *Child conscription and peace.* • **12.** The recruiting of child soldiers is a crime under inter-national law. The ICRC notes that child recruitment is a crime under customary international humanitarian law, Rule 136: 'Recruitment of Child Soldiers in Hostil-ities – Children must not be recruited into armed forces or armed groups.' The Statute of the 2002 International Criminal Court notes that conscripting or enlisting children into armed forces or groups constitutes a war crime in both international and non-international armed conflicts (ICC Statute, Article 8(2)(b) (xxvi) and (e)(vii)). • **13.** Richardson, *Paradise Poisoned*, pp. 495–501. • **14.** Ibid., p. 528. • **15.** Since its formation in 1949, the 6,000-man army had been dominated by Chris-tian officers. The plotters' motive was to preserve the apolitical character of the forces in the face of the Sinhalese nationalising programme of the Bandaranaike government. After protests in northern Tamil areas at the prime minister's vigorous introduction of the chauvinist provisions of the Sinhala Only Act in 1960, she had sent the army to quell the demonstrators, causing unrest in the ranks. Two Tamil artillery officers were relieved of command. The coup gave Mrs Bandaranaike an excuse to create a force dominated by Sinhalese Buddhists. She installed her cousin Colonel Richard A. Udagama as army head of staff. Between 1963 and 1969, 90 per cent of all officer recruits were Buddhist and Sinhalese. After 1960, every cadet selected for Sandhurst, where Ceylonese officers continued to train even after independence, was Sinhalese. Ibid., pp. 171 and 204–5. • **16.** Ibid., p. 510. The author describes particularly well the degradation, humiliation, terrible conditions and pariah status of the all-Sinhalese armed forces personnel serving in Tamil areas of Sri Lanka. • **17.** In 2007, this author interviewed a number of the families of people who had been killed just hours earlier in the Jaffna peninsula, when one of the nastier periods of low-level counter-insurgency was under way and killings were a daily affair. The panicked and angry modus operandi of the army seemed to bear many similarities with earlier recorded instances. In one funeral, held in a thatch house surrounded by wailing relatives, a school teacher had been shot dead along with a number of other civilians after soldiers opened fire randomly in the wake of a street bomb blast. Four such cases that actually reached the judicial stage are described by Pinto-Jayawardena, (January 2010); The *Kumarapuram Case* of 1996, in which 24 Tamil men, women, and children were killed, and which caused widespread public anger when it emerged; The 1998 *Thambalagamam Case*, in which 8 civilians were killed, and which were reprisal killings motivated by the bombing of the Temple of the Tooth in Kandy a week earlier; The *Mylanthanai Case* of 1992, in which soldiers killed 35 Tamils in the village of Mylanthani in retaliation for the LTTE killing of senior army officer Denzil Kobbekaduwa at Arali Point in Jaffna; The *Chemmani Case*, in which in the course of the prosecution of Lance Corporal Somaratne Rajapakse for the rape and murder of Krishanthi Kumaraswamy, and the killing of her mother, brother, and a neighbour, the mass killings by security forces of hundreds of Tamils in the Jaffna Peninsula in 1996 were revealed, shocking the country. There were few such cases that made their way to court, almost none that resulted in a successful prosecution and gaol time for the killers. • **18**. Of particular note are the Criminal Procedures (Special Provisions) Bill and the Prevention of Terrorism Act (Temporary Provisions) Bill, more commonly known as the PTA. The latter in particular, passed in 1979, meant that any policeman or soldier could arrest any person at any time based on a 'reasonable suspicion' that they had terrorist links. There was no longer any need to charge a suspect, nor even to level a specific accusation. Those arrested could be held incommunicado in secret locations, without access to legal counsel or family members, who need not be informed by the authorities. Police were shielded from criminal and civil liability under the PTA. It was a licence for torture and disappearance. • **19**. Narayan Swamy, *Tigers of Lanka*, p. 127. • **20**. Prabakharan was of the low-caste Karaiyar, or fisher caste, and his village was noted for the assertiveness of this caste against the higher Vellala caste. See Peiris, *Clandestine Transactions*. It is notable that the prominence of the Karaiyar caste as a result of its leadership of the secessionist movement has elevated it subtly to rival the higher castes. • **21**. Bose, *State, Nations, Sovereignity*, p. 64. • **22**. Pratap, 'If Jayawardene was a true Buddhist, I would not be carrying a gun'. • **23**. These cemeteries and monuments were bulldozed by the Sri Lankan army at the end of the war. The argument that the Tigers' ideology subsumed traditional Christian and Hindu worship is based partly on the fact that in the Hindu faith the dead are cremated. The Tigers in effect established new forms of memory, new modes of worship, and engraved the history of the Tiger movement in headstone and monument inscriptions. • **24**. Douglas Devananda, an early Tamil militant, an MP, a minister in the Rajapaksa government and the target of thirteen assassination attempts by the Tamil Tigers, trained in Lebanon in 1978 with the militant al-Fatah wing of the Palestine Liberation Organisation. From early episodes such as this, the government of Sri Lanka and a number of proxy 'experts' have creatively conflated the notion of links between the Tamil Tigers and al-Qaeda. 'Colonel' Karuna, a Tamil Tiger commander in the east, who split from the Tigers in 2004 along with 6,000 other activists, was also a trainee in the Middle East. There is some suggestion that Tamil Tiger arms purchases have benefited radical Islamic organisations, but there is no tangible evidence that these transactions were anything other than astute mercenary commercial package deals that helped the respective political ends of the contracting parties. One former key official in Scotland Yard's anti-terrorism division told the author that Sri Lankan intelligence – military and police – was inherently unreliable because of the nature of the conflict. Intelligence forces throughout the world, however, must largely rely on information obtained from these sources, and try to distinguish fact from fiction. • **25**. Pape, 'Tamil Tigers: Suicide Bombing Innovators'. According to Pape, during the same period Hamas sent 147 attackers on 117 missions. • **26**. Robert Pape, 'The Strategic Logic of Suicide Terrorism', *The American Political Science Review*, Vol.97, No.3, (August 2003). • **27**. See for example the Tamil Tiger video dedicated to the Black Tigers who attacked Anuradhapura military airport in 2007, when tens of millions of dollars' worth of aircraft were destroyed (YouTube, 'Tamil Tiger Attack to Anuradhapura Air Force Camp'); video of a Sea Tiger attack on a Sri Lankan naval vessel (YouTube, 'LTTE sea tigers sink israeli-made dvora FAC'); and YouTube, 'King of the Tamils', featuring a gun-toting Prabakharan. For a flavour of the kind of pride displayed by some parents in their Black Tiger children, see Tony Birtley's Al-Jazeera report, 'Suicide bombers in Sri Lanka'. • **28**. Perry, 'How Sri Lanka's Rebels Build a Suicide Bomber'. • **29**. See footage taken from CCTV inside the reception room of his offices showing the moment the female suicide attacker triggers her body vest, on YouTube, 'Sri Lankan Homicide/Suicide Bomber Attack terrorist'. • **30**. For more on the 'brown water' battles fought between the Sea Tigers and the Sri Lankan navy, see Tony Birtley's excellent 'Sri Lanka battles Tigers at sea'. See also Tiger propaganda piece on their brown-water capability, YouTube, 'Attack Boats of SeaTigers'. • **31**. They even thought to include a photographer amongst the assassination team sent to kill India's former prime minister Rajiv Gandhi. The photographer was killed in the explosion, but his camera and film survived. • **32**. On the evening of 29 April 2009, Sri Lanka was playing Australia in the final of the International Cricket Competition (ICC) in Barbados. With Australia in an unassailable position, the author retired to bed, only to wake at 1 a.m. to what sounded like celebratory fireworks. It was in fact an attack on Colombo by the Air Tigers. Soldiers were firing haphazardly into the air, and tracer fire arced across Colombo. One gun position opened up on a passing Thai Airways jet, forcing foreign carriers to cancel flights to Sri Lanka until a more coherent operational response from the Sri Lankan armed forces had been established. The Tigers successfully struck a Shell oil refinery, reportedly doing around $700,000 worth of damage to the facilities. The Air Tigers were more comparable to early First World War attempts at target bombing, but were remarkably successful given that context. • **33**. Within living memory, the Second World War provides almost innumerable examples on all sides of suicidal bravery. For example, the two young Czechoslovak soldiers who parachuted into German-occupied Prague in May 1942 to assassinate the Nazi Reinhard Heydrich had been extensively briefed by senior British officers on the insignificant chances that they might survive their mission. Having killed Heydrich, Jan Kubiš was mortally wounded, while Jozef Gabčík swallowed cyanide when surrounded. • **34**. In December 2010, Karuna, by then a minister in the government of Mahinda Rajapaksa, admitted that forces under his control had killed the police officers. See Charles Havilland, 'Sri Lankan Minister Admits Tamil Tiger Killings,' BBC, 13 December 2010. • **35**. In Colombo, the author's wife passed close by a bus that had been blown up moments earlier, and the vehicle of a friend was spattered with shrapnel from another bus blast. • **36**. There is no clearly agreed definition of terrorism under international law, and attempts to arrive at one have endured many years of frustrated negotiation in the antechambers of the UN. Under international law, however, the intentional terrorizing of a civilian population is outlawed in non-international conflicts such as Sri Lanka's. The second rule of the ICRC's compendium of customary international humanitarian law, runs as follows: 'Violence Aimed at Spreading Terror among the Civilian Population – Acts or threats of violence the primary purpose of which is to spread terror among the civilian population are prohibited.' There is a wider prohibition of 'acts of terrorism' contained in Article 4(2)(d) of Additional Protocol II to the Geneva Conventions, and the use of terror directed at civilians in war has been recently addressed at the International Criminal Tribunal for Rwanda and of the Special Court for Sierra Leone. Despite indications that many of these attacks had a certain strategic or tactical value, the author has erred far on one side to characterise these tiger attacks as primarily civilian in nature, simply by virtue of the fact that civilians were killed. This contentious categorising ranges from attacks targeting a single victim, in which many unintended or incidental civilian victims were killed, to attacks on villages, public transport or temples, where the intended victims could only have been civilians and the primary effect was to create a sense of terror throughout the broader community. This figure does not include the number of Tamils allegedly killed by the Tigers in the areas they controlled, nor the many hundreds of prisoners thought to have been killed in Tamil Tiger gulags. The University Teachers for Human Rights estimates that the latter figure is as high as 7,000 (email exchange between the author and the UTHR(J)'s Rajan Hoole, June 2010). See also UTHR(J), *Women Prisoners of the LTTE*, and *Human Rights and The Issues of War and Peace*. • **37**. As with the grand death tolls of the JVP uprisings, a figure for the thirty-year civil war between the Tamil Tigers and the Sri Lankan government remains elusive. Foreign reporters who attempted over the decades to arrive at realistic estimates always prefaced their reports with a warning that statistics could not be regarded as reliable when sourced from either side. A figure of

60,000 dead was being commonly reported in 2005. By the admission of government officials, army deaths may have been around 30,000, and an equivalent number estimated for the Tamil Tigers. The best count I have arrived at for the deaths of Sinhalese civilians might be as high as 5,000. This leaves the great unknown of civilian Tamil deaths, which range from the unrealistically low to extremely high. On 29 September 2010, Sri Lanka's minister for child development and women's affairs, M.L.A.M. Hizbullah, told reporters that Sri Lanka was seeking help for around 90,000 war widows from Tamil areas of Sri Lanka. He said that his ministry had a list of 49,000 widows from the island's eastern province and another 40,000 in the northern province where the final battles had been fought. A small proportion of these will be widows of Sinhalese and Muslim men killed by the Tamil Tigers. See AFP, 'Sri Lanka seeks help for 90,000 war widows: minister'. This tally excludes dead female fighters, who may have accounted for between one quarter and one third of the Tiger forces, and an unknown number of child soldiers, but which might have accounted some thousands of the Tamil Tigers fighters killed over thirty years of conflict. • **38**. Trincomalee was the linchpin in the Tamil Tiger strategic conception of the viability of an independent state, with similarities to Singapore or Taiwan. See Richardson, *Paradise Poisoned* p. 349. • **39**. Turlej, H. 'Turning a Blind Eye to Terrorism'. • **40**. For a flavour of this printed material, one might refer to the January–February issue of *Liberation Tigers*, published in the Vanni. Under the title 'What is Next? War or Peace!' is a picture of Prabakharan pointing at Jaffna on a map of Tamil Eelam with his left forefinger. Beneath it is printed the verse, 'Where Sooriya Thevan (Sun God) points with his finger, thither the sun rays will hasten, to enfold Thamil Eelam in the brightness of his glory!' See UTHR(J), *The Sun God's children and the big lie*. • **41**. In 2007, Intelsat Ltd, a satellite service provider, claimed that the Tamil Tigers had been using one of their satellites without permission. According to Peter Wonacott, in 'Sri Lanka Targets Tamil Tigers' Overseas Support Network', the organisation's satellite broadcasts had originated from at least two countries, France and Serbia. • **42**. The Internet was vital in the formation of, and to sustain, the revolutionary identity of the Tamil people across the globe, through websites, emails, chat rooms and bulletin boards, and extending latterly into Facebook, Twitter and blogging. This so-called computer-mediated communication has been vigorously combated by Sinhalese-dominated governments and Sinhalese diaspora communities. As has been the case in the physical domain, and regardless of the merits of the cause, the tactics of the protagonists in the virtual domain have mirrored each other. 'The Internet's "replicator technology" breeds infamy very easily and at great speed. More and more similar-thinking websites choose to reproduce . . . online slander and vilification [that] can have a debilitating effect on the writer thus "exterminating" the writer from cyberspace' and driving moderate voices either underground, or into the camps of the extreme. For an excellent introduction to the use of the Internet in this war between peoples, see

Ranganathan, 'Experiencing eelam.com: terror online'. • **43**. A twenty-seven-year-old woman named Shoba, who used the pseudonym 'Isaipriya', was one of the glamorous faces of the Tamil Tigers. She worked as a singer, songwriter and news presenter for the propaganda wing of the LTTE, and was allegedly executed by the SLA in the final days of the war (see Chapter Ten). Her videos can be found online. • **44**. So successful was this transmutation that cemeteries were regarded as sacred temples and monuments to war and struggle, rather than just cemeteries. For a more profound examination, see Roberts, 'Pragmatic Action and Enchanted Worlds'. • **45**. It was only in 2006 that the US-inspired Long Range Identification and Tracking (LRIT) satellite system became mandatory for cargo vessels plying international routes. It originated in a proposal put to the International Maritime Organisation by the US Coast Guard. Once again, the Tamil Tiger model for the business of war provided a frightening prospect for US Homeland Security officials. In the aftermath of the 2001 airborne al-Qaeda attacks, they contemplated the possibility of a seaborne nuclear attack on US harbour installations and realised that the ungoverned seas were one of the country's most vulnerable points. The LRIT satellite receives a beacon four times a day from all vessels over 300 tons, helping to keep tabs on the estimated 50,000 large vessels at sea. No doubt it contributed to the demise of the Sea Pigeons. • **46**. There are many videos of these actions online. For one example in early 2007, see the curiously titled 'Sri Lankan Navy blows up MIA Born Free Tamil Tiger TERRORIST LTTE weapons ship' on YouTube. • **47**. A great deal has been written about the alleged involvement of the Tamil Tigers in drug running. Some of the principal arms markets from where they probably sourced weapons were in the great drug production centres such as the 'Golden Crescent' of Afghanistan and Pakistan, and the 'Golden Triangle' of Myanmar, Laos, Thailand and Cambodia. Still, there is no definitive proof that drugs transactions were a substantial part of Tamil Tiger fund-raising, and the efforts of various Sri Lankan academics to piece together the evidence that exists amounts to at best a circumstantial picture. G.H. Peiris has written, 'As in our earlier analysis of the Tiger operations in Southeast Asia, the extent to which the LTTE has succeeded in its attempts to tap the potential of the Golden Crescent cannot be assessed with precision.' See Peiris, 'Clandestine Transactions of the LTTE and the Secessionist Campaign in Sri Lanka'. The author's own view is that despite the paucity of evidence for systemic drug running, it is likely that drugs were systematically trafficked by some segments of the Tamil resistance movement, and it would make sense that quantities of drugs were transported by the Sea Pigeons as a part, or by-product, of complex arms trading deals. • **48**. Joyce, 'Terrorist Financing in South East Asia'. • **49**. Jayasekara, 'Tamil Tiger Links with Islamist Terrorist groups'. • **50**. The Mackenzie Institute, 'Terrorism and Crime: A Natural Partnership'. • **51**. See Human Rights Watch, *Funding the Final War*. To Prabakharan, the Tamil diaspora was a source of revenue, but also a potential population pool for a future state. Intimidation and forced involvement in 'the

Movement', and the many visits of Tamil youths to the Vanni after the 2002 cease-fire, gave him hope that any future state, like Israel and Kosovo, would become a magnet for expatriates returning to a promised land, which, through work, agitation and contribution, they had helped to liberate. For a good introduction to the Tamil Tiger extortion network, see also Rotheroe and Ruhfus, 'Tiger Tax'. • 52. International developments played a considerable part. War preparations were boosted by the almost simultaneous election in May 2004 of a Congress government in New Delhi, backed by Rajiv Gandhi's widow Sonia. While occasionally calling for restraint and political efforts to resolve Tamil grievances, the Indian government gave the tacit go-ahead for Sri Lankan military action against the Tigers. The Tigers' intransigence in negotiations and their numerous ceasefire violations, including the August 2005 murder of the Sri Lankan foreign minister Lakshman Kadirigamar, angered the governments of the US, Japan and the EU, which had supported and funded the 2002–6 peace process. By May 2006, the Tigers had been banned as a terrorist organisation by the European Union. • 53. For more on Tamil v. Tamil violence during this period, see UTHR(J), *Political Killings and rituals of unreality*. • 54. In a country where 'foreign interference' or 'neo-colon-ialism' had long been used by all political parties as a political rallying cry, it was inevitable that the complexities (and considerable problems) of the international aid response following the tsunami led to a resurgence of anti-Western sentiment. Likewise, the fact that the Tamil Tigers took advantage of the aid flows to rearm came as no surprise to anybody familiar with the organisation's propensities. As one Sri Lanka specialist has put it, 'both the government and the LTTE sought to circumscribe the operations of aid agencies, while generating political and strategic capital from their presence'. But the backlash against the international agencies was also the fault of the agencies themselves, whose aid programmes were sometimes hamfisted, ran roughshod over local sensitivities and exacerbated elements of the root causes of the conflict. Indeed, it is not too extreme to claim that on one analysis, the international tsunami response was a major cause for the return to open conflict. See Goodhand, 'Stablising a victor's peace?' For more on the Tamil Tiger efforts to have all diaspora funding channelled through the Tamil Relief Organisation (TRO), see UTHR(J), *A Tale of Two Disasters and the Fickleness of Terror Politics*. • 55. See Wijesinha, *All Experience*, p. 196. A number of the Rajapaksa brothers display a taste for material acquisition and public exhibition quite different from the example of their father, whose life was marked by a determined simplicity and modesty. • 56. The eight points are: unwavering political will; disregard international opinion; no negotiations; control information; absence of political intervention; complete operational freedom for the security forces; accent on young commanders; keep international neighbours in the loop. See Shashikumar, 'Lessons from the War in Sri Lanka' and 'The Rajapaksa Model of Defeating Terror, Securing Peace and National Reconciliation'. • 57. According to Gotabaya, from 2006 the government acquired UAVs, ships, aircraft, armoured fighting vehicles, radars and a range of artillery pieces and mortars. The previous administration, under President Chandrika Kumaratunga, had first introduced Israeli-built Kfir jets, Russian MiG 27s, Czechoslovakian-built multi-barrel rocket launchers and UAVs. See *The Island*, 'Opposition's Claim Mahinda Bought Only Ammo Countered'; *Times of India*, 'Sri Lanka still sourcing arms from Pak, China'; *Sri Lanka Air Force News*, 'Pakistan Air Force chief arrives in Sri Lanka'. The commander of the Sri Lankan air force denied reports that Pakistan air force pilots had flown sorties during the war. See *Dawn*, 'Sri Lanka denies Pakistani pilots flew its planes'. • **58**. See Human Rights Watch, *Trapped and Mistreated: LTTE Abuses against Civilians in the Vanni*. • **59**. For a good introduction to the reconquest of eastern Sri Lanka by the Sri Lankan army in 2006–7, see Rotheroe and Ruhfus, 'How the East Was Won.' • **60**. See Rosenberg, 'Sri Lanka seen heading back to civil war'. The Tamil Tigers were in every sense a reactive popular movement that 'had the support of the Tamil people in general'. See Wilson, *Sri Lankan Tamil Nationalism*, p. 131. In a letter to the author from an influential member of the Australian Tamil community, Ana Pararajasinham, in August 2010, it was suggested that for many Tamils their loyalty to the Tamil Tigers included 'admiration, a sense of community, identification with the cause and . . . the fact that they were their own sons and daughters'.

Chapter Five: Convoy 11

1. There is a plausible case to argue that as many as 75,000 people are unaccounted for in the wake of the siege. See the International Crisis Group's *War Crimes in Sri Lanka*. The UTHR(J)'s director Rajan Hoole puts the figure at closer to 80,000. • **2**. The phrase is used to describe incidents in which, based on standards for the conduct of war described under international law, an investigative body might find prima facie evidence for war crimes. The premise of this book is that there were numerous such incidents during the final phase of the civil war. • **3**. See the press statement from the Sri Lankan Ministry of Foreign Affairs, 5 February 2009, which reads in part: 'The Government has also declared a "zero civilian casualty" policy in its military operations and at all times made every effort to ensure that civilians are supplied with food, medical supplies and other humanitarian assistance in collaboration with the UN and the ICRC.' • **4**. See OHCHR, 'Louise Arbour's address to Trinity College, Dublin'. By 2010, Arbour was president and CEO of the independent International Crisis Group based in Brussels. She had been a former justice of Canada's Supreme Court, former chief prosecutor for the International Criminal Tribunal for the former Yugoslavia and had most recently held the post of UN High Commissioner for Human Rights prior to Navanetham Pillay. • **5**. The Claymore mine was a versatile adaptation of the famous American mine. It was easily manufactured, reliable and could be set and triggered in a variety of ways,

and was used by both the Sri Lankan army and the Tamil Tigers. Most notoriously, the Tigers used it to strike civilian buses, or in remotely controlled assassinations in which a timer or mobile telephone trigger was used. It was also used
as a booby trap for forward defensive positions, as well as for locations vacated by
Tiger forces on to which the SLA was advancing. • 6. The term 'refugee' in this
context is technically incorrect, but is used because of its commonly understood
connotations. Under international law, a person forced to flee their home becomes
a refugee only after they have crossed an international border into foreign territory. If forced to flee their home within a country, they are more correctly called
'internally displaced persons'. • 7. Most of the 35.5 square kilometre No Fire Zone
was scrubby jungle, which meant that the vast majority of the people were
concentrated close to the A35 road, where they could easily obtain humanitarian
supplies. The Tamil Tigers located some of their artillery weapons inside the
No Fire Zone, but roughly three kilometers north of the main concentration of
people huddled near the road. According to the International Crisis Group, 'the
Defence Ministry's own website on 31 January showed that the LTTE artillery
positions, "plotted with accurate information received from technical and intelligence sources", were deep in the NFZ and far from the A35 road and the food
distribution centre.' The NFZ ran west along this major road from Manjal Palam
Bridge to Suthanthirapuram Junction, and included the Vallipunam hospital. It is
unclear whether the NFZ was contemplated as a 'Safety Zone' or as a 'Neutralized Zone'. Under international law, the former is meant to be located away from
fighting, whereas the latter can be used inside an area in which fighting it taking
place. The comments of the Defence Secretary suggest that it was seen by the
SLA as a 'Safety Zone'. In either case, attacks on these zones are clearly prohibited under international law, as discussed under Rule 35 of the ICRC's compendium of customary international humanitarian law: 'Hospital and Safety Zones
and Neutralized Zones – Directing an attack against a zone established to shelter
the wounded, the sick and civilians from the effects of hostilities is prohibited.'
In addition, Rule 24 of the compendium discusses the removal of civilians from
the vicinity of military objectives, where civilians 'cannot feasibly be separated
from densely populated areas according to Rule 23'. And yet, the government had
encouraged the civilian population to move to the NFZ, and then had mounted an
attack that appeared to indiscriminately strike that very concentration of civilians.
• 8. This tactic was widely used by the Americans in Vietnam. The intention to
attack a designated area would be declared, and a deadline set for non-combatants
to leave. The area would then be declared a 'free-fire zone', on the presumption
that anybody who remained had hostile intentions. The US repeated the strategy
prior to the second attack on the town of Fallujah, in Iraq, in November 2004.
It is a tactic that by definition is in part indiscriminate, and inherently prone to
lead to the widespread killing of civilians. It also contravenes a fundamental principle of customary international law, which requires positive identification of

combatants, in the absence of which the default is to assume that people are civilians. • **9.** The issue of 'proportionality' is discussed under Rule 14 of the ICRC's compendium of customary international humanitarian law, and is one of the fundamental principles governing international humanitarian law: 'Proportionality in Attack – Launching an attack which may be expected to cause incidental loss of civilian life, injury to civilians, damage to civilian objects, or a combination thereof, which would be excessive in relation to the concrete and direct military advantage anticipated, is prohibited.' Carrying out disproportional attacks is clearly prohibited. What is most often at issue is what constitutes an 'incidental loss', and discussions over the nature of what constitutes a direct military advantage. • **10.** As a military officer, Harun was aware of another of the fundamental customary principles of humanitarian law, which is that attacks must be discriminate. The ICRC, in its compendium of customary international humanitarian law, notes (in Rule 11) that indiscriminate attacks are prohibited. Rule 12 defines indiscriminate attacks as those that are: '(a) not directed at a specific military objective; (b) employ a method or means of combat which cannot be directed at a specific military objective; (c) employ a method or means of combat the effects of which cannot be limited as required by international humanitarian law, and consequently, in each such case, are of a nature to strike military objectives and civilians or civilian objects without distinction.' Rule 13 discusses area bombardment: 'Attacks by bombardment by any method or means which treats as a single military objective a number of clearly separated and distinct military objectives located in a city, town, village or other area containing a similar concentration of civilians or civilian objects are prohibited.'

Chapter Six: Inside the Cage

1. See Tamilnet, 'Cowardly Act says Vallipunam survivor.' • **2.** The official government version of events can be seen in defence.lk video presentations on YouTube. • **3.** The Sinhalese journalist Vilani Peiris had this to say: 'Stripped to its bare bones, Rambukwella's argument runs as follows: the LTTE trains child soldiers, the orphanage contained children, therefore it was a legitimate target. In other words, the entire population – children, as well as men and women – is being treated as the enemy. No one in the Colombo political and media establishment has called the Mullaitivu bombing by its right name: a war crime for which those responsible in the government and the military should be charged and prosecuted.' See Senewiratne, 'Senchcholai bombing – the legal dimension'. • **4.** The issue of the legality of the attack on the schoolgirls revolves around the highly contended interpretation of what constitutes 'direct participation in hostilities', in the context of a civil war, or a non-international armed conflict. This discussion can be read under Rule 6 of the 161 rules contained in the ICRC's compendium of

customary international humanitarian law. Coincidentally, just as events were
unfolding inside the Cage, the ICRC provided additional guidance on this issue in
the form of the adoption of the following: Interpretive Guidance on the Notion
of Direct Participation in Hostilities under International Humanitarian Law;
31-12-2008 Article, International Review of the Red Cross, No. 872, Adopted by
the Assembly of the International Committee of the Red Cross on 26 February
2009. • 5. See Sengupta, 'UN Leads Evacuation from Sri Lanka'. The full name of
the ministry is more correctly the Ministry for Disaster Management and Human
Rights. • 6. The author was the opposing speaker on the same live interview. • 7.
Sky News, 'Packed Sri Lanka hospital shelled'. • 8. The term 'medical unit' more
fully denotes the hospitals and makeshift medical tents that were established,
dismantled, shifted, and then re-established as the frontlines moved. Medical
units are protected under international law as, for example, outlined in Rules 35
(discussed above in endnote no. 7 in chapter 5) and 28 of the ICRC's compendium
of customary international humanitarian law: 'Rule 28. Medical Units – Medical
units exclusively assigned to medical purposes must be respected and protected in
all circumstances. They lose their protection if they are being used, outside their
humanitarian function, to commit acts harmful to the enemy.' The commentary
to Rule 28 also discusses the types of acts that would or would not remove the
particular protection afforded to medical units: 'While the Geneva Conventions
and Additional Protocols do not define "acts harmful to the enemy", they do
indicate several types of acts which do not constitute "acts harmful to the enemy",
for example, when the personnel of the unit is armed, when the unit is guarded,
when small arms and ammunition taken from the wounded and sick are found in
the unit and when wounded and sick combatants or civilians are inside the unit.
According to the Commentary on the First Geneva Convention, examples of acts
harmful to the enemy include the use of medical units to shelter able-bodied
combatants, to store arms or munitions, as a military observation post or as a
shield for military action.' • 9. This from Geneva Conventions, Protocol I (art
52(2)) which is accepted as reflective of customary law, as noted in the ICRC's
compendium of customary international humanitarian law, Rule 8: 'Definition
of Military Objectives – In so far as objects are concerned, military objectives are
limited to those objects which by their nature, location, purpose or use make an
effective contribution to military action and whose partial or total destruction,
capture or neutralization, in the circumstances ruling at the time, offers a definite
military advantage.' For a taste of the kinds of dilemmas faced by commanders
in the 'target selection' process, see for example, the US Air Force's (USAF) *Intelligence Targeting Guide*, which details many of the targeting dilemmas and the
guiding international law that commanders must face. • 10. The issue of
command criminal responsibility (commanders and their superiors) is dealt with
by two rules of customary international law, as listed in the ICRC's compendium
of customary international humanitarian law: Rule 152. 'Command Responsibility

for Orders to Commit War Crimes – Commanders and other superiors are criminally responsible for war crimes committed pursuant to their orders.' Rule 153: 'Command Responsibility for Failure to Prevent, Repress or Report War Crimes – Commanders and other superiors are criminally responsible for war crimes committed by their subordinates if they knew, or had reason to know, that the subordinates were about to commit or were committing such crimes and did not take all necessary and reasonable measures in their power to prevent their commission, or if such crimes had been committed, to punish the persons responsible.' Individual responsibility is dealt with under Rule 151. • **11.** Defence Secretary Rajapaksa has emphasised the broad use of UAVs: 'We gave all Commanders a direct connection to the UAV. Therefore, all Divisional Commanders could see what was going on in front, in the LTTE controlled areas. Throughout the Humanitarian Operations we gave this facility to the ground Commanders. Therefore, when they were planning and executing the operations it was very helpful for the ground Commanders to see in front; to see where the enemy concentrations were, to see and locate where the fire was coming from, to neutralise and act accordingly.' See *Business Today*, 'Defence Secretary Gotabaya Rajapaksa salutes the war heroes'. • **12.** Defence.lk, 'Former Puthukuddyiruppu hospital unharmed'. • **13.** UTHR(J), *Let Them Speak*, p. 40. • **14.** The immediate response from Sri Lanka's President Rajapaksa was to issue a bemusing proclamation of what was characterised as 'safe passage' over a forty-eight-hour period for civilians to leave the conflict area. The announcement unintentionally implied that civilians did not have safe passage at other times. The military also issued a standard response to the AP story, and denied that any civilian deaths had occurred. • **15.** The MBRL has a long history going back to the Korean peninsula in the fifteenth century, but the modern version might be dated from the famous Russian Katyusha system developed during the Second World War. An unguided weapon, using as many as four dozen rockets in a single firing, the MBRL is indiscriminate, and is designed to wreak devastation over a wide area of land. They are usually mobile and mounted on the back of trucks or wagons, and emit an unmistakable piercing shriek. The author listened to MBRLs being launched by the SLA during the attacks on the east in 2007. The Tamil Tigers also used them. • **16.** UTHR(J), *Let Them Speak*. • **17.** See for example, 'AAAS Satellite Image Analysis Points to New Graves, Shelling, and Human Displacement in Sri Lanka', accessed at www.aaas.org, and a more in-depth analysis at http://shr.aaas.org/geotech/srilanka/srilanka.shtml. • **18.** It is to serve as a counter-weight to this discretion that organisations such as Médecins Sans Frontières (MSF) were founded in the 1970s. The French organisation maintains a battlefield operational focus, but unlike the ICRC, it also has a reputation for pushing the limits of humanitarianism, and for speaking out forcefully and incessantly, to the discomfort of the protagonists, and sometimes that of its fellow humanitarian organisations. For this reason alone, and despite the high quality of its medical resources, MSF was excluded from access to the Sri Lankan battlefield by the government, and relegated to a small ad hoc role treating the wounded civilians who gradually came out from the siege. • **19**. Sri Lanka has been a prominent member of the Non-Aligned Movement (NAM), whose five 'principles of restraint', described by Indian prime minister Jawaharlal Nehru, in a speech given in Colombo in 1954, included: mutual respect for each other's territorial integrity and sovereignty; mutual non-aggression; mutual non-interference in domestic affairs; equality and mutual benefit; and peaceful co-existence. • **20**. Both these countries serve as early examples of unilateral interventionism by nations to deal with troublesome neighbours whose internal crimes threatened the stability of the intervener. In 1978–9, Tanzania invaded Uganda, and fought a combined Libyan and Ugandan force (as well as a small Palestinian contingent) to overthrow the murderous regime of Idi Amin, whose killings of civilians may have amounted to 300,000. The contemporaneous Vietnamese invasion of Cambodia ended the murderous rule of the Khmer Rouge, who are thought to have killed between one and two million Cambodians. In the context of Cold War machinations, the invasion was condemned by US-aligned nations, and by numerous UN resolutions. In the nineteenth century, there were several examples of Christian nations intervening in the affairs of Islamic states on humanitarian grounds. • **21**. The principle of distinction is a fundamental tenet of international humanitarian law. It requires that parties to a conflict must at all times distinguish between civilians and combatants and between civilian objects and military objectives. For civilians, see the first rule elucidated under the ICRC's compendium of customary international humanitarian law, Rule 1: 'The Principle of Distinction between Civilians and Combatants – The parties to the conflict must at all times distinguish between civilians and combatants. Attacks may only be directed against combatants. Attacks must not be directed against civilians.' See also Henckaerts, *Study on customary international humanitarian law*, p. 198. • **22**. IBN Live, 'Can't ensure safety of civilians in LTTE areas'. • **23**. In the same interview, the Minister added, 'there is absolutely no justification to use heavy weapons and, in fact, about ten days ago, the armed forces took a conscious decision not to use any heavy weapons. We have not been using heavy weapons'. On 13 March, a press release from his ministry titled 'High Commissioner for Human Rights' Statement is unfounded and lacks credibility', ran as follows: 'The Ministry also notes with regret that despite repeated assurances from the Government that the security forces were instructed to respect the no-fire zone and that they do not use long range weapons, the Office of the High Commissioner still continues to repeat unfounded claims of civilian casualties due to shelling'. • **24**. *Sunday Times*, 'Whereabouts Unknown'. • **25**. See *Der Spiegel Online*, 'Damning Report For UN Secretary-General', and Reuters, 'Norwegian memo sparks PR crisis for UN's Ban Ki-Moon'. A month earlier, a scathing and highly personal attack had been published in *Foreign Policy*: see Heilbrunn, 'Nowhere Man'. • **26**. By the time Eelam War IV was under way, the TRO had become widely regarded as a front organisation for the Tigers, and was proscribed as such by the US Treasury in November 2007. In August, nine people had been arrested by the FBI on suspicion of channelling funds to the Tigers. The Tamil Tigers had been proscribed as a foreign terrorist organisation by the US as far back as 1997. • **27**. It should be noted that there were a number of experienced, persistent, and resolute Indian journalists at work in Colombo. The Sri Lanka-based Murali Reddy of *The Hindu* contributed a body of excellent reporting, and attracted the ire of extremists as a result. • **28**. *Himal Magazine*, '13th Amendment will be implemented in full'. • **29**. Author interview with Louise Arbour, 24 June 2010. • **30**. Aleem, 'Interview with Sri Lanka's FM'.

Chapter Seven: The Struggle for Truth

1. Ayman al-Zawahiri, al-Qaeda senior commander, quoted in Marc Lynch, 'Al-Qaeda's media strategies', *National Interest* 83 (Spring 2006), extracted from O'Neill, *Confronting the Hydra*. • **2**. Author interview with Louise Arbour, 24 June 2010. • **3**. Throughout the months of the siege, the Tamil diaspora had mounted dramatic and overtly political protests, which, while focused on the impact of the army's bombardments, avoided mention of the devastation wrought on civilians by the Tigers' own brutality. As the crisis intensified, demonstrations were held across the globe, from Sydney to Toronto. Night after night in London, crowds of more than 100,000 people held vigils at Westminster, with hunger strikes splashed across the front pages of British papers. Yet whilst arousing sympathy for the plight of the civilians cornered inside the Cage, the protests had failed to trigger a concerted international response. As the battle raged inside Sri Lanka, and supporters rallied outside, the actual number of trapped civilians, and the impact on them of the Sri Lankan army's assault, remained uncertain. Norwegian paramilitary police forcibly evicted protesters who had invaded the Sri Lankan embassy in Oslo. The demonstrations backfired in Canada, where newspapers editorialised against the demonstrators. Tolerant Canadians tired of having their highways blocked by thousands of red-shirted youths waving placards bearing the oddly disjointed fatigue-wearing figure of Prabakharan. His face, so dear to many Sri Lankan Tamils, seemed to observers to belong to another age and another place. With internal threats already posed by extremists from Islamic immigrant communities, the space for additional political grievances had been narrowed. The defeat of the Tigers left the diaspora feeling 'powerless, betrayed by the West, demanding justice and, in some cases, wanting revenge'. See International Crisis Group, *The Sri Lankan Tamil Diaspora after the LTTE*. • **4**. In 2010, Poddala was awarded the Transparency International Integrity prize for his work during this time. • **5**. Monthly e-bulletin of the Free Media Movement (June 2008). • **6**. See Gunawardene, 'Goodbye, Lasantha Wickramatunga'. • **7**. International Crisis Group, *War Crimes in Sri Lanka*. • **8**. Journalists, writers and other dissenting voices who opposed the Tigers faced assassination. In areas controlled by the Tigers, dissent was virtually impossible, whilst in peripheral areas such as the Jaffna peninsula or Trincomallee, Tamils who published pieces critical of the the movement could expect to be reproached, threatened, beaten and otherwise intimidated, or killed. The full story of the Tamil Tiger programme of assassination and intimidation against voices of dissent or political moderation is beyond the scope of this book, but has been well documented in numerous UTHR(J) reports. A friend and colleague who worked for an international organisation inside Tiger-controlled Vanni, and who had spent seven years working in the Palestinian territory of Gaza, remarked that the Tiger regime might have been compared to the North Koreans running a forested section of the Gaza strip. • 9. In February 1990, for example, one of Sri Lanka's best-known journalists, Richard de Zoysa, was kidnapped from his mother's home. He was tortured, then shot, and his body dumped on a beach. His friend, the journalist Taraki Sivaram, was similarly murdered in 2005. Richard de Zoysa's mother said that she had seen two of the abductors, and some months later identified one of them on television as a high-ranking police officer. She received death threats. In 2005, charges were brought against three police officers, but were dismissed by the presiding magistrate for lack of evidence. • 10. In late 2010, Gotabaya Rajapaksa was using Sri Lanka's degraded judicial system in a bid to bankrupt the *Sunday Leader*. In two separate court actions, he has pursued claims for two billion Sri Lanka rupees, or the equivalent of approximately $US18 million, for defamation and the unauthorised use of his photograph. See *Sunday Leader*, 'Defence Secretary Suing The Sunday Leader for Rs 2 Billion'. • 11. See *Groundviews*, 'Mervyn Silva publicly admits to killing Lasantha Wickrematunghe'. The recording of Silva's 'speech' was sent to Mahinda Rajapaksa by journalists. • 12. A revealing account of one editor on the receiving end of extensive government efforts to snuff out a story is given by Frederica Jansz in 'Her Story'. This story details what happened after the *Sunday Leader* published an exclusive interview with Sareth Fonseka in which he accused the defence secretary of giving orders that the senior Tiger leadership should be executed if they attempted to surrender. • 13. Astrology is one of the elements of a complex system of metaphysical beliefs widely held and practised to varying degrees throughout Sri Lanka. Bradley Weerakoon, an adviser to nine Sri Lankan leaders, has said that President Premadasa and Prime Minister Sirimavo Bandaranaike were both guided in their daily decisions by what the stars purportedly held for them. The same is said of the current president, whose astrologer, Sumanadasa Abeygunawardene, says that he has even advised him on the best times to leave his house. Robert Knox noted in the seventeenth century of the Ceylonese that 'they are very superstitious in making Observations of any little Accidents, as *Omens* portending good to them or evil. *Sneezing* they reckon to import evil . . . There is a little Creature much like a *Lizzard*, which they look upon altogether as a *Prophet*, whatsoever work or business they are going about; if he

crys, they will cease for a space, reckoning that he tells them there is a bad Planet
rules at that instant. They take great notice in a Morning at their first going out,
who first appears in their sight: and if they see a *White* Man, or a big-bellied
Woman, they hold it *fortunate*: and to see any decrepit or deformed People, as
unfortunate.' Knox, *An Historical Relation*, pp. 63–4. • **14**. Months before Ekneligoda
was 'disappeared', Sri Lanka's new ambassador to the UN in New York, Palitha
Kohona (formerly secretary of the foreign ministry), had given the dubious reassurance that things were improving for journalists after the war, because 'there
hasn't been a single killing of a media person for the last 12 weeks'. See *Himal
Magazine*, '13th Amendment will be implemented in full'. • **15**. Razeen Sally, a Sri
Lankan teaching at the London School of Economics, has noted that the tone of
politics is matched by that of journalism: 'What passes for political debate is black
or white, hectoring and puerile. Journalistic standards are low and shoddy. Ceylon
was renowned throughout Asia for its liberal culture and high standards of journalism, with space enough for reasoned, nuanced and critical debate. That has
been almost extinguished – a symptom of extreme degeneration in public life and
an emasculated civil society.' See Transparency International interview The newspaper industry had long catered to a literate and engaged public. A 1964 survey
revealed that half of all Ceylonese men and a quarter of women were regular
newspaper readers and radio listeners. There were four daily newspapers, with an
average circulation of more than 50,000, and three weekly newspapers, with a
circulation of more than 100,000. There were also six other widely read dailies and
four more major weeklies. The newspapers were highly partisan, a far cry from
the more monochrome coverage seen in most English-language press and electronic media today (although greatly relieved by the newly vibrant Internet). See
Richardson, *Paradise Poisoned*, pp. 88 and 189–90. The author personally appreci-
ated the unique, if unfamiliar atmosphere of the Sri Lankan press, and particularly
the frequently intelligent and forcefully argued pieces that were a mixture of
opinion and facts artfully stretched to breaking point. Sri Lanka has a strong
history of investigative journalism, engaged in by hardy journalists even in the
most adverse of times and circumstances, and despite the generally poor pay scales
of the profession, but this is counter-balanced by its equally capacious taste for and
energetic manufacture of gutter journalism. See Richardson, op. cit., p. 411. • **16**.
Most of these exhaustive opinion pieces, since removed from Sri Lankan government portals, can be downloaded at www.box.net/shared/7uxy82bq41. • **17**. This
was not the first time that the BBC service had been jammed or dropped. The
government of Sirimavo Bandaranaike had set the benchmark as far back as 1960,
when it was similarly jammed during a politically inconvenient period. • **18**. Amos
Roberts filmed the exasperating process of trying to gain access to the conflict. See
Roberts, 'Hunting the Tigers'. • **19**. The figure is an approximation based on
reports filed with the UN, and compiled within Sri Lanka. A great deal of work has
been undertaken by the Committee for Investigation of the Disappeared. The

committee includes members who investigated the disappearances of Sri Lankan civilians during the second JVP uprising of the late 1980s. It was launched on 6 September 2006, in response to the sudden rise once more of disappearance as a method of state control. In August 2010, Amnesty International noted that 5,749 cases had made their way to the UN's permanently sitting Working Group on Enforced and Involuntary Disappearances, several hundred of which related to cases since 2006. This is unlikely to be an exhaustive list. The difficulty in reporting cases, or a simple lack of awareness of avenues of recourse for those whose relatives have been taken, means that a total figure for disappearances will almost certainly never be known. • **20**. The phrase is drawn from Ernesto Sabato, one of Argentina's leading intellectuals and writers, referring to his own country's tragic record of disappearances under the military triumvirate. • **21**. In fact, disappearances have been an irregular feature of Sri Lanka's political life since the 1950s. See Lionel Bopage, 'Political Violence in Sri Lanka', in Pararajasingham, *60 Years*. • **22**. It is important to note that there were a number of cases of Tamil Tiger infiltration into the UN and NGOs, and occasionally those operatives were caught, or contraband weapons and other illegal items were found on the premises of humanitarian agencies. The smuggling was militarily insignificant, however, and it was always unclear to what extent those involved were under pressure from the Tamil Tigers (or, alternatively, from the Sri Lankan security services). Regardless, and despite manifest shortcomings in some of their staff, the agencies had an important role to play that was continually undercut by an overemphasis by the government on, and indeed encouragement of, conspiracies surrounding these organisations. • **23**. The enemy, according to the government and its acolytes, included all foreign governments who opposed the conduct of their war, 'terrorist' UN officials, foreign and Sri Lankan non-governmental organisations and famous hallowed aid institutions such as UNICEF. By August 2007, more than thirty aid workers had been killed in Sri Lanka over the preceding eighteen months. After John Holmes, the UN's top humanitarian official, noted that Sri Lanka was one of the world's most dangerous places to be an aid worker, a senior government minister, Jeyeraj Fernandopulle, called him a terrorist, and suggested that he was in the pay of the LTTE: 'I would say Holmes is completely a terrorist, a terrorist who supports terrorism. We consider people who support terrorists also terrorists. So Holmes, who supports the LTTE, is also a terrorist. This person tries to tarnish the image of Sri Lanka internationally,' he added. 'I think the LTTE has bribed Holmes.' See Reuters, 'Top Sri Lanka official calls UN aid chief "terrorist"'. The Sinhalese-language *Divaina* newspaper, amongst others, regularly attacked by name UNICEF officials working in Sri Lanka. They were referred to as 'White Tigers', and accusations included the smuggling of food, drugs, explosives, armour-plating for vehicles and weapons. The children's agency was linked by government propaganda on government-sponsored websites like defence.lk to an international conspiracy to prevent the defeat of the Tamil Tigers. In 2009, Prime

Minister Ratnasiri Wickramanayaka, who had once branded the UN Secretary General 'a terrorist' in parliament, stood before the 64th General Assembly in New York and told the gathering that the UN must not at any time interfere in the internal workings of Sri Lanka. (Never short of irony, the prime minister's speech neglected the fifty years of UN development assistance and the billions of dollars of bilateral aid that his country had garnered from foreign donors. Less than a week later the country's human rights minister announced that Sri Lanka would be appealing for many times more than the $200 million it had just received from donors.) Relentless attacks discouraged the UN from speaking out, a factor that led to its relatively muted approach during early 2009. 'While outspoken international actors can suffer from a loss of access and therefore influence, those actors who get too close to the regime can also lose out in the long term, as was demonstrated after 1994 and 2002. Furthermore, criticism of a regime hostile to external engagement can easily be instrumentalized to bolster illiberal or belligerent agendas': Goodhand and Walton, 'The Limits of Liberal Peacebuilding?'. • **24**. In particular, see the government's Rajiva Wijesinha, 'A Tragedy waiting to happen', Secretary-General Secretariat for Coordinating the Peace Process, (1 September 2008). • **25**. UTHR(J), *Unfinished Business of the Five Students and ACF Cases*. • **26**. See the magisterial work of Kishali Pinto-Jaya-wardena, in this instance *Post-war Justice in Sri Lanka*. • **27**. See 'The Final Report of the IIGEP', 15 April 2008, accessed at www.ruleoflawsrilanka.org. • **28**. It is worth watching a CNN interview of 21 February 2009 ('The government of Sri Lanka does not use cluster bombs'), in which Kohona provides an almost pitch-perfect rational defence of the government's management of the war and a range of other issues. • **29**. See International Bar Association, *Justice in Retreat*. • **30**. See the website of the Sri Lankan Mission to Geneva, 'Sri Lanka government proves that the Channel 4 video is fabricated'. It is unlikely that the Tamil Tigers were any more restrained than government forces with regard to battlefield executions. In November 2010, the BBC reported an alleged confession by captured Tamil Tiger fighters of the torture and executions of twenty-six Sinhalese servicemen in January 2009. The confessions led to the recovery of remains from the battlefield. See BBC Online, 'Sri Lanka Police Send "Mass Grave" Ashes for Testing'. • **31**. AFP, 'Sri Lanka challenges war crimes allega-tions'. • **32**. Channel 4, 'Interview with Palitha Kohona'. • **33**. International Crisis Group, *Sri Lanka's Judiciary*. • **34**. See in particular the International Bar Associa-tion, *Justice in Retreat: A Report on the Independence of the Legal Profession and the Rule of Law in Sri Lanka*, an International Bar Association Human Rights Insti-tute report, pp. 31–37 (May 2009), and the International Crisis Group, *Sri Lanka's Judiciary: Politicized Courts, Compromised Rights*, pp. 10–13 (June 2009). • **35**. One Sri Lankan lawyer and analyst at Colombo's Centre for Policy Alternatives, addressing the International Bar Association Human Rights Institute on 25 June 2009, attributed the most overt politicisation of the judiciary to the appointment of C.J. Silva in 1999, who he said had 'engaged in a kind of judicial populism, which has ... undermined public confidence'. He added, 'We have a lack of confidence in and respect for democratic institutions that we've probably never had in post-independence Sri Lanka.' See the 2009 Annual Report of the International Bar Association. • **36**. It should be noted that after the war, and while the internment camps were still full, Justice Silva heavily criticised the internment of the Tamil population of the Vanni, and continued to do so after he retired in June 2009. • **37**. The UN Human Rights Committee is charged with supervising member state compliance with the International Covenant on Civil and Political Rights (ICCPR). The persistent litigant, Toby Fernando, had brought the case to the UNHRC upon his release after spending eight months in gaol. • **38**. See Asian Centre for Human Rights, *SAARC Human Rights Report 2006*. • **39**. Six Sri Lankan soldiers were convicted of the 1996 rape and murder of eighteen-year-old Krishanti Kumaraswamy, and a further five Sinhalese, including two police officers, of the 2000 massacre of twenty-eight Tamil detainees in the village of Bindunuwewa. In the latter case, all five convictions were eventually overturned. See Pinto-Jayawardena, *Post-War Justice in Sri Lanka*. In an ironic twist, a commission of inquiry established by President J.R. Jayawardene after his 1977 election victory over Sirimavo Bandaranaike was used to exact revenge on and humiliate the former prime minister, and to deprive her of her civic rights. Sirimavo Bandaranaike had very much set the pattern by the manner in which she privatised the police force for the use of the government and subverted the rule of law. With massive increases in police powers to include closing down presses, arresting UNP activists, heavily policing Tamil areas and stamping out strikes and demonstrations, the annual number of crimes and imprisonments under her second government increased respectively by 67 and 89 per cent. In 1972, Sri Lanka's senior police officer characterised the predominant public attitude towards the police as 'one of fear'. See Richardson, *Paradise Poisoned'* pp. 363–7. • **40**. Written exchange between author and Basil Fernando, January–March 2010. • **41**. The 1978 constitution was a reflection of both J.R. Jayawardene's political skills and his total hold over the ruling UNP. Many in his own party regarded the new constitution as inherently dangerous. As Wijesinha writes: 'Traditionally, as countries develop constitutionally, they introduce safeguards against absolute power [however, the 1978 constitution] consolidated power in the hands of one person [and] in effect made Parliament a rubber stamp for an Executive President.' See *All Experience*, pp. 12–13. According to Pinto-Jayawardena, in the 1978 constitution 'the subordination of the judiciary deepened'. See *Post-War Justice in Sri Lanka*, p. 38. • **42**. It is important to note that there are many thousands of policemen and women, as well as soldiers, who serve in the security forces of Sri Lanka with dedication to their oaths of office. In the preface to one of her reports, *The Rule of Law in Decline*, the legal academic Kishali Pinto-Jayawardena has noted 'the many honourable men and women who serve in the Sri Lanka

Police and the Army with integrity and honesty despite tremendous odds'. Many of them have resigned or been dismissed, while others have doggedly remained within the system doing their best. The author met a number of notable police officers during his time in Sri Lanka who exhibited the highest levels of professionalism and personal integrity. • **43**. International Commission of Jurists, *Emergency Laws and International Standards*, March 2009. • **44**. See the interview with Mangala Samaraweera, who had fallen foul of the Rajapaksas, and was forced from office in February 2007 after he objected to the government's actions following the killing of the ACF seventeen in August 2006. Samaraweera had also been the manager for Mahinda Rajapaksa's election campaign. Foster, 'The cost of war and the price of victory in Sri Lanka.' • **45**. Such was the case, for example, with the ever-colourful Mervyn Silva, whose son orchestrated the brutal nightclub assault of a young man at the hands of a squad of Silva's armed goons, while he stood over the melee waving a pistol. • **46**. The killings happened on 13 August 2009. See Coleman, 'Dirty Harry in Sri Lanka'. • **47**. The barrister, a Sinhalese former radical from the south, who cannot be named, explained his dilemma in a conversation with the author. • **48**. See *Sunday Leader*, 'Beggar Killings Continue'. • **49**. See, for example, *The Sunday Times*, 'Mr. 10%? Prove it, says Basil', 30 September 2007. • **50**. Hull, 'Factbox-Key political risks to watch in Sri Lanka'. William Easterly describes the black hole created by such widespread control of financial institutions as the 'Bermuda Triangle'. • **51**. Conversation with the author in December 2009, in Colombo. • **52**. See Lankanewspapers.com, 'DBS Jeyaraj quits Nation in dismay'. When the new editor of the *Sunday Leader*, Frederica Jansz, received a death threat, a report was allegedly pulled from one of the Rivira newspapers on the orders of the new Rajapaksa owner. • **53**. See Al-Jazeera, 'IMF sanctions $2.6bn Sri Lanka loan'. • **54**. De Silva, 'Geo-political reality and Sri Lankan Foreign Policy'. • **55**. See the interview with former Sri Lankan foreign minister Mangala Samaraweera in which he describes allegations around Mihin Air, a budget airline. Foster, 'The cost of war and the price of victory in Sri Lanka'. Ironically, after the post-war falling out between General Fonseka and the Rajapaksas, which will be dealt with in the following chapters, one of the first allegations levelled by investigators against Fonseka was that of corruption related to arms purchases. The government press gave great coverage to the police tracking down the riches allegedly stashed away by the fallen general and his extended family. • **56**. Page, 'Airline chief Peter Hill faces high jump'. Sri Lankan Airlines once again, began to run at a massive loss. • **57**. The editorial, 'And Then They Came for Me', can be accessed at thesundayleader. lk. • **58**. According to President Rajapaksa, the same held true for him. In an interview with *Time* magazine on 13 July 2009, he said that Lasantha, 'was a good friend of mine. He had informed somebody to inform me [that he was in danger]. But unfortunately, I didn't get that message. I would have told him to go to the nearest police station. No one knows what happened.' See, Jyoti Thottam, 'The Man Who Tamed the Tamil Tigers,' *Time*, 13 July 2010.

Chapter Eight: Managing the Siege

1. The number of inhabitants in the Tamil homeland remained a concern for Prabakharan. The author was told that in a private interview with a visiting member of the Tamil diaspora, the leader of the Tamil Tigers kept asking whether the man thought that expatriate Tamils would return to populate the area once independence had been won. • 2. ICRC international staff, who had the most constant – if not broadly spread – presence inside the Cage between late January and early May, believed that a population figure of 330,000 was the most likely number. The key UN official responsible for trying to make sense of all the conflicting numbers and accounts coming from the Vanni, and for tracking personnel, the aid effort, satellite imagery and anecdotal reports, continued to warn – despite the absence of firm evidence, and in the face of government efforts to reduce the figure – that there was a strong possibility that the true figure was 100,000 higher than the figure of 230,000 being used by the UN in early 2009. On 4 November 2010, the Government Agent for Jaffna, Mrs Imelda Sukumar, who had been trapped in PTK and elsewhere during the siege, appeared before the government's Lessons Learnt and Reconciliation Commission in Colombo, and said that she believed that there were 360,000 people in the Vanni caught up in the siege. It was a brave piece of testimony that contrasted with the later appearance before the commission of the Tamil government doctors, who mumbled, faltered, deferred and altogether (and justifiably) avoided providing coherent testimony in relation to what had happened to the Vanni Tamils between January and May 2009. If anything, the LLRC has once more underlined the dangers to witnesses in Sri Lanka. • 3. For the secretary to the foreign ministry's take on population in September 2008, which he put as thousands rather than hundreds of thousands, see the *Omni News 2* interview of 3 September 2008. • 4. Bell, 'Inside Sri Lanka'. • 5. See Borger, 'Sri Lanka says up to 5,000 civilians died in Tigers battle'. • 6. See Patranobis, 'Huge civilian toll in Lanka war'. The author visited the Indian army hospital during this time, and was shown by the head surgeon a metal bucket filled to the brim with thousands of shards of shrapnel and bullets extracted from civilians inside the internment camps. The surgeon said that there were another two buckets of the same size, similarly filled. • 7. See, for example Swaminathan Natarajan, 'Sri Lanka civilians talk of war ordeal', *BBC*, 7 April 2009. • 8. This zone ran from the north of Vadduvakal past Putumattalan. See Defence.lk, '"No fire zone" declared further facilitating civilian safety'. • 9. While the Tigers controlled the Vanni and provided the police, courts and 'customs service', the Sri Lankan government was responsible for most other services, including registration of births, deaths and marriages; health and hospital facilities; education; water supply; sanitation; and transport of essential food and non-food items to the area. The government's staff in the Vanni were formally prohibited from communicating with the Tamil Tigers, but – as the government accepted – had to liaise with them

on a practical level in order to carry out their duties. As in the rest of Sri Lanka, each district had a government agent and subsidiary bureaucrats, reporting to Colombo and administering government services even in the Tiger-controlled areas. • 10. Whereas the 1863 Lieber Code had effectively allowed for the use of starvation as a military tactic that could be deployed against a besieged population, by 1919 it was recognised that this was illegal. Starvation as a tactic is now clearly prohibited under customary international law (Rule 53 of the ICRC's compendium on customary international humanitarian law). The Statute of the 2002 International criminal Court says that intentionally using starvation of civilians as a method of warfare is a war crime in international armed conflicts, but the prohibition, although as yet not tested, almost certainly extends to internal armed conflicts. See ICC Statute, Article 8(2)(b)(xxv), *ibid.*, § 3. In a later exercise, the author and the UN official responsible for tracking supplies, Vincent Hubin, created a graphic 'timeline map' after the style of the famous Charles Joseph Minard map of Napoleon's march to and retreat from Moscow. Our modest imitation and tribute shows the reduction of food and the rise of injuries coming together like closing pincers as the months advance from January to May and people are forced back into a smaller and smaller space. The supplies of food graphically fail to keep pace with the number of people trapped inside the siege zone. • 11. Customary law is considered a primary source of international law. Many of the provisions of the Hague and Geneva Conventions were long considered customary, their origins lost in the mists of time or so widely accepted that they were assumed, and thus took the form of custom – 'evidence of a general practice of law' (Statute of the International Court of Justice Article 38 (1)(b)). Customary law, universally practised in varying degrees across cultures and time, was only recently examined, sorted and systematically compiled by the ICRC in Geneva into a single compendium. See the International Committee of the Red Cross, *Customary International Humanitarian Law.* • 12. Sri Lanka's reliance on and mastery of the use of drones over the small battlefield was driven by the 'geek' proclivities of defence secretary Rajapaksa. Just as the author has experienced personally in Gaza, drones were evidently a constant menacing presence, even without the capacity to fire missiles at targets. • 13. Sounder minds eventually prevailed, and the council soon modified its resolution to include crimes committed by either party during the course of the invasion. Prior to the inquiry resolution, the Human Rights Council had already passed a dozen resolutions condemning the invasion. It passed none against Sri Lanka or the Tamil Tigers during this time. • 14. Under international law, the legal burden is equal for all parties to a conflict. The argument here is that a sovereign government has a higher burden of ethical responsibility precisely because they are the legally recognised sovereign authority of a given geographical area. • 15. The UN Human Rights Council is the principal human rights deliberative body of the UN, reporting to the General Assembly. It has no real powers of its own, but its findings and resolutions carry considerable weight. Founded in 2006, it was supposedly a reform initiative, replacing as it did the UN Human Rights Commission, whose deliberations had been so mired in politicised double standards – chiefly directed at Israel – that former UN Secretary General Kofi Annan had felt impelled to recommend its abolition. It was a reform that has failed in essence. In January 2008, Dutch foreign minister Maxime Verhagen commented in reference to the Human Rights Council's resolutions: 'At the United Nations, censuring Israel has become something of a habit, while Hamas's terror is referred to in coded language or not at all.' A host of other statespeople and countries acknowledge the failure of the Human Rights Council, while human rights groups point to the control of the body by a bloc of countries with poor human rights records, backed by China and Russia. • 16. The Fourth Geneva Convention and the 1977 Additional Protocol provide a number of exceptions that can be used to deny humanitarian aid. Article 23 of the Fourth Convention states, for example, that an army must be satisfied that there are no 'serious reasons' to believe that supplies will be diverted, or that the enemy will not derive a substantial benefit or have its economy supported by humanitarian aid. But instances of denial must be justified on an individual basis. The sweeping denial of humanitarian aid is prohibited, particularly given the circumstances of this siege, when two independent organisations like the UN and ICRC were capable of identifying, transporting, distributing, and monitoring aid to civilians in need.

Chapter Nine: The Watching World

1. Conversely, the UN had been instrumental in the counting of bodies during the invasion of Gaza, albeit that it was in a much superior position to do so there because of the comparatively unfettered access it had to the Palestinian territories. • 2. In June 2009, the authorities refused entry to Canadian Liberal MP Bob Rae upon his arrival on the island, despite his holding a valid visa. Rae was the shadow foreign minister at the time, an extraordinary diplomatic insult even to a nation less important to Sri Lanka's interests than Canada is, with its enormous expatriate Tamil and Sinhalese communities. • 3. See the New York Times, 'China Builds, India Frets'. In 2010 alone, China allocated $25 billion in aid to ASEAN nations. See UPI, 'China unveils 25b in ASEAN aid, credit'. See also Kaplan, 'China's Grand map'. • 4. This from The Economist, which also made the point that China's foreign affairs are complicated by the relatively low importance accorded to the role of foreign minister Yang Jiechi, who is not only absent from the politburo's nine-member standing committee, but does not even figure in the twenty-five-member central committee. See The Economist, 'Banyan: Great disorder under heaven'. • 5. Lee, 'Why China won't be a "responsible stakeholder"'. One good example is the following. In October 2007, as donor governments were preparing to punish Guinea for the football stadium massacre of opposition supporters, the Guinean

government announced a $7 billion deal with the China International Fund. • 6. Following a visit by President Rajapaksa to Tehran in November 2007, Iran agreed to provide a credit facility to Sri Lanka as of January 2008. Iranian soft loans and grants of $1.9 billion for a hydroelectric and irrigation scheme and for an upgrade to Sri Lanka's main oil refinery followed. According to the BBC that year, 'Iran is emerging as a major economic donor in Sri Lanka which is under pressure on human rights issues as war has resumed with the Tamil Tigers.' See the BBC, 'Iran Boosts Major Refinery'. See also *Tehran Times*, 'Iran extends import credit line to Sri Lanka', and Bloomberg, 'Sri Lanka Says Iran May Lend $1.5 Billion to Double Oil Refinery Capacity'. • 7. See the US Senate, Committee on Foreign Relations, 'Sri Lanka: Recharting US Strategy After the War'. The report also recommended that the Sri Lankan government should repeal emergency laws; share reconstruction and resettlement plans; discuss land tenure issues; initiate a reconciliation programme; welcome back journalists who had fled abroad, and investigate threats, abuse and the killings of journalists; and treat all internally displaced people according to international standards. In January 2011, a newly published Wikileak revealed that on 8 May 2009, the US embassy in Colombo had raised the prospect of sanctions on the Rajapaksa government because of contemplated or completed arms purchases from North Korea. The cable also noted 'an Iranian Revolutionary Guard Corp force element located in Sri Lanka provided details to an Iranian shipping company for the sale of weapons to the Sri Lanka army', and that, 'any arms purchase contracts entered into by Sri Lankan entities with North Korea or Iran, if implemented, could trigger sanctions against the entities involved under the Iran, North Korea, and Syria Nonproliferation Act (INKSNA)'. Purchases of weapons from either country would have been in violation of UN sanctions on both. See Colum Lynch, 'Sri Lanka Seeks Weapons from Rogue States, Earns US Ire', *Foreign Policy*, 5 January 2011. • 8. Commercially available satellite imagery is increasingly used by human rights organisations. Human Rights Watch used satellite images of Sri Lanka from the American Association for the Advancement of Science, which also helped to expose rights abuses in Myanmar, Zimbabwe, Chad and the Darfur region of Sudan. The images are analysed by experts who are often former military officers. • 9. The government, contradicting its earlier statements, announced on 27 April that it was once again ending the use of heavy weapons. See Sengupta, 'Sri Lanka Halts Heavy Weapon Attacks on Rebels'. • 10. See AFP, 'Sri Lanka wants to arrest 50,000 army deserters'. • 11. UTHR(J); *Let Them Speak*. • 12. See for example the Rupavahini TV Corporation report 'World's Largest Rescue Operation Launched'. • 13. AFP, 'UN's Holmes in Sri Lanka for Crisis Talks'. • 14. Murari, 'India demands Sri Lanka end war on Tamil Tigers'. Shortly before this book went to press, the *Hindu* published a series of astonishing Wikileaks US embassy cables that revealed the dilemmas of the Indian Government and its efforts to balance its interests. The *Hindu* noted that: 'In the closing stages of the war, New Delhi played all sides, always sharing the concern of the international community over the humanitarian situation and alleged civilian casualties in the Sri Lankan military campaign, but discouraging any move by the West to halt the operations.' Among other things, the cables detail the Indian government's view that India's elections made any Indian efforts to encourage negotiations between the Tigers and the Sri Lankan government impossible; that if left unchecked, the Sri Lankan government would try to keep the captive Tamil population in internment camps and would avoid rehabilitation of the devastated Vanni; that Indian intelligence inside the siege zone rivalled that of the Sri Lankan government; that the Indians believed that the first No Fire Zone was dysfunctional, with the army firing into the zone and killing large numbers of civilians; that President Rajapaksa made pledges to Delhi to halt the firing of heavy weapons into civilian areas, and then reneged; and that China alone failed to intervene diplomatically, in an effort to further its relationship with Colombo. There were more US embassy cables yet to be published by Wikileaks. See Subramanian, 'How India kept pressure off Sri Lanka'. • **15**. In December 2010, Wikileaks released a 2007 cable from the US embassy in Colombo, in which the then US Ambassador to Sri Lanka Robert Blake (now Assistant Secretary of State for South and Central Asian Affairs), wrote that 'it appears that this involvement [with the Tamil paramilitaries] goes beyond merely turning a blind eye . . . these accounts suggest that top leaders in its [Sri Lanka's] security establishment may be providing direction to these paramilitaries'. The cable went on to suggest that defence secretary Gotabaya Rajapaksa had ordered military officers not to interfere with the activities of the paramilitaries, on the grounds that 'they are doing work that the military cannot do because of international scrutiny'. See AFP, 'US cable points to S. Lanka links with paramilitaries'. The Karuna group and the paramilitary Eelam People's Democratic Party (EPDP) were also allowed to forcibly conscript child soldiers, and to fund themselves by kidnapping and the provision for SLA troops of Tamil prostitutes drawn from the 130,000 Tamils in refugee camps in eastern Sri Lanka as a result of the 2006–7 campaign against the Tigers. They were also given free rein to extort money from Tamil businessmen, which the embassy believed 'may account for the sharp rise in lawlessness, especially extortion and kidnapping that many have documented in Vavuniya and Colombo'. See *Hindustan Times*, 'Lanka govt allowed paramilitary groups to run sex rackets'. The same cable accused the Nordic Sri Lanka Monitoring Mission, charged with supervising the 2002 Ceasefire Agreement (CFA), and its thousands of infringements, of turning a blind eye to forced recruitment in the east. • **16**. By late June, when all civilians were inside the camps, a collection of aid agencies had made a preliminary calculation of 15,000–20,000 wounded civilians, including roughly 2,000 children with amputations. • **17**. Bland, 'Sri Lanka ends "combat operations" on Tamil rebels'. • **18**. Nessman, 'UN condemns "bloodbath" in northern Sri Lanka'. The government responded by attacking the author, in his capacity as UN spokesman. It was one of a number of occasions during 2009 when ministers, newspapers, television and radio reports and even street demonstrations fashioned personal attacks that were calculated to deter such statements. • **19**. Nessman, 'UN deplores killing of Sri Lanka civilians', quoting Suresh Premachandran. • **20**. The defence ministry's own records suggest that Tiger fighters continued to be killed through to 21 May. It is not clear if this was because of continuing mopping-up of resistance, or because of alleged battle-field executions. • **21**. This seems to be the most credible version, and is borne out by a television report from Sri Lanka's Rupavahini TV channel. The video shows the location close to where Prabakharan's body was retrieved, and features the commanders of the 53rd and 58th Divisions looking at the bodies, surrounded by their troops, as well as Karuna viewing the weapon and holster of his former comrade and confirming his death. See YouTube, 'Special Force Hero who Killed the Prabakharan with the Leaders'. Another version that was reported held that Prabakharan was captured and tortured at 53rd Division headquarters in the presence of senior officers and his nemesis Colonel Karuna. See also Jeyaraj, 'The Last Days of Thiruvenkadam Veluppillai'. Many Tamils I spoke with during research still harbour doubts that Prabakharan was killed at all. • **22**. UTHR(J), *A Marred Victory and a Defeat Pregnant with Foreboding*. • **23**. Human Rights Watch issued another call for an investigation into allegations of war crimes in the wake of the Channel 4 story. For an authoritative list of the SLA's version of the identities of senior leaders and their dates of death, see Defence.lk, 'Identified LTTE Leaders who were killed during the Last Battle'. • **24**. In his triumphalist pamphlet published shortly after the end of the war, the JHU minister Champika Ranawaka appears to provide confirmation of and justification for the executions along the lines that any surving family members of the senior leadership would leave 'roots' that would inevitably have to be excised at a later date. See Ranawaka, *Charge of the Lion Brigade*. Aside from his various writings, Ranawaka was a courageous and resourceful activist who, like so many other impassioned Sri Lankans, had been imprisoned during the 1980s for his political activities. • **25**. Sanjana Hattotuwa, 'Those who forget the past'.

Chapter Ten: Aftermath

1. See Philp and Evans, 'Times photographs expose Sri Lanka's lie on civilian deaths at beach'. • **2**. See the press statement from Human Rights Watch, 'Sri Lanka: UN Rights Council Fails Victims' (27 May 2009). The text of the final resolution can be found at ohchr.org. Sri Lanka's minister for human rights said, 'The support of the international community at the UNHRC is a clear endorse-ment of our effort to eliminate terrorism without a civilian bloodbath', while the country's ambassador to the UN in Geneva, Dayan Jayatilleka, said, 'This was a lesson that a handful of countries which depict themselves as the international community do not really constitute the majority.' See Philp, 'UN Human Rights

Council praises Sri Lanka's defeat of Tamil Tigers'. • **3.** On 18 May 2009, Minister for Disaster Management and Human Rights Mahinda Samarasinghe had also announced: 'All Tamil civilians have been rescued without shedding a drop of blood.' • **4.** In 2010, half of the African Union countries said that they would not arrest Sudan's president Omar Hassan Al-Bashir, wanted by the International Criminal Court for genocide in Darfur, should he set foot on their soil. • **5.** The doctors' modest new estimates conflicted with the facts as related by President Rajapaksa in an interview with *Time* magazine on 13 July: 'Seven thousand? No way. In the eastern province, zero casualties. I won't say there are zero casualties in the north. The LTTE shot some of them when they tried to escape.' Jyoti Thottam, 'The Man Who Tamed the Tamil Tigers,' *Time*, 13 July 2010. • **6.** One of the doctors was a pediatrician called Tathagata Bose, who later wrote an account of his work: 'We were managing scores of infants with bullet/shell blast injuries [some festering, mostly healed]. It gives an idea of the extent of collateral damage suffered by the civilians caught in the last days of the conflict. If an infant could not be protected, imagine the plight of older children and adults. The so-called "Sri Lankan Solution" being touted as the panacea for dealing with terrorism world-wide needs a thorough relook.' See *Groundviews*, 'The End of War: Reflections and challenges'. • **7.** Pathirana, 'Sri Lanka pressure over murders'. Persuading victims to issue letters absolving the perpetrators seems to form an unfortunate part of 'due process' in Sri Lanka. In August 2010, President Rajapaksa was forced to remove Mervyn Silva, by now handling the deputy minister of highways portfolio, after he was filmed on TV tying a government civil servant to a mango tree. According to *The Hindu*, the man had failed to prevent the spread of the mosquito-born dengue fever. At a later news conference, and by way of explanation for his actions, Silva alleged that the man had written a letter asking him to tie him to the tree. • **8.** Page, 'Archaeology sparks new conflict between Sri Lankan Tamils and Sinhalese'. It is said that in Sri Lanka, Sinhalese archaeologists dig horizontally, while their Tamil counterparts dig vertically. • **9.** See Reuters, 'Sri Lanka seeks extra 20pc for '09 defence budget' and 'Sri Lanka says 18pc of 2009 budget for defence'. • **10.** In a 2010 interview, Gotabaya Rajapaksa put the combined strength of the army, navy and air force at 450,000 in 2009, 300,000 of whom were SLA. See Shashikumar, 'Winning wars'. • **11.** Harim Peiris, an adviser to former President Kumaratunga, said, 'Sri Lanka is by far the most militarized society in South Asia.' See, J. Sri Raman, 'Sri Lanka: After the "War on Terror"', *Truthout* (27 February 2010). • **12.** Low-level thuggery had always constituted a part of electioneering in Sri Lanka, but it was Sirimavo Bandaranaike who institutionalised the repression of political opposition and shanghaied the police and armed forces to do the dirty work. J.R. Jayawardene adopted those practices, and many of the victims during the suppression of the JVP in the late 1980s were SLFP activists. • **13.** See *Sunday Leader*, 'I will be the Common Candidate'. • **14.** As told to the author by Ganesan in December 2009. • **15.** See Nizam, 'PNM requests Gen. Fonseka not to contest

Presidential elections'. See also BBC Online, 'Profile: Gen Sarath Fonseka'. • **16**. The foreign minister, prime minister, and defence secretary all accused foreign governments of directly funding the Fonseka campaign. In February 2010, Gota-baya Rajapaksa told Singapore's *Straits Times* that he had proof that the Norwe-gian and US governments had funded the fallen general. In October 2009, Fonseka had travelled to Oklahoma to visit his two daughters, who are permanent United States residents. En route, inside the US, he was approached by Department of Homeland Security officials who wanted to question him on allegations of war crimes related to the war in Sri Lanka. The request provoked protests from the Sri Lankan government, and Fonseka was ordered home – reportedly without acceding to the request. • **17**. See Jansz, 'Gota Ordered Them to Be Shot'. In this initial interview, later repudiated by Fonseka, he accused Sri Lanka's current deputy ambassador to the UN in New York, Brigadier Shavendra Silva, then commander of the 58th Division, of accepting orders from Gotabaya Rajapaksa that any Tamil Tiger leaders attempting to surrender 'must all be killed'. • **18**. See *Sunday Leader*, 'From Hero to Villain'. In September 2010, the president confirmed Fonseka's thirty-month gaol sentence for fraud, allegedly related to arms purchases. He had already been dishonourably discharged, and stripped of his rank, pension, privileges and medals. • **19**. The old council had once issued an order allowing the publication of a letter advocating that convicted rapists be let loose on lesbians, on the basis that 'misguided and erratic women should be corrected and allowed to understand the true sense and reality of life'. • **20**. Tissainayagam was released from gaol on health grounds in January 2010, and as a gesture to mark World Press Freedom Day in May 2010 it was announced that he would be formally pardoned by President Rajapaksa. Six months later, his pardon was still to be officially prom-ulgated. • **21**. For an insight into the kind of pressure brought to bear on humani-tarian officials, see the press conference held by the human rights minister Mahinda Samarasinghe and the secretary to the foreign ministry Palitha Kohona, available on YouTube, 'UN Spokesman Gordon Weiss will be summoned to explain about the civilian bloodbath'. • **22**. Just weeks earlier, *The Times* of London had published the results of an expert study that also concluded the video was genuine. See Blakely, 'Sri Lankan war crimes video is authentic'. • **23**. See Russell Lee, 'At UN, ICC's Map of Crimes Includes Sri Lanka'. In 2002, the Rome treaty established the International Criminal Court (ICC), a permanent tribunal for the prosecution of war crimes, genocide and crimes against humanity in cases where countries are either unwilling or unable to investigate or prosecute grave crimes committed within their territory. Based in The Hague, this court can try cases involving the citizens of states that are party to the treaty (of which there are now around 110), as well as cases referred to it by the UN Security Council, such as Sudan, which was investigated over its war in Darfur. Like Sudan, Sri Lanka is not a party to the treaty and therefore not subject to its jurisdiction unless referred to the ICC by the Security Council. • **24**. The US Office of War Crimes Issues, created under the

Clinton administration in 1996 as a response to the Balkan wars and the Rwandan genocide, was another example of the development of international humanitarian law during the 1990s, the growing willingness to prosecute charges of war crimes against political office holders and the potential application by US courts of the doctrine of universal jurisdiction. The appointment of Stephen Rapp, the ambassador-at-large attached to that office, was regarded as a sign that the Obama administration was serious in its commitment to uphold and extend the reach of international law, and to redress some of the damage done to American standing by the Abu Ghraib scandal and the treatment of detainees in Guantanamo Bay. In December 2010, the first of a series of more than 3,000 cables leaked to the online site Wikileaks was released. In a frank confidential assessment to the US State Department, the new US ambassador to Sri Lanka, Patricia Butenis, claimed that 'responsibility for many of the alleged crimes rests with the country's senior civilian and military leadership, including President Rajapaksa and his brothers and opposition candidate General Fonseka'. • **25**. See Miller, 'Sri Lanka war crimes video'. Neither side held the monopoly on atrocities. One instance of the execution of 140 Sinhalese, Tamil and Muslim prisoners at the behest of Tiger intelligence chief Pottu Amman is referred to by UTHR(J) (*Let Them Speak*), but there were many more cases. The Tamil Tigers had long maintained a nasty chain of secret prisons and after the fall of Kilinochchi had murdered most of the prisoners they still held. The majority of the Tiger leaders could not, however, be brought to justice for their decades of vicious assaults on Sinhalese, Muslim and Tamil civilians, and for the liquidation of alternative Tamil political voices. • **26**. The JVP politburo has stated that 'a genuine national "truth and reconciliation commission" should be established to look into injustices various communities have been subjected to and aiming at removing resentments among communities'. Currently the JVP is the only political party to call for a truth commission. See JVP, 'A practical initiative to overcome challenges'. • **27**. Slightly different details are provided in this newspaper story by Anthony David, Chris Kamalendran, Asif Fuard and Damith Wickremasekera, 'Freedom at High price', the *Sunday Times*, 5 September 2009. • **28**. The sudden appearance of a gleaming white Western Union office inside the camps within weeks of the end of the war served as an unsettling counterpoint to the misery of the internees, providing them with an efficient means to obtain money from their relatives abroad. It was an unsubtle extortion, couched as a 'service' to the captives. The poor languished and became even more destitute, while those with relatives abroad were able to purchase their exit, or at least food from the few shops that did finally open – run by Sinhalese businesspeople. • **29**. Pratap, 'A Tiger Changes his Stripes'. • **30**. Determinations on the political (that is, 'liberation') v. criminal (that is, 'terrorist') dilemma are of course complex. On 27 August 2010, the Supreme Court of New Zealand, in an appeal decision (SC 107/2009 [2010] NZSC 107), noted at [90] that in determining whether a crime is political, 'the context, methods, motivation and proportionality of a crime related to a claimant's political objectives are accordingly all important in determination of whether a serious crime committed by a claimant was of a political nature'. The NZSC quoted approvingly at [91] Justice Kirby of the Australian High Court: 'The [Refugee] Convention was intended to operate in a wider world. It was adopted to address the realities of "political crimes" in societies quite different from our own. What is a "political crime" must be judged, not in the context of the institutions of the typical "country of refuge" but, on the contrary, in the circumstances of the typical country from which applicants for refugee status derive.' The NZSC noted the following at [92]: 'At all relevant times the Tamil Tigers was an organisation having the goals of self-determination for Tamils and securing an independent Tamil state in northeast Sri Lanka. The principal objective was to induce the government of Sri Lanka to concede such political change. These characteristics made the Tamil Tigers a political organisation notwithstanding its use, at times, of proscribed methods of advancing its cause. That much is not in dispute.' The full transcript of the judgement can be accessed at jdo.justice.govt.nz • **31.** See Ellis, 'Sri Lankan Brotherhood'. • **32.** See *The Economist*, 'Sri Lanka's Powerful President'.

Chapter Eleven: Post-Mortem

1. 'External balances are strong,' the IMF stated in its review of Sri Lanka's finances, '[and] remittance inflows continue at a high rate, tourism prospects continue to improve rapidly, and gross reserves remain at comfortable levels. The end of the 30-year war has led to a surge in investor enthusiasm, bolstered by the decline in the risk of a short-term balance of payments crisis – and future growth prospects have improved markedly.' See IMF press statement. The government's statistics office said that the country's agriculture sector had grown by 5.1 per cent, manufacturing by 8.9 per cent, construction by 9.3 per cent and services by 8.8 per cent from a year earlier. See Sri Lankan government's press note on quarterly estimates of gross domestic product for the second quarter of 2010. • **2.** In defence of his firm's so-called reputation laundering, Tim Bell said, 'I am not an international ethics body.' See Booth, 'PR firms make London world capital of reputation laundering'. • **3.** By the end of 2010, in what must have been an extraordinary if discombobulating boon for the earnings of the Tamil population, hundreds of thousands of local tourists inundated Jaffna each weekend. • **4.** According to the European Trade Commission, 'The decision to withdraw GSP+ from Sri Lanka is based on the findings of an exhaustive Commission investigation launched in October 2008 and completed in October 2009. This investigation relied heavily on reports and statements by UN Special Rapporteurs and Representatives, other UN bodies and reputable human rights NGOs and identified significant shortcomings in respect of Sri Lanka's implementation of three UN human rights conventions – the International Covenant on Civil and Political Rights (ICCPR), the Convention against

Torture (CAT) and the Convention on the Rights of the Child (CRC) – effective implementation of which forms part of the substantive qualifying criteria for GSP+.' See The European Trade Commission, 'The decision to withdraw GSP+ from Sri Lanka'. • **5.** January 2011 saw an upswing in unexplained killings and abductions on the Jaffna Peninsula, despite the presence of an estimated 50,000 troops and police. See Krishan Francis, 'Lawmakers: Violence returns to northern Sri Lanka,' *AP*, 6 January 2011. In July 2010 the private TV station Siyatha was attacked by 12 masked men who firebombed it and menaced the staff with guns. The owner had fled abroad some months before, having been a supporter of Sarath Fonseka's presidential bid. In March, a mob arrived by bus and attacked the Colombo offices of Sirasa TV and Radio. • **6.** Mackey, 'Desmond Tutu Rebukes Sri Lanka'. Speaking of Sri Lanka's 'disdain for human rights', Tutu, on behalf of the group of statesmen known collectively as 'the Elders', singled out the following: the persecution, intimidation, assassination and disappearance of government critics, political opponents, journalists and human rights defenders; the ongoing detention of an estimated 12,000 suspected ex-combatants without charge or access to legal representation, their families or independent monitors; the government's failure to withdraw wartime emergency laws more than a year after the end of the conflict with the LTTE; the lack of action by the government to address the political marginalisation of ethnic minorities that was at the root of Sri Lanka's thirty years of war; unacceptable behaviour towards the UN – including a siege by demonstrators of the UN offices in Colombo, led by a cabinet minister – following the Secretary General's appointment of a panel of experts to advise him on accountability issues relating to alleged violations of international human rights and humanitarian law committed by both sides during the final stages of the conflict in Sri Lanka. • **7.** Trade between India and Sri Lanka had increased by almost 40 per cent by September 2010. See *Sunday Observer* (19 September 2010). • **8.** Louise Arbour, conversation with the author, 24 June 2010. • **9.** Power, *Chasing the Flame*, p. 189. The noted Canadian political philosopher John Ralston Saul has described this tendency of bureaucrats to sustain the machinery of management at all costs as 'the marginalisation of ethics in the name of smooth process'. See Saul, *Equilibrium*, p.73. • **10.** Defence.lk, quoting an article in the *Daily News*, (14 May 2010). It is notable that the testimony of Jayantha Dhanapala, former UN Under Secretary General and a Sri Lankan diplomat since 1965, was distorted by the government press, which ignored his plea to the LLRC that it should examine the use of violence by the state extending back many decades. • **11.** Louise Arbour, interview with Britain's Channel 4 (18 May 2010). Arbour also noted that a credible international investigation was important if for no other reason than to 'collect the evidence that will tell the people of Sri Lanka themselves their own history'. Philip Alston, the UN's Special Rapporteur on Extrajudicial, Summary or Arbitrary Executions, who had pressed home an inquiry into the videoed executions of Tamil captives, said, 'The President has indicated that the Commission should look forward, which is generally a way of saying that past violations should be ignored.' See Najmuddin, 'Alston questions Lanka's stand'. In December 2010, as President Rajapaksa began a private visit to Britain, where he had been invited to address the Oxford Union, Channel 4 once again broadcast allegations of war crimes, based on an extended version of the video it had used in its earlier report. The reporter, Jonathan Miller, said that the report would be forwarded to the UN Secretary General's panel on Sri Lanka. If there is a 'smoking gun', it is the thousands of Tamils who witnessed the siege, who escaped from Sri Lanka and whose testimony is now being gathered under the auspices of the Australian chapter of the International Commission of Jurists. This will form a compelling brief for further action internationally. During the war, there were moves to bring criminal prosecutions against Sri Lankan leaders in foreign jurisdictions. Former US Associate Deputy Attorney General Bruce Fein, then representing a group called Tamils Against Genocide, formulated a model indictment under the Genocide Accountability Act of 2007 (GAA), and the War Crimes Act, which accused General Sarath Fonseka (a US green card holder) and Gotabaya Rajapaksa (a US passport holder) of genocide (an interesting side note is that the GAA had been sponsored in its passage through the Senate in 2007 by senators Obama, Clinton and Biden). In January 2011 Fein filed a civil action under the Alien Tort Claims Act on behalf of two Tamil groups in the Federal Court of Texas against President Mahinda Rajapaksa, who was visiting the US at the time. The claim related to the alleged mass killing of civilians during the final siege of 2009, to the killing by security forces of five Tamils in Trincomallee in January 2006 and to the killing of the 17 ACF workers in August 2006. In March 2011, following criticism by former ambassador to Sri Lanka and now US assistant secretary of state for South and Central Asian affairs, Robert Blake of the flawed LLRC process, the US Senate passed a resolution calling for the Sri Lankan government, the UN and the international community to establish an 'independent international accountability mechanism' that would examine allegations of war crimes committed by both sides during and after the war. For more on possible sources of future judicial review, see International Crisis Group, *War Crimes in Sri Lanka*. • **12**. The Sri Lankan parliamentarian and leader of the TNA, Mr. R. Sampanthan, in a speech delivered to the Sri Lankan parliament during a debate on the emergency, 10 September 2008. • **13**. As Owen Harries has written of the distinctions between liberal democracy and other states that claim the mantle of democracy, corruption, human rights abuses, nepotism and the abuse of power often exist comfortably within a democratic framework. By the same token, liberalism thrived in undemocratic England throughout the eighteenth and much of the nineteenth centuries. In Sri Lanka, the mere existence of institutions of democracy, whether or not they function, is held up as proof of the healthy state of the democratic polity. See Harries, *Benign or Imperial?*, p. 39. • **14**. Gunasekara, 'Rajapaksas Bared'. This was not the first time that Sri Lanka had seen this sort of constitutional *coup d'état*. President J.R. Jayawardene had used a compliant Supreme Court to achieve a similarly favourable ruling from a judge who in 1982 found that Jayawardene's bid to illegally extend his time in office did not amount to a fundamental change to the country's constitution that would require going to a referendum. Jayawardene held power for a further six years until 1988. • **15**. Aruna, 'Resisting the Loss of Citizenship in Sri Lanka'. • **16**. Throughout 2010, as it extended the country's emergency regulations and consolidated the recaptured areas with the expanded armed forces, the Sri Lankan government continued to assert that the Tamil Tigers posed a threat. This contradicted earlier assertions by people like Sarath Fonseka and Palitha Kohona. In July 2009, Kohona had said, 'There is no LTTE left, the leadership is gone ... The vast majority of people who were supporters of the LTTE will, in the next few months, drift away.' See *Himal Magazine* (30 July 2009). Nevertheless, in 2010, Sri Lanka's diplomatic missions in Canada and Australia continued to promote the Tamil Tigers as an abiding threat in the context of immigration and 'boat people' controversies in those two countries. They pressed for all refugees to be sent back to Sri Lanka. See Weiss, 'Tamils of a different stripe'. In addition, one should view the 'comments' that follow this article in order to get a sense of the bitterness of the debate between Tamil and Sinhalese expatriates resident in Canada. • **17**. See Jeyaraj, 'Will there be a violent resurgence of the LTTE soon?'. • **18**. Louise Arbour, interview with Britain's Channel 4 TV (18 May 2010), in which she described the government's management of the 'information war'. • **19**. The author has favoured the word 'grievance' throughout the text, but 'anger' might be just as good a word. See Keen, *Endless War*. • **20**. As the Sinhalese nationalist newspaper *The Island* has said, 'The hardliners in the government are arguing that these provinces no longer need [devolution] because more Tamils are now living outside these provinces.' See Philips, 'The aftermaths of the war'. • **21**. The role of international development bureaucrats in providing support to demographic changes – 'a calibration between aid donor practices and the nationalist goals of the Sri Lankan state' – is beyond the scope of this book. It is described by David Rampton in 'Colonization', in Pararajasingham, *60 Years*. After the east had been wrested from the Tamil Tigers in 2007, President Rajapaksa said: 'Economic freedom is as important as freeing territory. We expect to launch an all out development war, throughout the country, giving priority to agriculture ... I believe with optimism that our international friends would help us in this task. Friends, please come to the east.' The friends came, to both the eastern and northen reconstruction party. According to Jonathan Goodhand, 'Donors have probably never had so limited leverage in relation to government policy on humanitarian action, development or peace-building. The constant attacks on international actors in the media and by government officials have had the effect of cowing the donor community.' Major donors have supported a range of huge infrastructure programmes, with no conditionality that will actually encourage a political settlement, or discourage the Sinhalese nationalist programme and personal enrichment of the Rajapaksas. See

Goodhand, 'Stabilising a victor's peace?'. The net effect is that the 'good donor practice' and 'conflict sensitivity' on which Western governments pride themselves have been blindsided by the 'Beijing Consensus'. Aid agencies are as much victim to the centralisation of power in Sri Lanka as is the state of democratic governance. The effective use by successive governments of international funding to alter demography was detailed by a Sinhalese government civil servant, Herman Gunaratne, in his book *For a Sovereign State*, which is extensively quoted by the University Teachers for Human Rights. Using the development framework, and some of the large-scale hydroelectric and irrigation schemes backed by the World Bank, the government speeded programmes to place soldier-settlers at strategic points along the Tamil coastline in the 1980s and 1990s, such as Madura Oya, south of Trincomalee Harbour. These strategic settlements explain (but do not excuse) the counter-strategy of Tamil Tiger attacks on Sinhalese villages in these zones. Former prime minister of Singapore Lee Kuan Yew was scathing in his criticism of the colonisation schemes in Sri Lanka, and of President Jayawardene's failure to stop them, despite his apparent commitment to solving the Tamil problem. On development ideology, see Bhagwati, 'Banned Aid'. Richardson (*Paradise Poisoned*, pp. 575–87 and 597) makes the point that for many years, World Bank programmes were predicated on apolitical assumptions, with decisions made by economists using a few select indicators – inflation, money supply growth, interest rates, and budget and trade deficits. The long list of Sri Lankan government development failures, mired in and flavoured by chauvinist policies, were faithfully supported by aid agencies whose own myopic goals are often far too short term, and politely divorced from the reality of a beneficiary state's political ideology. William Easterly characterises the ill-intended effects of foreign aid as the 'Paradox of Evil', and asks why if foreign aid works on behalf of the poor and excluded and is effective at resolving their problems, so many bad things happen to them. The danger of large development loans to governments in the wake of civil wars (such as the IMF loans to Sri Lanka) is that one 'deals with even worse gangsters than under peacetime conditions. And what incentive does it create to give aid money to the men of violence in post-conflict societies, many of whom committed war crimes?' See Easterly, *The White Man's Burden*, pp. 151 and 240. • **22.** The 13th constitutional amendment, which made Tamil an official language and established provincial councils, was one of the provisions of the Indo-Sri Lanka Accord, negotiated by Indian prime minister Rajiv Gandhi just prior to the entry into Sri Lanka of Indian forces in July 1987. • **23.** Dayan Jayatilleka, 'Tamil politics tomorrow'. • **24.** Sanjana Hattotuwa, various writings at sanjanah.wordpress.com. • **25.** Hattotuwa, 'One Year On', quoting a BBC interview by Charles Haviland on 19 May 2010. Jayatilleka, in the weeks following the end of the war, also called the 13th constitutional amendment 'the cornerstone of our postwar relationship with India, the relationship with which is the cornerstone of our international relations . . . [and] the minimum cost of accommodation between the Sinhalese . . . and the Tamils'.

Jayatilleka was the most lucid of the vocal government of Sri Lanka representatives. His father was a noted political journalist. He had been embroiled in radical politics even as a teenager, and was involved in the violence of the Sinhalese insurgency of the 1980s. No friend of Sinhalese chauvinism, he also blamed the 'ancient historical tendency within the Tamil psyche' that led it to favour 'secession and incorporation with India'. See Jayatilleka, '2007: The Road Ahead'. • **26**. Walzer, *Just and Unjust Wars*, p. 204. As one Tamil man who had lived under Tamil Tiger authority said, 'The LTTE had harmed the people. They extorted our money and appropriated our land for their purposes. What is worse, there was no freedom of thought. We even feared to talk privately . . . But nobody dared to go before them and criticize them. They would get arrested or killed.' See Amnesty International, 'The tragic tale of a displaced Tamil family in Sri Lanka'. • **27**. O'Neill, *Confronting the Hydra*, p. 19. • **28**. Garton Ash, 'Crusading is not the answer'. • **29**. According to the UN Secretary General's spokesperson, the panel will examine 'the modalities, applicable international standards and comparative experience with regard to accountability processes, taking into account the nature and scope of any alleged violations in Sri Lanka'. • **30**. Former Sri Lankan foreign minister Mangala Samaraweera had this to say: 'Unlike in a war with an external aggressor, in a conflict of this nature – a conflict between two ethnic groups within one country, there are no winners and losers. I strongly believe that the only way to defeat terrorism and to usher in a lasting peace is to address the genuine grievances of the Tamil people. The majority of Tamils do not demand a separate state; a convincing power sharing arrangement within an undivided Sri Lanka is what they seek. Therefore the most potent weapon in defeating the separatist terror of the Tamil tigers is to come up with political solutions acceptable to all the peoples of Sri Lanka. Sinhala chauvinistic politics has always been the raison d'être of extremist Tamil politics and the openly Sinhala supremacist policies of the present regime are driving even the moderate Tamils to extreme positions. Even if Prabakharan is eliminated, many more Prabakharans may have been created.' Foster, 'The cost of war and the price of victory in Sri Lanka'. • **31**. Philip Bobbit succinctly identifies this as the tension that must be sustained between law and strategy in order to cope with the unprecedented challenges thrown up on the shores of the twenty-first century by the collapse of the old bipolar order and the headlong rush of globalisation. See his concluding remarks in *Terror and Consent*. • **32**. Hobsbawm, *The New Century*, p. 9.

Bibliography

Books and Chapters

Abeysekara, Ananada, *Colors of the Robe: Religion, Identity and Difference* (South Carolina, 2002)

Agrawal, Bina, *A Field of One's Own: Gender and Land Rights in South Asia* (Cambridge, 1994)

Anderson, Jon Lee, *Guerrillas: Journeys in the Insurgent World* (London, 2004)

Anderson, Mary, *Do No Harm: How Aid Can Support Peace – or War* (London, 1999)

Arendt, Hannah, 'The Revolutionary Tradition and its Lost Treasures', in *The Portable Hannah Arendt* (New York, 2000); *The Origins of Totalitarianism* (New York, 1951)

Bandarage, Asoka, *The Separatist Conflict in Sri Lanka: Terrorism, Ethnicity, Political Economy* (Colombo, 2009)

Bastian, S., 'How development undermined peace', in K. Rupesinghe (ed.), *Negotiating Peace in Sri Lanka: Efforts, Failures and Lessons* (Volume II), Foundation for Co-existence, pp. 245–78 (Colombo, 2006); *The Politics of Foreign Aid in Sri Lanka: Promoting Markets and Supporting Peace*. International Centre for Ethnic Studies (Colombo, 2007)

Bellamy, Alex J., *Responsibility to Protect: The Global Effort to End Mass Atrocities* (Cambridge, 2009)

Bobbit, Philip, *Terror and Consent: The Wars for the Twenty-First Century* (London, 2009)

Bose, Sumantra, *State, Nations, Sovereignty: Sri Lanka, India, and the Tamil Eelam Movement* (London, 1994)

Burgan, Michael, *Buddhist Faith in America* (New York, 2003)

Buruma, Ian, *The Wages of Guilt* (London, 2009)

De Silva, K.M., *Reaping the Whirlwind: Ethnic Conflict, Ethnic Politics in Sri Lanka* (New Delhi, 1998); *A History of Sri Lanka* (Colombo, 2005); *Managing Ethnic Tensions in Multi-ethnic Societies: Sri Lanka, 1880–1985* (Maryland,1986)

Easterly, William, *The White Man's Burden: Why the West's Efforts to Aid the Rest Have Done So Much Ill and So Little Good* (London, 2006)

Edrisinha, Rohan, Mario Gomez, V.T. Thamilmaram and Asanga Welikala, *Power-Sharing in Sri Lanka: Constitutional and Political Documents 1926–2008* (Colombo, 2008)

Eliot, J., B. Imhasly and S. Denyer, *Fifty Years of Reporting South Asia* (New Delhi, 2008)

Fanon, Frantz, *A Dying Colonialism* (London, 1965)

Fukuyama, Francis, *State Building: Governance and World Order in the Twenty-first Century* (London, 2004)

Gardner, Katey, and Filippo Osella (eds, *Migration, Modernity, and Social Transformation in South Asia* (New Delhi, 2004)

Geiger, Wilhelm, *Mahavamsa: The Great Chronicle of Ceylon* (Colombo, 2003)

Glantz, David, *The Siege of Leningrad* (London, 2001)

Gombrich, R.F., and G. Obeysekere, *Buddhism Transformed: Religious Change in Sri Lanka* (Princeton, 1988)

Grayling, A.C., *Towards the Light: The Story of the Struggles for Liberty and Rights That Made the Modern West* (London, 2007)

Gunaratne, Malinga, *For a Sovereign State* (Colombo, 2009)

Gunawardana, R.A.L.H., *Historiography in a Time of Ethnic Conflict: Construction of the Past in Contemporary Sri Lanka* (Colombo, 1995)

Guruge, A., *Return to Righteousness: A Collection of Speeches, Essays and Letters of the Anagarike Dharmapala* (Colombo, 1965)

Hanson, V., *A War Like No Other* (New York, 2005)

Harries, Owen, *Benign or Imperial? Reflections on American Hegemony* (Sydney, 2004)

Henckaerts, Jean-Marie and Doswald-Beck, Louise, *Customary International Humanitarian Law*, Volume I. Rules, liii + 621 pp., Volume II. Practice (two parts), xxxiv + 4411 pp., International Committee of the Red Cross and Cambridge University Press, (Cambridge, 2005)

Hoare, Philip, *England's Lost Eden: Adventures in a Victorian Utopia* (London, 2005)

Hobsbawm, Eric, *Bandits* (London, 1969): *The New Century* (London, 2000); *Globalization, Democracy and Terrorism* (London, 2008)

Hoole, Rajan, *The Arrogance of Power: Myths, Decadence, and Power* (Colombo, 2001); *The Linkages of State Terror: The Vijaya Kumaratunge Assassination in Perspective* (ND)

Indrapala, K., *The Evolution of an Ethnic Identity: The Tamils in Sri Lanka* (Colombo, 2007)

Ivan, Victor, *Paradise in Tears: A Journey Through History and Conflict* (Colombo, 2008)

Jayawardene, Kumari, *Nobodies to Somebodies: The Rise of the Bourgeoisie in Colonial Sri Lanka* (Colombo, 2000); *Erasure of the Euro-Asian* (Colombo, 2007)

Johnson, Paul, *The Birth of the Modern: World Society 1815–30* (New York, 1991)

Judt, Tony, *Postwar: A History of Europe Since 1945* (London, 2007)

Kalshoven, Frits, and Liesbeth Zegveld, *Constraints on the Waging of War: An Introduction to International Humanitarian Law* (Geneva, 2009)

Kaplan, Robert D., *Monsoon* (Melbourne, 2010)

Keegan, John, *The Mask of Command* (London, 1988)

Keen, David, *Endless War: Hidden Functions of the War on Terror* (Cambridge, 2006)

Knox, Robert, *An Historical Relation Of The Island Ceylon In The East Indies Together With An Account Of The Detaining In Captivity The Author And Divers Other Englishmen Now Living There, And Of The Author's Miraculous Escape* (Project Gutenberg, 2004)

Lewis, Milton, 'A Brief History of Human Dignity: Ideas and Application', in Jeff Malpas, and Norelle Lickiss (eds.), *Perspectives on Human Dignity: A Conversation* (Dordrecht, 2007)

Malte-Brun, Conrad, *A System of Universal Geography*, Chapter XLIX (Boston, 1834), accessed at http://lakdiva.org/maltebrun/ceylon_1834.html

Mandela, Nelson, *The Long Walk to Freedom* (London, 2000)

Manogaran, Chelvadurai, 'Colonization as Politics: Political use of Space in Sri Lanka's Ethnic Conflict', in Chelvadurai Manogaran and Brian Pfaffenberger (eds.), *The Sri Lankan Tamils: Ethnicity and Identity* (Colorado,1994)

Martin, H., *Kings of Peace Pawns of War: the Untold Story of Peace-making* (London, 2006)

Murray Li, Tania, *The Will to Improve: Governmentality, Development and the Practice of Politics* (North Carolina, 2007)

Narayan Swamy, M.R., *Tigers of Lanka: From Boys to Guerrillas* (Colombo, 2008)

Ondaatje, Michael, *Anil's Ghost* (Canada, 2000)

Pararajasingham, Ana (ed.), *Sri Lanka: 60 Years of Independence and Beyond* (Sydney, 2009), including Lionel Bopage, 'Political Violence in Sri Lanka'; Guy de Fontgalland, 'State aided colonization: The destruction of the Tamil Homeland'; Bruce Kapferer, 'From the Crime of War to the Crime of Peace?'; V. Nithiyanandam, 'Sri Lanka: The politics of development'; David Rampton, 'Colonization, Securitized Development and the Crisis of Civic Identity in Sri Lanka'; Neil De Votta, 'Back to the Future: Sri Lanka's 1956 Election, Sinhalese Buddhist Nationalist Ideology, and the Consolidation of Ethnocracy'

Peebles, Patrick, *The Plantation Tamils of Ceylon* (Leicester, 2001)

Peiris, G.H., 'Secessionist War and Terrorism in Sri Lanka: Transnational Impulses', in K.P.S. Gill and Sahai Ajay (eds.), *Global Threat of Terror*, Institute of Conflict Studies (New Delhi, 2003)

Ponnambalam, Arunachalam, *Sketches of Ceylon History* (New Delhi, 2004)

Power, Samantha, *Chasing the Flame: Sergio Vieira de Mello and the Fight to Save the world* (London, 2008)

Prothero, Stephen R., *The White Buddhist: The Asian odyssey of Henry Steel Olcott* (Indiana, 1996)

Rahula, Walpola, *The Heritage of the Bhikkhu: A Short History of the Bhikkhu in Educational, Cultural, Social and Political Life* (Wellampitiya, 2003)

Ranawaka, Champika, *Charge of the Lion Brigade: Sri Lanka's Epic Victory Over Terrorism* (Colombo, 2009)

Richardson, John, *Paradise Poisoned: Learning about Conflict, Terrorism, and Development From Sri Lanka's Civil Wars* (Kandy, 2007)

Rieff, David, *A Bed for the Night: Humanitarianism in crisis* (London, 2002)

Roberts, Michael, *Confrontations in Sri Lanka: Sinhalese, LTTE and Others* (Colombo, 2009)

Robertson, Geoffrey, *Crimes Against Humanity* (Melbourne, 2008)

Ryan, Bryce, *Caste in Modern Ceylon* (New Delhi, 2004)

Saul, John Ralston, *On Equilibrium: Six Qualities of the New Humanism* (New York, 2004)
—*The Collapse of Globalization: And the Reinvention of the World* (Melbourne, 2005)

Schmidt, Bettina, and Ingo Schröeder (eds.), *Anthropology of Violence and Conflict* (New York, 2001)

Selvadurai, Shyam, *Funny Boy* (London, 1994)

Seneviratne, H.L., *The Work of Kings: The New Buddhism in Sri Lanka* (Chicago, 1999); *Buddhism, Identity, and Conflict* (Colombo, 2004)

Silberman, Neil Asher, *Between Past and Present: Archeology, Ideology, and Nationalism in the Modern Middle East* (New York, 1989)

Siriweera, W.I., *History of Sri Lanka* (Colombo, 2002)

Smith, General Sir Rupert, *The Utility of Force: The Art of War in the Modern World* (London, 2005)

Spencer, J., (ed.), *Sri Lanka: History and the Roots of Conflict* (London, 1990)

Snyder, Craig (ed.), *Contemporary Security and Strategy* (New York, 1999)

Spittel, R.L., *Wild White Boy* (Colombo, 2001)

Tambiah, Stanley, *Sri Lanka: Ethnic Fratricide and the Dismantling of Democracy* (Chicago, 1991); *Buddhism Betrayed: Religion, Politics and Violence in Sri Lanka* (Chicago, 1992)

Thiranagama, Rajani, *The Broken Palmyra* (Colombo, 1990)

Uyangoda, J., *The Way We are: Politics of Sri Lanka 2007–2008*, Social Scientists Association (Colombo, 2008)

Vidal, Gore, *Perpetual War for Perpetual Peace* (Forest Row, 2002)

Walzer, Michael, *Just and Unjust Wars: A Moral Argument with Historical Illustrations* (New York, 1977)

Wickramasinghe, Nira, *Sri Lanka in the Modern Age: A History of Contested Identities* (Colombo, 2006)

Wijesinha, Sam, *All Experience: Essays and Reflections* (Colombo, 2001)

Wilson, A.J., *Sri Lankan Tamil Nationalism* (New Delhi, 2001).

Wright, Arnold (ed.), *Twentieth Century Impressions of Ceylon: Its History, People, Commerce, Industries and Resources*, first published in 1907 (New Delhi, 1999)

Zakaria, Fareed, *The Post-American World: And the Rise of the Rest* (New York, 2008)

Journals and Organisation Reports

Amnesty International, *Twenty Years of Make-Believe: Sri Lanka's Commissions of Inquiries* (June 2009)

Anderson, Morten Koch, and Basil Fernando, *The Phantom Limb: A Study of Police Torture in Sri Lanka* (Hong Kong, 2009)

Asian Centre for Human Rights, *SAARC Human Rights Report 2006*

Atran, Scott, 'Mishandling Suicide Terrorism', *Washington Quarterly*, 27:3, pp. 67–90, The Center for Strategic and International Studies (2004)

Calvert, P., 'Revolution: The politics of violence', *Political Studies*, Vol. 15, No. 1, 1967, pp. 1–11

Centre for Policy Alternatives, *A Profile of Human Rights and Humanitarian Issues in the Vanni and Vavuniya* (Colombo, March 2009)

Chalk, Peter, *Liberation Tigers of Tamil Eelam's (LTTE) International Organization and Operations: A preliminary analysis*, Commentary no.77, a Canadian Security Intelligence Publication (Winter 1999)

Cronin, Audrey Kurth, 'Behind the Curve: Globalization and International Terrorism', *International Security*, Vol.27, No.3 (Winter 2002/3), pp. 30–58

Diamond, Larry, 'The Democratic Rollback', *Foreign Affairs* (March/April 2008)

Feith, David, 'Tamil and Sinhala Relations in Sri Lanka: A historical and contemporary perspective', in *Global Change, Peace and Security*, Vol. 22, No.3 (October 2010), pp. 45–53

Free Media Movement, monthly e-Bulletin (June 2008)

Goodhand, Jonathan, 'Stabilising a victor's peace? Humanitarian action and reconstruction in eastern Sri Lanka', *Disasters*, Vol.34, pp. 342–67 (2010)

Goodhand, Jonathan, and Oliver Walton, 'The Limits of Liberal Peacebuilding? International Engagement in the Sri Lankan Peace Process', *Journal of Intervention and State-building*, 3:3, pp. 303–23 (2009)

Green, Michael, 'America's Grand Strategy in Asia: What Would Mahan Do?', *Strategic Snapshots*, The Lowy Institute (Sydney, September 2010)

Groundviews, 'Special Edition: The end of war: Reflections and challenges' (19–27 May, 2010)

Gunasekara, Tisaranee, 'Insurrectionary Violence in Sri Lanka: The Janatha Vimukthi Peramuna Insurgencies of 1971 and 1987–1989', *Ethnic Studies Report*, ICES, Vol. XVII, no. 1 (January 1990)

Harries, Owen, *Morality and Foreign Policy*, Occasional Paper No. 94, The Centre for Independent Studies (Sydney, 2005)

Henckaerts, Jean-Marie, 'Study on customary international humanitarian law: A contribution to the understanding and respect for the rule of law in armed conflict', *International Review of the Red Cross 87*, No. 857 (March 2005)

Hughes, James J., 'Buddhist Monks and Politics in Sri Lanka', research paper, Institute for Social Science Research (Chicago, Spring 1987)

Human Rights Watch, *Funding the Final War: LTTE Intimidation and Extortion in the Tamil Diaspora* (March 2006); *Trapped and Mistreated: LTTE Abuses Against Civilians in the Wanni* (December 2008); *Recurring Nightmare: State Responsibility for 'Disappearances' and Abductions in Sri Lanka* (August 2008)

IIGEP, 'The Final Report of the IIGEP', www.ruleoflawsrilanka.org (15 April 2008)

International Bar Association, *Justice in Retreat: A Report on the Independence of the Legal Profession and the Rule of Law in Sri Lanka*, An International Bar Association Human Rights Institute Report (May 2009)

International Commission of Jurists, *Emergency Laws and International Standards* (March 2009); *Beyond Lawful Constraints: Sri Lanka's Mass Detention of LTTE Suspects* (September 2010)

International Commission on Intervention and State Sovereignty (ICISS), *The Responsibility to Protect: Report of the International Commission on Intervention and State Sovereignty* (December 2001)

International Committee of the Red Cross, *International Humanitarian Law and the Challenges of Contemporary Armed Conflicts* (September 2003)

International Crisis Group, *Sri Lanka's Judiciary: Politicized Courts, Compromised Rights* (June 2009); *Development Assistance and Conflict in Sri Lanka: Lessons from the Eastern Province*, Asia Report No. 165 (Brussels, 2009); *The Sri Lankan Tamil Diaspora after the LTTE*, Asia Report No. 186 (23 February 2010); *War Crimes in Sri Lanka*, Asia Report No. 191 (May 2010)

Kadirigamar, Ahilan, 'Sri Lanka's post war political economy and the question of minorities', *Economic and Political Weekly*, 44(24), pp. 72–8 (2009)

Kiribamune, Sirima, 'Tamils in Ancient and Medieval Sri Lanka: The Historical Roots of Ethnic Identity', in *Ethnic Studies Report*, Vol.XXII, No.1, The International Centre for Ethnic Studies (January 2004)

O'Neill, Mark, *Confronting the Hydra: Big Problems with Small Wars*, Lowy Institute Paper No. 28, The Lowy Institute for International Policy (Sydney, 2009)

Pape, Robert A., 'The Strategic Logic of Suicide Terrorism', *The American Political Science Review*, Vol. 97, No. 3 (August 2003), pp. 343–61

Peiris, G.H., 'Clandestine Transactions of the LTTE and the Secessionist Campaign in Sri Lanka', *Ethnic Studies Report*, Vol. XIX, No.1, Independent Centre for Ethnic Studies (Colombo 2001)

Pinto-Jayawardena, Kishali, *The Rule of Law in Decline: Study on Prevalence, Determinants and Causes of Torture and Other Forms of Cruel, Inhuman or Degrading Treatment or Punishment in Sri Lanka* (Colombo, 2009); *Post-War Justice in Sri Lanka: Rule of law, the Criminal Justice System, and Commissions of Inquiry*, The International Commission of Jurists (January 2010)

Rampton, David, and Asanga Welikala, 'The Politics of the South', in *Strategic Conflict Assessment*, Vol. 3, Asia Foundation (Colombo, 2005)

Ranganathan, Maya, 'Experiencing eelam.com: terror online', *South Asian History and Culture*, 1:1, pp. 71–85 (2010)

Richmond, O.P., 'The problem of peace: understanding the "liberal peace"', *Conflict, Security and Development*, 6 (3), 291–314 (2006)

Roberts, Michael, *Exploring Confrontation in Sri Lanka: Politics, Culture, and History* (1994); 'Pragmatic Action and Enchanted Worlds: A Black Tiger rite of communication', *Social Analysis*, Vol. 50, Issue 1, 73–102 (Spring 2006)

Ross, Russell, *Sri Lanka: A Country Study*, US Library of Congress (Washington, 1988)

Stack-O'Conner, Alisa, 'Lions, Tigers, and Freedom Birds: How and why the Liberation Tigers of Tamil Eelam employs women', *Terrorism and Political Violence*, 19:1, 43–63 (March 2007)

Stoddard, A., A. Harmer and V. DiDomenico, *Providing Aid in Insecure Environments: 2009 Update*' HPG Policy Brief 34. April 2009, Overseas Development Institute (London, 2009)

US Department of State, *Report to Congress on Incidents During the Recent Conflict in Sri Lanka*, accessed at http://www.state.gov/documents/organization/131025.pdf

UTHR(J) (University Teachers for Human Rights, Jaffna), 'The Sri Lankan Forces' Response', in *Human Rights and The Issues of War and Peace*, briefing paper no.1 (August 1992); *Women Prisoners of the LTTE*, Information Bulletin No. 5 (8 March 1995); *The tragedy of Vanni Civilians and Total Militarization*, Bulletin No. 20 (19 May 1999); *The Sun God's Children and the Big Lie*, Information Bulletin No. 23 (11 July 2000); *Child Conscription and Peace: A Tragedy of Contradictions*, Special Report No. 16 (18 March 2003); *A Tale of Two Disasters and the Fickleness of Terror Politics*, Information Bulletin No. 37 (10 January 2005); *Political Killings and Rituals of Unreality*, Information Bulletin No. 38 (21 July 2005); *Unfinished Business of the Five Students and ACF Cases: A Time to call the Bluff*, Special Report No. 30 (1 April 2008); *Pawns of an Un-Heroic War*, Special Report No. 31 (28 October 2008); *A Marred Victory and a Defeat Pregnant with Foreboding*, Special Report No. 32 (10 June 2009): *Let Them Speak: Truth about Sri Lanka's Victims of War*, Special Report No. 34 (13 December 2009)

News Reports

AFP, 'UN's Holmes in Sri Lanka for Crisis Talks' (24 April 2009); 'Sri Lanka challenges war crimes allegations' (16 June 2010); 'Sri Lanka seeks help for 90,000 war widows: minister' (29 September 2010); 'Sri Lanka wants to arrest 50,000 army deserters' (14 December 2010); 'US cable points to S. Lanka links with paramilitaries' (18 December 2010)

Aleem, Zeesham, 'Interview with Sri Lanka's FM', *Politico* (27 May 2010)

Al-Jazeera, 'IMF sanctions $2.6bn Sri Lanka loan', english.aljazeera.net (25 July 2009)

Amarasuriya, Rajeev, 'Lee Kuan Yew's impressions of Sri Lanka', *Sunday Observer* (31 August 2003)

Arbour, Louise, interview with Britain's Channel 4 TV (18 May 2010)

Aruna, T., 'Resisting the Loss of Citizenship in Sri Lanka', *Groundviews* (6 September 2010)

BBC, 'Iran Boosts Major Refinery' (29 April 2008); 'Profile: Gen Sarath Fonseka', BBC Online (17 September 2010); 'Sri Lanka Police Send "Mass Grave" Ashes for Testing', BBC Online (25 November 2010); 'Sri Lankan Minister Admits Tamil Tiger Killings' (13 December 2010)

Bell, Stewart, 'Inside Sri Lanka: A life Given Over to War', *National Post* (23 September 2008)

Bhagwati, Jagdish, 'Banned Aid: Why international assistance does not alleviate poverty', *Foreign Affairs* (January/February 2010)

Birtley, Tony, 'Sri Lanka battles Tigers at sea', Al-Jazeera (11 June 2007); 'Suicide bombers in Sri Lanka', Al-Jazeera, (28 November 2007)

Blakely, Rhys, 'Sri Lankan war crimes video is authentic, Times investigation finds', *The Times* (15 December 2009)

Bland, Archie, 'Sri Lanka ends "combat operations" on Tamil rebels', *Independent* (28 April 2009)

Bloomberg, 'Sri Lanka Says Iran May Lend $1.5 Billion to Double Oil Refinery Capacity' (24 October 2010)

Booth, Robert, 'PR firms make London world capital of reputation laundering', *Guardian* (3 August 2010)

Borger, Julian, 'Sri Lanka says up to 5,000 civilians died in Tigers battle', *Guardian* (4 June 2009)

Business Today (Sri Lanka), 'Defence Secretary Gotabaya Rajapaksa salutes the war heroes' (June 2009)

Channel 4 (UK), 'Interview with Palitha Kohona' (21 May 2010)

CNN, 'The government of Sri Lanka does not use cluster bombs' (21 February 2009)

Coleman, Padraig, 'Dirty Harry in Sri Lanka', *Le Monde Diplomatique* (September 2009.

David, Anthony, and Chris Kamalendran, Asif Fuard and Damith Wickremasekera, 'Freedom at High price,' *Sunday Times* (5 September 2009)

Dawn (Pakistan), 'Sri Lanka denies Pakistani pilots flew its planes' (29 May 2009)

Der Spiegel Online, 'Damning Report For UN Secretary-General' (19 August 2009)

De Silva, Jayatilleke, 'Geo-political reality and Sri Lankan Foreign Policy', *Daily News* (12 August 2009).

The Economist, 'Sri Lanka's Powerful President: Putting the raj in Rajapaksa' (20 May 2010); 'Banyan: Great disorder under heaven' (18 December 2010)

Ellis, Eric, 'Sri Lankan Brotherhood', *Sydney Morning Herald* (24 June 2010)

Foster, Peter, 'The cost of war and the price of victory in Sri Lanka', *Telegraph* (16 February 2009)

Francis, Krishan, 'Lawmakers: Violence Returns to Northern Sri Lanka', AP (6 January 2011)

Garton Ash, Timothy, 'Crusading is not the answer, but nor is pulling up the drawbridge', *Guardian* (3 July 2008)

Groundviews, 'Mervyn Silva publicly admits to killing Lasantha Wickrematunghe and grievously attacking another journalist' (13 July 2009); 'Jayantha Dhanapala responds to erroneous and selective media reports of his submission to LLRC' (30 August 2010)

Gunasekara, Tisaranee, 'Rajapaksa Bared', *Sunday Leader* (5 September 2010)

Gunawardene, Nalaka, 'Goodbye, Lasantha Wickramatunga – and long live Siribiris!', worldpress.com (12 January 2009)

Hattotuwa, Sanjana, 'One Year On' and various writings at sanjanah.wordpress.com; 'Those who forget the past', *Sunday Leader* (24 May 2009)

Havilland, Charles, 'Sri Lanka's Historic Jaffna Library "Vandalised"', BBC Online (2 November 2010)

Heilbrunn, Jacob, 'Nowhere Man', *Foreign Policy* (July–August 2009)

Himal Magazine, '13th Amendment will be implemented in full: Dr Kohona' (31 July 2009)

Hindustan Times, 'Lanka govt allowed paramilitary groups to run sex rackets' (17 December 2010)

Hull, Bryson C., 'Factbox-Key political risks to watch in Sri Lanka', *Reuters* (2 August 2010)

IBNLive TV (India), 'Can't ensure safety of civilians in LTTE areas: Sri Lanka' (3 February 2009)

The Island, 'Opposition's Claim Mahinda Bought Only Ammo Countered' (4 January 2010)

Jansz, Frederica, 'Gota Ordered Them to Be Shot – General Sarath Fonseka', *Sunday Leader* (13 December 2009); 'Her Story', *Sunday Leader* (3 January 2010)

Jayasekara, S., 'Tamil Tiger Links with Islamist Terrorist groups', International Institute for Counter-Terrorism (2 March 2008)

Jayatilleka, Dayan, '2007: The Road Ahead', Asian Tribune, (28 December 2006); 'Tamil politics tomorrow: Options, challenges and pitfalls', Groundviews (5 February 2009); 'Mervyn de Silva and the Lankan condition', Daily News (22 June 2009)

Jeyaraj, D.B.S., 'The Last Days of Thiruvenkadam Veluppillai' (22 May 2009); 'Will there be a violent resurgence of the LTTE soon' (5 November 2010) at dbsjeyaraj.com

Joyce, Brian, 'Terrorist Financing in South East Asia', Jane's Intelligence Review (1 November 2002)

Kaplan, Robert, 'Buddha's Savage Peace', Atlantic (September 2009); 'China's Grand map: How far will Beijing reach on land and at sea?', Foreign Affairs (May/June 2010)

Lankanewspapers.com, 'DBS Jeyaraj quits Nation in dismay' (6 September 2008)

Lee, John, 'Why China won't be a "responsible stakeholder"', Wall Street Journal (2 February 2010)

Lynch, Colum, 'Sri Lanka Seeks Weapons from Rogue States, Earns US Ire', Foreign Policy (5 January 2011)

Mackey, Robert, 'Desmond Tutu Rebukes Sri Lanka', New York Times (3 August 2010)

Miller, Jonathan, 'Sri Lanka war crimes video: Woman's body identified', Channel 4 (UK) (8 December 2010)

Morris, Chris, 'gotabhaya: you are either with us or against us', BBC interview available on YouTube (8 February 2009)

Murari, S., 'India demands Sri Lanka end war on Tamil Tigers', Reuters (23 April 2009)

Najmuddin, Jamila, 'Alston questions Lanka's stand', Daily Mirror (15 June 2010)

Natarajan, Swaminathan, 'Sri Lanka civilians talk of war ordeal', BBC (7 April 2009)

Nessman, Ravi, 'UN condemns "bloodbath" in northern Sri Lanka: Doctor estimates up', AP (9 May 2009); 'UN deplores killing of Sri Lanka civilians', AP (10 May 2009)

New York Times, 'China Builds, India Frets', editorial (15 February 2010)

Nizam, Ifham, 'PNM requests Gen. Fonseka not to contest Presidential elections', The Island (10 November 2009).

Omni News 2 (Canada), 'Interview with Palitha Kohona' (3 September 2008)

Page, Jeremy, 'Airline chief Peter Hill faces high jump for refusing to kick off tourists for President Rajapaksa', The Times (7 December 2007); 'Archaeology sparks new conflict between Sri Lankan Tamils and Sinhalese', The Times (6 April 2010)

Pape, Robert, 'Tamil Tigers: Suicide Bombing Innovators', interview on National Public Radio (21 May 2009)

Pathirana, Saroj, 'Sri Lanka pressure over murders', BBC (26 July 2009); 'King Mahinda Rajapaksa' (23 September 2009)

Patranobis, Sutirtho, 'Huge civilian toll in Lanka war: Indian doc', Hindustan Times (1 June 2010)

Perry, Alex, 'How Sri Lanka's Rebels Build a Suicide Bomber', Time (12 May 2006)

Philips, Rajan, 'The aftermaths of the war', The Island (June 2009)

Philp, Catherine, 'UN Human Rights Council praises Sri Lanka's defeat of Tamil Tigers', The Times, (27 May 2009)

Philp, Catherine, and Michael Evans, 'Times photographs expose Sri Lanka's lie on civilian deaths at beach', The Times (29 May 2009).

Pratap, Anita, 'If Jayawardene was a true Buddhist, I would not be carrying a gun', Sunday Magazine (Calcutta) (11–17 March, 1984); 'A Tiger Changes his Stripes', Time (9 April 1990)

Reuters, 'Top Sri Lanka official calls UN aid chief "terrorist"' (15 August 2007); 'Sri Lanka says 18pc of 2009 budget for defence' (9 October 2008); 'Norwegian memo sparks PR crisis for UN's Ban Ki-Moon' (21 August 2009); 'Sri Lanka seeks extra 20pc for '09 defence budget' (8 October 2010)

Roberts, Amos, 'Hunting the Tigers', SBS Australia (15 March 2009)

Rosenberg, Matthew, 'Sri Lanka seen heading back to civil war', AP (4 May 2007)

Rotheroe, Dom, and Juliana Ruhfus, 'How the East Was Won', Al-Jazeera (2007); 'Tiger Tax', Al-Jazeera (2007); 'Monks of War', Al-Jazeera (2007)

Rupavahini TV Corporation, 'World's Largest Rescue Operation Launched' (20 April 2009)

Russell Lee, Matthew, 'At UN, ICC's Map of Crimes Includes Sri Lanka, Myanmar and Zimbabwe, Unacted On by Victor's Justice', Inner City Press (9 September 2009)

Sackur, Stephen, 'Sri Lanka's defence secretary, Gotabaya Rajapaksa, says General Sarath Fonseka will be executed', BBC Hardtalk interview, available on YouTube (7 June 2010)

Senewiratne, Brian, 'Senchcholai bombing – the legal dimension', www.tamilcanadian (14 August 2007)

Sengupta, Somini, 'UN Leads Evacuation from Sri Lanka', New York Times (29 January 2009); 'Sri Lanka Halts Heavy Weapon Attacks on Rebels', New York Times (27 April 2009)

Shashikumar, V.K., 'Lessons from the War in Sri Lanka', Indian Defence Review 24, No. 3 (July–September 2009); 'The Rajapaksa Model of Defeating Terror, Securing Peace and National Reconciliation', Indian Defence Review 24, No. 4 (October–December 2009); 'Sri Lanka: After the "War on Terror"', Truthout (27 February 2010); 'Winning wars: political will is the key', Indian Defence Review 25, No. 2 (April–June 2010)

Sky news, 'Packed Sri Lanka hospital shelled' (2 February 2009)

Subramanian, Nirupama, 'How India kept pressure off Sri Lanka', The Hindu (16 March 2011)

The Sunday Leader, 'I will be the Common Candidate – General Sarath Fonseka' (30 November 2009); 'From Hero to Villain: The rise and fall of General Fonseka' (14 March 2010); 'Beggar Killings Continue' (20 June 2010); 'Defence Secretary Suing The Sunday Leader for Rs 2 Billion' (30 November 2010)

The Sunday Times, 'Whereabouts Unknown', editorial (26 March 2009)

The Tehran Times, 'Iran extends import credit line to Sri Lanka' (22 September 2009)

Thottam, Jyoti, 'The Man Who Tamed the Tamil Tigers', Time (13 July 2010)

The Times of India, 'Sri Lanka still sourcing arms from Pak, China' (4 March 2009)

UPI, 'China unveils 25b in ASEAN aid, credit' (12 April 2009)

Weiss, G., 'Tamils of a different stripe', Globe and Mail (28 August 2010)

Wickrematunghe, Lasantha, 'And Then They Came for Me', Sunday Leader (11 January 2009)

Wonacott, Peter, 'Sri Lanka Targets Tamil Tigers' Overseas Support Network', Wall Street Journal (11 June, 2009)

Websites and Miscellaneous

AAAS, 'AAAS Satellite Image Analysis Points to New Graves, Shelling, and Human Displacement in Sri Lanka,' accessed at www.aaas.org

Amnesty International, 'The tragic tale of a displaced Tamil family in Sri Lanka', Amnesty.org

Defence.lk, 'Former Puthukudduyiruppu hospital unharmed; Air Force Beechcraft exposes how LTTE has taken UN for ride' (6 February 2009); '"No fire zone" declared further facilitating civilian safety' (12 February 2009); 'Identified LTTE Leaders who were killed during the Last Battle' (ND)

The European Trade Commission, 'The decision to withdraw GSP+ from Sri Lanka', at trade.ec.europa.eu

Human Rights Watch, 'Sri Lanka: UN Rights Council Fails Victims', press statement (27 May 2009).

IMF press statement, 25 February 2010

JVP, 'A practical initiative to overcome challenges Motherland is confronted with after defeating separatist terrorism', at jvpsrilanka.com (27 May 2009)

The Mackenzie Institute, 'Terrorism and Crime: A Natural Partnership', in *Other People's Wars: A Review of Overseas Terrorism in Canada* (2003)

Ministry of Foreign Affairs, Sri Lanka, press statement (5 February 2009)

OHCHR, 'Louise Arbour's address to Trinity College, Dublin', www.ohchr.org, (23 November 2007)

Sampathan, R., MP and leader of Tamil National Alliance (TNA), speech delivered to the Sri Lankan parliament during a debate on the emergency (10 September 2008)

Sri Lanka Air Force News, 'Pakistan Air Force chief arrives in Sri Lanka' (12 November 2009)

Sri Lankan Mission to Geneva, 'Sri Lanka government proves that the Channel 4 video is fabricated' (10 September 2009)

The Supreme Court of New Zealand, in an appeal decision, SC 107/2009 [2010] NZSC 107, noted at [90]

Tamilnet, 'Cowardly Act says Vallipunam survivor' (24 August 2006)

Transparency International, interview with Razeen Sally (16 September 2009)

Turlej, J., 'Turning a Blind Eye to Terrorism', The Mackenzie Institute (April 2000)

US Senate, Committee on Foreign Relations, 'Sri Lanka: Recharting US Strategy After the War' (7 December 2009)

Universal Declaration of Human Rights, 1948, preamble

Wijesinha, Rajiva, 'A Tragedy waiting to happen', Secretary-General Secretariat for Coordinating the Peace Process, (1 September 2008)

YouTube, 'LTTE sea tigers sink israeli-made dvora FAC' (9 November 2006); 'LTTE Special Operations Assault Against Sri Lankan Army' (15 July 2007); 'King of the Tamils' (21 July 2007); 'Sri Lankan Navy blows up MIA Born Free Tamil Tiger TERRORIST LTTE weapons ship' (2007); 'Sri Lankan Homicide/Suicide Bomber Attack terrorist' (2 December 2007); 'Attack Boats of Sea Tigers' (24 December 2007); 'UN Spokesman Gordon Weiss will be summoned to explain about the civilian bloodbath' (15 May 2009); 'Special Force Hero who Killed the Prabakharan with the Leaders' (1 June 2009); 'Tamil Tiger Attack to Anuradhapura Air Force Camp' (9 July 2009)

Index